Southside Virginia

Wright Families

1755-1820

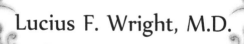

Lucius F. Wright, M.D.

HERITAGE BOOKS
2014

HERITAGE BOOKS

AN IMPRINT OF HERITAGE BOOKS, INC.

Books, CDs, and more—Worldwide

For our listing of thousands of titles see our website
at
www.HeritageBooks.com

Published 2014 by
HERITAGE BOOKS, INC.
Publishing Division
5810 Ruatan Street
Berwyn Heights, Md. 20740

International Standard Book Numbers
Paperbound: 978-0-7884-5536-0
Clothbound: 978-0-7884-9081-1

Table of Contents

Preface

This book started as a simple search for the antecedents of John Wright, who died in Clarke County, Georgia in 1832, leaving a wife and an infant son, John Andrew Wright. Evidence pointed toward Mecklenburg Co., Virginia, but early research showed that there were as many as eight different men named John Wright living in Southside Virginia (Brunswick, Lunenburg, and Mecklenburg Counties) at the time of the first personal property tax lists in 1782. The results of efforts to sort these men out are presented here.

Since I started the effort, Y-DNA studies have become more readily available, and, somewhat to my surprise, I was a complete match to another man who can trace his ancestry to yet another John Wright, who died in Goochland County, Virginia, about 1772. The descendants of John Wright, Goochland County carpenter, have been published by Robert N. Grant,[1] who is a lineal descendant of this man, and first cousin to the man whose Y-DNA matches mine. I have included a brief description of his studies on "John the carpenter" as a way of postulating a line of descent for my Wright family, but those interested in these connections are referred to his work. Bob and I have corresponded often about our parallel lines of research, and I am appreciative of the generosity with which he has shared the results of his more than forty years of study of the Wright families of Virginia in the 1700's.

I have tried to base my conclusions on the surviving public documents, supplemented by contemporaneous documents held in private hands. In some cases, the results of internet searches on sites such as Rootsweb.com and Ancestry.com have been used as guides. I have used a mix of traditional generational numbers and Robert Grant's nomenclature where connections are less certain, listing the year of death, name, and place of death.

My primary interest was in the John Wrights still living in the area in 1810 and before, although I extended the work through 1820. Sadly, most of the men named Wright had either died or moved away before this date, and, since they had common names

---

[1] Grant, Robert N. *Sorting some of the Wrights of southern Virginia. Part 2, John Wright (Goochland County carpenter), his wife Judith (Easly) Wright, and their descendants.* Menlo Park, Calif.: Grant, 2004. 5 vols.

like John and Thomas, I have not been able to trace their descendants in the migration from Southside Virginia. Perhaps others, working back from their own parents will find connections here.

These studies show that 1832 (year of death) John Wright of Clarke Co., Ga., (place of death), was the man listed in the Mecklenburg Co., Va., records as John Wright (Fox), who married Sarah Fox in 1797. This John Wright is the son of 1795 John Wright of Brunswick Co., Va., who appeared there before 1762, likely from King William Co., Va. So, in addition to a detailed discussion of the records of the four counties, I also present a probable ancestry from 1832 John Wright of Clarke Co., Ga., detail the immediate ancestry of his first wife, Sarah Fox, and a study of their five children: 1865 Richard W. Wright of Decatur Co., Ga., 1890 Isham B. Wright of Putnam Co., Ga., 1855 Puritha Bass, about 1842 Frances Barksdale of Muscogee Co., Ga., and after 1870 Mary Gossett of Fort Bend Co., Texas.

John Wright married as either a second or third wife, Lucy Garland Andrew, daughter of John Andrew and Mary Overton Cosby. The Andrew and Cosby lines have been worked out by others and are not presented here. They had one child, John Andrew Wright, who left an archive of letters now housed at Emory University. These letters are presented in context. He married, first, Sarah Camp, but she died without children. He married, second, 1907 Thyrza Frances (Fleming) Wright of Troup Co., Ga. Finally, I consider the descendants of their son, 1911 Henry S. Wright of Fulton Co., Ga.

Given the duplication of names in the public records, the lack of wills, and the overlapping geography, I have almost certainly made errors in linking parents and children where family records were not available to supplement those data. So, as always, use these studies as a guide to further research.

Chapter 1: The Search for John Wright

In 1965, I had a chance to review information collected by my great aunt, Kathleen F. Wright. She stated without documentation that John Wright, her great-grandfather, had married Lucy Garland Andrew, daughter of John Andrew and sister of Bishop James Osgood Andrew. She noted he was "99 years old" when he died, and that he had five children by a first marriage, Richard, Isham, Polly, Puritha, and Frances, who had lived in Putnam Co., Georgia. Here the matter rested for thirty years until my father, Lucius F. Wright, Jr., decided he wanted to try locating John Wright. He was able to identify Isham Wright in the Putnam Co., Ga., census of 1830, 1840, 1850, 1860, and 1880, and eventually found him in the 1870 census for Hancock Co., Ga. The census records after 1850 listed him as being born in Virginia sometime between 1803 and 1809, depending upon his stated age. He also found Isham Wright was a "fortunate drawer" in the 1832 Georgia Land Lottery as "heir of John Wright." Kathleen F. Wright gave a large number of family papers to her cousin, George P. Cuttino, Professor of History at Emory University, who placed these documents in the special collections archive.[1] In 1999, we examined the collection, and found two letters from Puritha Bass to "Mother" that we had not seen previously.[2]

The Letters

Eatonton GA Putnam
February 24, 1854

Dear Mother,
    I take this one opportunity of addressing you a few lines, hoping that they may find you and your family all well. Probably I had better let you no who it is addressing you, it is Puritha Bass, the daughter of John Wright, your

---

[1] Woodruff Library, Emory University, Atlanta, Ga. Papers of Lucius Horace Featherston.
[2] "Mother" can be established as Lucy Garland Andrew as she married secondly, as his second wife, William Roe Henry 28 November 1843 in Newton Co., Ga. [Georgia Marriages, 1699-1944. Online database at ancestry.com.]

first husband. You married a Mr. Henry, I understand, the last time you married, dear Mother. I am very much afflicted and have been for eleven years, so that I cannot get around the house, but am some better at this time, Mother. The reason that I have never rote to you before now, I did not no where you were recently, until Brother John rote to me in his letter. I suppose you no where he lives Brother John Wright, your son, Brother Isham Wright lives about twelve miles from Eatonton. I live in Eatonton. Sister Polly Forseth (?) lives about nine miles from me, Brother Richard lives down there in the lower part of this state, I do not no exactly where. Mother, I have often heard from you, but not lately. I have already stated the reason that I have not rote to you before, Mother. You must come to see me and don't let it be long before you come. I am more than anxious to see you and your (and your) family, but more especially you. You must be certain to, and see me, for I am not able to come to see you, Mother. I have not heard or seen you in about eleven years. I send my love to you and your family. Mother, you must excuse my short letter this time, I could rite a great more to you but I will stop for the present. You must answer my letter just as soon as you can, and let me no when I may look for you. I direct your letter to Eatonton, I believe that I have stated in my letter that I live in Eatonton, (and that?) nothing more at present, but I remain your affectionate daughter in law.

Puritha Bass

Eatonton, GA Putnam County
June 7th, 1854
Dear Mother,

I take this one more opportunity of addressing you a few more lines to inform you that my family is all well excepting myself. My health is no better than it was when I last rote to you, but I am up and about. I am in hopes that these few lines my find you and your family all well. I should be very glad to see you and your family and to be with you all. I often think of you Mother. This is the third letter that I have rote to you, but I have not received one about or from one of these and that was the first one. I thought nothing of it, my son rote the last letter to you for me. He rote two at the same time, one to you and one to Brother John Wright. He rote them in great haste and I thought that probably that he might of made a mistake in (lacking?) of them. If he did, he did not do it intentionally. I must bring my letter to a close. I send my best love to you and your family. Sister Polly was well the last time I saw her. Brother Isham was at my house yesterday, he was well. Sister Frances is dead, she died in Harris about nine or ten years ago. You must answer my letter just as soon as you get it and let me hear from you, for I am (very?) anxious to hear from you. Nothing more at preset, I remain you affectionate step daughter.

Puritha Bass

Of the five children of John Wright listed by Puritha Bass, I was able to positively identify three in the 1850 Census for Putnam Co., Georgia: 1865 (year of death) Richard W. Wright of Decatur Co., Georgia, (place of death),[3] 1890 Isham B. Wright of Putnam Co., Georgia, and 1856 Puritha (Wright) Bass of Putnam Co., Georgia. All listed their birthplace as Virginia. Isham, the youngest, was born about 1809.

1810 Census for Virginia

The 1810 Census for Virginia is not complete, but a total of 36 men named John Wright were recorded. Data on the household structure was available on 35 of these men. Assuming that Isham was the youngest of five children, all but four of the households could be eliminated. Only John Wright of Lunenburg County had the correct number of children, although both of the boys were under 10 years of age. The other three, John Wright of Caroline, Fauquier, and Nelson Co., had too many children, but these were not excluded.

---

[3] I am indebted to Robert N. Grant, a cousin, for this nomenclature, which does not depend upon the generational identifiers used in genealogy reports when the line of descent is well established.

There were 11 counties in which tax lists are used as a substitute for the 1810 Census and a total of 15 men named John Wright were present.[4] The tax lists and available records for these 11 counties were examined. Those counties in whom John Wright was still present in that county in 1816,[5] or those where his death was on record were eliminated. This process left four candidates: John Wright of Louisa Co., John Wright of Lunenburg Co., and one of the two John Wrights of the Mecklenburg Co. tax list.[6]

John Wright of Louisa Co. is present in 1810 and 1814, but not in 1815-1817. In 1814, he had a second tithable, not named, probably a son 16-21. This did not match the known data, so he was excluded from further consideration.

John Wright of Lunenburg Co. had two boys and three girls, all less than 10 years old listed on the 1810 census. He appears in the tax lists, and in various deeds in association with Parsons Wright. Parsons and John Wright left the tax lists after 1811. Parsons Wright appears in Putnam Co., Ga., where he bought land from Anderson Mize, probably one of his Virginia neighbors and kin.[7] Parsons Wright died in Putnam Co., Ga., before 28 September 1818. In this will, he left his property to Susan Messervey Mize, daughter of James and Elizabeth Mize after the death of his wife Mary. He also left $2 to his brothers and sisters "John Wright, James Wright, David Wright, Henry Wright, Rosa Wright, Amy Shell, and Chastity Scott."[8] Since the children

---

[4] Amelia Co., King William Co., (2), Louisa Co., Mecklenburg Co., (2), Nansemond Co., (2), Orange Co., (3), and Pittsylvania Co.

[5] Data presented later suggested "our" John Wright had moved to Franklin Co., N. C., by then.

[6] John Wright of Amelia Co. was present through 1817. John Wright's estate was taxed in Caroline Co. in 1812 and 1813. John Wright was present in Fauquier Co. in 1814, 1816, and 1817. John Wright, Sr., and John Wright, Jr., were both present in King William Co. at least through 1817. Both men named John Wright are present in Nansemond Co. through 1817. Nelson Co. records were not examined since it is now in West Virginia. All three men named John Wright were present in Orange Co. in 1814, and only two were present in 1815 and 1816. Land records show the missing John Wright was in Shenandoah Co., Va. Both men named John Wright of Pittsylvania Co. were present in 1813, 1814, but only one in 1816 and one in 1818. Examination of local records in Danville, Va., indicates that one of these men died, and the other moved to Ohio.

[7] See in particular the discussions in Evans, June Banks. Long Ago in Lunenburg on Stony Creek of the Meherrin. (New Orleans: Bryn Ffyliad Publ, 1993.) Parsons and Mary Wright sold their land to Julius Hite on 11 November 1813. On 30 December 1814, he bought 50 acres of land, part of lot 235 in the 14th District from Anderson Mize. [Putnam Co., Ga., DB E:137]

[8] Putnam Co., Ga., Will Book A:104-105.

of 1832 John Wright of Clarke Co., Ga., were living in Putnam County, this suggested a connection.

The Lunenburg County data are considered in detail in Chapter 4, but Parsons Wright sold land to Julius Hite on 11 March 1813 and signed with a mark.[9] Since 1832 John Wright of Clarke Co., Ga., signed his name to his will, I discarded the notion that these Wrights were related to 1832 John Wright.

The Three John Wrights of Mecklenburg County before 1810

John Wright appears on the Upper District list in 1789,[10] associated with Job Wright, but disappears after 1791. John Wright appears in the household of Augustine Wright in 1793 and 1794 and then disappears.[11] John Wright appears next in 1797.[12] The same John Wright appears in 1798, this time with one slave, named Chancey, and John Wright, son of Reuben also appears.[13] In 1799 there are three men named John Wright, two with slaves.[14] In 1800 only two men are listed: John (Fox) Wright and John Wright.[15] The same is true in 1801.[16] In 1802, we are again three men: John (Fox) Wright, John Wright (son of Austin), and John Wright.[17] Finally, in 1803, the three men are all given identifiers: John (Fox) Wright, John Wright, (son of Austin), and John Wright (son of Reuben.)[18] In 1804, John (Fox) Wright and John Wright (son of Austin,) appear,[19] but in 1805 all three men are again listed with their separate identifiers.[20] John Wright (son of Austin) does not again appear, but John (Fox) Wright and John Wright, (son of

---

[9] Lunenburg Co., Va., Deed Book 23:143.

[10] Mecklenburg Co., Va., 1789 Tax List A, p.38.

[11] Mecklenburg Co., Va., 1792 Tax List A, p. 29 (lists were reversed in some years. Job Wright lived in the Upper district, while all the other Wrights lived in the Lower District.)

[12] Mecklenburg Co., Va., 1797 Tax List B, p. 39. Augustine Wright and Reuben Wright are on p. 41. Since I think this is our John Wright, I note that he paid one poll and tax on one horse.

[13] Mecklenburg Co., Va., 1798 Tax List A, p. 49; Lower District.

[14] Mecklenburg Co., Va., 1799 Tax List B, pp. 64, 67, and 68.

[15] Mecklenburg Co., Va., 1800 Tax List A, p. 24; Lower District. John (Fox) Wright's slave is named Eady H.

[16] Mecklenburg Co., Va., 1801 Tax List B, p. 42.

[17] Mecklenburg Co., Va., 1802 Tax List B, pp. 39, 40, and 41.

[18] Mecklenburg Co., Va., 1803 Tax List A, pp. 46, 48.

[19] Mecklenburg Co., Va., 1804 Tax List B, pp. 49, 52.

[20] Mecklenburg Co., Va., 1805 Tax List A, pp. 52, 53, 54 Lower District.

Reuben) are still so listed in 1806.[21] In 1807 John (Fox) Wright is listed alone, and has three slaves, compared to none the year before.[22] In 1809 John (Fox) Wright was present with no slaves and John Wright was present with one slave.[23] The 1810 and 1811 list showed John Wright and John Wright (son of Reuben.)[24] The former, who is almost surely John (Fox) Wright from the company he keeps on the rolls, has no slaves, while the latter, has at least one in every list. After 1811, all of the entries are for a single John Wright.[25]

Wright-Fox Connections in Mecklenburg County, Virginia

John Wright witnessed the will of Mary (Kendrick) Fox in Mecklenburg Co., Virginia on 9 October 1795.[26] The loose marriage bonds of Mecklenburg Co., Va., include the following:

Know all men by these presents that we John Wright and Wm. Taylor _____, are held and firmly bound unto his Excellency James Wood, Esq., Governor or Chief Magistrate of the Commonwealth of Virginia in the just sum on one hundred and fifty dollars to the which payment well and truly to be made to the said Governor and his successors for the use of the Commonwealth, we bind our and each of our heirs, excrs., & admors. jointly and severally firmly by these presents sealed with our seals and dated this 3rd day of Oct. 1797.
The Condition of the above obligation is such that if there be no lawful cause to obstruct a marriage intended to be heard (?) and solemnized between the above bound John Wright and Sarah Fox then the above obligation to be void else to remain in full force and virtue.

John Wright

Sealed and Delivered   Wm. Taylor (Speed)

---

[21] Mecklenburg Co., Va., 1806 Tax List B, pp. 45, and 46.

[22] Mecklenburg Co., Va., 1807 Tax List B, p. 40.

[23] Mecklenburg Co., Va., 1809 Tax List B, pp. 45, 46.

[24] Mecklenburg Co., Va., 1811 Tax List B, pp. 33,35.

[25] This is clearly 1820 John Wright of Mecklenburg Co., Va., son of 1819 Reuben Wright of Mecklenburg Co., Va. Mecklenburg Co., Va., Will Book 9:135-136.

[26] Mecklenburg Co., Va., Will Book 3:311-312.

In presence of
E. Baskerville

Sir:

Please grant the Bearer John Wright a Matrimonial License to Marry My Daughter Sarah Fox, as witness my hand, this 3rd day Oct. 1797

Wm. Taylor (Speed)   Richard Fox
Myles Lunsford
Mary Lunsford

Mr. William Baskerville, Clk, Meckbg county
Mecklenburg County ____
This certificate was sworn to by William Taylor (Speed) the rest.
Teste: E. Baskerville, Dep.

In 1791, the town of St Tammany was laid out on fifty acres on the Roanoke River owned by James Blanton to serve as a warehouse for tobacco inspection. Grief Harwell, Richard Fox, and Stephen Mabry (who was Grief's brother-in-law, a brother to Jordan and Joshua Mabry, Jr.), were the first inspectors appointed. Grief Harwell and Richard Fox would be reappointed every year up until 1807. Between 9 February 1795 and September 1800, Richard Fox was involved in seven transactions with the Commonwealth of Virginia.[27]

In 1801, the warehouse was constructed at St Tammany under the name of Samuel Lambert & Company with Samuel Lambert, Grief Harwell and Richard Fox as business partners.[28]

Richard Fox's financial affairs began a downward spiral in 1803, as witnessed by the following records

On 10 November 1803 Ebenezer McGowan filed a suit *in fiere facias* against Richard Fox and John Wright (Fox), which was not contested. A judgment was rendered for the plaintiff in the

---

[27] Mecklenburg Co., Va., DB 8:493; 9:151; 9:336; 10:70; 10:227; and 10:384. (Deeds not examined) There are additional transactions up until 1808, when they stop.

[28] Bracey, Susan L. Life By the Roaring Roanoke: A History of Mecklenburg County, Virginia. (Mecklenburg Bicentennial Committee, 1977,) pp. 117-118.

amount of £596.19.71/2d. As was the pattern at that time, the judgment could be satisfied by paying one half of the debt, or £295.18.3 "and three farthings," plus costs and an annual interest rate of 6% from 5 October 1803.[29] This judgment was appealed to the next district court to be held at Brunswick.

On 7 January 1804 Pleasant Allen & Co. obtained a judgment against Richard Fox and John Wright for defaulting on a bond in the amount of £86.13.2. This judgment would also be satisfied by payment of half the debt plus costs and 6% annual interest from 20 November 1803.[30]

Richard Fox entered a Deed Poll of Trust with Presley Hinton on 9 July 1804.[31] Ebenezer McGowan filed suit against Walter Pennington and Richard Fox on 12 August 1804, and the defendants were ordered to pay or go to jail. The same day Grief Harwell, acting as administrator for John Davis filed suit against John Wright and Richard Fox, although there was a dispute as to whether the debt had already been paid or not.

On 10 March 1806, Edward Davis brought suit against John Wright, Richard Fox, and Lewis Wright in fiere facias and obtained a judgment in the amount of £67.7.3.[32] The same day the case of Edward Delony against John Wright (Fox) was heard, and a judgment against John Wright for non-performance of the assumption was levied for £7.6 plus costs.[33]

On 14 April 1806 a deed poll of trust between Richard Fox and Samuel Lambert of the first part and Grief Harwell of the second part was recorded.[34] This likely refers to Richard[4], (William[3]) Fox rather than Richard[3] (Richard[2]) Fox, since Samuel Holmes would have been a brother in law to the former.

On 12 May 1806 William Wright was granted a judgment against Grief Harwell as executor of John Davis, deceased, for £77.7.1.[35] The next day Grief Harwell, acting as executor of John Davis, deceased, had his case against John Wright and Richard Fox for debt heard and obtained a judgment of £13 Virginia

[29] Mecklenburg Co., Va., Court Order Book 12:58.
[30] Mecklenburg Co., Va., Court Order Book 12:97.
[31] Mecklenburg Co., Va., Court Order Book 12:194; cf. also DB 12:282.
[32] Mecklenburg Co., Va., Court Order Book 13:102.
[33] Mecklenburg Co., Va., Court Order Book 13:103.
[34] Mecklenburg Co., Va., Court Order Book 13:145.
[35] Mecklenburg Co., Va., Court Order Book 13:175.

money, the debt to be satisfied by the payment of £6.10 plus costs, and 6% interest from 16 November 1803.[36] The same day Grief Harwell was ordered to pay Richard Fox $3.18 for six days as a witness in his suit against William Wright.[37] Ebenezer McGowan, as assignee of John Wright was awarded £40.2 in a suit against Richard Fox and Walter Pennington.[38]

Finally, again on 13 May 1806 Richard Fox, as the assignee of Samuel Lark in his suit against Edmund Wall and Samuel Simmons was awarded a judgment for £40.[39] In this case, I suspect this is Richard[5] (William) Fox rather than Richard[4] Fox, because of the latter's association with the Lark family. This suspicion is heightened by the suit of Robert Fox, assignee of Samuel Lark, Jr., against Edmund and Benjamin Wall in which he obtained a judgment for £102.13.0.[40]

On 8 September 1806 Richard Fox and Jacob Bugg were security in the amount of $5000 for John Wright's application for letters of administration for the estate of Roderick Wright. Smith Collier, Daniel Taylor, Elijah Rideout and Stephen Mabry were appointed to appraise the estate.[41] The same day Richard Fox with Grief Harwell and Ebenezer McGowan as his securities for a $5000 bond, received a certificate for letters of administration of the estate of Moses Lunsford.[42] Richard Fox appears several times in his capacity as administrator of Moses Lunsford.

On 13 October 1806 Grief Harwell, again in his capacity as administrator for John Davis, deceased, was awarded a judgment for £21.9.6 against John Wright, Richard Fox, and Isham Fox, the penalty of the bond they had made.

On 14 September 1807 Richard Fox and Grief Harwell were appointed inspectors of tobacco at St. Tammany one last time.[43]

---

[36] Mecklenburg Co., Va., Court Order Book 13:185.

[37] Mecklenburg Co., Va., Court Order Book 13:186.

[38] Mecklenburg Co., Va., Court Order Book 13:191.

[39] Mecklenburg Co., Va., Court Order Book 13:187.

[40] Mecklenburg Co., Va., Court Order Book 13:295.

[41] Mecklenburg Co., Va., Court Order Book 13:303.

[42] Mecklenburg Co., Va., Court Order Book 13:301. Mecklenburg Co., Va., Guardian Bond Book, 1765-1850 shows no entries for Roderick Wright. Since Roderick Wright married Martha Cleaton in 1795 and died about 11 years later, there were probably no children from this marriage.

[43] Mecklenburg Co., Va., Court Order Book 14:215.

Further evidence of economic hard times are the suits of Samuel Lambert, Grief Harwell, and Richard Fox, doing business as Samuel Lambert & Co., against William Blanton and Judson Burnett,[44] and William Baskerville against Richard Fox and Henry Watson in which judgment against the defendant Fox in a suit *fiere facias* for £211.8.6 was obtained.[45] Finally a deed poll of trust between John Wright of the first part, Richard Fox of the second part, and Evan Evans of the third part was entered 12 Sep. 1808.[46]

All of these financial losses, which are enormous, led the nearly 75 year old Richard[4] Fox to throw in the towel, by selling his land to William Baskerville in a deed recorded 11 June 1810.[47]

Mecklenburg Co., Va.—Putnam Co., Ga., Connections

Putnam Co., Ga. records suggests that Richard W. Wright had at least two uncles in Putnam Co., Ga., when he arrived there about 1822: Richard W. Fox and Abner Ragland, and probably also Lewis Wright. What is the evidence concerning these three men?

Richard Fox married Nancy Wright 4 October 1792 in Mecklenburg Co., Va.[48] From this date, I estimate a birth year of about 1762. Richard Fox is present in the household of his father in the 1800 Tax List for the lower district of Mecklenburg Co., Va. The tax lists will need to be examined to determine his departure from the area.

On 4 December 1809 in Hancock Co., Ga., it was "ordered that tavern license be granted to Richard W. Fox to retail spirituous liquors at his place of residence for one year."[49]

On 2 April 1810 it was "ordered that license to retail Spirituous Liquors be granted to Phebe Carr and Richard W. Fox, the former at her place of residence, and the latter at his store

---

[44] Mecklenburg Co., Va., Court Order Book 14:96. [11 May 1807]

[45] Mecklenburg Co., Va., Court Order Book 14:299. [14 Jan 1808]

[46] Mecklenburg Co., Va., Court Order Book 14:454.

[47] Mecklenburg Co., Va., Court Order Book 15:224. cf. DB 14:292. (not examined.)

[48] Nancy Wright is probably the daughter of 1829 Austin Wright of Mecklenburg Co., Va., and his first wife, Lark. Austin Wright is probably a first cousin to John Wright (Fox).

[49] Brantley, J. Kenneth. Hancock County, Georgia Inferior Court Minutes, 1809-1833. (2000); p. 24. Personal communication from Walker Baumgardner 5 March 2004.

called Mount Hope in this county for one year. Commencing the 1st of March the latter."[50]

The Minutes of 14th Regiment of Militia, 1804-1862, (Hancock Co., Ga.,) show that on 15 June 1810 at a regimental court of inquiry held at Sparta, Ga., "Joseph Cooper and Richard W. Fox of Capt. Harper's Company being duly returned and called as delinquent for failing to appear at the Regimental Muster held at Sparta on the 5th last were fined each three dollars."[51]

He was taxed for 11 slaves in 1810 Putnam Co., Georgia.[52] He appears in the tax lists for 1813, 1815, and the 1820 Census for Putnam Co., Ga.

On 3 August 1814 a tract of 101½ acres of land of the second quality, part of lot 364 on Beaver Dam Creek held in 1813 by Richard W. Fox was sold to pay taxes.[53] On 1 May 1827 a tract of land containing 303½ acres "whereon Richard W. Fox now lives, adjacent to Laird W. Harris, Alford Clopton, & others" was sold by the Sheriff at the Courthouse door to settle a writ of fiere facias. On 28 January 1828 a tract of 202½ acres "whereon Richard Fox lives" was seized by the Sheriff and sold to satisfy a writ of *fiere facias*.

I have found no record of his death, but a family manuscript reported his death as occurring on 15 March 1828 in Putnam Co., Ga.[54] The only estate papers on file in Putnam Co. show an account for tuition (3 Feb 1830) and a receipt for payment of tuition (16 Mar 1830) for Quintana Fox and Charles James Fox, minor children of R. W. Fox, deceased.[55]

Abner Ragland married Nancy Fox 3 March 1799 in Mecklenburg Co., Va.[56] She is probably a sister of Sarah Fox, wife of John Wright (Fox.)

---

[50] Brantley, p. 24. (Baumgardner.)

[51] Walker Baumgardner, personal communication, 5 March 2004.

[52] http://files.usgwarchives.net/ga/putnam/taxlists/1810taxd.txt

[53] This and the following items were in a collection of newspaper cutting from Putnam Co., newspapers in the Albany, Ga., library and were sent to me by Marialis Hamlett, 11 Mar 2004.

[54] Walker Baumgardner, personal communication 11 Feb 2004.

[55] Putnam Co., Ga., Miscellaneous Probate Records.

[56] Nottingham, Stratton. Marriage License Bonds of Mecklenburg County, Virginia from 1765 to 1810. (Onancock, Va.: 1928,) p. 42. (Located on ancestry.com.) This work shows the security as Thomas Fox, whereas the other information shows that Richard Fox was the security.

Abner Ragland is present in Putnam Co., Ga., on the 1813 tax list for Capt. John Brodnax. Also listed are Richard Fox and Lewis Wright. He also listed in 1815, (wk) as is Lewis Wright, (jb and di) , and Richard W. Fox. (jb).[57]

Abner Ragland is in the 1820 Census for Capt. Matthew Leggett's Company. He is shown as over 45 years of age, with five sons and two daughters. His wife is shown as 26-45 years of age, which is consistent with the marriage date above.

Children of Abner Ragland reportedly include Reuben, Richard, Williamson, Edward, John, Nancy, and Polly.[58] The 1830 Census for Putnam Co., Ga., (p. 209) shows Wilmouth Fox along with Richard Ragland 20-30 with one male, (brother?), 15-20, and one female 15-20, presumably Richard's wife. Also shown is Reuben Ragland, 20-30, with one female, also 20-30.[59] I have not found Abner Ragland in the 1830 Census, and presume that he died before that date. He was certainly dead in 1833 as attested by the chancery court case in Hanover Co., Va., involving his father's estate.[60]

Lewis Wright appears on the tax list of Brunswick Co., Va., in 1794,[61] and in the lower district of Mecklenburg Co., Va., in 1804, 1806, and 1809.[62] Lewis Wright married Fanny Dortch 12 December 1806 in Warren Co., N. C.[63]

---

[57] Taylor, Robert J. An Index to Georgia Tax Digests. Vol. V. (1814-1817.) (Spartanburg, SC: The Reprint Co., 1986.)

[58] Walker Baumgardner, citing melba, who cited p. 194 in the Charles J. Ragland book.

[59] Shown on this page, also, is Mary Wright, 30-40, with two girls 15-20, and one 5-10, and two boys, one 10-15, and one 15-20. This does not match with Lewis Wright, however. She is probably the widow of 1826 John Wright of Putnam Co., Ga.

[60] Cocke, William R. Hanover County Chancery Court Wills and Notes. (copy located on books.google.com, accessed 17 January 2013. Gideon Ragland wrote his last will and testament in Hanover Co., Va., 24 July 1795 and it was proved 1 October 1795. He named Abner as his executor, but he failed to qualify, perhaps because he was in Mecklenburg County by then. His mother, Mary, was executor but the estate, which included land on Stoney Run and 19 slaves was not settled at the time of her death in 1833. His widow, Nancy, was alive and living in Putnam Co., Ga. His sons Reuben and Richard were in Putnam Co., Ga., and his daughter Polly was the wife of Nelson C. Elliott of Putnam Co. Son William was living in Monroe Co., Ga., and named William B. Wright of Pittsylvania Co., Va., as his attorney. Son Edward was a minor in 1836 living in Monroe Co., Ga., and son John was a minor in 1839 and living in Pike Co., Ga. Daughter Nancy was alive and living in Putnam Co., Ga., in 1833, unmarried.

[61] Brunswick Co., Va., Tax List A:29. He appears with one tithable and one horse.

[62] Mecklenburg Co., Va., Tax List B:50 (1804); B:47 (1806); and B:46.

[63] Marriage records located on http://usgenweb.org/~ncwarren.

Lewis Wright appeared on the 1813 tax list[64] (and subsequently) often in the same company as Richard W. Fox and Abner Ragland. In the 1820 Census, he is in Captain Matthew Leggett's company (along with Abner Ragland). His age is 26 to 45, with his wife is also 26-45 and has either five or eight sons and no daughters.[65]

On 7 March 1820 Lewis Wright had recorded a sorrel mare appraised by Jones and Harry Kendrick for $50 "tolled" by Alford Clopton, J. P. on 25 September 1819. On the same day in 1820, Merida Kendrick said he possessed "three notes on Lewis Wright for $305." It was also noted that on the 1st Tuesday of April, 1820, 81 acres of land "on which Lewis Wright now lives," was seized by the Sheriff to be sold to satisfy a writ of fiere facias obtained by Avera Buckner.

Lewis Wright served as security on the apprenticeship of George W. Crowder to Richard W. Fox in 1823. Alexander Crowder fled his apprenticeship and a notice appeared in the Putnam Co., Journal in 1824.

> "Eloped from the subscriber on the 4th of January last, a boy by the name of Alexander Crowder about 14 years of age. He is of dark complexion, stammers in his speech…It is supposed he was sent away from my employ by Briggs Allums to his mother who was secreted in the neighborhood and carried away by her into Henry County. I will give $5 reward to any person that will bring the said boy to me in Putnam County."[66]

Alexander Crowder was an orphan of George Crowder and Sally Wright, who married in Mecklenburg Co., Va., 28 October 1803. George Crowder is presumed to have died in Virginia, for he does not appear in the Putnam Co., Ga. records. It appears that Sarah (Wright) Crowder married a Mr. Millirons (Millians). Interestingly, Lot 25 in the 6th district, Henry Co., Ga.,

---

[64] http://files.usgwarchives.net/ga/putnam/taxlists/1813taxd.txt.

[65] My copy of the census looks like five boys under ten, but it could be two. There are three boys 10-16.

[66] Georgia Journal, Vol. 3 (1809-1840). Cited by Marialis Hamlett, personal communication 8 March 2004. She also reports that Briggs Allum had married Martha Crowder, Alexander Crowder's sister.

was sold by Sion Lassiter Hill to Edward Allums, in a deed witnessed by Richard Fox, and then sold by him to his brother, Briggs Allums.

"Briggs Allums sold to Sarah Millirons, both of the said Co. (Henry) on Sept. 22, 1827 for the sum of $200, Lot 25, District 6, 202½ acres of land lying on the waters of Cotton River, and this land to Sarah during her lifetime, then to her children: Briggs Allums, George, Alexander, Christopher, Nancy, James, and Leonard. Wit: A. Doss and Wm. P. Newell. Recorded Dec. 12, 1833."[67]

Since Lewis Wright stood as security on the indenture to Richard W. Fox, it seems reasonable to conclude he was Alexander Crowder's maternal uncle. It seems reasonable, although not certain, that Richard W. Fox, Abner Ragland, and Lewis Wright, and their families traveled to Georgia about 1809 from Mecklenburg Co., Va. This would also explain why Richard W. Wright and Isham B. Wright arrived in Putnam Co., Ga., as young men, Richard being about 22 and Isham about 13, without their father, John Wright. These connections, in turn, lend support to the identification of 1832 John Wright of Clarke Co., Ga., as the man known as John Wright (Fox) in the Mecklenburg Co., Va., records.

Conclusion

In 2013, I received a copy of the following letter:[68]

Columbus, Ga., Nov. 25, 1932

Mr. L. S. Wheeler
Monroe, Ga.

Dear Mr. Wheeler—

My information about the Wrights is not as full as I wish, but I take pleasure in telling you what I have found out.

Richard Fox was an inhabitant either of Mecklenburg County or of Petersburg, in Virginia. He had one daughter,

---

[67] Data provided by Marialis Hamlett, personal communication 11 March 2004.
[68] John Wheeler, a lineal descendant of 1890 Isham Wright of Putnam County, Ga., and a grandson of L. S. Wheeler, provided me with this letter.

Nancy, who married Abner Ragland at Petersburg. Another daughter, Sarah, married John Wright in Mecklenburg County. All of these came to Georgia together. John Wright had the following children: Richard, Isham, Mary, Polly, and John, and Sam, and maybe Purity.

Richard W. Wright married Mary Ann Harrison. Their son, Alexander Harrison Wright married Sarah Arnold. Their daughter is my mother, who married John H. Ellis. My brothers are Fred Ellis of Phoenix, Arizona, Paul Ellis of Sarasota, Florida, Earl M. Ellis of Phoenix, Arizona. My sisters are Mrs. Annie Brannan of Port Arthur, Texas, Mrs. C. Z. Smith of Atlanta, and Mrs. Oscar Flor of Demorest, Ga. My mother's name was Mary Cullen Wright.

Isham Brooks Wright married a Barksdale. Their children were Sarah Fox Wright, who married a Bomgartel, Mrs. Elizabeth Ross, William, John, James, Joseph, and Mary, who married E. Wheeler. Paul Wheeler, their son, married Della McNatt, whose children are Earnest, Pauline (Bryant), Owen, L. Sidney, Lucy, Kate, Eula (Blackburn), Eva (Reid), and Marion.

Mary Wright, daughter of John and Sarah Wright married John Bass, or this may have been Purity Wright who married John Bass. Another daughter, either Mary or Polly, married a John Gossit. The Gossits went to Texas. John Bass raised a considerable family. I wish I had this part of my record in better shape.

It seems the original John Wright had also had a daughter named Frances who married one William Barksdale—perhaps a relative of your grandmother.

Another son of the original John Wright was named John. He lived in Clark County, Georgia.

My ancestor, Richard Wright, had a daughter, Rebecca, who married Jimmie Rogers. This family lived in Putnam County. They had two daughters, Georgia and Jimmie. Georgia married a Bellflower; she died, and her sister Jimmie married the husband. Jimmie Rogers, their father, was an uncle of Mrs. Paul Wheeler. After the death of Jimmie Rogers, his widow married an Edwards whose family lived in Terrell County.

This is all the information I have that would be of use to you. If you find any of these records incorrect, or if you have any further information as to the family, I would greatly appreciate your giving it to me. I think it could be established that both John Wright and Richard Fox were soldiers in the Revolutionary War. I have not gone to the trouble, owing to the fact that we have other ancestors whose records were more easily traced. But I would like any information in this regard also.

I assure you that I am proud of the family relationship, and I hope to have the pleasure of meeting you sometime. My mother and I had a most delightful time at your father's home some years ago. Write me for any further information I may give you.

With many good wishes I remain,
Yours very sincerely
S/ John E. Ellis
PS I happen to be out of stationery.

This letter confirms the conclusions made from the detailed studies presented in this chapter that John (Fox) Wright of Mecklenburg Co., Va., is, indeed, 1832 John Wright of Clarke Co., Ga.

Chapter 2: Wrights of Waqua Creek, Brunswick Co., Virginia

John Wright's first appearance in the Mecklenburg Co., Va., records was as an adult member of Augustine (Austin) Wright's household.[1] Austin Wright was the son of 1783 Robert Wright of Brunswick Co., Va., which indicates that John Wright likely also came from there.[2]

There were at least five men named John Wright in Brunswick Co., Va., during the years from 1782 to 1800, but the connection to Austin Wright led to a focus on the Wright families living on Waqua Creek. John Wright was first recorded in the records of Brunswick Co., Va., when he appeared on the list of tithables for St. Andrew's Parish taken in 1762.[3] He appears with Jeremiah Wright, who has two tithables, Robert Wright and Uriah Wright.[4]

On 26 October 1772 John Batten Dobyns wrote his last will and testament, a document witnessed by signature of John Wright, the mark of Mary Wright, and Richard Littlepage.[5] This will, proved on 22 March 1773 describes two parcels of land left to his sons: a tract of 100 acres described as adjacent Matthews, Martin, and Williams, and a 100 acre tract described as adjacent Stith and Atkinson.

On 15 June 1778 John Wright bought 101 acres of land from Jonathan Williams and his wife Elizabeth. The indenture was witnessed by Robert Wright, Robert Kennedy, and Henry Martin.[6]

---

[1] Mecklenburg Co., Va., 1792 Tax List "A", p. 29.

[2] For a more detailed discussion of Austin Wright see my post 6 September 2004. Located at http://genforum.genealogy.com/wright/messages/17887.html. On 4 September 1786 "Augustin" Wright of Mecklenburg Co., Va., sold to John Penn of Brunswick Co. for £106 a tract of 175 acres beginning "at Walker's line where it crosses the gum branch, thence along the said line to Samuel Briggs' spring branch...to Stith's line...." This indenture was signed by "Austin" Wright and witnessed by Samuel Briggs, Reuben Wright, and Robert Wright. It is this sale, which is probably his inheritance from the estate of Robert Wright that establishes his connection. [Brunswick Co., Va., Deed Book 14:257.]

[3] Brunswick Co., Va., Deed Book 11:138.

[4] These can be identified as 1783 Robert Wright of Brunswick Co., Va., and 1784 Uriah Wright of Brunswick Co., Va.

[5] Brunswick Co., Va., Will Book 4:160. Cited in Bradley, Stephen E. Brunswick County, Virginia Will Books, Vol. 2, 1761-1780. (Lawrenceville, VA, 1997,) pp. 27-28.

[6] Brunswick Co., Va., Deed Book 13:351.

The land was described as "adjoining the land of John Williams, Ch. Withers and William Townsend..." Robert Wright can be shown to be 1783 Robert Wright of Brunswick Co., Virginia, who also bought land on Waqua Creek in the northern half of Brunswick Co., Virginia.

On 14 May 1785 John Wright, Thomas Penn and Joseph "Dameon" were witnesses to the last will and testament of Mary Lightfooot.[7] John Wright and Thomas Daniel were witnesses to the will of William Daniel on 28 January 1786.[8] The will was proved in court by the oath of John Wright on 25 September 1786.

On 11 June 1785 William Briggs and Elizabeth his wife sold to John Haskins 180 acres of land "on the South side of Waqua Creek bounded by...John Haskins South to the Great Branch as it meanders to the said creek."[9] This indenture was witnessed by John Green, Randolph Rhodes, Millie Patlow, and William Wright.

On 28 December 1785 Richard Ramsey and Amy Ramsey, his wife sold to Thomas Hailey 100 acres of land bounded by Roger Atkinson, Moses Dobbins, and Richard Littlepage.[10] This indenture was witnessed by John Wright, William Stanhope Wright, and Martha Hailey, and proved by them in court 25 September 1786.

On 7 April 1786 Robert Daniel sold to John Gilliam 140 acres of land adjacent to Gilliam's own land and "to a gum in the licking branch thence along the said branch to Reuben Wright's corner red oak...to Edmund's line...."[11] The land was described as part of tract previously owned by Thomas Daniel, deceased. This indenture was witnessed by John Flood Edmunds, Hincha Gilliam, and Robert Kenneday.

On 17 April 1788, John Potts and Susanna, his wife sold to John Gilliam 100 acres "the whole of the widows dower [of] Susanna Potts" "on the south side of Waqua Creek," which apparently lay adjacent to John Gilliam's land.[12] This indenture

---

[7] Brunswick Co., Va., Will Book 5:149. Cited in Bradley, Stephen E. Brunswick County, Virginia Will Books, Vol. 3. (Lawrenceville, VA, 1997,) p. 9.

[8] Brunswick Co., Va., Will Book 5:183. Cited in Bradley, Stephen E. Brunswick County, Virginia Will Books, Vol. 3. (Lawrenceville, VA, 1997,) p. 14.

[9] Brunswick Co., Va., Deed Book 14:126. Proved 22 August 1785.

[10] Brunswick Co., Va., Deed Book 14, 223.

[11] Brunswick Co., Va., Deed Book 14, 232. Proved 23 October 1786.

[12] Brunswick Co., Va., Deed Book 14:381.

was witnessed by John Wright and Hincha Gilliam, and was proved in court 28 July 1788 by oath of John Wright and Richard Bagwell, and apparently a written deposition by Hincha Gilliam.

On 1 March 1791, John "Right" and his wife Mary "Right" sold to John Gilliam a tract of land for "£22 10s, current money of Virginia:

> ...containing 100 acres more or less, and bounded as follows: to Wit: Beginning at _____ pine thence by his line south one hundred seventy four poles to his corner on Gilliam's line, thence by his line north 60 degrees west one hundred and seventy eight poles to a "whight" oak thence north fifty three degrees east two hundred and thirty poles to the beginning....

The indenture was signed by John Wright, while Mary "Right" made her mark "+". The deed was witnessed by Robert "+ his mark" Daniel, William Roberts, and Hincha Gilliam.[13]

The Brunswick County Tax Lists show John Wright in the upper district in 1782 with one tithable and four white males under 16. In 1784, he appears as John Wright and John Wright, under 21.[14] In 1785, the notation is made for John Wright (Taylor) and John Wright, under 21,[15] apparently to distinguish him from John Wright with one white and one black male, who appear on the same list with James Wright.[16]

John Wright and John Wright appear together on the lists through 1788. In 1789, John Wright (tailor) appears with two polls, but the latter are not named,[17] and again in 1790.[18] The John Wright who has been present in association with Reuben Wright is not present in 1791 or thereafter, which is consistent with the deed of sale noted above.[19] The appearance of John Wright, Jr., in the 1784 list implies he had turned 16 the year previously, which implies a birth year of 1768, but his disappearance in 1789 would

---

[13] Brunswick Co., Va., Deed Book 15:180, proved 27 Feb 1792.

[14] Brunswick Co., Va. Tax List, Upper District, 1784, p. 8.

[15] Brunswick Co., Va. Tax List, Upper District. 1785, p. 31.

[16] Brunswick Co., Va. Tax List, Upper District, 1785, p. 61.

[17] Brunswick Co., Va. Tax List, Upper District, 1789, p. 32.

[18] Brunswick Co., Va. Tax List, Upper District, 1790, p. 31.

[19] In 1787 John Wright sued Reuben Wright for unstated reasons. The case was dismissed by agreement. [Brunswick Co., Va., Court Order Book 14:473]

imply he was 21 and on his own, which also supports a birth year of 1768.

On 28 August 1787 John Wright was in suit against John Allen. Listed as witnesses for John Wright were Robert Hailey and John Wright. Robert Wright appeared as a witness for John Allen.[20] On 24 March 1788 John Wright was in suit against John Allen and John Ingram, and a reply bond was posted.[21]

Purchasers at the estate sale of George Walker in 1795 include John Wright, Taylor Wright, and William Wright.[22]

From these data, I have concluded that John Wright had a son, named John Wright who was born about 1764, which suggests a birth year for the father of about 1735. The tax lists also imply at least two more sons, whose names are not shown. The notation for "Taylor Wright" in 1795 suggests that John Wright (Taylor) was still alive, although not in Brunswick Co., Virginia. John Wright appeared in the same area as Jeremiah Wright and his two relatives, Robert and Uriah, who were brothers.

Genealogical Summary

1. JOHN WRIGHT died after 1795 Brunswick Co., Virginia. He married MARY (Taylor?)

In Chapter 5 I will show a probable ancestry for this man, based on the work of Robert N. Grant.

Children of JOHN WRIGHT and MARY are:

    i.   JOHN[2] WRIGHT,b. about 1764 Brunswick Co., Virginia; d. before 22 October 1832 Clarke Co., Georgia; m. (1) SARAH[5] FOX 27 October 1797 Mecklenburg Co., Va.,

---

[20] Brunswick Co., Va., Court Order Book 14:567

[21] Brunswick Co., Va., Court Order Book 14:620 There is a deed written 5 Feb 1779 in which William Loftin sold a tract of land to William Collingsworth (Brunswick Co, Va., DB 13:239. Collingsworth turned around and sold the tract to Owen Myrick on 4 March 1779. (Brunswick Co., Va., DB 13:240. In both indentures the tract of 315 acres was described as originally granted to Thomas Gilliam 13 Aug 1763 and lying adjacent to Myrick and John Taylor. The former deed also says adjacent to Amos Nanney and Rattlesnake Creek. I have assumed that the John Wright who appears on Rattlesnake Creek 1790-1806 is a son of 1789 Reuben Wright of Brunswick Co., Va., but these deeds were witnessed by Parsons Wright, who is 1818 Parsons Wright of Putnam Co., Ga., and a member of the Wright family of Stony Creek, Lunenburg Co., Va. On the other hand, this John Wright was associated with lands of the Gilliam and Briggs families, who were intermarried.

[22] Brunswick Co., Va., Will Book 5:626. Cited in Bradley, Stephen E. Brunswick County, Virginia Will Books, Vol. 3, (1780-1795.) (Lawrenceville, Va., 1997.) pp. 90-91.

daughter of RICHARD[4] FOX and MARY (DAVIS) RAINEY; b. about 1776 Mecklenburg Co., Virginia; d. about 1812 Mecklenburg Co., Virginia; m. (2) PAMELIA BRANTLEY 17 December 1812 Warren Co., N. C.; m. (3) LUCY GARLAND ANDREW 10 May 1830 Clarke Co., Ga., daughter of JOHN ANDREW and MARY OVERTON COSBY; b. 25 August 1799 Elbert Co., Ga.; d. 8 July 1870 Campbell Co., Ga.; m. (2) WILLIAM R. HENRY 28 November 1844 Henry Co., Ga. (See Chapter 7).

ii. RODERICK[2] WRIGHT b. about 1770 Brunswick Co., Va.,; d. before 8 September 1806 Mecklenburg Co., Va.; m. MARTHA CLEATON 24 September 1795 Mecklenburg Co., Va.

Roderick Wright does not appear in the tax lists for Brunswick, Lunenburg, or Mecklenburg Co., Va., and I have not been able to locate a probate for his will.

2. iii. LEWIS[2] WRIGHT was born 1775-1780, Brunswick Co., Va.; d. after 1824 Putnam Co., Ga.[23]; m. (1) FANNY DORTCH 12 December 1806 Warren Co., N. C.; m. (2) MARY (KENDRICK) CARTER about 1820 Putnam Co., Ga., daughter of JOHN[4] KENDRICK and MARTHA MONTGOMERY, widow of JOHN CARTER; b. about 1789; d. after 1844 Putnam Co., Ga.

iv. NANCY[2] WRIGHT was born about 1777 Brunswick Co., Va.; m. DAVID WRIGHT 29 December 1797 Brunswick Co., Va., son of THOMAS WRIGHT and HANNAH MIZE.

See discussion in Chapter 4 in the entry for 1804 Thomas Wright of Lunenburg Co., Virginia.

v. SARAH[2] WRIGHT was born about 1783 Brunswick Co., Va.; d. Henry Co., Ga.; m. (1) GEORGE CROWDER 28 October 1803 Mecklenburg Co., Va.; m. (2) ___ MILLIANS about 1825 Henry Co., Ga.

2. LEWIS[2] (*JOHN[1],*) WRIGHT was born between 1775 and 1780 in Brunswick Co., Va., and died in Putnam Co., Ga., after 1824. He married (1) FANNY DORTCH 12 December 1806 Warren Co., N. C. He married (2) MARY (KENDRICK) CARTER about 1821 in

---

[23] It is possible he is the Lewis Wright who appears in the 1840 Census for Putnam Co., but I cannot be certain from the neighbors and associates listed.

Putnam Co., Ga., daughter of JOHN[4] KENDRICK and MARTHA MONTGOMERY, and widow of JOHN CARTER. She was born about 1789 and died after 1844 in Putnam Co., Ga.

Lewis Wright appears on the tax list of Brunswick Co., Va., in 1794,[24] and in the lower district of Mecklenburg Co., Va., in 1804, 1806, and 1809. [25] Lewis Wright married Fanny Dortch December 12, 1806 in Warren Co., N. C.[26]

Lewis Wright appeared on the 1813 tax list (and subsequently) often in the same company as Richard W. Fox and Abner Ragland. In the 1820 Census, he is in Captain Matthew Leggett's company (along with Abner Ragland). His age is 26 to 45, with his wife is also 26-45 and has either five or eight sons and no daughters.[27]

On 7 March 1820 Lewis Wright had recorded a sorrel mare appraised by Jones and Harry Kendrick for $50 "tolled" by Alford Clopton, J. P. on 25 September 1819. On the same day in 1820, Merida Kendrick said he possessed "three notes on Lewis Wright for $305." It was also noted that on the 1st Tuesday of April, 1820, 81 acres of land "on which Lewis Wright now lives, was seized by the Sheriff to be sold to satisfy a writ of fiere facias obtained by Avera Buckner."

The Last Will and Testament of Martha Kendrick[28]
Georgia, Putnam County) I Martha Kendrick in perfect mind and memory in the presence of Almighty God do make this my last will and testament. I do give and bequeath unto my beloved daughter Betty A. Kendrick my bay mare.

I give and bequeath unto my four grandchildren, John W. Carter, William B. Carter, Walton T. Carter, and Robert M. Carter fifty dollars in cash to be equally

---

[24] Brunswick Co., Va., Tax List A:29. He appears with one tithable and one horse.

[25] Mecklenburg Co., Va., Tax List B:50 (1804); B:47 (1806); and B:46.

[26] Marriage records located on http://usgenweb.org/~ncwarren.

[27] My copy of the census looks like five boys under ten, but it could be two. There are three boys 10-16.

[28] Putnam Co., Ga., Will Book B:2. Martha Kendrick's husband was a cousin of Mary (Kendrick) Fox, whose 1795 will was witnessed by John Wright (Fox) in Mecklenburg Co., Va., as discussed above.

22

divided between them. I bequeath unto my son-in-law Lewis Wright five dollars in cash.

I do further give and bequeath my real and personal Estate and all debt due me at this ___ after paying all my just debts the balance of my property to be equally divided into five equal parts (as follows:)

I do give and bequeath unto my four grandchildren, John W. Carter, William B. Carter, Walton J. Carter, and Robert M. Carter one fifth of my estate to by Equally divided between them.

I do given and bequeath the balance of my Estate unto John Monk, Meredith Kendrick, Priscilla Goode and Betty A. Kendrick to be equally divided between them. And do further nominate and appoint John Monk and Meredith Kendrick my lawful executors. This 6th day of March 1822.

Signed in the presence of   Martha (x) Kendrick

Harvey Kendrick

Richard Wright

Silas Monk.

Georgia, Putnam County) The above within will was duly proven in open court by Harvey Kendrick and Richard Wright subscribing witnesses to the same this 6th day of May 1822.   Coleman Pendleton, C. C. A.

The appearance of Lewis Wright and Richard Wright in the will of Martha Kendrick is consistent with the notion that Lewis Wright was an uncle to Richard W. Wright.[29]

There is a Lewis Wright, age 50-60 living in Putnam Co., Ga., in 1840, listed on the same page with Meredith Kendrick and, as it turns out, his niece and her husband, John and Mary Gossett.[30] This may or may not be the same man.

Child of LEWIS WRIGHT and FANNY DORTCH is:

3.   i. BENJAMIN HARVEY[3] WRIGHT born 7 February 1819 Putnam Co., Va.; d. 28 April 1903 Coweta Co., Ga.

---

[29] Unfortunately, there were two men named Richard Wright in Putnam Co., Ga. at this time: 1865 Richard W. Wright of Decatur Co., Ga., and Richard J. Wright.

[30] 1840 Census Putnam Co., Ga., District 310, p. 195.

3. BENJAMIN HARVEY[3] WRIGHT was born 7 February 1819 in Putnam Co., Ga., and died 28 April 1903 in Newnan, Coweta Co., Ga.[31] He married EMILY EUBANKS TOMPKINS 22 November 1846 Putnam Co., Ga., daughter of NICHOLAS TOMPKINS and KATHARINE GRIFFIN LEVERETT. She was born 5 July 1829 in Putnam Co., Ga., and died 3 March 1914 Newnan, Coweta Co., Ga.

It seems likely that Lewis Wright, was the father of Benjamin Harvey Wright, who was born in Putnam Co., Ga., 7 February 1819. However, his son, William C. Wright, in a biography published in 1917, was described as the grandson of James Wright.[32]

James Wright and his wife moved from Northern Virginia, early in the nineteenth century, to Eastern Georgia, where they reared their family. He was a planter and slave-holder, a man of prominence in his section. A staunch democrat, he took an active interest in political affairs. His vigorous life closed in Putnam County, after seventy-five years of independent and forceful activity.

Benjamin Wright, born February 1819, is living with his son, William C. Wright, in the 1900 Census.[33] Emily E., 70, is there as well. Benjamin Wright's obituary appeared in *The Newnan Herald & Advertiser* on 1 May 1903.[34]

The death of Judge B. H. Wright, which occurred Tuesday afternoon, was an event which cast a gloom over the entire community. It was known that he had been in poor health for some time, and that he was also fettered to the point of helplessness by the enfeeblements of age, yet the announcement of his death came at last as a distinct shock to his friends. He had a sudden attack last Sunday and was completely prostrated. Physicians were

---

[31] Obituary published 1 May 1903 in *The Newnan Herald & Advertiser*. Transcribed by Beth Collins. Located at http://files.usgwarchives.net/ga/coweta/obits/wrightbh.txt.

[32] Knight, Lucian L. A Standard History of Georgia and Georgians, Vol. V. (Chicago: Lewis Publ. Co., 1917,) pp. 2506-2507. Cited hereafter as "Knight, Lucian L."

[33] 1900 Census Newnan, Coweta Co., Ga., ED 18, p. 4, #74/87.

[34] Collins, Beth. Located at http://files.usgwarchives.net/ga/coweta/obits/wrightbh.txt.

summoned, and all was done for his relief that medical skill could suggest, but without avail. He never rallied from the attack, and at 4 o'clock Tuesday afternoon breathed his last.

Judge Wright was a remarkable man in many respects. He was born in Putnam county Feb. 7, 1819, and on Nov. 22, 1846, was married in the same county. In 1849 he moved to Carroll county, and during his residence there was one of its most prominent and useful citizens. In 1851 he was chosen to represent his district in the State Senate, and was also sent as a delegate from Carroll county to the Secession Convention in 1861. In 1864 he entered the Confederate service as a member of the State militia, and remained until the close of the war. In 1870 he moved to Newnan, and continued to reside here until his death. He was a deacon in the Baptist church, having been set apart to this office when quite a young man, and during his long and eventful life never wavered in his fealty to the church of his choice. He was, in all respects, a good man and useful citizen, and will be sadly missed in the community.

He is survived by his aged wife and six children—B. H. Wright, of Atlanta; N. T. Wright, W. C. Wright and Mrs. J. C. Gibson, of Newnan; Mrs. T. S. Roberts, of Seville; Mrs. E. S. Roberts, of Cordele - all of whom were present at the funeral, which occurred Wednesday afternoon at the First Baptist church.

Services were conducted by his pastor, Dr. Nunnally, assisted by all
the ministers of the city. The interment was at Oak Hill.

Benjamin[35] (who lived to become the father of William Carter Wright) was of Putnam County birth. There he was reared. He married Miss Emily Eubanks Tompkins,[36] also a native of Putnam County. Soon after their lives and fortunes were united, they removed to

---

[35] Knight, Lucian L.

[36] Her eldest sister, Maria Ann Tompkins, married Lucius H. Featherston. They lived in Heard County until after the Civil War, when they moved to Newnan, Ga. Their daughter, Mary Emma Featherston, married Henry S. Wright, who is discussed in Chapter 9. My father had no family memory of the connection between these two Wright lines, other than visiting with an elderly "Wright" relative in Newnan when he was a child.

Carroll County, which was the scene of their long and eventful life together. Benjamin Wright became a man of purposive political activities. His strong individuality made him a noteworthy figure in the Georgia State Legislature, of which he was a member, both in Senate and House, representing the Carroll County district. He was, moreover, a member of the historical secession convention of Milledgeville, which severed the southern states from the Union. Vocationally, Benjamin Wright was a planter. He and his wife, Emily Wright, lived to an unusually ripe old age. Despite the service he had given to the Confederate army, Colonel Wright lived to number his years as eighty-three, one year less than those attained by Mrs. Wright, who died in 1914, at the age of eighty-four. Both were active members of the Baptist Church. They reared four sons and three daughters. Tompkins Wright, the eldest, was but sixteen years of age when he joined Captain Beall's companies of the Confederate army; while in service he contracted pneumonia, which soon cut short his promising young life. Mary C. Wright became Mrs. J. C. Gibson, of Newnan, Georgia. Giles B. Wright is a resident of Atlanta, Georgia. Nicholas T. Wright died in 1909, at Newnan, Georgia. Emma Wright and Ada K. Wright married brothers—the former lady becoming Mrs. E. S. Roberts and the latter Mrs. T. S. Roberts, both families establishing homes in Crisp, Ben Hill County, Georgia.

Children of BENJAMIN WRIGHT and EMILY TOMPKINS are:[37]

i. EUBANKS TOMPKINS[4] WRIGHT, b. 9 December 1847 Heard Co., Ga.; d. 16 Jan 1865 Newnan, Coweta Co., Ga.
    "Tompkins Wright, the eldest, was but sixteen years of age when he joined Captain Beall's companies of the Confederate army; while in service he contracted pneumonia, which soon cut short his promising young life."[38]

[37] Collins, Beth. Jones/Roberts Tree. 5 July 2008. Located at http://wc.rootsweb.ancestry.com, (db. 300601).
[38] Knight, Lucian L.

ii. MARY CATHERINE[4] WRIGHT, b. 1 December 1849 Carroll Co., Ga.; d. 15 March 1920 Newnan, Coweta Co., Ga.; m. JOSHUA CALLAWAY GIBSON 16 April 1871 Carroll Co., Ga.; b. 1 December 1845; d. 2 February 1914 Newnan, Coweta Co., Ga.

4. iii. GILES BENJAMIN[4] WRIGHT, b. 28 October 1851 Carroll Co., Ga.; d. 7 June 1923 Newnan, Coweta Co., Ga.; m. ALLIE DICKSON; b. 29 October 1854; d. 11 April 1899 Newnan.

iv. NICHOLAS TOMPKINS[4] WRIGHT, b. 23 January 1854 Carroll Co., Ga.; d. 17 October 1907 Newnan; m. SUE PINSON; b. 20 September 1856; d. 12 August 1935 Newnan.

Sue P. Wright is head of household in the 1910 Census with Martha, 22, and Mary E., 19. She is listed as a librarian.[39] In 1920, "Emily" is 26 and Martha is not in the household.[40]

N. T. Wright's obituary was published in *The Newnan Herald & Advertiser* 17 October 1907.[41]

"It is with a feeling of deep sorrow and regret that the Herald & Advertiser chronicles this week the death of another good citizen, Mr. N. T. Wright, this sad event occurring yesterday morning about 6 o'clock. Mr. Wright had been in poor health for several months, but did not take to his bed until about three weeks ago. He was seriously ill from the first, the complication of ailments from which he suffered causing his family much uneasiness, although it was hoped that he would ultimately rally from the attack. It was soon apparent however that his condition was critical and but little hope was held out by his loved ones that he would survive the attack. He lingered until yesterday morning when death ended his sufferings. Mr. Wright was a good man and useful citizen and his death causes the deepest sorrow in the community. His numerous admirable traits and genial disposition drew to him

---

[39] 1910 Census Militia District 646, Coweta Co., Ga., ED 32, p. 12A, #745/767.
[40] 1920 Census Newnan, Coweta Co., Ga., ED 33, #253/283.
[41] Gravelle, Candace. Accessed 23 October 2008. Located at http://files.usgwarchives.net/ga/coweta/newspapers/nw1676newspape.txt.

27

many warm friends who were as strongly attached to him as he was loyal to them. To those friends his death comes as a personal bereavement while the community at large mourns the loss of a useful and popular citizen. Deceased was 52 years of age. Besides his aged mother, two brothers and three sisters, he is survived by his wife and two children, who have the sincere sympathy of everyone in their sad affliction. The funeral took place this afternoon at half past two, from the Central Baptist church and was largely attended. Services were conducted by his pastor, Dr. J. S. Hardaway, assisted by Rev. F. J. Amis and Rev. W. J. Cotter, after which the body was laid to rest in Oak Hill Cemetery."

"It is with deep regret that we learned of the death of Mr. Nick Wright of Newnan.[42] Some years ago he taught school in Turin and by his faithful work and Christian deportment won the admiration and confidence of the entire community. The sweet songs he used to sing with us still ring in our memory and yet in nobler, sweeter strains he joins now in anthems of paraise around the Throne of God. Our deepest sympathy goes out to the family in their bereavement."

Children of NICHOLAS WRIGHT and SUE PINSON are:

1. MARTHA[5] WRIGHT, b. 1888.
2. MARY EMILY[5] WRIGHT, b. 24 September 1892; d. 29 March 1929.
3. WILLIAM PINSON[5], b. 15 October 1882; d. 10 October 1884.
4. TOMPKINS[5] WRIGHT, b. 9 February 1884; d. 6 May 1903.

v. EMILY ELIZABETH[4] WRIGHT, b. 24 November 1856 Heard Co., Ga.; d. 17 August 1953 Crisp Co., Ga.; m. EUGENE SUMMERFIELD ROBERTS, SR. 5 November 1879 Newnan, son of GRANT ROBERTS and ELIZA GARLAND DAVENPORT; b. 13 September 1849 Whitesburg, Carroll Co., Ga.; d. 20 March 1916 Hatley, Crisp Co., Ga.

---

[42] In the edition of 25 October 1907, "Turin News."

"Emma Wright and Ada K. Wright married brothers—the former lady becoming Mrs. E. S. Roberts and the latter Mrs. T. S. Roberts, both families establishing homes in Crisp, Ben Hill County, Georgia."[43]

5.   vi. WILLIAM CARTER[4] WRIGHT, b. 6 January 1866; d. 11 June 1933; m. PAULINE E. ARNOLD 14 September 1892; b. 29 November 1868; d. 17 April 1918; m. (2) ROSA MAE (FEATHERSTON) BUNN October 1919.

   vii. ADA KENDRICK[4] WRIGHT, b. 18 April 1863; d. 23 December 1954; m. THOMAS SANFORD ROBERTS 15 December 1886 Newnan, son of GRANT ROBERTS and ELIZA GARLAND DAVENPORT; b. 7 April 1860; d. 24 August 1919.

4. GILES BENJAMIN[4] WRIGHT was born 28 October 1851 in Carroll Co., Ga., and died 7 June 1923 in Newnan, Coweta Co., Ga. He married ALAMEDA CALIFORNIA DICKSON 13 September 1885 Carroll Co., Ga. She was born 29 October 1854 and died 11 April 1899 in Newnan.

Giles Wright was listed as "Chas." B. Wright in the 1900 Census for Fulton Co., Ga., where he was listed as a railroad agent.[44] His birth date was listed as October 1850, and he had three children, Emily, b. July 1887, Lou, b. August 1888, and Dickson, b. April 1890. Also present in the same dwelling as a separate head of household was Texas Dickson, b. June 1844, who is presumably his deceased wife's mother or aunt.

In 1910, Giles B. Wright, 59, is a railroad clerk, and his wife is Anna T. Wright, also 59. Emily, 21, is not employed, Lou, 20, is a stenographer for the railroad, and Dickson, 19, is a shipping clerk in a grocery.[45]

Children of GILES WRIGHT and ALLIE DICKSON are:

   i. EMILY[5] WRIGHT, b. 11 July 1886; d. 23 February 1980 Newnan.

---

[43] Knight, Lucian L.

[44] 1900 Census Ward 1, Atlanta, Fulton Co., Ga., ED 44, p. 4, #76/77.

[45] 1910 Census Ward 1, Atlanta, Fulton Co., Ga., ED 46, p. 16B, #153/238.

ii. LOU[5] WRIGHT, b. 7 August 1887; d. 24 February 1982 Newnan.

iii. DICKSON[5] WRIGHT, b. 30 April 1889; d. 6 March 1960 Newnan; m. MAIE EVERETT

Child of DICKSON WRIGHT and MAIE EVERETT is:

1. MARY EVERETT[6] WRIGHT, b. 28 October 1915

5. WILLIAM CARTER[4] WRIGHT was born 6 January 1866 Carroll Co., Ga., and died 11 June 1933 in Newnan, Coweta Co., Ga. He married (1) PAULINE E. ARNOLD 14 September 1892 Coweta Co., Ga. She was born 29 November 1868 and died 17 April 1918 in Newnan. He married (2) ROSA MAE (FEATHERSTON) BUNN October 1919 in Newnan, Coweta Co., Ga., daughter of GILES WINFIELD FEATHERSTON and ROSA RICHARDSON, and widow of FRANK SWANSON BUNN. She was born 30 September 1872 Newnan, Coweta Co., Ga., and died 1972 in Cedartown, Polk Co., Ga.

Representative from Georgia; born on a farm in Carroll County, Ga., January 6, 1866; moved with his parents to Newnan, Coweta County, Ga., in 1869; attended the common and high schools of Newnan; studied law; was admitted to the bar in 1886; lawyer, private practice; banker; farmer; city attorney for Newnan, Ga., 1892-1895; solicitor of the city court of Newnan, Ga., 1894-1903; member of the board of education, 1910-1918; chairman of the Democratic Georgia state executive committees, 1910 and 1911; elected as a Democrat to the Sixty-fifth Congress to fill the vacancy caused by the resignation of United States Representative William C. Adamson; reelected to the Sixty-sixth and to the six succeeding Congresses (January 16, 1918-March 3, 1933); did not seek re-nomination to the Seventy-third Congress in 1932; died on June 11, 1933, in Newnan, Ga.; interment in Oak Hill Cemetery.[46]

---

[46] http://bioguide.congress.gov/scripts/biodisplay.pl?index=W000773. Accessed 13 Dec 2008.

William C. Wright is head of household in the 1900 census with his wife, Pauline E., b. November 1868, daughters Evelyn M., b. November 1893, and Pauline A., b. May 1900, along with his parents, Benjamin Wright, and Emily E. Wright.[47]

In the 1910 Census, he is head of household with Pauline, 40, Evelyn, 16, Arnold 8, and William C., 1 7/12, are living with Emily E. Wright, 80, Lizzie Arnold, 38, Lucile Arnold, 30, and James Wisdom, 14.[48] I have not located him in the 1920 Census, presumably because he was living in the District of Columbia. In 1930 he and Rosa were living alone without children in Newnan.[49]

A self-made, educated man is William C. Wright, whose fortunate combination of native gifts and consistent ambition have led him from point to point of his successful career.[50] Carroll County was the scene of his nativity, the date of that event being January 6, 1866. Showing at an early age an interest in books and public affairs, as well as a talent for persuasive oratory, he continued his studies through the high school and soon after became a popular young schoolmaster in the educational institutions of Carroll County. Such work, pursued by a young person of character, soon develops individuality and initiative to a practical degree; those were the qualities which guided William Wright to the choice of the law as a life-work and those have been as well notable characteristics of its performance.

Mr. Wright's first tutor in legal lore was Gen. L. H. Featherstone,[51] whose office our subject entered at Newnan, Georgia. When those studies were cut short by General Featherstone's death, they were resumed under ex- Governor William Y. Adkinson, of Newnan, Georgia. After this period of training was concluded, Mr. Wright was formally admitted to the practice of law in 1886.

---

[47] 1900 Census Newnan, Coweta Co., Ga., ED 18, p. 4, #74/87.

[48] 1910 Census Newnan, Coweta Co., Ga., ED 32, p. 17B.

[49] 1930 Census Newnan, Coweta Co., Ga., ED 3, p. 2A, #31/34.

[50] Knight, Lucian L.

[51] He is my great-great-grandfather, and namesake, but he spelled his last name Featherston, not Featherstone, even though my grandfather had the "e" added by his mother.

Attorney Wright's first professional partnership was formed with the Hon. P. S. Willcoxon. After five years spent as junior partner of the firm, Mr. Wright entered another professional relation, becoming the head of the partnership of Wright and Farmer, his junior partner being L. W. Farmer of Newnan. Two years of legal practice in this connection were followed by another change. At that time our subject became associated with the Hon. R. W. Freeman and the firm thus formed was known for the eight years of its existence as the leading legal office of the City of Newnan. This association was not to be permanent, however, for Mr. Freeman was eventually called to the bench, as superior judge for Coweta Circuit. Attorney Wright has since continued to administer independently the legal business of the large class of clients acquired and his is conceded to be the most important practice of the community. Mr. Wright has in the interim been honored with the office of solicitor of City Court of Newnan, Coweta County, holding that office for eight years and demonstrating his ability as one of the ablest prosecutors who have been known in the history of the county. With all his heavy professional business, he finds time for practical participation in affairs educational and matters agricultural. He has served for several years on the Newnan Board of Education, having a sincere and deep interest in this phase of civic life. Mr. Wright, like every true Southerner, has a genuine affection for "our mother, the earth," and takes delight in managing the business of his farm. He has a genius for getting results from the soil and holds the record of having raised forty bales of cotton with the use of but two plows.

The attractive and efficient mistress of Attorney Wright's home is Pauline Arnold Wright, to whom he was married September 15, 1892. Mrs. Wright is a daughter of William P. and Mary (Harris) Buford, well-known citizens of the community. Several children have come to the home of Mr. and Mrs. Wright. Evelyn, the eldest, was born in 1893; Emily, the second, died at the age of four years and her little sister Pauline was called by "the reaper of the flowers" at the age of two years. Arnold, the first son, and William C. Wright, junior, are the other members of the family, and all were born in Newnan, Georgia.

Fraternal and religious life have their due share in the life of the Wright family. Mrs. Wright is a loyal and helpful member of the Methodist Church, to whose interests she devotes both time and talent; while her husband continues his allegiance to the Baptist division of the church, so faithfully adhered to by his ancestors. He is a popular Mason, having been honored by all chairs to that of Shrine. The Elks also claim his membership as a genial and distinguished member. A well-rounded life is William C. Wright's, one of fully deserved success, of broad interests, of admirable character, of substantial qualities well worthy of emulation.

Children of WILLIAM WRIGHT and PAULINE ARNOLD are:

   i. EVELYN[5] WRIGHT, b. November 1893 Newnan, Coweta Co., Ga.; m. WILLIAM N. BANKS.

        In 1920 they were living in Grantville, Coweta Co., Ga., and had no children.[52]

  ii. EMILY[5] WRIGHT, b. 20 April 1895; d. 4 December 1899.

 iii. PAULINE[5] WRIGHT, b. 4 May 1900; d. 7 November 1901.

 iv. ARNOLD[5] WRIGHT, b. about 1902 Newnan, Coweta Co., Ga.

  v. WILLIAM CARTER[5] WRIGHT, JR., b. 16 Sep 1908; d. 11 July 1971 Newnan[53]; m. GWENDOLYN ADAMS; b. 16 December 1910; d. 27 June 1980 Newnan.

        William C. Wright was living with his sister, Evelyn Banks, in the 1920 Census in Grantville, Coweta Co., Ga.[54] William N. Banks was a bookkeeper and his household included his wife, his mother, Theopa Bobo Banks, 62, his brother, Donald Banks, 24, and his sister, Emma E. Banks, 22, as well as his brother-in-law.

---

[52] 1920 Census Grantville, Coweta Co., Ga., ED 44, p. 4A, #66/66.
[53] SSDI lists his residence at the time of death as Grantville, Coweta Co., Ga., and death as June 1971. Accessed on http://www.familysearch.org 13 December 2008.
[54] 1920 Census Grantville, Coweta Co., Ga., ED 44, p. 4A, #66/66.

1783 Robert Wright of Brunswick County, Virginia

On 20 February 1777, Thomas Briggs and his wife Betty and Robert Briggs and his wife, Ruth, sold 280 acres to Robert Wright, described as:

> beginning S... line where it corners the Gum Clark [Creek?] thence along his line to corner at Briggs living Black [gum?] thence up this said branch, to head to a corner red oak thence by a line of marked trees to Mathis line thence up the said to the Garden Branch, thence down the said branch to the beginning....[55]

This indenture was witnessed by Reuben Wright, Joshua Wright, and William Walker.

On 15 October 1777 Reuben Wright, "of King William Co.," bought 150 acres in Brunswick Co., Va., from Thomas Briggs and his wife Elizabeth, described as:

> beginning on beginning at a small hickory on a Branch thence up the meanders of the said branch to a red oak on the same thence south three hundred and eight pole to a red oak on the line Hensley his line ...two hundred two poles to his corner on Mathis [Martin?]...thence by a line of marked trees to the land of M... Branch and David H... in the said branch to Walker's Line thence along his line to the beginning....[56]

Witnesses to this indenture included Robert Wright, Samuel Briggs and Joshua Wright.

On 15 June 1778 John Wright bought 101 acres, from Jonathan Williams and his wife Elizabeth, which was described as bounded by John Williams, Ch. Matthews and William Townsend. The indenture was witnessed by Robert Wright, Robert Kennedy, and Henry Martin.[57]

The indenture just prior to the deed above shows Abraham Martin sold 100 ac. of land on the north side of Waqua Creek to Robert Kennedy in an indenture witnessed by Thomas Briggs,

---

[55] Brunswick Co., Va., Deed Book 13:69.
[56] Brunswick Co., Va., Deed Book 13:67.
[57] Brunswick Co., Va., Deed Book 13:351.

Henry Martin, and Samuel Stegall.[58] This seems to establish a connection between John and Robert, and by implication, with John and Reuben.

On 27 March 1780, Samuel Briggs and Betty Briggs, his wife, and Robert Briggs and Ruth Briggs, his wife, sold to Richard Lamb 70 acres of land described as "….along the line of William Walker on the north, …along the line of Robert Wright on the west…"[59] The indenture was witnessed by Thomas Penn, John Allen, Robert Kennedy and David Thomas.

These deeds establish that Reuben Wright, of King William Co., Va., Robert Wright, and John Wright all took up residence on Waqua Creek, Brunswick Co., Va., near the Briggs, Walker, and Kennedy (or Cannaday) family in late 1777 and early 1778.

The Brunswick County Tax List makes it clear that Robert Wright, living near John and Reuben Wright, was dead by 1783.[60] The list shows five taxable individuals, who are not named, ten slaves listed by name, and two white males under 21.

On motion of Reubin Wright, Certificate granted him to obtain Letters of Administration on est of Robert Wright, decd. Bartholomew Ingram and Thomas Penn securities for £2000. William Walker, Richard Lamb, John Haskins, and George Trotter to appraise the estate and the same persons to lay off to the widow her dower.[61]

A writing purporting to be the Last Will and Testament of Robert Wright decd. was presented…Executors named refused, and Austin Wright with Thomas Penn and Robert Wright securities for £2000 were named.[62]

---

[58] Brunswick Co., Va., Deed Book 13:350.

[59] Brunswick Co., Va., Deed Book 14:74. Proved 23 October 1780.

[60] Brunswick Co., Va. Tax List 1st District, 1783, p. 13. The total tax was £5.12.9 which was quite substantial compared to his neighbors.

[61] Brunswick Co., Va., Court Order Book 2:138. [Mon. 28 Apr 1783] The dower is recorded on Order Book 2:162 for Mary Wright.

[62] Brunswick Co., Va., Court Order Book 2:157. [Mon. 26 May 1783]

Last Will and Testament of Robert Wright of Brunswick Co., Va. [63]

I Robert Wright of Brunswick County do make this my last will and Testament after all my just debts are paid as followeth—I give unto Mary wife one negro man named George one woman saddle one feather bed and furniture.

Item I give unto my son Robt. Wright one negro woman named Milley and her youngest child Silvia.

Item I give unto my daughter Jane Featherston one negro girl named Fib to her and her heirs I give unto my son Thomas Wright one Negro man named Daniel to him and his heirs.

I give unto my son Joshua one Negro boy named Jacob to him and his heirs. My will and desire is that where I have given Negroes they shall have _right to keep them. Also my will and desire is the remaining part of my estate be equally divided amongst my wife and children that are now living, the negroes that are not mentioned here I desire may not go out of the family, my desire is that my land should be sold my widow having a third part my desire is that Uriah's children may have an equal part of my movable estate. I give unto son Reubin Wright my two work steers. I do appoint my sons Reubin and Joshua my Executors of this my last will and Testament this 11th Day August 1781.

s/ Robert Wright

Brunswick County Court 26th May 1783

This writing was produced as the last will and Testament of Robert Wright decd. and on examining sundry witnesses the Court are of opinion the same was wholly wrote by said Testator and that same ought to be recorded as his agreed [?] last will and Testament, and the Executors therein named having refused thereto[?] on the motion of Austin Wright and he having given bond with security and taken the oath according to Law certificate was granted him for obtaining Letters of Administration of the said estate with this his will annexed.

Ex teste Drury Stith ClC

---

[63] Brunswick County, Va., Court Order Book 2:438-439. (Transcription by Carol York.)

This will shows Robert Wright was literate and apparently drew this will without benefit of counsel. He neglected to have the will witnessed, so when his heirs entered the will into court, the Court had to investigate to determine that this was a true holographic will. Third, the two sons named executors, Joshua and Reuben, declined to perform the duty and deferred to an unnamed brother, Austin (Augustine.)[64] Yet another son, Robert served as security for his brother. The will also implies that there are children who have pre-deceased Robert. Unfortunately, he did not name those deceased children. He also had given slaves to others, and he wished to confirm their ownership of his gift, but he did not list the recipients. The will implies that he had at least one brother, Uriah, who had children, as he wished for Uriah's children to share in the division of his estate.

Austin Wright is named as a defendant in Brunswick Co., Court 1769,[65] and bought land in Mecklenburg Co., Va., on 10 September 1771, so Austin Wright was born before June 1748. Robert[3] Wright appears to be the youngest son, but he was able to act as security for Austin in 1783, so was born before 1762. Reuben[3] Wright appears to be the eldest son, as he has adult children in the tax lists of 1783-1785, and is therefore likely to be about 55 years old himself, or born about 1730 to 1735. The available estimates, then, suggest that Robert Wright was born no later than 1710, and that he had children spread over more than two decades.

On 4 September 1786 "Augustin" Wright of Mecklenburg Co., Va., sold to John Penn of Brunswick Co. for £106 a tract of 175 acres beginning "at Walker's line where it crosses the gum branch, thence along the said line to Samuel Briggs' spring branch...to Stith's line..."[66] This indenture was signed by "Austin" Wright and witnessed by Samuel Briggs, Reuben Wright, and Robert Wright. This 175 acres leaves 105 acres of his father's purchase unaccounted for.

Thomas Penn applied for letters of administration on the estate of Mary Wright 22 September 1794. He posted bond for

---

[64] The fact that Augustine is not named might imply that he was a brother, rather than a son, but the data for him, (c.f. 1829 Austin Wright of Mecklenburg Co., Va.) makes it clear that he is too young to be anything other than a son.

[65] Brunswick County, Va., Court Order Book 11:74 [27 June 1769] Petition of Charnel Hightower v Augustine Wright is ordered to abate.

[66] Brunswick Co., Va., Deed Book 14:257.

£300 with John Penn as his security. John Payne, William Orgain, William M. Johnson and George Trotter were appointed to appraise the estate.[67] An appraisal of the estate of Mary Wright was returned in Brunswick County, Virginia, 26 October 1794 by George Trotter, William D. Orgain, and William M. Johnson.[68] The inventory was returned 28 September 1795.[69]

Genealogical Summary

1. ROBERT[1] WRIGHT was born before 1710 possibly in King William Co., Va., and died before 26 May 1783 in Brunswick Co., Virginia. He married MARY (PENN?). She died before 22 September 1794 Brunswick Co., Va.

Children of ROBERT WRIGHT and MARY are:

   i. REUBEN[2] WRIGHT was b. say 1735 perhaps in King William Co., Va.; d. 1789 Brunswick Co., Va.

   ii. JANE[2] WRIGHT, b. about 1738 in Va.; d. 16 November 1812 Charlotte Co., Va.; m. CHARLES FEATHERSTON; d. before 25 January 1790 Brunswick Co., Va.

      The will of Charles Featherstone was written 3 April 1788 and proved 25 January 1790 in Brunswick Co., Va. [70]

Children of JANE WRIGHT and CHARLES FEATHERSTON are:[71]

   1. FAITH[3] FEATHERSTON, m. DAVID GRANT.

   2. CHARLOTTE[3] FEATHERSTON, m. BURWELL GRANT.

   3. HEZEKIAH[3] FEATHERSTON, b. about 1760 Brunswick Co., Va., d. between 22 May 1827 and 4 June 1827, Charlotte Co., Va.; m. NANCY TARPLEY 26 August 1794 Charlotte Co., Va., daughter of JAMES TARPLEY.

---

[67] Brunswick Co., Va., Court Order Book 16:320.

[68] Brunswick Co., Va., Will Book 5:650. Cited in Bradley, Stephen E. Brunswick County, Virginia Will Books, Vol. 3, (1780-1795.) (Lawrenceville, VA: 1997,) p. 92.

[69] Brunswick Co., Va., Court Order Book 16:500.

[70] Brunswick Co. Va., Will Book 5:342.

[71] Featherston Findings, Vol. 1:11. Located at http://Featherstone_society.org. His connection to the descendants of 1682 Charles Featherston of Henrico Co., Va., who is the ancestor of the Featherstons who married descendants of 1832 John Wright of Clarke Co., Ga., is uncertain.

4. CAROLUS[3] FEATHERSTON, d. after April 1830 Franklin Co., Ky.; m. (1) GILLEY BRUMFIELD 21 Nov. 1782, Brunswick Co., Va., daughter of WILLIAM BRUMFIELD; m. (2) LUCY ELMORE 10 December 1787 Charlotte Co., Va.; m. (3) ALVA LUCY, Charlotte Co., Va.

Carolus Featherston was a planter. He moved to Fayette Co., Ky., about 1815.

5. JEREMIAH[3] FEATHERSTON, b. 4 November 1776 Brunswick Co., Va.; d. 11 July 1854 Fayette Co., Kentucky; m. ELIZABETH ELMORE 4 January 1796 Charlotte Co., Va.

iii. JOSHUA[2] WRIGHT.

Joshua[3] Wright appears in conjunction with the deeds listed above, but does not appear in the tax lists of Brunswick County from 1783 to 1815. There is no will of record, so it seems fair to assume that he died or left area about the time of his father's death in 1783, which may be why Austin Wright replaced him as administrator.

iii. AUGUSTINE[2] (AUSTIN) WRIGHT, b. about 1748; d. 1829 Mecklenburg Co., Va.; m. (1) SARAH LARK about 1775, Mecklenburg Co., Va.; m. (2) LUCY HOLLOWAY 1 May 1806, Mecklenburg Co., Va.

iv. THOMAS[2] WRIGHT

Thomas Wright does not appear on the tax rolls for Brunswick Co., Va. The first time a Thomas Wright appears on the Mecklenburg Co., Va., tax roll was 1799.[72] The evidence convinces me this man is the eldest son of 1829 Austin Wright of Mecklenburg Co., Virginia. Thomas Wright is a witness to the will of William Briggs 5 July 1805 Brunswick Co., Va.[73]

Thomas Wright appears on the tithe lists for Lunenburg Co., Va., which was originally part of

---

[72] Mecklenburg Co., Va., Tax List, Lower District, 1799, p. 68. In 1798 Thomas is shown as a son of Reuben Wright, (p. 49) and again in 1801 (p.40). Interstingly 1819 Reuben Wright of Mecklenburg Co., Va., does not mention a son named Thomas, although he went to some pains to mention his deceased son Robert, and to disinherit his son Joshua's wife. (See 1819 Reuben Wright of Mecklenburg Co., Va.)

[73] Brunswick Co., Va., Will Book 7:137 [23 Dec 1805.] In: Bradley, Stephen E. Brunswick County, Virginia Will Books, Vol. 5: 1804-1812. (Lawrenceville, Va.: 1998.)

Brunswick Co., in 1749 in conjunction with John Wright.[74] (See discussion in Chapter 4 under 1804 Thomas Wright of Lunenburg Co., Virginia.)

v. ROBERT[3] WRIGHT, b. say 1762 Mecklenburg Co., Va.; d. before 1820 Mecklenburg Co., Va.; m. NANCY WRIGHT 16 November 1792 Mecklenburg Co., Va., daughter of AUSTIN WRIGHT?

Robert Wright with one poll appears in conjunction with Reuben Wright and John Wright (tailor) in 1790.[75] In 1791 he appears with no taxables, and one under 21,[76] while in 1792 he is back to paying one poll.[77] His last appearance on this tax list was in 1793.[78] Robert Wright of Brunswick Co., married Nancy Wright 16 November 1792 in Mecklenburg County, Va., with Austin Wright as his bondsman.[79] This certainly suggests that Austin and Robert Wright were related. This Austin Wright is almost certainly 1829 Austin Wright of Mecklenburg County, Va., who was a son of 1783 Robert Wright of Brunswick County. This Robert Wright, then, may be the youngest son of 1782 Robert Wright.

The family connection seems strengthened by analysis of the Mecklenburg County deeds. There is a deed, not examined, in which William Price sold land to Robert Wright on 13 January 1794 in Mecklenburg County, Va.[80]

Robert Wright appears on the Mecklenburg Co., Va., tax lists in 1796, when he had one poll and two slaves.[81] He appears on the same page with 1819 Reuben Wright and 1829 Austin Wright. He appears

[74] Bell, Landon C. Sunlight on the Southside. (Lists of Tithes: Lunenburg Co., Virginia, 1748-1783.) (Baltimore: Genealogical Publishing Co., 1974,) p. 67. Cited hereafter as Bell.

[75] Brunswick Co., Va. Tax List, Upper District, 1790, p. 31.

[76] Brunswick Co., Va. Tax List, Upper District, 1791, p. 66.

[77] Brunswick Co., Va. Tax List, Upper District, 1792, p. 64.

[78] Brunswick Co., Va. Tax List, Upper District, 1793, p. 66.

[79] Elliott, Katherine B. Marriage Records 1765-1810, Mecklenburg County, Virginia. (Easley, S. C.: Southern Historical Press, repr. 1984.) p. 136.

[80] Mecklenburg Co., Va., Deed Book 8:376.

[81] Mecklenburg Co., Va. Tax List, Lower District, 1796, p. 32.

through 1799,[82] but is not present in 1800 or 1801. He reappears in 1802, and stays through 1805, after which he again disappears.[83]

The 1820 Census does show a Nancy Wright with herself and four young children, one boy under 10, one girl under 10, and two girls 10-16.[84] This could be the Nancy Wright who married David Wright in 1797, except the data suggest she was born before 1775, which is why I have placed the information here.

The deed books of Mecklenburg Co. contain information relevant to the problems of Robert Wright. Robert Wright entered an indenture with Richard Russell and Kirby Langford on 19 November 1801.[85] On 14 March 1803 Robert Wright of Mecklenburg Co., Va., and Richard Russell of Warren Co., N. C., and Kirby ("Curby") Langford of Warren Co., N. C., made and indenture "said Robert Wright is indebted to Richard Russell for £89 14s. 3d., this plus the 5s. for 172 acres...."[86] The land was described as "Beginning at a corner black gum on the county line on a Branch on Amasa Palmer's, Reuben Wright's, and Jacob Short's corner, thence west along said county line to a corner on Curb Langford's line, thence North along said Langford's line to Lucy Cunningham's corner, thence East along said Cunningham's line to a corner pine on Reuben Wright's line, near the head of a Branch, thence east along said branch to the beginning; also including on Bed and furniture, one Colt, thirteen head Hogs, all my corn now cribbed, supposed to be 30 barrels, two stack blades, and all my tobacco now hanging in my Barn supposed to be twelve hundred weight...." All of this was sold to Curby Langford with the proviso that if Robert Wright repaid the money, plus interest, before 1 April 1803, he could have the property back, and that if

---

[82] Mecklenburg Co., Va. Tax List, Lower District, 1797, p. 38; 1798, p. 49; 1799, p. 64.

[83] Mecklenburg Co., Va. Tax List, Lower District, 1802, p. 40; 1803, p. 46; 1804, p. 50; 1805, p. 54.

[84] 1820 Census Mecklenburg Co., Va., p. 158A, 10000-12001, no slaves.

[85] Mecklenburg Co., Va., Court Order Book 11:130.

[86] Mecklenburg Co., Va., Deed Book 11:349.

the money was not repaid, then Langford could sell the property, with the excess over the amount owed, plus interest, to go to Robert Wright. Robert Wright signed with a mark, while Russell and Langford signed their names. Witnesses were Presley Hinton, William B. Langley, Thomas Wright, and Sterling Pitchford.

On 14 May 1804 Robert Wright and Nancy Wright, his wife sold to Donaldson Potter for £129 a tract of unspecified acreage described as "beginning at a corner Gum in the County line on the Round Hill Branch, thence West on the County line to Corner where (formerly Fields) now line of Samuel Hopkins, jr. intersects the said County line thence by the line of the said Samuel Hopkins, Junr., until it Intersects the line of (formerly William Price) now John Hopkins,[87] thence on the said John Hopkins line until it Corners on a line on the Round Hill Branch thence down the Branch as it Meanders to the first Station...." [88]This deed was purportedly signed by Robert Wright and Nancy Wright and witnessed by Curby Langford, Joseph F. Speed, Austin Wright, Jr., and Isham Fox.

Robert Wright and Nancy, his wife, sued Austin Wright in chancery in July 1805, when they received the right to depose Mary Lark.[89] The case appears to have been settled out of court, as no record of it appears later.

There are scattered later references to Robert Wright, but it is less clear these refer to the same man. Robert Wright acquired slaves in a deed entered 16 March 1812.[90] Robert Wright reappears on the tax rolls in 1812 with one son under 21.[91] In 1813, he appears with Robert Wright, Jr.[92] The tax rolls after 1814 have not been examined. The 1810 Census shows a Robert

---

[87] On 8 Feb 1796 Austin Wright replaced John Hopkins as surveyor of the road because the latter had moved. (Mecklenburg Co., Va., Court Order Book 9:11.

[88] Mecklenburg Co., Va., Deed Book 12:22.

[89] Mecklenburg Co., Va., Court Order Book 12:439.

[90] Mecklenburg Co., Va., Deed Book 14:544.

[91] Mecklenburg Co., Va. Tax List, 1812, p. 52.

[92] Mecklenburg Co., Va. Tax List, 1813, p. 55. Unfortunately, 1819 Reuben Wright also has a son named Robert, so it is not perfectly clear that this is the same person.

Wright living in Lunenburg County, but no one of that name is in either Brunswick or Mecklenburg County. The 1820 Census does not show anyone named Robert Wright in any of the three counties. There is a Robert Wright in Warren County, who is 26-45, and might be Robert[4] Wright, Jr., grandson of 1783 Robert Wright of Brunswick Co., Va.[93] However, it appears that Robert[3] Wright, son of the same died without a will or left the area sometime before 1820.

Children of ROBERT WRIGHT and NANCY WRIGHT:

1. ROBERT[4] WRIGHT, b. 1793 Mecklenburg Co., Va.; m. REBECCA TURNER 28 November 1810 Warren Co., N. C.

    Robert Wright, Jr., was grantee of James Whitlow, Sr., on 16 March 1812.[94] Robert Wright and Rebecca were grantors to Marley Taylor on 15 July 1816.[95] Robert Wright was also grantor to Robert H. Jones, et al., on 14 December 1820.[96]

    There is evidence from the Warren Co., N. C., Court Order Books that suggest he belongs here, as on 24 Feb 1812, Stephen Turner gave evidence that Robert Wright, Jr., of Mecklenburg Co., Virginia was entitled to two slaves by virtue of his intermarriage with Rebecca Turner, now Rebecca Wright, formerly of Warren Co., N. C.[97]

2. Other unknown children

---

[93] Robert Wright is shows with two sons under five, two daughters under five, one female 10-15, and seven slaves. This suggests that Robert's wife is dead—with four children in four years, it seems probable.

[94] Mecklenburg Co., Va., Deed Book 14:376.

[95] Mecklenburg Co., Va., Deed Book 16:253.

[96] Mecklenburg Co., Va., Deed Book 18:420). Robert Wright, Jr., appears on the tax lists in 1813 only, which is certainly consistent with the idea that he is living elsewhere. Without examining the deeds, I cannot tell if the deed to Robert Jones is by this man, or by Robert[4], (Reuben[3], Reuben[2]) Wright.

[97] Warren Co., Va., Court Order Book , p 270, [24 Feb 1812]. Cited by Christmas-Beattie, Ginger. Warren County, North Carolina Minutes to the Court of Pleas and Quarter Sessions, Vol. VII (1810-1813). (Forest Grove, OR: Ancestral Tracks, 2001,) p. 76.

1784 Uriah Wright of Brunswick Co., Va.

Uriah Wright appears on the 1762 tithe list for Brunswick Co., Va., along with Robert Wright, John Wright, and Jeremiah Wright. Uriah Wright, Jeremiah Wright, Robert Wright and John Wright also appear on 24 May 1773 petition for release from the levies of St. Andrew's Parish.[98]

Uriah Wright appears in several suits with members of the Price family. On 27 June 1769 a suit by Edmunds & Rose against Uriah Wright and Joseph Price was dismissed by agreement.[99] On 22 Aug 1769 John Ezell was appointed overseer of the highway from Lucas' quarter to Pennington's ford with the hands of Joseph Wilkes, John and William Price, Uriah Wright, Thomas Twitty Jr., Jesse Edwards, Lazarus Williams, John and Francis Hagood, & hands of Edmund Ruffin under Thomas Adams.[100] I have found no land records for Uriah Wright. Finally, Uriah Wright witnessed the will of John Price, written 11 May 1772 and proved 25 May 1772.[101] A student of this man reports that John Price's children were 1814 William Price of Green Co., Ky., and his wife, Elizabeth Wright; Catherine Price who married David J. Moss, Sr.; Mary Price; and Joseph Price.[102] This author states that Elizabeth Wright was from Halifax Co., Va., but does not provide documentation and has some apparent conflicts in his statement about John Price, which does record his will and estate. I think it possible that Elizabeth Wright was a child of Uriah Wright.

On 28 March 1774 a petition of "Bottom Steagall v. Thomas Penn, admr. Philip Penn, decd. Debt. Bottom Steagall to pay Uriah Wright and John Jones as wits for him" was recorded.[103] Jeremiah Wright and Robert Wright participated in the estate sale of Philip Penn, as documented in the account filed 28 March 1774.[104] Robert Wright and Reuben Wright were assigned to

---

[98] Brunswick Co., Va., Deed Book 11:138. Cited in Bradley, Stephen E. Brunswick Co., Va., Deed Books. Vol. 5. (Lawrenceville, Va., 1998) p. 62.

[99] Brunswick Co,, Va., Court Order Book 11:83 [27 June 1769].

[100] Brunswick Co,, Va., Court Order Book 11:182 (22 Aug. 1769).

[101] Brunswick Co., Va., Will Book 4:88. Cited in Bradley, Stephen E. Brunswick County, Virginia Will Books, Vol. 2, (1761-1780). (Lawrenceville VA: 1997,) p. 17.

[102] Downs, Freddie. Re: John Price of VA. 20 January 2005. Located at http://genforum.genealogy.com/price/messages/12305.html.

[103] Brunswick Co,, Va., Court Order Book 12:530 (Mon. 28 March 1774)

[104] Brunswick Co., Va., Will Book 4:196. Cited in Bradley, Stephen E. Brunswick County, Virginia Will Books, Vol. 2, (1761-1780). (Lawrenceville VA: 1997,) p. 35.

appraise the estate of Moses Penn, deceased, in 1782.[105] Thomas Penn was security for Reuben Wright when he applied for letters of administration on the estate of his father 1783 Robert Wright of Brunswick Co., Va.[106] These also suggest connection with the family of Moses Penn.

I have found no land deeds for Uriah Wright. However, deeds for others mentioned in these suits establish that he was resident in the upper district of Brunswick Co., Va.[107]

The will of 1783 Robert Wright of Brunswick Co. Va., stated: "My desire is that my land should be sold my widow having a third part my desire is that Uriah's children may have an equal part of my movable estate"[108] It clear Uriah and Elizabeth Wright had children, but they were not named. I have no indications from the tax lists as to who these children might be.

---

[105] Brunswick Co., Va., Court Order Book 13:459. [27 May 1782.]

[106] Brunswick Co., Va., Court Order Book 2:138. [Mon. 28 Apr 1783] The dower is recorded on Order Book 2:162 for Mary Wright.

[107] On 27 May 1791 Edmond Harrison and Mary, his wife, of Prince George Co., Va., sold to Sterling Edmonds of Brunswick Co., for £297, 16 shillings, 10 d., a 325 acre tract of land. "Beginning at Thomas Penns line where it crosses Great Creek...South 50 deg. West eighty-four and a half poles to a corner white oak on the said Edmonds line thence along the said Edmonds line South 12 deg. East one hundred and eighty-two poles to a red oak thence south 19 deg. East sixteen poles to William Johnstons corner black oak thence South 53 deg. East one hundred and fifty-four poles along said Johnstons line to a red oak on the main road thence along the hedge row on the North side of said row North eighty-one degrees East fifty-four poles North 74 East 12 poles North 56 East 26 poles North 33 East fifty- four poles to a small red oak in the said hedge row thence leaving the hedge row North 43 deg. East sixteen poles to a white oak on Great Creek thence up the said creek as it meanders to the Beginning." This indenture was signed by both Edmond and Mary Harrison and witnessed by Mary Gilliam, Sally Harrison, and Jane Harrison. Edmond Harrison's signature was further witnessed before Samuel (x) Hudgins, James Parrish, Thos. Fowlkes and Bennitt (x) Goodrum at the Brunswick County Court 29 November 1791. [Brunswick Co., Va., Deed Book 15:174, 25 Jul 1791] On January 1, 1794 Jesse Briggs of Stokes Co., N. C. sold to Jesse Penn of Brunswick Co., Va., for £100 a 100 acre tract of land beginning: "on John Haskins's line on a small poplar thence near a West course to a branch to corner poplar thence up the said branch as it meanders to a white oak on a large path, thence a South course to corner maple on Stith's line thence along Stith's line to Haskins's corner hiccory [sic] thence along Haskins's line to the Beginning." This indenture was signed by Jesse Briggs and witnessed by Thomas Edmunds, Thomas Penn, James Ogburn, and John Orgain. [Brunswick Co., Va., Deed Book 15:532, 28 Apr 1794].

Thomas Briggs sold tracts of land to 1783 Robert Wright and 1788 Reuben Wright of Brunswick Co., Va., in 1777. [Brunswick Co., Va., Deed Book 13:67, 69.] The will of William Briggs says that John Penn was his brother-in-law, further evidence of interconnection. [Brunswick Co., Va., Will Book 7:137, 5 Jul 1805/23 Dec 1805].

The 1788 tax lists show William Thomas Penn, Jesse Penn, John Penn, and Thomas Penn all living in the Upper District of Brunswick Co., Va. [Brunswick Co., Va., Tax List B (1788) pp. 20,21.]

[108] Last Will and Testament of Robert Wright, 11 Aug 1781. Brunswick Co., Va., Court Order Book 2:438-439. [26 May 1783.]

Uriah Wright died before 24 May 1784 when an inventory of his estate was returned by Elizabeth Wright, administratrix.[109] She had some difficulty settling his estate, for on 28 March 1785 Edward Goodrum, as assignee of Moses Dobbins, filed suit for debt against Elizabeth Wright as administratrix of Uriah Wright, deceased, and John Holman, a suit to which the defendants did not appear.[110] In December 1787, John Williams posted security for an appearance bond of Elizabeth Wright in a suit brought by William Call, surviving partner of Thomas Field.[111]

Elizabeth Wright died before 27 May 1790 when Elisha Clark filed for letters of administration on the estate of Elizabeth Wright, deceased. Bond was posted in the amount of £100 with Peter Williams as security.[112] John Williams, Jones Williams and Lewelling Williams were ordered to appraise the estate.[113] This may have been a formality, though, as no inventory was filed, and it is clear that Elizabeth Wright was impecunious at the time of her death, as the minutes of the annual meeting for the Overseers of the Poor on 25 October 1790 show that Elisha Clark was paid £2, 3sh, 9d on 4 November 1789 for six days care and burying Elizabeth Wright.

Jeremiah Wright

Jeremiah Wright is associated with 1783 Robert Wright and 1784 Uriah Wright, but the record does not allow any statement as to the relationship. Jeremiah Wright and Robert Wright participated in the estate sale of Philip Penn.[114] Jeremiah Wright does not appear in the tax lists, which began in 1782.

William Stanhope Wright

William Stanhope Wright appears on the tax list of 1782 with himself and four sons under 21.[115] He is on the same list with John Wright. There are no records of land purchases or sales

---

[109] Brunswick Co., Va., Will Book 2:231. Brunswick County, VA, Order Book 8 p. 407 (24 May 1784)

[110] Brunswick Co., Va., Court Order Book 14:p.. 95 (28 March 1785)

[111] Brunswick Co., Va., Court Order Book 14 p. 405. (Dec 1787)

[112] Brunswick Co., Va., Court Order Book 15 p. 369 (27 May 1790).

[113] Brunswick Co., Va., Court Order Book 15 p. 370. 27 May 1790

[114] Brunswick Co., Va., Will Book 4:196, 28 March 1744. Cited in Bradley, Stephen E. Brunswick County, Virginia Will Books, Vol. 2, (1761-1780). (Lawrenceville VA: 1997,) p. 35.

[115] Brunswick Co., Va. Tax List, Upper District, 1782, p. 9.

involving William Wright. On 11 June 1785 William Briggs and Elizabeth his wife sold to John Haskins 180 acres of land "on the South side of Waqua Creek bounded by "...John Haskins South to the Great Branch as it meanders to the said creek."[116] This indenture was witnessed by John Green, Randolph Rhodes, Millie Patlow, and William Wright. The indenture makes it clear that William Wright was living in the Waqua Creek area, and is thus presumed to be related.

William Stanhope Wright and John Wright were witnesses to the deed executed by Richard Ramsey and wife Amy, of St. Andrew Parish, Brunswick Co., Va., to Thomas Hailey of the sale for £60 of a 100 acre tract of land bounded by Roger Atkinson, Moses Dobbins, and Richard Littlepage.[117]

The notation William Wright/William Wright with no polls appears on the tax lists for 1787[118] and 1788.[119] This suggests that William Stanhope Wright died about 1786, and that his son William is living, but less than 16 years of age. These are also the years when "Elizabeth" appears and there seems to be some mixing of the Wrights in the upper district. I speculate that William Stanhope Wright was the husband of Elizabeth,[120]

William Stanhope Wright witnessed the will of George Walker written 4 February 1779 and proved 25 December 1780. He also witnessed the codicil written 1 October 1780. It seems likely that the William Wright who participated in his estate sale, as discussed above under John (Taylor) Wright is the same man, but could, of course, be his son.

1788 Reuben Wright of Brunswick Co., Virginia

On 15 October 1777, Reuben Wright, "of King William Co.," bought 150 acres in Brunswick Co., Va., from Thomas Briggs and his wife Elizabeth, described as:

beginning on beginning at a small hickory on a Branch thence up the meanders of the said branch to a red oak on

---

[116] Brunswick Co., Va., Deed Book 14:126. Proved 22 August 1785.

[117] Brunswick Co., Va., Deed Book 14:223, 8 December 1785, proved by both witnesses 25 September 1786. http://files.usgwarchives.net/va/brunswick/deeds/db14-250.txt. Accessed 20 June 2010.

[118] Brunswick Co., Va. Tax List, Upper District, 1787, p. 26.

[119] Brunswick Co., Va. Tax List, Upper District, 1788, p. 31.

[120] She may be the widow of Uriah Wright, also. See below.

the same thence south three hundred and eight pole to a red oak on the line Hensley his line ...two hundred two poles to his corner on Mathis [Martin?]...thence by a line of marked trees to the land of M... Branch and David H... in the said branch to Walker's Line thence along his line to the beginning...[121]

Witnesses to this indenture included Robert Wright, Samuel Briggs and Joshua Wright.

On 16 October 1795, Reuben Wright and Charlotte, his wife, sold to Leonard Ward Walker for £100 Virginia money, 150 acres of land in Brunswick Co., Va.[122] Reuben Wright signed this indenture, and Charlotte made her mark. This is the land acquired by Reuben Wright from Thomas Briggs in 1777 as evidence by the fact that this land bounded on "Walker's" line.

The date of the land sale explains Reuben Wright's disappearance from Brunswick and his appearance in Mecklenburg County. If John is his eldest son,[123] born about 1777, then he is most likely the Reuben Wright, Jr., of the tax rolls in 1787, as the Reuben Wright of the 1783 tax roll had a significant number of white polls, including one named Reuben. Reuben, Jr., was born say 1765 or earlier, based upon the appearance of his son, John. Given the estimated birth year of 1783 Robert Wright as say 1710, I believe there are two Reuben Wright's—father and son, who I will denote as Reuben Wright of Waqua Creek, and his son, 1819 Reuben Wright. (see below).

Child of REUBEN WRIGHT and unknown are:

    i. REUBEN[2] WRIGHT, b. about 1755; d. 1819 Mecklenburg Co., Va.; m. CHARLOTTE _____ about 1776 Brunswick Co., Va. She died 1823 Mecklenburg County, Va.[124]

    ii. others, not known

1829 Augustine (Austin) Wright of Mecklenburg Co., Va.

Austin, also called Augustine, first appears in the land records of Mecklenburg County in 1770. On 19 May 1770

---

[121] Brunswick Co., Va., Deed Book 13:67.
[122] Brunswick Co., Va., Deed Book 16:172.
[123] John Wright, son of Reuben, from the Mecklenburg County tax lists.
[124] Mecklenburg Co., Va., Will Book 9:469.

Stephen Hatchell sold to Austin Wright, "of Mecklenburg County" 150 acres of land, "bounded by Flatt Creek, Robert Good, Ned's Branch, Laban Wright, and said Hatchell."[125] This tract of land was sold to Hatchell by Laban Wright on 11 October 1764 150 acres of land, "part of 386 acres patent by John Wright 10 Jan 1748, Flatt Creek, adj. Haw Branch and Rock Branch, to Stephen Hatschel."[126]

On 4 September 1786 "Augustin" Wright of Mecklenburg Co., Va., sold to John Penn of Brunswick Co. for £106 a tract of 175 acres beginning "at Walker's line where it crosses the gum branch, thence along the said line to Samuel Briggs' spring branch...to Stith's line..."[127] This indenture was signed by "Austin" Wright and witnessed by Samuel Briggs, Reuben Wright, and Robert Wright. It is this sale, which is probably his inheritance from the estate of Robert Wright that establishes his connection.

Austin Wright appears on the 1784 tax list with ten Negroes.[128] He appears regularly through the years. In the 1790 tax list he is shows as "Augustine" Wright (1-6-1-5) implying that he had himself as his tithe, and still had several slaves.[129] In 1791 he is with two tithes[130], and in 1792, he is shown with the second tithe being for John Wright.[131] John Wright is still with Austin Wright in 1793,[132] but is gone in 1794, but there is a William Wright with one poll nearby.[133] Austin Wright appears with one poll until 1798, when he is shown with two polls, himself and son John Wright.[134] John Wright, son of Austin, is clearly identified with three slaves in 1802.[135] He makes his last appearance on the

---

[125] Mecklenburg County, Virginia Deeds, 1765-1771. (Miami Beach: TLC Genealogy, 1990,) p. 106.

[126] Ibid., p. 45. Laban Wright appears to have been his first cousin, as I think he was a son of 1788 Reuben Wright of Brunswick Co., Virginia.

[127] Brunswick Co., Va., Deed Book 14:257.

[128] Mecklenburg Co., Va., Tax List 1784, Lower District, p. 17.

[129] Mecklenburg Co., Va., Tax List 1790, Lower District, p. 47. The only other Wright in the Lower District was James, who can be shown to be in a different area, away from the Roanoke River, and is probably connected with the Wrights of Stony Creek in Lunenburg County.

[130] Mecklenburg Co., Va., Tax List 1791, Lower District, p. 14.

[131] Mecklenburg Co., Va., Tax List 1792, Lower District, p. 29. He is shown as (2-6-1-6).

[132] Mecklenburg Co., Va., Tax List 1793, Lower District, p. 35.

[133] Mecklenburg Co., Va., Tax List 1794, Lower District, p. 29. William in on p. 28.

[134] Mecklenburg Co., Va., Tax List 1798, Lower District, p. 49.

[135] Mecklenburg Co., Va., Tax List 1802, Lower District, p. 40.

lists in 1805. Austin Wright, Jr., son of Austin Wright makes his first appearance in 1803.[136]

Austin Wright, Sr., married Lucy Holloway on 1 May 1806 in Mecklenburg Co., Va., with Francis Ballard as his security.[137] Clearly, this is a second marriage for him, as he has grown sons. His first wife's name was Sally, as evidenced by her release of dower rights in a sale of land by Austin Wright to Sherwood Bugg recorded 10 May 1790 in Mecklenburg Co., Va.[138]

The last will and testament of Robert Lark was written 8 February 1793 and proved 10 June 1793. He mentions his daughter, Elizabeth Fox, wife of Jacob Fox, daughter Sarah Wright, daughter Joyce Taylor, daughter Anne Collier, and son Samuel Lark.[139]

On 13 July 1795, suit was filed by Frederick Collier and Ann, his wife, against Samuel Lark, Jacob Fox and Elizabeth, his wife, Augustine Wright and Sarah, his wife, John Holmes, Walter Leigh, and Joshua Smith. Notation was made that Jacob Fox and Elizabeth, Walter Leigh, and Joshua Smith were not inhabitants of the Commonwealth of Virginia.[140] This suit establishes that Frederick Collier's wife was Ann Lark, and that Augustine Wright's wife was Sarah Lark.

> The claim of Austin Wright against the public for his services in collecting cattle seventy days for Continental use, for which he received four hundred & fifty pounds in October 1781 is examined and allowed by the Court.[141]

On 13 October 1787 Austin Wright was appointed ensign in the county's militia, with Stephen Mabry as Captain and William

---

[136] Mecklenburg Co., Va., Tax List 1803, Lower District, p. 46.

[137] Elliott, Katherine B. Marriage Records 1765-1810, Mecklenburg Co., Virginia. (Easley, SC: Southern Historical Press, 1984,) p. 135.

[138] Mecklenburg Co., Va., DB 7:583. Release of dower right by Sally Wright, wife of Austin Wright in Mecklenburg Co., Va., Court Order Book 7:592.

[139] Mecklenburg Co., Va., Will Book 3:163.

[140] Mecklenburg Co., Va., Court Order Book 8:475. See also Mecklenburg Co., Va., Court Order Book 8:223. [10 Feb 1794.] The suit was abated 13 May 1799 on the death of the plaintiffs. [Mecklenburg Co., Va., Court Order Book 10:170.]

[141] Mecklenburg Co., Va., Court Order Book 6:604. (9 Oct 1786)

Blanton as lieutenant.[142] On 10 August 1790 Austin Wright brought suit against Ray Moss for trespass, assault and battery. The case was referred to the District Court, (no record of the outcome.) On 8 August 1803 Austin Wright was sued by Ebenezer McGowan for non-performance as security on a bond in the amount of £ 3.15.8½.[143]

Austin Wright's suit against Richard Russell[144] in 1804 indicates possible family relationships. On 9 October 1804:

> By consent of the parties aforementioned is awarded the plt to examine and take the deposition of Robert Huddleston, William Turner, Stephen Turner, David Moss, Joshua Wright and Phebe Wright witness in this cause of Warren County and State of North Carolina before any two magistrates of that County giving the dft legal notice of the time and place of execution of service.[145]

> The defendant granted permission to take the deposition of James William Daniel Pitchford, and John Baird all of Warren Co., N. C., and the plt. to take the deposition of Edmund Webb, John Baird, Thomas Newman, Daniel Newman and Philemon Hawkins all of Warren Co., N. C.[146]

A jury was finally selected to hear this case on 11 March 1806,[147] and found in favor of the plaintiff (Austin Wright) the next day. That same day, though, Austin Wright was found in debt to Presley Hinton Brothers for just over £35.[148]

---

[142] Mecklenburg Co., Va., Court Order Book 7:129.

[143] Mecklenburg Co., Va., Court Order Book 12:18. McGowan was a Methodist preacher who emigrated from England and was apparently involved in a number of money transactions, as he was actively suing for collection of debts in the records for these years. The suit against Austin Wright was one of the smaller sums.

[144] Robert Wright of Mecklenburg Co., Va., owed £89.14.3 to Richard Russell of Warren Co., NC, (Mecklenburg Co., Va., Deed Book 11:349 [14 Mar 1803]. The extant records do not make it clear if Austin Wright was attempting to recoup any of this money with this suit, but it is possible as the sum of money involved is comparable and Sterling Pitchford and Presley Hinton were witnesses to this indenture.

[145] Mecklenburg Co., Va., Court Order Book 12:251.

[146] Mecklenburg Co., Va., Court Order Book 13:50, 9 December 1805.

[147] Mecklenburg Co., Va., Court Order Book 13:119.

[148] Mecklenburg Co., Va., Court Order Book 13:274.

At some point, Austin Wright moved from the land he had acquired in the purchase from Hatchell, which was along Flatt Creek, north of the Roanoke to land south of the Roanoke, as shown in the following road work order.

> Daniel Taylor appointed surveyor of road from county line to Blanton's Ferry in room of Presley Hinton with the hands of sd. Daniel, Hinton, Amasa Palmer, Reuben Wright, Charles King, Henry King, Edward Davis, William Davis, Baxter Davis, Wms (?) Davis, Thomas H. Davis, Richard Fox, Richard Marshall, Jacob Bugg, Elijah Rideout, Edmund Webb, Wesley Webb, Edward Palmer, John Read, Walter Pennington, Austin Wright, William Hamilton, Jeremiah Griffin, Joseph King, Richard Glenn, and William S. Collier.[149]

Richard[4] Fox, (son of 1771 Richard Fox of Mecklenburg Co., Va.,) sold a parcel of land inherited from his father's claim on the south side of the Roanoke River to James Blanton in 1777.[150] Amasa Palmer's land was on the county line near the present Palmer's Spring.[151] Since Richard Fox is listed in the middle of the above detail, it seems likely that the clerk went down one side of the road from the county line to Blanton's Ferry over the Roanoke and then back up the other side of the road to the county line.

The deed index shows a purchase by Austin Wright from the Town of St. Tammany, which was located on the parcel purchased by James Blanton.[152] He also bought land from Zachariah Spurlock[153] and Sam Hopkins, et al.[154]

The will of Austin Wright was written 11 May 1829 and proved 21 December 1829 in Mecklenburg Co., Va.[155] He named his son-in-law William H. Farrar as his executor. William H.

---

[149] Mecklenburg Co., Va., Court Order Book 12:481 [14 Oct 1805].

[150] Mecklenburg Co., Va., Deed Book 5:20 [10 March 1777].

[151] Bracey, Susan L. Life By the Roaring Roanoke: A History of Mecklenburg County, Virginia. (Mecklenburg Bicentennial Committee, 1977,) p. 324.

[152] Mecklenburg Co., Va., Deed Book 8:175 [10 Sep 1792].

[153] Mecklenburg Co., Va., Deed Book 8:6 [14 Feb 1791]

[154] Mecklenburg Co., Va., Deed Book 9:340 [9 Oct 1797].

[155] Mecklenburg Co., Va., Will Book 12:72-75. Proved by the oaths of John Smith and William Freeman 21 December 1829. My transcription from FHL microfilm # 0,032,381.

Farrar posted a $6,000 bond for letters of administration on the estate of Austin Wright, Sr., 21 August 1829.[156]

In the name of God, Amen. I Austin Wright, Senr., of Mecklenburg County and state of Virginia being sound of mind, memory, and understanding do make and publish these present instruments as my last will and testament revoking and annulling all or any other will or wills by me at any time heretofore made. I will and direct that my just debts of which there are few, be paid as soon as practicable by my Executor hereinafter named.

Imprimis: I give and bequeath unto my beloved wife Lucy Wright and her heirs forever one feather bed and furniture, first choice. I lend unto my said wife Lucy one Negro man named Nicholas & one Negro boy named Cesar during her natural life or widowhood, and at her death I give, devise and bequeath the said two Negroes above named to my daughter Rebecca B. Farrar and to her heirs forever. I further lend unto my said wife Lucy as aforesaid one Negro named Jacob and one Negro woman named Phillis and it is my will and desired that should these last named Negroes or either of them survive my wife they shall have a choice of guardianship & discretion of my Executor hereinafter named after fulfillment of the conditions above named.

I give devise and bequeath unto my son Samuel Wright one feather bed and furniture, second choice, to him and then finally I give and bequeath unto my daughters Nancy Wright, Betsey Kendrick, Polly Holloway, Martha Turner, Jenny Potter and Sally Clements each one dollar.

I give and bequeath unto my sons Austin Wright and Robert Wright as also the heir or heirs of my deceased son John Wright, the like sum of one dollar in memory of having heretofore given to each aforementioned a part of my estate for this and other reasons, I add nothing more.

---

[156] Mecklenburg Co., Va., Fiduciary Book 1765-1850. Library of Virginia microfilm #JR 694.

I give and bequeath unto my daughter Rebecca B. Farmer my dark & large dining table to her and her heirs forever.

I further will and direct that my Executor hereinafter named shall as soon after my decease as may be [considered] proper procedure to sell on such credit or otherwise as he may think must conducive to the interest of the [estate] and to the just and speedy payment of any debt or debts that may remain due by me at the time of my death, the entire of my landed estates, the following Negroes, Amon, Daniel, William, Edmond, Fanny & her youngest child & all their increase at the time of my death, with the whole of my share of ____ household and kitchen furniture not otherwise disposed of, [share of crops, etc.]—the amount of such sales together with any Bonds, judgments, or debts that may be due me, I will and direct that my just debts shall be paid and satisfied and the balance remaining shall be divided as follows: one third unto my wife Lucy, one third I give and bequeath unto my son Samuel Wright to be placed by my Executor in the hands of my friend and neighbor Nathl. Alexander, Esq., with an earnest request from me that he will hold & dispose of it from time to time for the sole use and benefit of my said son Samuel, and one third I hereby give and bequeath unto my said daughter Rebecca B. Farmer to her & her heirs forever.

Lastly I appoint my son-in-law William H. Farrar without security or appraisment specifically my sole Executor of this my last will and testament. In testimony whereof I have hereunto set my hand and seal this eleventh day of May in the year of our Lord one thousand eight hundred and twenty nine.

S/ Austin Wright

W. S. Bailey
Jno. Smith
Jno. Owen, Jr.

A codicil to my last will and testament which I have solemnly appended and desire may constitute and made part of my said will within written and subscribed, that is to say that instead of one third the amount of sales after payment of my just debts, I give and bequeath unto my son Samuel Wright one half the amount thereof the remainder or the other half I will and direct shall be equally divided between my said wife Lucy Wright and my daughter Rebecca B. Farrar to these and their heirs forever I give the same. In testimony whereof I have hereunto set my hand and seal this eleventh day of May 1829.

In presence of
Wm. S. Bailey
    s/ Austin Wright
John Smith
Jno. Owen, Jr.

Mecklenburg County, State of Virginia
    Whereas I Austin Wright, Senr., of the county and state aforesaid having by my will made no provision for a home for the wife and children of my son Austin Wright, Junr., and knowing at my death they will be without one, do now prompted by the natural love and affection I bear them make this a codicil to be amended to my will now in the possession of Nathaniel Alexander. It is my desire and I do by these presents lend to my said son Austin during the life of himself and wife all the land I have below and East of Hicks Ferry Road containing by recent survey sixty two acres and after the death of himself and wife it is my desire that the said land be equally divided between his two youngest sons Paldy Wright and Mark Wright to whom I give in fee simple. In testimony whereof I have hereunto set my hand and affixed my seal this 29th day of October 1829.

Signed, sealed, and delivered in the presence of
    s/ Austin Wright, Senr.
John Smith
Wm. Freeman
James Burroughs.

Genealogical Summary

1. AUSTIN[2] (ROBERT[1]) WRIGHT, b. 1745-1749, d. between 11 May 1829 and 21 December 1829 Mecklenburg Co., Va.; m. (1) SARAH LARK, daughter of ROBERT LARK and MARY; m. (2) LUCY HOLLOWAY 1 May 1806 Mecklenburg Co., Va.

Children of AUSTIN WRIGHT and SARAH LARK are:

i. JOHN[3] WRIGHT, b. 1777, Mecklenburg Co., Va.; m. 21 SALLY HOLMES May 1801 Mecklenburg Co., Va.;[157] d. before 11 May 1829.

John Wright sued Isaac Holmes and Edward Holmes for trespass in 1801. The case was heard by a jury 12 August 1801[158] and was decided in John Wright's favor in the amount of £3 plus costs. He was ordered to pay the daily rate ($0.53) to Henry Creedle, Robert Fox, Francis Ballard and William Evans. The Holmes paid costs for Samuel Lark and Ezekiel Redding.

John Wright and John Holmes were sued by William Patrick Davis, executor of the estate of William Davis, deceased, on 8 August 1803 for debt.[159] The defendants acknowledged a debt in the amount of £12.8 due 14 October 1801, and agreed to repay plus 6% interest and costs. The judgment was stayed until the November court.

John Wright, son of Austin, disappears from the tax rolls of Mecklenburg Co., Va., after 1805. This departure is probably connected to a deed recorded 11 July 1803 Mecklenburg Co., Va.,[160] between John Wright, (son of Austin) and William Baskerville, and Noah Dortch and James Whitlow, Jr., for a debt £41 17 shillings, which John Wright owed to William

---

[157] Elliott, Katherine B. Marriage Records 1765-1810 Mecklenburg County, Virginia. (Easley, S. C.: Southern Historical Press, repr. 1984,) p. 135. The bond was issued 13 May 1801 with John Holmes as surety, and the ceremony was performed by Ebenezer McGowan. The John Wright who married Rebecca Oslin in 1820 John Wright of Mecklenburg Co., Va., who was a son of 1819 Reuben Wright of Mecklenburg Co., Va. The John Wright who m. Sarah Fox is, I contend, the man identified in the tax rolls as John Wright (Fox). I believe this man to be 1832 John Wright of Clarke Co., Ga.

[158] Mecklenburg Co., Va., Court Order Book 11:50-51.

[159] Mecklenburg Co., Va., Court Order Book 12:2.

[160] Mecklenburg Co., Va., Deed Book 11:449 [11 Jul 1803].

Baskerville, "so Noah Dortch and James Whitlow, Jr., have paid to John Wright....one Negro man, Phil, one feather bed, and furniture, one dozen Windsor chairs, his crop of Corn, wheat and tobacco,...one cow and one calf..."

He had until 1 January 1804 to repay the debt, otherwise Dortch and Whitlow could sell the property on the courthouse steps, pay Baskerville the debt, with the excess going to John Wright after payment of interest, which was specified in steps depending upon when the sale took place. This indenture was signed by John Wright and witnessed by Daniel Hicks and Robert Rainey. In a memorandum attached the Indenture was modified to explicitly allow deduction of the cost of the sale from the "overplus" obtained from the sale of the property before repaying John Wright. This indenture was also signed by John Wright.

John Wright was deceased when his father wrote his will in 1829. The place of his death is not known to me.

ii. AUSTIN[3] WRIGHT, b. 1782, Mecklenburg Co., Va.; m. MARY NICHOLSON 28 June 1811 Mecklenburg Co., Va.

Austin Wright, Jr., was a witness to the deed of sale between Robert Wright and Nancy, his wife who sold to Donaldson Potter for £129 a tract of land on 14 May 1804. He was therefore born before that date in 1783, which is consistent with the 1782 date estimated from his appearance on the tax lists. Austin Wright, Jr., was still living in Mecklenburg Co., Va., at the time of the 1820 Census.[161] His father must have been living with him by then, as Austin Wright, Sr., is not listed in that report. (There are no young children in the household, so the other two people in the household may be his youngest brother and sister.)

The 1830 Census shows two men named Austin Wright. One is living in Spartanburg, S. C.,[162] the other

[161] 1820 Census Mecklenburg Co., Va., p. 158A; 00111-01011, 17 slaves.

[162] 1830 Census Spartanburg Co., S. C., p. 247. He is 50-59 years old. He was also present in Spartanburg District, S. C., in the1800 Census age 26-44, (p. 247,) so his birth year can be restricted to 1771-1774. He appears to be associated with yet another John

is living in Hopkins Co., Kentucky.[163] Presently, I have no information to connect either of these men with Austin Wright, son of 1829 Augustine Wright of Mecklenburg Co., Virginia.

From his father's granting of a life estate to him with his two younger sons, Paul and Mark, to inherit, I presume he was something of a wastrel.

iii. ROBERT[3] WRIGHT

It is difficult to separate this Robert Wright from his uncle, son of 1782 Robert Wright of Brunswick Co., Va. (see data under his entry.)

iv. SAMUEL[3] WRIGHT.

Samuel appears to have been a minor in 1829, but I have found no other reliable information about him at this point.

v. REBECCA B.[3] WRIGHT, m. WILLIAM H. FARRAR 1 August 1825 Mecklenburg Co., Va., son of JOHN FARRAR and ANN BASKERVILLE.[164]

William H. Farrar is living in Mecklenburg Co., Va., in 1830, age 20-30, with two males 15-19, one woman 50-60, and one woman also 20-30. There seem to be no children.[165] It seems probable that John Farrar had died before the census and his wife and perhaps two younger sons are living with this couple. I have not been able to locate them with certainty in either 1840 or 1850.

vi. NANCY[3] WRIGHT, m. DAVID WRIGHT 28 December 1797 Mecklenburg Co., Virginia.

Wright, who was born before 1755, (p. 185,) and a Thomas Wright, age 16-26 (p. 211). While it is tempting to link these men to the Wrights of Waqua Creek, I have seen no evidence to justify doing this.

[163] 1830 Census Hopkins Co., Ky., p. 62. He is age 60-69, which is older than I have calculated, but his family structure suggests he is living with two younger married couples who have six small children between them. [100020001=50002001]. Also in the county are George Wright with five whites and 15 slaves, John Wright, and Lindsey Wright.

[164] Doyle, Marian June. Mrs. 21 May 2003. Located on http://worldconnect.rootsweb.com. (db ghf1).

[165] 1830 Census Mecklenburg Co., Va., part 1, (District of Lewis F. Hicks,), p. 13. There is also a William Farrar in part 2, p. 49, who is also 20-29 with a wife the same age and one boy and one girl both under 5. They had 13 slaves and 6 free persons of color in the household. This William Farrar may be the same as the William G. Farrar who appeared in Putnam Co., Ga., 1840-1860, with a second marriage of record.

Nancy Wright and Robert Wright of Brunswick Co., Va., were married in Mecklenburg Co., Va., on 16 November 1792 with Austin Wright as security. I have attributed this marriage to Robert Wright, son of 1783 Robert Wright of Brunswick Co., Va. This would make Robert Wright the uncle of this Nancy Wright which is not credible. I think Nancy Wright is a daughter of Laban Wright. Also, it appears that most of Austin's children were born after 1775, so his daughter Nancy would have been underage in 1792 and her father's permission would have been noted.

Nancy Wright and David Wright of Lunenburg Co., Va., were married in Mecklenburg Co., Va., on 28 December 1797, with Roderick Wright as security. Roderick Wright is probably a son of John Wright of Brunswick Co., Va., and brother of John Wright (Fox). I have taken the view that she is probably their sister.

The 1820 Census for Mecklenburg Co., Va., shows Nancy Wright as head of household with three children, but she is over 45 years old, suggesting a birth date before 1775. I think this is probably the Nancy Wright who married Robert Wright.

vii. ELIZABETH[3] WRIGHT, m. JAMES KENDRICK 12 December 1797 Mecklenburg Co., Va.,[166] son of JOHN KENDRICK and AMY FOX. He was born about 1772 Mecklenburg Co., Va., and died before 16 June 1811, Mecklenburg Co., Va.

His will was written 16 May 1811 and proved 16 June 16 1811. He names his wife Elizabeth and his children, all under age, Dennis, James, and Polly.[167]

viii. MARY[3] WRIGHT, m. DAVID HOLLOWAY 21 December 1799 Mecklenburg Co., Va.[168]

An undocumented online source says that David Holloway was a sister to Lucy Holloway who m. Austin

---

[166] John Wright, security. Mecklenburg Co., Va., Marriage Bonds. (courtesy of Carol York.)

[167] Oberlies, Denise. Denise's Research Files. 30 Aug 2003. Located on http://worldconnect.rootsweb.com. (db :2648461.) This is a well documented source of information on the branches of the Kendrick family.

[168] John Holmes, security. Minister Ebenezer McGowan. Mecklenburg Co., Va., Marriage Bonds. (courtesy of Carol York.)

Wright as his second wife. There were two other sisters, Martha, who m. William Bailey and Nancy, who m. Henry Burger.[169]

ix. MARTHA[3] WRIGHT, m. STEPHEN TURNER 11 March 1801 Mecklenburg Co., Va.[170]

Stephen Turner was living in Warren Co., N. C., in 1804 when he was deposed as part of Austin Wright's suit against Richard Russell.[171]

x. JANE[3] WRIGHT, m. DONALDSON POTTER 6 September 1804 Mecklenburg Co., Va.[172]

Donaldson Potter purchased land from Robert Wright and Nancy his wife on May 14, 1804 in a transaction witnessed by Austin Wright, Jr.[173]

xi. SARAH L.[3] WRIGHT, m. EDMUND CLEMMONS 12 November 1805 Mecklenburg Co., Va.[174]

1819 Reuben Wright of Mecklenburg Co., Virginia

The Brunswick Co., Va., tax lists, show a Reuben Wright, with three white males, two under 21, and threes black males, present in the upper district in 1783.[175] He appears with a son, Reuben Wright, Jr., in 1787.[176] In 1789, only one Reuben appears.[177] This Reuben Wright appears every year through 1795, when he paid tax on himself, one white under 21, and two black males,[178] and then disappearing from the tax lists.

---

[169] Pike, Sharon. Holloway family of Kentucky. 10 Jun 2003. Located on http://worldconnect.rootsweb.com. (db holloway-sharon). An undocumented file states that David Holloway died 21 December 1851 in Lincoln Co., Tenn. I have not been able to confirm this.

[170] Austin Wright, security. Mecklenburg Co., Va., Marriage Bonds. (courtesy of Carol York.)

[171] Mecklenburg Co., Va., Court Order Book 12:251.

[172] Edmund Clements, security, Minister James Meacham. Mecklenburg Co., Va., Marriage Bonds. (courtesy of Carol York.) There is online information that a Donaldson Potter m. Catherine Ellis 22 Dec. 1796. She was b. 19 Sep 1764 in Sussex Co., Va. An undocumented file says she was born in 1782 and died in 1807 and that he was born 24 June 1767 in Ireland and died 5 May 1849 in Spring Hill, Williamson Co., Tennessee. I have not been able to confirm this.

[173] Mecklenburg Co., Va., Deed Book 12:22.

[174] Richard Moss, security. Mecklenburg Co., Va., Marriage Bonds. (courtesy of Carol York.)

[175] Brunswick Co., Va. Tax List, Upper District, 1783 p. 13.

[176] Brunswick Co., Va. Tax List, Upper District, 1787, p. 26.

[177] Brunswick Co., Va. Tax List, Upper District, 1789, p. 31.

[178] Brunswick Co., Va. Tax List, Upper District, 1795, p. 43.

Reuben Wright appears on the tax rolls of Mecklenburg Co., Virginia, in 1796, where he appears near Austin Wright, paying tax on one white male and five black.[179] In 1798, John Wright, son of Reuben, makes his first appearance on the tax lists.[180] The appearance of John Wright, son of Reuben, on the tax list of 1798 implies he turned 21, so giving an estimated birth year of 1777. Assuming his father, himself, was at least 21, this implies a birth year for Reuben of before 1756.

Reuben, subsequently Reuben, Sr., makes an appearance on the Mecklenburg Co., Va., tax lists at least through 1814.[181] Reuben Wright on 16 September 1816,[182] purchased land from Austin Wright, Jr., Mary Wright, and others. Reuben Wright, Jr., on 16 August 1824 purchased land from John Hopkins.[183] Reuben Wright bought two slaves from his son-in-law, Reuben Dunnington 24 November 1807.[184] The debt with Reuben Dunnington was returned to his daughter "Polly" in Reuben's will.

On 21 April 1817, Reuben Wright and Charlotte, his wife, sold land to Joseph Bennett.[185] The administrators of Reuben Wright sold his lands 15 March 1824 the same day that lands inherited by his son William Wright were sold by his administrators.[186] Reuben had extensive slave holdings, so he surely had lands to go with it, yet there is no record of land purchase in Mecklenburg Co., Va., to account for this. I think he inherited the land, probably in 1795 or so, when he moved to Mecklenburg County. Secondary sources suggest his land was near the present-day Palmer Springs[187], on the south side of the Roanoke. This may be a clue that Charlotte's maiden name is Palmer, as this name occurs among their children.

---

[179] Mecklenburg Co., Va., Tax List Lower District, 1796, p. 32.

[180] Mecklenburg Co., Va., Tax List Lower District, 1798, p. 49.

[181] Mecklenburg Co., Va., Tax List Lower District, 1814, p. 31.

[182] Mecklenburg Co., Va., Deed Book 16:317.

[183] Mecklenburg Co., Va., Deed Book 21:95.

[184] Brunswick Co. Va., Deed Book 20:324. I read the name as Drummington, but have since corresponded with descendants of his and the name should have been read as Dunnington.

[185] Mecklenburg Co., Va., Deed Book 16:434.

[186] Mecklenburg Co., Va., Deed Book 20:488.

[187] Bracey, Susan L. Life By the Roaring Roanoke: A History of Mecklenburg County, Virginia. (Mecklenburg Bicentennial Committee, 1977, p 324.

The Last Will and Testament of Reuben Wright of Mecklenburg Co., Va.[188]

In the Name of God Amen I Reuben Wright of Mecklenburg County and State of Virginia being of sound mind and memory but calling to mind the mortality of man and knowing it is appointed for all men once to die and being desirous to dispose of the worldly goods wherewith it has pleased God to bless me do make and ordain this my last will and testament in manner and form as following:

Imprimis: I give and bequeath to all the surviving children of my son Robert Wright, deceased one Seventh part of all the property I leave in possession of my wife after her death to them and their heirs forever.

Item: I give and bequeath to my son John Wright two negro boys named Duke and Griffin to him and his heirs forever.

Item: I give and bequeath to the heirs of my daughter Polly Dunnington the judgment I obtained against Reuben Dunnington in Brunswick Co., State of Virginia, and further I give and bequeath to the heirs of my daughter Polly Drummington twenty five pounds instead of a little negro girl to make it equal with that I intend giving to William Wright to them and their heirs forever after my wife's death.

Item: I give and bequeath to my son William Wright two negroes named Park and Silvy and her increase to him and his heirs forever.

Item: I lend to my son Joshua Wright one negro boy named Anderson (?) and one negro girl named Suckey with the condition that if my son Joshua should depart this life before his wife Feoby (sic) then for the said negroes to be returned and equally divided among the rest of my children, but if Feoby his wife should depart this life first, then I give my son Joshua the two negroes above mentioned to be disposed of as he may think best.

---

[188] Mecklenburg Co., Va., Will Book 9:40-41.

Item: I give and bequeath to my daughter Nancy Davis two negro boys named Harrison and Sam to her and her heirs forever.

Item: I give and bequeath to my son Reuben Wright two negro boys named ___ and ____ to him and his heirs forever.

Item: I give to my dear and loving wife during her natural life or widowhood all my land and cash on hand and the crop...and all the stock consisting of horses, cattle, hogs, and sheep and all the plantation ___ of any description, and all my household and kitchen furniture, and also nine negroes named Jack, ___, ____, ____, Spencer, Isham, Dolph, Milly, and Sarah. I give my loving wife all this property as before inscribed after paying my just debts ....and after paying one seventh to the children of my son Robert Wright, {the remainder to be divided among the surviving children equally, with the exception that Phoebe, wife of Joshua, is not to inherit anything if Joshua dies first. The copy is too faded to read fully.} Lastly, I constitute and appoint my son William Wright and Reuben Wright executors of this my last will and testament revoking all others by me heretofore made, In witness whereof I have hereunder set my hand and affixed my seal this 10th day of December 1816.

Signed, sealed and acknowledged in the presence of

Jesse Dortch   Reuben (X) Wright

Isaac S. Langley

At a court held for Mecklenburg County the 17th day of May 1819 the above written last will and testament of Reuben Wright, deceased, was exhibited in Court and proved by the oaths of two witnesses thereto subscribed and ordered to be recorded. When after on motion of William Wright one of the executors therein named and made oath according to law Certificate is granted him for obtaining ___ thereof, in due form, he having given security. Whereupon he, together with Smith Palmer and Thomas Palmer his securities acknowledge there bond in the penalty of fifteen thousand dollars conditioned as the law directs for that purpose. Teste: Edward S. Babb

William Wright posted a $10,000 bond for letters of administration on the estate of Reuben Wright with Thomas Palmer and Smith Palmer as his securities 17 May 1819.[189]

Charlotte Wright is listed as head of household in the 1820 Census along with one adult male and nine slaves.[190]

Genealogical Summary

REUBEN[2] WRIGHT was born about 1755 probably in King William Co., Va., and died before 17 May 1819 in Mecklenburg Co., Va. He married CHARLOTTE _____ about 1776 Brunswick Co., Va. She died 1823 Mecklenburg County, Va.[191]

Children of REUBEN WRIGHT and CHARLOTTE _____ are:

i. JOHN[3] WRIGHT, b. about 1777 Brunswick Co., Va., d. before 21 August 1820 Mecklenburg Co., Va.; m. REBECCA OSLIN 19 June 1802 Mecklenburg Co., Va.[192]

Rebecca Wright is listed as head of household in the 1820 Census, along with six males and one adult woman besides herself.[193] This exceeds the number of children listed in his will, so there must be members of the extended family living there as well.

Rebecca Wright posted a $10,000 bond for letters of administration on the estate of John Wright 21 August 1820 with Drury Pennington, Joseph A. Arnold, and William P. Oslin as her securities.[194]

Children of JOHN WRIGHT and REBECCA OSLIN are:

1. REBECCA[4] WRIGHT
2. FRANCES L.[4] WRIGHT
3. JOHN M.[4] WRIGHT, b. 1808 Mecklenburg Co., Va.; d. 24 October 1867 Mecklenburg Co., Va.; m. JANE H. Davis 21 March 1838 Mecklenburg Co.,

---

[189] Mecklenburg Co., Va., Fiduciary Book 1765-1850. Library of Virginia microfilm #JR 694.

[190] 1820 Census Mecklenburg Co., Va., p. 150A; 00010-00001.

[191] Mecklenburg Co., Va., Will Book 9:469.

[192] Elliott, Katherine B. Marriage Records 1765-1810 Mecklenburg County, Virginia. (Easley, S. C.: Southern Historical Press, repr. 1984,) p. 136.

[193] 1820 Census Mecklenburg Co., Va., p. 159; 031200-00011 and eight slaves.

[194] Mecklenburg Co., Va., Fiduciary Book 1765-1850, Library of Virginia microfilm #JR694.

Va.; b. 1814 Mecklenburg Co., Va.,[195] d. 2 November 1898 Mecklenburg Co., Va.[196]

John M. Wright also received letters of administration on the estates of Abner P. Wright 17 October 1836,[197] and Amasa P. Wright 19 June 1845.[198] His Bible record has been published.[199]

Children of JOHN M. WRIGHT and JANE H. DAVIS are:

    a.   MARTHA ANN[5] WRIGHT, b. 18 May 1839 Mecklenburg Co., Va.; d. 29 August 1846 Mecklenburg Co., Va.

    b.   MARY[5] WRIGHT, b. 3 March 1841 Mecklenburg Co., Va.; m. STEPHEN P. READ 23 October 1864 Mecklenburg Co., Va.

    c.   AMASA P. [5] WRIGHT, b. 6 March 1843 Mecklenburg Co., Va.; d. 25 August 1864 Shepherdstown, West Virginia.[200]

    d.   SALLY B. [5] WRIGHT, b. 4 May 1849 Mecklenburg Co., Va.

    e.   WILLIE[5] WRIGHT, b. 13 August 1856 Mecklenburg Co., Va.;

4. REUBEN N.[4] WRIGHT, died before 19 September 1831 Mecklenburg Co., Va.[201]

5. WILLIAM R.[4] WRIGHT.[202]

---

[195] 1850 Census Mecklenburg Co., Va., 98th Regt., p. 92A, #707/707.

[196] Tombstone record Union Chapel Methodist Church Cemetery. [Moore, M. M., and Moore, M.: Cemetery and Tombstone Records of Mecklenburg County, Virginia. (Chase City, Va.: Munsey Moore Publ., 1982,) p. 147.

[197] Mecklenburg Co., Va., Fiduciary Book 1765-1850. Library of Virginia microfilm #JR 695. Bond was for $6,000 and securities were Amasa P. Wright and George Rogers.

[198] Mecklenburg Co., Va., Fiduciary Book 1765-1850. Library of Virginia microfilm #JR 695. Bond was for $60,000 and no securities were listed.

[199] Sheppard, Susan B., Corker, Carol B. Family Records, Mecklenburg County, Virginia. (South Hill, Va.: DAR Prestwould Chapter, 1997,) pp. 169-171.

[200] Listed as a battle casualty. Relationships amongst the Amasa P. Wrights of record is obscure to me.

[201] Mecklenburg Co., Va., Fiduciary Book 1765-1850. Library of Virginia microfilm #JR 694. John M. Wright posted a $10,000 bond for letters of administration on the estate of Reuben Wright with William Kendrick and William Wright as his securities 19 September 1831.

[202] He may be the William R. Wright, 42, laborer, living in Petersburg, Va., in the 1850 Census, along with wife Ann, son Edward, 19, and daughters Martha, 17, and Mary,15. 1850 Census, Petersburg, Virginia, p.353B, #501/442.

ii. JOSHUA[3] WRIGHT, b. 1781 Brunswick Co., Va. He married PHOEBE SHORT, widow of JACOB SHORT before 1804.

Joshua Wright and Phoebe Wright were witnesses for Austin Wright in his suit against Richard Russell in 1804, at which time they were resident in Warren Co., N. C.[203] In 1811 Joshua Wright and his wife Phoebe Short, widow and relict of Jacob Short filed suit for slander against George Tucker and Edith, his wife, because they had said Jacob Short was not deceased when Phoebe married Joshua Wright.[204] The suit was dismissed by the court for lack of evidence of slander.[205] However, the will of 1819 Reuben Wright makes it clear that he does not want her to benefit from her marriage to Joshua, at least as far as inheriting from him. Obviously, he did not approve of the marriage.

Joshua Wright is listed twice in the 1820 Census,[206] but the arrangement of the listing makes it probable that he and Phoebe are not living together, so he was listed as head of her household. This suggests a legal separation as opposed to a divorce.

Joshua Wright and Phoebe Wright were grantors to Elizabeth H. Wall on 19 March 1821. (Mecklenburg Co., Va., Deed Book 19:43.) Joshua Wright was grantor to Bartlett Hubbard on 22 August 1826, (Mecklenburg Co., Va., Deed Book 22:76.)

The 1820 Census also shows a couple of young men that I cannot account for, who may be sons of Joshua Wright: James Wright[207] and John Wright, although the latter seems less likely.[208]

He may be the Joshua Wright listed as a laborer in the 1850 Census for Mecklenburg Co., Virginia, since he appears near John N. and John E. Wright.[209]

iii. ROBERT[3] WRIGHT d. before 10 December 1816.

---

[203] Mecklenburg Co., Va., Court Order Book 12:251 [9 October 1804.]

[204] Mecklenburg Co., Va., Court Order Book 15:388 [20 February 1811.]

[205] Mecklenburg Co., Va., Court Order Book 16:297 [18 May 1812.]

[206] 1820 Census Mecklenburg Co., Va., p. 150, 1 male over 45 and three slaves; p. 158A, 1 female over 45 and two slaves.

[207] 1820 Census Mecklenburg Co., Va., p. 153, 00100-0000.

[208] 1820 Census Mecklenburg Co., Va., p. 163; 10010-00100.

[209] 1850 Census Mecklenburg Co., Va., 98th Regt., p.93A, #717/717. He has in his household Nina Baskervill, 50 BF and Nina Baskervill 15 BF.

I have not found definite evidence of this man. As discussed elsewhere, the tax lists and the other documents strongly suggest to me that the Robert Wright and Robert Wright, Jr., of the tax lists of 1812 and 1813 are not this man, who does not appear in his own name before 1814, when I stopped examining the tax lists. This does not leave him much time to marry and have children. If, on the other hand, Robert Wright, Jr., is actually Robert Wright, the younger, he might be this son of Reuben Wright, although he still does not have much time to marry and beget a family.

iv. REUBEN[3] WRIGHT, b. about 1791 Brunswick Co., Va.; d. before 15 March 1824 Mecklenburg Co., Va.; m. CATHERINE _____; d. before 15 February 1813 Mecklenburg Co., Va.

Reuben Wright posted a $10,000 bond for letters of administration on the estate of Catherine Wright 15 February 1813 with William Langley and Amasa Palmer as his securities.[210]

Reuben Wright is living in Mecklenburg Co., Va., in the 1820 Census near his other family.[211] He appears to have three sons and two daughters, but has one extra adult female in his household

Reuben Wright purchased land from John Hopkins on 16 August 1824.[212] John Hopkins' land was adjacent to that sold by Robert[3] Wright in 1803, as discussed under his entry.

v. WILLIAM[3] WRIGHT, d. before 15 March 1824 Mecklenburg Co., Va.

On 15 March 1824 the executors of William Wright and the executors of Reuben Wright of Mecklenburg Co., Va., sold land to William Marshall.[213] William Wright was purchaser of two tracts of land in 1821. On 16 July 1821 he purchased a tract from Thomas Palmer.[214] On 19 November 1821 he

[210] Mecklenburg Co., Va., Fiduciary Book 1765-1850. Library of Virginia microfilm #JR 694.

[211] 1820 Census Mecklenburg Co., Va., p. 159A, 21010-20020, with 13 slaves.

[212] Mecklenburg Co., Va., Deed Book 21:95.

[213] Mecklenburg Co., Va., Deed Book 20:488.

[214] Mecklenburg Co., Va., Deed Book 19:140.

purchased a tract from Reuben Dunnington et. al.[215] Interestingly, he is also listed as a grantee on an indenture from John C. Carroll which was recorded May 17, 1824. I suspect examination of the deed would show that the indenture was executed earlier than the date of its recording, and would probably allow us to narrow the probable date of death of William Wright.

vi. POLLY[3] WRIGHT, b. about 1780 Va.; d. before 10 December 1816 Anderson Co., Tenn., m. REUBEN DUNNINGTON 11 July 1798 Mecklenburg Co., Va.; b. December 1772 in Va.; d. about 1852 Morgan Co., Tenn.; m. (2) LUCINDA _____ probably about 1824 Morgan Co., Tenn.; b. about 1806 Tennessee.

In 2011 I was in contacted by Jerry James, who had compiled a summary of the descendants of this marriage for his family from private letters with descendants of this couple. I am using his information here. His information showed that the couple had 11 children and that they moved in 1810 from Mecklenburg Co., Va., to Anderson Co., Tennessee.

Morgan Co., was set off from Anderson County in 1817 and Reuben Dunnington and he appears there after 1820. Without examination of land titles, I cannot say if he moved, or if his land was partitioned into the new county. He died about 1852 in Morgan Co., Tennessee. Polly was clearly deceased when her father wrote his will on 10 December 1816, and Lucinda is thought by census data (1850 Morgan Co., Tenn.) to have been born about 1808 in Tennessee. It is unlikely she married much before age 16, and so likely did not marry until at least 1824, by which time Reuben Dunnington and family had moved to Morgan Co., Tennessee. As a result, I think the children he attributed to this marriage, Bronson, b. 1818, and Palatiah, (male) b. 5 November 1821, probably in Morgan Co., Tenn., were from another marriage, as Lucinda would have been too young to be the mother of either if she were born in 1808, and we can be sure that Polly was dead by

[215] Mecklenburg Co., Va., Deed Book 19:276.

December 1816, and likely at least a couple of months prior to that. He also had family records listing Calvin Dunnington, Elizabeth Dunnington, and Lawson Dunnington as children of this marriage. The 1850 census shows two children, Alexander W., 11, and Mary F., 7.[216] Mr. James is not sure these are children, as opposed to grandchildren, but Lucinda would have been about 35 when Mary was born in 1843, so it is certainly possible. However, the large gap between Palatiah's known date of birth and Alexander's birth in 1839 makes me suspicious that there was either a third marriage, or these were not Reuben's children, but rather his grandchildren.

Reuben Dunnington served under Zachary Taylor during the War of 1812, and was in Mobile at the time of the battle of New Orleans in January 1815.

Reuben Dunnington appears to have moved to Missouri on his own, but soon joined the family, most of whom appear in the 1850 Census.[217]

Children of MARY WRIGHT and REUBEN DUNNINGTON are:

1. JOSHUA DUNNINGTON, b. 1799 Mecklenburg Co., Va.; d. 1845 Eureka, Illinois; m. Tennessee MARY SPENCER, b. 1809 Tennessee; d. 1875 Eureka.

2. ELIZABETH DUNNINGTON, b. 1800 Mecklenburg Co., Va.; d. ca. 1850 Macon Co., Mo.; m. _____ SHELTON.

3. JOHN DUNNINGTON, b. 1803 Mecklenburg Co., Va.; d. 20 January 1850 Macon Co., Mo.; m. ELLEN (_____) HOLLEY; d. before 1850.

4. WILLIAM DUNNINGTON, b. 28 June 1806 Mecklenburg Co., Va.; d. 5 February 1870 Hendricks Co., Indiana.[218]

5. HENDLEY DUNNINGTON, b. 1808 Mecklenburg Co., Va.; d. ; m. MARY DAVIDSON about 1833

---

[216] 1850 Census Morgan Co., Tenn., 19th Civil District, #307/307.

[217] 1850 Census Macon Co., Mo., 22nd Civil District, p. 130, #160/165 and ff.

[218] Mr. James was not able to confirm these dates.

Morgan Co., Tenn., dau. of SAMUEL C. DAVIDSON.

6. CHARLOTTE DUNNINGTON, b. 1809 Mecklenburg Co., Va.; d. 23 May 1874 Macon Co., Mo.; m. JOHN C. RICHARDSON 14 April 1842 Macon Co., Mo.

7. REUBEN DUNNINGTON, b. 26 January 1810 Mecklenburg Co., Va.; m. TALITHA CATHERINE DAVIDSON, dau. of SAMUEL C. DAVIDSON 18 July 1838 Cooper Co., Mo.

vii. NANCY[3] WRIGHT, m. DAVIS

viii. THOMAS[3] WRIGHT, b. about 1778 Virginia.

Thomas Wright is listed as a son of Reuben Wright in the tax lists of 1798 and 1801, and 1802. He is present in 1799 and 1800 in his own right.[219] He appears continuously through 1812, but then is not listed.

I have found no record of a marriage for Thomas Wright in Mecklenburg, Lunenburg, or Brunswick Co., Va.

Thomas Wright was grantor on three deeds in Mecklenburg Co., Va., after the death of Reuben Wright.[220] However, I have not examined these deeds to prove that these were the lands of Reuben Wright that were being sold.[221]

---

[219] Mecklenburg Co., Va., Tax Lists: A:49 (1798); B:68 (1799); A:26 (1800); B:40 (1801); B:39 (1802); B:46 (1806); B:40 (1807); B:46 (1809); B:36 (1811); B:55 (1812.)

[220] Mecklenburg Co., Va., Deed Book 20:66 and 20:76 [July 15, 1822]; 20:372 [December 4, 1823]; 22:21 [February 20, 1826]; 23:193 [May 12, 1828].

[221] There is a reference to a Rev. Thomas Wright in a WB 12:401, which I have not examined. It should be about 1830. There is no clue as to why he was not listed in his father's will, since the tax lists are explicit.

Chapter 3: Other Wrights of Brunswick Co., Virginia

Joseph Wright

On 7 April 1737 Joseph Wright helped to settle an estate.[1] On 2 Jun 1743, Joseph Wright, who signed with a "J", witnessed a series of transactions involving 100 acres of land on Fountains Creek. In the first two Henry Ivey sold land to Burrell Brown, and in the second two Jeremiah Brown sold land to John Tooke.[2]

On 30 December 1751 Joseph Wright "of Granville County, North Carolina" sold to John Cumbow, Jr., of Brunswick Co., Va., for £14 a tract of 238 acres "on the south side of Reedy Branch..." granted by patent to Joseph Wright on 1 August 1745.[3] The deed was signed by the mark of Joseph Wright and witnessed by George Brewer, Gabriel Peterson, Lanier Brewer, and William Vaughn.

On 6 August 1760 John Cumbo of Meherrin Parish sold to Peter Avent for £35 a tract of 238 acres which he bought from Joseph "Right" and was bounded as by patent to Joseph Wright 1 August 1745.[4]

Joseph Wright married Judith Marshall, widow of Matthew Marshall before September 1742, in Brunswick County. Matthew Marshall's will was proved there 2 September 1742, and his executor, Lewis Dupay, resigned in favor of Judith Wright, relict of Matthew Marshall and her husband, Joseph Wright.[5]

---

[1] Brunswick Co., Va., Deed Book/Will Book 1:316. Cited in Bradley, Stephen E. Brunswick County, Virginia Deed Books, Vol. 1: 1732-1745. (Lawrenceville, Va.:1997,) p. 35.

[2] Brunswick Co., Va., Deed Book 2:306; 2:307; 2:310; 2:311. Cited in Bradley, Stephen E. Brunswick County, Virginia Deed Books, Vol. 1: 1732-1745. (Lawrenceville, Va.:1997,) pp. 75-76.

[3] Brunswick Co., Va., Deed Book 5:135. Cited in Bradley, Stephen E. Brunswick County, Virginia Deed Books, Vol. 1: 1732-1745. (Lawrenceville, Va.:1997,) pp. 75-76.

[4] Brunswick Co., Va., Deed Book 6:595. Cited in Bradley, Stephen E. Brunswick County, Virginia Deed Books, Vol. 3: 1755-1764. (Lawrenceville, Va.: 1998.)

[5] Brunswick Co., Va., Will Book 2:47. Cited in Bradley, Stephen E. Brunswick County, Virginia Will Books, Vol. 1, (1739-1769; 1783-1785.) (Lawrenceville, VA: 1997,) p. 7.

Joseph Wright, Sr., Joseph Wright, Jr., and John Wright were living together and taxed in Granville Co., N. C., in 1753.[6] Joseph Wright and son were taxed there in 1757.[7]

There is a John Wright taxed in Granville County in 1750 with one tithe.[8] John Wright had one tithable in the Bear Swamp District of Granville County in 1761.[9] The muster roll recorded 8 October 1754 confirms there were two men named John Wright present. John Wright is present in Capt. Osbourn Jeffreys' company, while in Capt. Benjamin Sims' company are Joseph Wright, John Wright, and Joseph Wright, Jr.[10]

1780 Dionysius Wright of Richmond Co., Georgia

"Dionysius" Wright, name spelled many ways, first appears in the Brunswick Co. Deeds on 5 September 1747 as a witness.[11] Shortly thereafter he witnessed the sale of 100 acres of land on Fountains Creek,[12] and the sale of 350 acres 350 ac. on s. side of Nottoway Creek joining south side of Rocky Run (probably adjacent to Mabry's land, bought from Richard and Hannah (Williamson) Fox.)[13]

On 3 June 1752, Abraham Peebles sold to David Meredith, of Dinwiddie County, 100 acres of land, part of a patent to Charles Kimball, on the north side of Three Creeks in an indenture witnessed by Dionysius Wright.[14] On 8 June 1752 Joel Threewits sold to David Meredith for £20 a tract of 100 acres, part of a 450 acre patent to Bartholomew Peterson made in 1746 and sold to John Threewits in April 1749 and willed to Joel Threewits

---

[6] List of Osborn Jeffreys, Esq. Accessed 9 March 2013 at http://files.usgwarchives.net/nc/granville/court/tax1753.txt.

[7] List of John Martin. Accessed 9 March 2013 at http://files.usgwarchives.net/nc/granville/court/tax1757.txt.

[8] List of Lemuel Lanier. Accessed 9 March 2013 at http://files.usgwarchives.net/nc/granville/court/tax1750.txt.

[9] List of Solomon Alston. Accessed 9 March 2013 at http://files.usgwarchives.net/nc/granville/census/1761tax.txt.

[10] http://files.usgwarchives.net/nc/granville/military/eaton01.txt.

[11] Brunswick Co., Va., Deed Book 3:356. Cited in Bradley, Stephen E. Brunswick County, Virginia Deed Books, Vol. 2: 1744-1755. (Lawrenceville, Va., 1997.)

[12] Brunswick Co., Va., Deed Book 3:562. Cited in Cited in Bradley, Stephen E. Brunswick County, Virginia Deed Books, Vol. 2: 1744-1755. (Lawrenceville, Va., 1997.)

[13] Brunswick Co., Va., Deed Book 3:615. Cited in Bradley, Stephen E. Brunswick County, Virginia Deed Books, Vol. 2: 1744-1755. (Lawrenceville, Va., 1997.)

[14] Brunswick Co., Va., Deed Book 5:249. Cited in Cited in Bradley, Stephen E. Brunswick County, Virginia Deed Books, Vol. 2: 1744-1755. (Lawrenceville, Va., 1997.)

in 1749.[15] The land was located on the north side of the Three Creeks joining Mabry, John Collier, and Dionysius Wright.

On 28 June 1754 Dionysius Wright patented 400 acres of land "on the branches of Crab Louce Creek adjacent Peter Daniels, Francis Lett and Kimble...."[16] And on 16 August 1656, Dionysius Wright patented 138 acres of land "adjacent the Glebe, his own line and Lett."[17]

On 25 April 1758 Dionysius Wright sold to Randal Daniel for £35 a tract of 538 acres obtained by patent to Wright and described as adjoining the lands of the Glebe, Lett and Noble. Witnesses were John Daniel, Jr., Robert Gee, Jr., and James Daniel.[18] The land was further described in an indenture made 24 March 1760 between William House and William Eppes, Attorney at Law of Dinwiddie County, who sold two tracts of land containing 538 acres granted by patent to Dionysius Wright and conveyed by Wright to Randall Daniel. One tract was described as having 400 acres adjoining the land of Peter Daniel, Crablouse Creek, Francis Lett, and Kimball. The other tract, containing 138 acres, adjoined the 400 acre tract, the Glebe line and the land of Lett.[19]

On 25 May 1767 a tract of land was sold and described as joining D. Wright, Vaughn, Isaac House, Daniel, Crablouse Branch.[20] Dionysius Wright again witnessed a sale involving the Threewits tract on 28 September 1767,[21] but in a poll of voters taken 2 December 1768, only James and Samuel Wright were listed.[22] These deeds suggest Dionysius Wright still had land in Brunswick County, even after sale of his two large tracts in 1758. It also suggests he left the area in late 1767 or 1768.

Dionysius Wright had land on Big Kiokee Creek in Richmond Co., Ga., by 23 April 1775 when Daniel Reese of South

[15] Brunswick Co., Va., Deed Book 5:252. Bradley, Stephen E. Brunswick County, Virginia Deed Books, Vol. 2: 1744-1755. (Lawrenceville, Va., 1997.)

[16] Virginia Land Patent Book 31:434.

[17] Virginia Land Patent Book 33:340.

[18] Brunswick Co., Va., Deed Book 6:282.

[19] Brunswick Co., Va., Deed Book 6:440.

[20] Brunswick Co., Va., Deed Book 8:517. Bradley, Stephen E. Brunswick County, Virginia Deed Books, Vol. 4: 1765-1770. (Lawrenceville, Va.: 1998.)

[21] Brunswick Co., Va., Deed Book 8:70. Bradley, Stephen E. Brunswick County, Virginia Deed Books, Vol. 4: 1765-1770. (Lawrenceville, Va.: 1998.)

[22] Brunswick Co., Va., Deed Book 9:279. Bradley, Stephen E. Brunswick County, Virginia Deed Books, Vol. 4: 1765-1770. (Lawrenceville, Va.: 1998.)

Carolina sold a 140 acre tract there to Nathan Harris.[23] The land was described as acquired by him in 1772 and adjacent Dionysius Wright and Nathan Harris.

There is a will for Dionysius Wright proved 22 March 1780 in Richmond Co., Georgia, but also filed in 96 District, South Carolina.[24] The double filing, may have been necessary because of the War, but, it may have been considered important to maintain title to the land in South Carolina.

Genealogical Summary[25]

1. DIONYSIUS[1] WRIGHT was born before 5 September 1726 and died before 22 March 1780 Richmond Co., Ga. He married ELIZABETH _____.

Children of DIONYSIUS WRIGHT and ELIZABETH are:

i. ABEDNEGO[2] WRIGHT, d. December 1824; m. ELIZABETH JONES 19 June 1791 Columbia Co., Ga.

Abednego Wright obtained patents on substantial tracts of land in Richmond County, Georgia, including 150 acres in 1785, 333 in 1787, and 200 in 1794. He also obtained a 575 acre tract in Washington County in 1785, and 19 acres in Columbia County in 1799.[26]

ii. ALBERT[2] WRIGHT, d. before 12 May 1857 Columbia Co., Ga.

---

[23] Mitchell, Carol. 27 January 2003. Located at http://genforum.genealogy.com/wright/messages/15585.html.

[24] Mitchell. Wright, Dionysius - of Ninety-Six Dist S. C. to Sons Shadrach and Mesech sons in law John Cotten and Charity his wife, Abner Willingham and Peace his wife, Wm. Mims and Naoni his wife five shillings each. To son Abednego Wright, slave, son Habakkuk Wright 100 lbs etc; to son Isaah Wright 400 acres in GA being part of plantation whereon I lived, adjoining William Saterwhite. To son Albeart Wright, land and dwellings whereon I lived. To dau.Concord and Elizabeth Penny Wright a slave. To wife Elizabeth Wright, residue for life at her death to dau. Unity Wright. Wife Elizabeth and son Abednego. Exrs. Land on Kiokee Creek in GA to son Shadrach Wright upon his paying Habakkuk Wright 75 lbs. Signed May 9 1779. Probated Mar 20 1780 before Wm Chandler, J. P. Richmond Co., Wit. Lewis Gardner, James Harvey, Richard Harvey. 9 May 1779-20 Mar 1780 Richmond Co., GA

[25] Kisabeth, Craig. Re: Dionysius Wright. 23 February 2002. Located at http://genforum.genealogy.com/wright/messages/13728.html.

[26] Georgia Colonial and Headright Plat Index, 1735-1866. Accessed 8 March 2013 at http://cdm.sos.state.ga.us:8888/cdm4/platindex.php. Cited hereafter as Virtual Vault.

Albert Wright sold 300 acres of land on Big Kiokee Creek to Abednego Wright 21 December 1793.[27] The land was described as including 150 acres originally acquired by William Holliday, Sr., and sold by him to Dionysius Wright, and bequeathed by the latter in his will to Albert Wright.

iii. MESHACK[2] WRIGHT, d. before 1 November 1814 Edgefield District, S. C.[28]

In the name of God Amen. I Meshack Wright of the State of South Carolina & District of Edgefield Planter do make and ordain this my last Will and Testament in manner & form following VIZ. First I give and bequeath to Lud Harris, Sen. five shillings in full for his share of my estate. Secondly I give and bequeath to Lud Harris, Jun. son of my daughter Sarah one half of all my Personal Estate during his natural life and should he die possessed of living and lawful issue to him and his heirs forever. Third I give and bequeath to Dionecious Zenn Wright, son of Ann Zenn all my lands and remaining half of all my Personal Estate during his natural life and should he die Possessed of living lawful issue then to him and his heirs forever. Fourthly, my desire is that if either Lud Harris, Jr., or Dionecious Zenn Wright either should die without living lawful Issue then it is my desire that the surviving one shall have the whole of my estate and if they both die without living lawful issue then my desire is that their shares shall go to the male heirs of Habackeech Wright, dec'd., and be equally divided amongst them to them and their heirs forever. Fifthly also my desire that my Excr hire my Negroes at private hire and to such persons as they may think proper and that they will sell at public auction any part of my Stock and household furniture that they may

[27] Richmond Co., Ga., Deed Book 1:166. Recorded 18 February 1795. Cited by Carol Mitchell.

[28] Edgefield Co., S. C., Will Book A:336-337, 11 January 1815. Accessed 8 March 2013, http://www.archivesindex.sc.gov/onlinearchives/Thumbnails.aspx?recordId=301180 . The date of death was derived from the attestation in court of Casper Nail when he presented the will for probate. Meshack Wright and David Meyer were appointed executors of the will of Catherine Meyer of Edgefield Dist., S. C., 25 May 1789/27 March 1800. Edgefield Dist., S. C., Will Book A:36.

think best and than when the legatees come of age my Excrs divide to each as the will directs. Sixthly, I nominate and appoint my trusty friends Casper Nail, Sr., John Miller, and Dionecious Zenn Wright as my sole and lawful executors and also guardians to the legatees and that no legatee shall have it in their power to choose a Guardian nor the Court to choose for them. In witness whereof I have hereunto set my hand and affixed my seal this 21st day of June 1814. Meshack Wright

> Signed sealed and delivered in the presence of
> John Nail
> Casper Nail, Jr.
> Rebecca Nail

iv. SHADRACK^2 WRIGHT.

> Shadrack Wright obtained a patent on a 690 acre tract in Washington Co., Ga., in 1784.[29]

v. ISAIAH^2 WRIGHT, b. 1748 Virginia; d. 1820 Georgia; m. REBECCA BRISCOE 27 November 1787 Columbia Co., Ga.

vi. HABBAKUK^2 WRIGHT, d. 1805; m. SUSANNAH BACON 18 June 1787 Richmond Co., Ga.

> Habbakuk Wright obtained patents on a 250 acre tract in Richmond County in 1783 and a 575 acre tract in Washington County, Georgia, in 1784.[30]

vii. CHARITY^2 WRIGHT, m. (1) _____ SCHULTZ; m. (2) JOHN COTTON.

viii. NAOMI^2 WRIGHT, m. WILLIAM MIMS.

ix. CONCORD^2 WRIGHT.

x. PEACE^2 WRIGHT, m. ABNER WILLINGHAM.

xi. UNITY^2 WRIGHT, d. before 23 April 1788 Richmond Co., Ga.[31] d. s. p.

---

[29] Virtual Vault.

[30] Virtual Vault.

[31] Mitchell, Carol. 26 January 2003. Located at http://genforum.genealogy.com/wright/messages/15582.html.

1810 John Wright of Brunswick Co., Va.

The tax lists show John Wright in the Lower District for the first time in 1787, when his tax was paid by Thomas Washington.[32] In 1788 he is on his own with one poll.[33] This implies a birth year of about 1762, and also implies that John's father was dead in 1787.

On 23 February 1801 John Wright and Nancy, formerly Nancy Smith, widow of James Smith, deceased, sold to Pleasant Smith, for £10 sell "the land belonging to James Smith, dec'd..." The boundaries were not described. The indenture was signed by both John Wright and Nancy (_____) (Smith) Wright and proved by them in court on the same date. No witnesses were listed.

On 14 February 1809, John Wright wrote a will leaving his estate to his wife Nancy during her lifetime, and then to be divided amongst his four youngest children: James Wright, Wyatt Wright, Lucy Wright, and "Tyny" Wright.[34] He signed the will and it was probated 25 June 1810. Unfortunately, he does not name his "older" children, probably born of his first wife, only his "younger" children.

Nancy Wright is the head of household in the 1810 Census for Brunswick County.[35] She is 26-45 years old, and she has one son under five, one son five to ten, and two daughters under five. This makes it clear that John Wright and Nancy were the parents of the four children named in the will he wrote in 1809.

The will suggests he had children by his first wife. The "older children" would have been in their teens or early twenties at most by the time of his death in 1810. He does not appear with any named sons in the tax rolls, so it seems probable that his older children were daughters, and they may have married by the time he wrote his will, freeing him from the need to specifically provide for them. The only "Wright" bride of record in Brunswick Co., Va., prior to 1810 is Sally Wright who married Josias Wright 28

[32] Brunswick Co., Va. Tax List, Lower District, 1787, p. 15.

[33] Brunswick Co., Va. Tax List, Lower District, 1788, p. 22.

[34] Brunswick Co., Va., Will Book 7:418. In: Bradley, Stephen E. Brunswick County, Virginia Will Books, Vol. 5: 1804-1812. (Lawrenceville, Va.: 1998,) p. 84.

[35] 1810 Census Brunswick Co., Va., Meherrin Dist., p. 765. The list is alphabetized, so no conclusions about neighbors is possible.

November 1808, with Wesley Wright as bondsman.[36] The ceremony was performed by Edward Dromgoole.

Genealogical Summary

1. JOHN WRIGHT, d. before 25 June 1810 Brunswick Co., Va.; m. (1) UNKNOWN; m. (2) NANCY (_____) SMITH, widow of JAMES SMITH before 23 February 1801 Brunswick Co., Va.

Child of JOHN WRIGHT and NANCY is:

   i. JOHN N.[2] WRIGHT, b. 1805 Brunswick Co., Va.; d. 14 April 1885 Brunswick Co., Va.; m. ANN ELIZA SMITH 27 September 1836 Brunswick Co., Va.; b. 1815 Virginia; d. March 1893 Brunswick Co., Va.[37]

      John N. Wright is present in the 1850 Census,[38] 1860,[39] 1870,[40] and 1880.[41] His death record states that his father was John Wright.[42]

Children of JOHN WRIGHT and ELIZA SMITH are:

  1. MARY E.[3] WRIGHT, b. 1837 Brunswick Co., Va.

  2. REBECCA E.[3] WRIGHT, b. 1838

  3. MARTHA[3] WRIGHT, b. 1839

  4. PAMELIA[3] WRIGHT, b. 1842

  5. JOHN N.[3] WRIGHT, b. 1845 Brunswick Co., Va.; d. 13 September 1877 Brunswick Co., Va.[43]

  6. VIRGINIA[3] WRIGHT, b. 1847

  7. WILLIAM R.[3] WRIGHT, b. 1849

  8. ORIAN A.[3] WRIGHT, b. 1857

---

[36] Knorr, Catherine L. Marriage Records and Ministers Returns of Brunswick County, Virginia, 1750-1810. (Pine Bluff, Ark.1953,) p. 109.

[37] Virginia Deaths and Burials Index, 1853-1917. Online database located at Ancestry.com, accessed 1 June 2013.

[38] 1850 Census Brunswick Co., Va., Southern District, p. 348B, #532.

[39] 1860 Census Brunswick Co., Va., Meherrin Dist., Crichton's Store P. O., p. 626, #98/97. His wife was listed as Ann E. Wright, 43, and he had one more child, Orian A., b. 1857. William M. Wortman was living in the household as a farm hand.

[40] 1870 Census Brunswick Co., Va., Meherrin Dist., p. 13B, #242/242. John J., William R., and Orian were still at home.

[41] 1880 Census Brunswick Co., Va., Meherrin Dist., p. 330B, ED 195, #272/272. Orian W. Wright, 22, is still at home. He stated that he and both parents were born in Virginia.

[42] Virginia Death and Burial Index 1853-1917. Ancestry.com 1 June 2013.

[43] Virginia Death and Burial Index 1853-1917. Ancestry.com 1 June 2013.

1825 James Wright of Newberry District, S. C.

The Bible of Mary Wright Shell was transcribed by Mrs. W. L. Martin, Jr., of Hogansville (Coweta Co.), Georgia, and a copy was placed in the files of the Coweta Co., Genealogical Society in Grantville, Ga.[44] This record states that James Wright and his wife, Lucy, were married 23 January 1774. The place is not mentioned, but the record appears in Surry Co., Virginia. James Wright was born 27 November 1745 and died 3 January 1825. Lucy Wright was born 27 November 1756 and died 27 November 1824.

The Bible record did not list any locations, but a reading of the Old Tranquil Methodist Cemetery in Newberry Co., South Carolina, records James Wright died 3 January 1825, aged 79, and Lucy Wright died 27 September 1824, aged 67.[45] The matching of the dates with the Bible record makes it certain that these are the same people. James Wright, resident of Newberry Co., S. C., applied for naturalization in 1808, stating he was born in Ireland and had been resident in the state for 10 years.[46]

His will was written 27 December 1823 and mentions his sons William and "Tacker." The Bible record suggests his name was Zaccheus. He also mentions daughter Mary Shell and daughter Lucy Shell, who was dead in 1823.[47]

William Shell executed a power of attorney in Brunswick Co., Va., to his son, Lemmon Shell, upon his departure to South Carolina on 29 October 1797.[48] A history of these families shows their land lay along the waters of Pigeon Roost Creek, where William Shell and his wife, Amelia Ellis, came in 1765.[49] This

---

[44] Accessed 21 October 2008. The page numbers suggest this was part of the Georgia DAR Bible collection, but I have not yet located a copy in that work. The Bible was owned by Mrs. Lucius Arnold, Jr., of Hogansville at the time of transcription.

[45] Shell, Dan. Old Tranquil Cemetery, Newberry, S. C. Accessed 23 October 2008 at http://files.usgwarchives.net/sc/newberry/cemteries/tranquil.txt.

[46] O'Sullivan, Nancy. http://archiver.rootsweb.ancestry.com/th/read/scnewber/1999-11/0941766481. Accessed 23 October 2008.

[47] South Carolina Probate Records Box 60, p. 31. Cited online at http://wc.rootsweb.ancestry.com, (db. :ah10687.) A search of online South Carolina records did not show this file on 23 October 2008. [http://www.archivesindex.sc.gov/].

[48] Brunswick Co., Va., Deed Book 17:225. Cited in South Carolina Magazine for Ancestral Research 12:97, (Spring) 1984. Quoted by Donna Carpenter. Southern Ancestors. 13 July 2002. Located at http://wc.rootsweb.ancestry.com, (db. :2165387.)

[49] Sheek, Ann Ellis. History of Twelve Generations of the Ellis Family. (1974), p. 26. Cited by Pinnix, Grant. Yadkin County, NC, and Caswell County, NC. 28 September 2008. Located at http://wc.rootsweb.ancestry.com, (db. grantpinnix.)

Creek arises in Brunswick Co., Va., but flows into the Roanoke River in Warren Co., N. C., (which was formed from Bute Co., N. C., in 1779.)[50] William Shell subsequently established himself on the West Branch of Poplar Creek, which is actually the easternmost branch, but passes through the very southwestern part of Brunswick County.

Harmon Shell of Newberry District petitioned the Washington District Court of Equity 29 February 1808 for partition and sale of the property of his father, William Shell, who died intestate August 1807 leaving a widow and ten children while seized of 130 acres of land on the waters of the Enoree River in Newberry District. The children were listed, including Lucy, wife of James Wright.[51]

Genealogical Summary

1. JAMES[1] WRIGHT was born 27 November 1745 in Ireland and died 3 January 1825 Newberry Dist., S. C. He married LUCY SHELL 23 January 1774 Surry Co., Va. She was born 27 November 1756 and died 27 November 1824 Newberry Dist., S. C.

Children of JAMES WRIGHT and LUCY SHELL are:[52]

2. i. WILLIAM[2] WRIGHT, b. 29 January 1775 Brunswick Co., Va.; d. 6 February 1855 Coweta Co., Ga.; m. (1) LUCY TUCKER 1 September 1803 Newberry Co., S. C., dau. of JOSEPH TUCKER and LUCY BUFORD; b. 15 January 1782[53]; d. 28 June 1811 Newberry Co., S. C.; m. (2) MARY TUCKER 3 July 1812 Union Co., S. C.[54], dau. of JOSEPH TUCKER and LUCY BUFORD; b. 20 September 1788; d. 19 November 1843 Newberry Co., S. C.[55]

   ii. MILLY[2] WRIGHT, b. 13 January 1777; d. 22 August 1785.

   iii. JOSEPH[2] WRIGHT, b. 7 January 1779; d. 9 January 1779.

---

[50] The other area mentioned was along Leath's branch, which arises in Mecklenburg Co., Va., crosses into Brunswick Co., Va., and empties into the Roanoke River in Warren Co., N. C.

[51] SC Magazine Ancestral Research 3:10-11a, (Winter) 1975. (Donna Carpenter.)

[52] Based on Mary Wright Shell's Bible record, unless otherwise noted.

[53] Foley.

[54] Foley.

[55] Old Tranquil Methodist Cemetery.

3. iv. ZACCHEUS[2] WRIGHT, b. 9 January 1783; d. 21 March 1862 Newberry Co., S. C.[56]; m. MARY GLASGOW 7 December 1809; b. 17 September 1785; d. 6 September 1841 Newberry Co., S. C.[57]

4. v. ELIZABETH L.[2] WRIGHT, b. 12 February 1787; m. WILLIAM DUGAN 17 December 1807;

5. vi. MARY[2] WRIGHT, b. 18 December 1788; d. 21 May 1880; m. ISHAM MALONE SHELL 16 April 1818; d. 5 October 1871.

6. vii. LUCY[2] WRIGHT, b. 9 November 1792; d. 21 October 1819 Newberry Co., S. C.; m. EDMOND SHELL 9 November 1815; d. September 1832.

viii. JAMES[2] WRIGHT, b. 29 June 1797; d. 17 September 1797.

2. WILLIAM[2] WRIGHT was born 29 January 1775 in Brunswick Co., Virginia and died 6 February 1855 in Coweta Co., Georgia. He married (1) LUCY TUCKER 1 September 1803 in Newberry Co., South Carolina, daughter of JOSEPH TUCKER and LUCY BUFORD. She was born 15 January 1782 and died 28 June 1811 in Newberry Co., S. C. He married (2) MARY TUCKER 3 July 1812 Union Co., S. C., daughter of JOSEPH TUCKER and LUCY BUFORD. She was born 20 September 1788 and died 19 November 1843 in Newberry Co., S. C.

The Bible record records the birth of William Wright on 29 January 1775, and his marriage to Lucy Tucker on 1 September 1803. She died 28 June 1811. There is a tombstone in the Old Tranquil Methodist Cemetery for Lucy Wright dated 28 June 1817, aged 29 years, which appears likely to be Lucy (Tucker) Wright. The difference in dates is likely a transcription issue, but marriage records indicate that William Wright married, secondly, Mary Tucker 1812, so the Bible record is likely correct. Mary Wright is also buried in Old Tranquil Methodist Cemetery with her date of birth as 17 September 1785 and date of death 6 September 1841.

---

[56] Old Tranquil Methodist Cemetery.
[57] Old Tranquil Methodist Cemetery.

William Wright's death 6 February 1855 at age 81 was recorded in the Southern Christian Advocate for 30 March 1855.[58] It stated he was born in Brunswick Co., Va., and moved to South Carolina in his 21st year. These statements are consistent with William Wright, b. 29 January 1775, and would make 1796 the year of his removal to South Carolina. William Wright appears as a new name in the Brunswick Co., Va., personal property tax records for 1797,[59] but he disappears, along with James after 1798.[60] There are no deeds of sale involving James Wright at this time, and there are no deeds at all involving William Wright that have been found. However, the tax records support the statements in the obituary.

Children of WILLIAM WRIGHT and LUCY TUCKER (b. Newberry Co., S. C.) are:[61]

   i. JAMES L.[3] WRIGHT, b. 24 August 1804; d. 9 May 1844.

  ii. NANCY R.[3] WRIGHT, b. 6 January 1806; m. WILLIAM BROWN.

 iii. MARY W.[3] WRIGHT, b. 14 April 1807; d. 8 June 1882 Clinton, Laurens Co., S. C.; m. HUGH MCKELVEY son of JOHN MCKELVEY and MARY STEWART; b. 9 December 1803 Laurens Co., S. C.; d. 4 December 1859 Laurens Co., S. C.[62]

 iv. ELIZABETH A.[3] WRIGHT, b. 10 June 1809; d. 15 September 1836.

  v. LUCY[3] WRIGHT, b. 21 March 1811; m. JAMES LEAKE.

Children of WILLIAM WRIGHT and MARY TUCKER are:[63]

---

[58] Holcombe, Brent H. Marriage and Death Notices from the Southern Christian Advocate, Vol. 1, (1837-1860). (Easley, S. C., Southern Historical Press, 1979,) p. 373.

[59] Brunswick Co., Va., Tax List, Lower District, (1797), p. 25.

[60] Brunswick Co., Va., Tax List, Lower District, (1798), p. 25.

[61] Mary (Wright) Shell Bible Record lists the births of the children of Lucy Wright, and makes it clear she died in childbirth with her daughter, Lucy. The remainder of the information is from Foley.

[62] McKelvey, Reba. McKelvey Family. 24 Jan 2003. Located at http://wc.rootsweb.ancestry.com, (db. :2402426.) She reports they are buried in the Mt. Zion Methodist Cemetery, and that the church moved into Clinton, S. C., in 1855, and after two more moves, is now the Broad Street United Methodist Church. The markers at the old cemetery in town were moved to Rosemont Cemetery and she cites a transcription from the South Carolina Magazine of Ancestral Research. She also notes that Mary was a sister of Rebecca Parram Wright who married Jabez McKelvey.

[63] Foley.

vi. REBECCA PARRAM[3] WRIGHT, b. 29 November 1813; m. JABEZ MCKELVEY 3 December 1833 Laurens Co., S. C., son of JOHN MCKELVEY and MARY STEWART; b. 27 June 1802 Laurens Co., S. C.; d. 14 January 1862 Nevada Co., Arkansas.[64]

vii. HILLIARD J.[3] WRIGHT, b. 6 December 1815; d. 1 June 1844; m. SERENA LEAKE 21 January 1836 dau. of JOHN LEAKE and MARY CLARA DENDY; b. 4 October 1814 Laurens Co., S. C.; d. 23 January 1899 Adairsville, Bartow Co., Ga.[65]

viii. WILLIAM C.[3] WRIGHT, b. 23 November 1817.

ix. JOSEPH ASBURY[3] WRIGHT, b. 29 June 1819; d. about 1878 DeKalb Co., Ala.;[66] m. NANCY BELLAH 3 September 1841 Coweta Co., Ga., dau. of JOHN BELLAH and NANCY MCLIN; b. 23 May 1823 in Georgia; d. 18 August 1906 Jackson Co., Ala.

x. MILTON FLETCHER[3] WRIGHT, b. 9 February 1821; d. 4 October 1902 Wynnville, Blount Co., Ala.; m. MARY NANCE SHELL 14 December 1848 Coweta Co., Ga., dau. of WILLIAM BAUGH SHELL and NANCY SIMS NANCE; b. 1 June 1832 Coweta Co., Ga.; d. 27 November 1906 Wynnville, Blount Co., Ala.

xi. MARGARET FRANCES ANN[3] WRIGHT, b. 1 August 1822; d. 1 Jan 1892 Logan, Cullman Co.,. Ala.; m. SAMUEL LEAKE son of JAMES LEAKE and MARTHA NEILL; b. 3 May 1812 Laurens Co., S. C., d. 1896 Cullman Co., Ala.[67]

xii. MARTHA A. S.[3] WRIGHT, b. 10 February 1825; d. 23 May 1826.

xiii. MARTHA A. S.[3] WRIGHT, b. 14 March 1827;

xiv. SARAH EMALINE[3] WRIGHT, b. 10 March 1829.

---

[64] McKelvey, Reba.

[65] Buried in Poplar Springs Methodist Church Cemetery. Heard, John W. Heard and Allied Families from PA to SC and West to AR, MO, & TX. 1 October 2008. Located at http://wc.rootsweb.ancestry.com, (db. poole.)

[66] Family Group Sheet of Hilda King of Apopka, FL, copy located at the Coweta Co., Ga., Genealogical Society Library, Grantville, Ga., 21 October 2008.

[67] He was a Methodist minister and is buried in Shady Grove Methodist Church Cemetery, Cullman, Alabama. Miner, Robin K. Knowles-Miner Family Tree. 14 October 2005. Located at http://wc.rootsweb.ancestry.com, (db. robinkminer.)

3. ZACCHEUS[2] WRIGHT was born 9 January 1783 and died 21 March 1862 in Newberry Co., South Carolina. He married MARY GLASGOW 7 December 1809 Newberry Co., S. C., daughter of ROBERT GLASGOW and ELIZABETH KINNARD. She was born 17 September 1785 in Newberry Co., S. C., and died 6 September 1841 in Newberry Co., South Carolina.

Children of ZACCHEUS WRIGHT and MARY GLASGOW (b. Newberry Co., S. C.) are:[68]

   i. MARTHA ANN[3] WRIGHT, b. 25 October 1810[69]; d. 12 August 1815.

  ii. ABNER FLETCHER[3] WRIGHT, b. 9 October 1812; d. 8 August 1815.

 iii. ELIZABETH MELINDA[3] WRIGHT, b. 7 February 1815; d. 1894 Newberry Co., S. C.; m. ISAAC KELLER 6 December 1855 son of JACOB KELLER and SUSANNAH BOSHART; b. 7 December 1790; d. 2 June 1871 Newberry Co., S. C.[70]

 iv. LUCY CAROLINE[3] WRIGHT, b. 21 February 1817; d. 2 September 1909 Newberry Co., S. C.; m. JOHN ADAM BEDENBAUGH 25 July 1845 Newberry Co., S. C. son of HENRY BEDENBAUGH and ELIZABETH BRIGHT; b. 11 July 1816; d. 5 January 1899 Prosperity, Newberry Co., S. C.[71]

  v. JAMES MARION[3] WRIGHT, b. 25 February 1819; d. 30 August 1899; m. MARY ANN LITTLE; d. 30 August 1889.

 vi. MARY EUSEBIA[3] WRIGHT, b. 13 March 1821; d. 20 August 1889 Newberry Co., S. C.; m. JAMES B. WILSON, b. 25 December 1805; d. 8 October 1864 Newberry Co., S. C.

 vii. WILLIAM N.[3] WRIGHT, b. 24 March 1823.

viii. ZACCHEUS FRANKLIN[3] WRIGHT, b. 25 September 1825; d. 9 October 1885 Newberry Co., S. C.; m. ISABELLA JANE BYRD.

---

[68] Glasgow, Ann. Life's Weaving. 9 October 2008. Located at http://wc.rootsweb.ancestry.com, (db. lifesweaving.)

[69] Mary (Wright) Shell Bible Record.

[70] He is buried in Gilder's Creek Cemetery.

[71] Both are buried in St. Luke's Lutheran Cemetery, Newberry Co., S. C. (Foley.)

ix. ROBERT HERMAN[3] WRIGHT, b. 30 July 1828; d. 11 March 1896; m. MARY FRANCES BOWERS 23 August 1866 Newberry Co., S. C., dau. of JACOB STEPHEN BOWERS and SARAH ELIZABETH CHAPMAN; b. 16 January 1846 Newberry Co., S. C.; d. 17 March 1924.

4. ELIZABETH LEMMON[2] WRIGHT was born 12 February 1787 in Brunswick Co., Va., and died 13 March 1856 in Newberry Co., South Carolina. She married WILLIAM DUGAN 17 December 1807 in Newberry Co., S. C., son of THOMAS DUGAN and MARY JOHNSTON. He was born 3 April 1782 in Newberry Co., S. C., and died 20 September 1831 in Newberry Co., S. C.

Children of ELIZABETH WRIGHT and WILLIAM DUGAN are:

i. LUCINDA[3] DUGAN, b. 14 February 1809.[72]
ii. MARIA[3] DUGAN, b. 30 January 1813.[73]
iii. MARY A. E.[3] DUGAN, b. 11 February 1814; m. ROBERT CAMPBELL; b. 21 November 1808; d. 26 February 1846 Newberry Co., S. C.[74]
iv. MARGARET FRANCES[3] DUGAN, b. 28 March 1818; d. 6 November 1888 Emmett, Nevada Co., Arkansas; m. JOHN T. BOYD 22 April 1838 Newberry Co., S. C.; b. 10 February 1815 Newberry Co., S. C.; d. 25 July 1848 Florida.[75]

5. MARY[2] WRIGHT was born 18 December 1788 and died 5 October 1871 Coweta Co., Georgia. She married ISHAM MALONE SHELL 16 April 1818 in Newberry Co., South Carolina, son of JOHN ELLIS SHELL and ELIZABETH MALONE.[76] He was

---

[72] Mary (Wright) Shell Bible Record.

[73] Foley.

[74] Buried at Gilder's Creek Presbyterian Cemetery, Newberry Co., S. C. Cited by Judith. Fowler, Blake, Owen, Norris, Dorman, McWhorter, Payne, Boyd, and Allied Southern Families. 8 August 2008. Located at http://wc.rootsweb.ancestry.com, (db. judyk.)

[75] Ouzts, H. C. The Ouzts Family in America. 24 October 2008. Located at http://wc.rootsweb.ancestry.com, (db. hcouzts.)

[76] The Mary (Wright) Shell Bible Record shows she died 6 April 1867.

born 30 March 1785 Mecklenburg Co., Virginia, and died 5 October 1871 in Coweta Co., Georgia.

Children of MARY WRIGHT and ISHAM SHELL are:[77]

    i. LAURA ANN L.[3] SHELL, b. 15 June 1819;

    ii. JAMES G. C.[3] SHELL, b. 18 September 1820;

    iii. ISHAM ABNER FLETCHER[3] SHELL, b. 11 August 1822; d. 5 August 1827.

    iv. LUCY ELIZABETH MALVINEY[4] SHELL, b. 25 June 1824; m. WILLIAM J. HARDY.[78]

    v. IVERY ISHAM MALONE[3] SHELL, b. 5 November 1826; d. 30 May 1906 Turin, Coweta Co., Ga.; m. (1) HANNAH AMANDA DOMINIC; m. (2) TEXANA ISABEL KIRK 5 March 1858 Heard Co., Ga.; d. 21 March 1929 Heard Co., Ga.

    vi. JOHN ABNER ZACCHEUS[3] SHELL, b. 10 January 1829; d. 7 May 1918 Coweta Co., Ga.

    vii. RUFUS HARMON[3] SHELL, b. 1 January 1834; d. 10 June 1886 Coweta Co., Ga.; m. SARAH HARIETT ANN HEAD 22 March 1866 Coweta Co., Ga.

6. LUCY[2] WRIGHT was born 9 November 1792 and died 21 October 1819 Newton Co., Georgia. She married EDMOND SHELL son of JOHN ELLIS SHELL and ELIZABETH MALONE. He was born about 1792 in Brunswick Co., Virginia, and died 1 September 1832.

Children of LUCY WRIGHT and EDMOND SHELL are:

    i. HENRY W.[3] SHELL;

    ii. MARTHA ANN[3] SHELL;

    iii. JOHN A.[3] SHELL;

---

[77] Mary (Wright) Shell Bible Record.

[78] Foley. He lists a different date of birth than that in the Bible record. Rufus Shell's birth was not listed, but his marriage and death were.

1791 James Wright of Brunswick Co., Virginia

The 1768 tax list for Brunswick Co., Virginia showed one man named James Wright.[79] James Wright was mentioned in a deed dated 28 March 1763 when John Gibbs sold 200 acres to Charles Sullivant lying on the "south side of Hayses Creek" joining James Wright and Steep Br.[80] When Charles Sullivant sold this land to William Bailey on 26 January 1767, it was described as 250 acres on the south side of the Meherrin river, part of a patent to John Gibbs, 16 June 1756. This indenture was witnessed by Josias Wright.[81]

When James Wright was listed in the 1783 tax list, he had himself and two sons under 21.[82] The 6th district list was missing in 1784. In 1785, James is on the long list, probably equivalent to the upper district, with himself, Laban Wright, and David Wright, all over 21, and three males under 21.[83] The lower district showed George Wright and Sarah Wright with one male under 21.[84] In 1786, James Wright is in the Lower District, (Meherrin Parish), along with John Wright.[85] George Wright and Sarah Wright are in the same district, but apparently not that close to the James and John.[86] The 1787 list shows James and James Jr., both over 21, with a third poll not named, David, son of James Wright, and shows John Wright as under 21, the tax paid by Thomas Washington.[87]

The 1788 tax list again shows George Wright living in the lower district,[88] but somewhat distant from James, who has four polls, James with one poll,[89] John Wright with one poll,[90] and Sarah with two polls.[91] The same people, with the same number of

---

[79] Brunswick Co., Va., Deed Book 9:279-283.

[80] Brunswick Co., Va., Deed Book 7:265. Bradley, Stephen E. Brunswick County, Virginia Deed Books, Vol. 3: 1755-1764. (Lawrenceville, Va.: 1998.)

[81] Brunswick Co., Va., Deed Book 8:532. Bradley, Stephen E. Brunswick County, Virginia Deed Books, Vol. 4: 1765-1770. (Lawrenceville, Va.: 1998.)

[82] Brunswick Co., Va. Tax List District 6, (1783) p. 8. George Wright (4th District) p. 9.

[83] Brunswick Co., Va. Tax List, (1785) p. 15.

[84] Brunswick Co., Va., Tax List, 4th District, (1785), p. 28.

[85] Brunswick Co., Va., Tax List, Lower District, (1786), p. 61.

[86] Brunswick Co., Va., Tax List, Lower District. (1786), p. 48.

[87] Brunswick Co., Va., Tax List, Lower District. (1787), p. 15.

[88] Brunswick Co., Va., Tax List, Lower District. (1788), p. 19.

[89] Brunswick Co., Va., Tax List, Lower District, (1788), p. 21.

[90] Brunswick Co., Va., Tax List, Lower District, (1788), p. 22.

[91] Brunswick Co., Va., Tax List, Lower District. (1788), p. 23.

polls are shown on the 1789 tax list, although without major space in their appearance.[92]

The 1790 tax list was too faded to decipher, but in 1791, James Wright with two polls now, has been joined by Samuel Wright with one poll, Sarah Wright has no polls, but one male under 21, Nancy Wright appears with one poll, John Wright is still present with one poll, and George Wright is still present with one poll.[93] The most likely explanation is that Nancy is the relict of James. James Wright persists in the tax lists with two polls until 1795, when he has only one poll. There is no new name on the 1795 tax list that might be the "missing" poll. The remaining James Wright disappears from the tax lists after 1798.

On 26 October 1778 James Wright sold to John Kimbrel or Kimble, for £35 sterling a tract of 50 acres, "being part of the land granted by patent to James Wright bearing date the third day of March one thousand seven hundred and seventy ..."[94] The land was described as "beginning at a corner poplar at the Mouth of the Little branch on Little Creek and Gibbs line thence along his line to a corner red oak on James Wright line thence along a line of Marked trees to a (?) scrub white oak on James Wright's line thence along a line of marked trees to the head of the spring branch thence down said branch to the Creek and thence down the said Creek to the Beginning...." The deed was signed by both James Wright and Nancy Wright. No witnesses were named. This is surely the tract described previously.

This deed shows that James Wright had a wife named Nancy, and that he was likely related to Josias (Josiah) Wright, which is the basis for identifying this man as 1791 James Wright of Brunswick Co., Virginia. It must be noted, however, that there are probably two different men: one named Josiah, the other named Josias. Keeping them separate has not been possible.

Additional deeds for James Wright are of record, most showing land along Rattlesnake Creek with recurring abutters named Randle, Brewer, and Ledbetter. Review of maps shows Rattlesnake Creek is generally east flowing, and at one point is one ridge south and west of Hayes Creek. The Creek flows into Fountain Creek and eventually into the Roanoke River in Warren

---

[92] Brunswick Co., Va., Tax List, Lower District, (1789), pp. 59-62.
[93] Brunswick Co., Va., Tax List, Lower District, (1791), pp. 28, 29, 32.
[94] Brunswick Co., Va., Deed Book 13:192.

Co., N. C. These deeds show relationships with a number of other men named Wright.

In 1782 James Wright sold land to Samuel Scott.[95] (*Deed not examined.*)

On 29 December 1787, John Randle sold to Henry Ledbetter[96] "...a parcel of land lying and being in the County of Brunswick beginning on Rattlesnake Creek...to James Wright's line, thence along Wright's line to a birch stump on Rattlesnake Creek," containing 130 acres.[97] The indenture also describes the property running along Henry Ledbetter's on line, so he was clearly purchasing adjoining land.

On 4 September 1789 Henry Ledbetter and "Winnifred," his wife sold to James Wright for £80 current money "one certain tract or parcel of Land containing by estimation two hundred and twelve acres be the same more or less, lying and being in the County of Brunswick aforesaid and bounded as follows: Viz: Beginning at a white Oak Tree John Brewer Corner, thence along the said Brewer Line to a corner scrub Oak, thence up Brewer's Branch to a corner turkey Oak thence along a line of chopt trees to Bowles Dobbins line, thence along Dobbins line to the Long Branch, thence down the said Branch to Rattlesnake Creek thence along the said creek to a corner, J Harrison, thence along a line of chopt trees to a corner sweet Gum on the creek thence down the meanders of the Creek to the beginning..."[98] The indenture was witnessed by Edward King, John Harrison, and John Wright. Since this indenture transfers 212 acres, whereas the former covered only 130 acres, the bounds do not match, but certainly appear to include the former tract.

On 20 October 1790, John Brewer and William Brewer sold to William Vaughn a nine acre tract "on Rattlesnake Creek"

---

[95] Brunswick Co., Va., Deed Book 2:249.

[96] Brunswick Co., Va., Deed Book 2:204 [2 Dec 1742] Hollum Sturdivant and Elizabeth of Surry Co., John Rottenbury & Susannah of same, Henry Ledbetter and Edith of Brunswick Co., Richard (R) Fox and Hannah, alias Joanna (X) Fox, and Sarah Mabry to George Mabry of St. Andrew's Parish in Brunswick Co., £30 280 ac. patented by John Williamson 18 Feb 1722 and left to his daughters upon his death, the land being on the south side of Nottoway River joining the n. side of Rocky Run. This land is in the upper district, but does serve to show that Henry Ledbetter's wife, Williamson, was a sister to Hannah Fox, wife of Richard Fox. This Henry Ledbetter is probably the son of Henry and Edith (Williamson) Ledbetter.

[97] Brunswick Co., Va., Deed Book 14:380. Proved 28 July 1778.

[98] Brunswick Co., Va., Deed Book 14:532.

that ran "up the creek to a White Oak James Wrights corner thence south along said Wrights line..."[99] Also noted was William Vaughn's land, so clearly he was buying a small piece of property, presumably to adjust his own lines.

In the 1930's Harvey Elam wrote a history of his Wright family who migrated to the area around Xenia, Greene Co., Ohio, and were prominent Methodists in that area.[100] He identified the progenitor as George Wright, but I have not found definite information about him. He reportedly had four sons, John, Samuel, Josiah, and James, about whom information was found in Brunswick Co., Va., records. According to Mr. Elam, the family had land on Hayes Creek. Review of Brunswick County, Va., maps shows Hayes Creek as a short, north flowing river, which drains into the Meherrin River just west of present-day Virginia Rte. 46, near Fort Hill and Fort Christiana. However, I have chosen to examine each of these men separately, since I have not seen the documentation that they are brothers and sons of a George Wright.

Genealogical Summary

1. JAMES[2] WRIGHT died about 1791 Brunswick Co., Va. He married NANCY _____.

Children of JAMES WRIGHT are:

i. JOSIAH[3] WRIGHT, b. about 1765; d. 1814 Xenia, Greene Co., Ohio; m. SARAH NELSON WRIGHT 28 November 1808 Brunswick Co., Va., daughter of GEORGE WRIGHT and SOPHIA OWENS; b. 3 December 1788; d. 25 April 1862 Xenia.

Josias Wright makes his appearance on the tax list for 1806, (p. 21) with one poll. All of the other Wrights that year were listed on p. 19. In 1807, he is again by himself (p. 21) with the rest of the Wrights on p. 19. No tax was collected in 1808. Josias Wright married Salley

---

[99] Brunswick Co., Va., Deed Book 15, p. 73. Proved 25 April 1791.

[100] The work exists as a manuscript in the public library of Xenia, Ohio. I have not personally reviewed a copy, but it was used as the basis for a report by Lola Galloway. Jeff Galloway. 9 October 2008. Located at http://worldconnect.rootsweb.com, (db. jlgalloway.) I have accepted her reading of the work, pending reviewing the original. Cited hereafter as Elam.

Wright 28 November 1808 Brunswick Co., Va., with Wesley Wright as bondsman.[101] In 1809, Josias Wright is by himself on p. 21, while Merritt Wright and Samuel Wright (Rattlesnake Creek) are on p. 22, while George Wright, "Willie" Wright, and 1810 John Wright are on p. 20. The ceremony was performed by Edward Dromgoole. In 1810 he is "Josiah" Wright, (p. 22) and again, on a separate page. He is again present in 1811, (p. 16) but disappears thereafter. There is another man named Josias Wright, who is discussed separately.

ii. TABITHA[3] WRIGHT.

iii. REUBEN[3] WRIGHT.

   Reuben Wright appears on the 1801 tax list (p. 22) with one poll just after John Wright, Sr. (p. 21) In 1802 he again appears just after John Wright, Sr., (1810 John Wright) (p. 24). In 1803 there are two men named Reuben Wright. One (p. 22) is under 21 as he owes no poll, and is listed after John (Brewer) Wright. The other Reuben Wright (p. 23) is listed after John Wright, Sr. Neither Reuben Wright appears again on the tax list. There is no certainty, of course, that these listings apply to this particular Reuben Wright.

iv. MERRITT[3] WRIGHT, b. about 1788; d. 10 April 1855 Xenia; m. (1) NANCY OWENS 17 January 1809 Brunswick Co., Va., dau. of WILLIAM OWENS and SARAH BATCHELOR; d. 11 September 1839 Xenia.; m. (2) MARTHA (BONNER) PERKINS 1840 Xenia.

   Samuel Wright was bondsman for Merritt Wright when he married Nancy Owens 17 January 1809 Brunswick Co., Va., in a ceremony conducted by Edward Dromgoole.[102]

   Merritt Wright appears in the 1810 Census for Brunswick Co., age 16-26, with his wife, also 16-26, and two daughters under the age of 5.[103] The children

---

[101] Knorr, Catherine L. Marriage Records and Ministers Returns of Brunswick County, Virginia, 1750-1810. (Pine Bluff, Ark.: NPD, 1953,) p. 109.

[102] Knorr, Catherine L. Marriage Records and Ministers Returns of Brunswick County, Virginia, 1750-1810. (Pine Bluff, Ark.: NPD, 1953,) p. 109.

[103] 1810 Census, Meherrin Parish, Brunswick Co., Va., p. 755.

listed in Elam do not match this, suggesting at least one daughter died in infancy.

In the 1820 Census Merritt Wright is 26-45, with one male under ten, two girls under ten, and one 10-16, with his wife, also 26-45.[104]

Merritt Wright first appears on the tax list adjacent to Samuel Wright in 1809.[105] This suggests a birth year of 1788, which would make him 21 at marriage, and 22 in 1810. Merritt Wright also disappears from the tax list after 1811, suggesting he went with Samuel Wright and his family. Since Samuel did not marry until 1795 and his family on the 1810 census is young, he is not the father of Merritt Wright. He is probably his cousin, Samuel³ (Samuel²) Wright.

- viii. TEMPERANCE³ WRIGHT.
- ix. ELIZABETH³ WRIGHT.
- x. MARTHA³ WRIGHT.
- xi. DICEY ANN³ WRIGHT, m. HAMLIN LEDBETTER 22 October 1804 Brunswick Co., Va.
- xii. REBECCA³ WRIGHT.

1775 Samuel Wright of Brunswick Co., Virginia

On 3 March 1760 Samuel Wright patented 300 acres of land in Brunswick Co, described as being "down the little creek."[106] On 27 August 1762, Samuel Wright and Sarah, his wife, sold 100 acres of the patent land "on the south side of Little Creek joining Samuel Wright's branch..." for £12 Virginia money to their son James Wright.[107]

On 22 April 1762 Samuel Wright witnessed a sale from Jacob Woolsey to John Moore of a 270 acre tract of land on "both sides of the Great Creek and adjoining Lick Branch, and being part of a tract granted to Francis Ellidge by patent dated July 25, 1741..."[108]

On 9 September 1766 Matthew Parham, Jr. sold to James Mize, "of Lunenburg Co." a tract of 200 acres adjoining "Samuel

---

[104] 1820 Census, Xenia Twp., Greene Co., Ohio, p. 148.
[105] Brunswick Co., Va. Tax List, Lower District, 1809, p. 22.
[106] Va. Land Patent Book 33:761.
[107] Brunswick Co., Va., Deed Book 7:178.
[108] Brunswick Co., Va., Deed Book 7:98.

92

Wright, Hayes, the mouth of Great Branch, Morgan." The indenture was witnessed by Aaron Hudgins, John (x) Wright, and John Moore.[109]

There is an inventory on record for Samuel Wright 27 November 1775.[110]

Genealogical Summary

1. SAMUEL[2] WRIGHT died before 27 November 1775 Brunswick Co., Virginia. He married SARAH NELSON.

Children of SAMUEL WRIGHT and SARAH NELSON are:

  i. GEORGE[3] WRIGHT, b. 4 February 1756 Brunswick Co., Va.; d. 25 September 1829 Xenia, Greene Co., Ohio;[111] m. SOPHIA OWENS 1784 Brunswick Co., Va., dau. of WILLIAM OWENS and MARY BATCHELOR; b. 30 June 1766 Brunswick Co., Va.; d. 3 October 1846 Xenia.

   George Wright appears in the tax lists with two sons 16-21.[112] The earliest land transaction I find involving George Wright is the sale 25 June 1787 of seventy acres of land to William James for £38 10s. "current money of Virginia."[113] The land is described as bounded "Beginning at a corner poplar, thence North to a corner red oak on the said William James' line, from thence East to a corner white oak, thence southwest on the new line to a sweet gum in the head of the branch, thence down the branch as it runs to the beginning poplar..." This indenture was signed by both George Wright and his wife Sophia Wright. Witnesses were not named by the clerk, and the indenture was apparently proved by George and Sophia Wright personally.

   On April 25, 1794, William Owens and Mary, his wife, sold to George Wright of Brunswick County for £45 Virginia money, a tract of land containing 100

---

[109] Brunswick Co., Va., Deed Book 8:370 Cited in Bradley, Stephen E. Brunswick County, Virginia Deed Books, Vol. 4: 1765-1770. (Lawrenceville, Va.: 1998.)

[110] Brunswick Co., Va., Will Book 4:475.

[111] Woodland Cemetery, Xenia, Greene Co., Ohio. http://www.findagrave.com, memorials #21217951 and #21218032.

[112] Brunswick Co., Va. Tax List, 4th District, 1783, p. 9. In 1784, he had no sons under 21 counted. (p. 35)

[113] Brunswick Co., Va., Deed Book 14:291. Proved 20 Apr 1794.

acres bounded "Beginning at a pine the Corner tree between William Owens, & Briggs, Goodrich from thence a South Course to a White Oak on Middleton Fletcher's land from thence a S. E. course to a red Oak, from thence to a White Oak on Sd. Road from thence down the said Road to a White Oak, a Corner Tree and from thence a N.W. course to the first station... This indenture was witnessed by Thomas Goodrich, Owen M. Fletcher, and Micajah Lane, and was signed by William Owens, and Mary (x, her mark) Owens.

George Wright applied for letters of administration and posted a £50 bond on the estate of Lewis Wright with Benjamin Lashley as his security on 28 April 1795.[114] I assume this was one of his sons, particularly given the small amount of bond required. William James, John Hauser, Jesse Braswell, and John A. James were appointed to appraise the estate.[115]

On 6 February 1798, George Wright and Sophia Wright, his wife, made two indentures. In the first, George and Sophia Wright sell to Samuel Wright for one shilling a tract of land containing 95 acres.

"Beginning at a corner sweet gum on a branch at William James' line thence along said line north east to a corner scrub oak thence South East on said line to a corner Spanish oak on Howser's ? line thence West on the Said line to a corner Spanish oak on Wm James' new line thence north on the said line to the beginning Sweet gum..."[116]

The indenture was signed by both George and Sophia Wright, and proved in court by their own testimony on 26 Feb 1798. Sophia released her dower rights at that hearing.

In the second indenture, George Wright sold to William James for £48 "current money of Virginia" a tract containing 35 acres..."Beginning at a corner white oak on Hases Creek thence east on Elizabeth Howser's line to a corner Spanish oak from thence north to a

[114] Brunswick Co., Va., Court Order Book 16:405-406, 28 April 1795.

[115] Brunswick Co., Va., Court Order Book 16:406, 28 April 1795.

[116] Brunswick Co., Va., Deed Book 17:182.

sweet gum on the said William James' line on a branch, thence down the said branch west to the above said corner, from thence South up the said Creek to the beginning White oak..."[117] This indenture, too, was signed by both George and Sophia Wright, was not witnessed, but proved in court by their oath on 26 Feb 1798. Sophia again released her dower rights.

The Brunswick Co., Va., tax lists show George Wright present from 1783 through 1814, and he does not appear in the 1820 Census. George Wright sold land to John Carpenter in 1815.[118] I have not examined this deed, but it may mark the time he moved to Ohio.

George Wright is present in the 1810 Census for Brunswick Co., Va., age greater than 45, with his wife being 26-45, and two sons 16-26, two sons under 16 and two sons under five, two daughters 16-26 and one daughter under 16.

ii. SAMUEL[3] WRIGHT, b. 27 October 1767 Brunswick Co., Va.; d. 1 June 1859 Xenia; m. SARAH OWENS 15 January 1795 Brunswick Co., Va., dau. of WILLIAM OWENS and MARY BATCHELOR; b. 27 Oct 1775 Brunswick Co., Va.; d. 3 May 1844 Xenia.

Samuel Wright makes his first appearance on the tax lists in 1791, when he appears with George Wright.[119]

Samuel Wright married Sally Owens on 3 January 1795 in Brunswick Co., Va., with George Wright and Sophia as his bond.[120] The ceremony was performed by Edward Dromgoole, Methodist minister.

On 23 July 1800 Samuel Wright and Sally Wright, his wife, sold to Cary James, Ira Ellis, William Manning, Sr., William Manning, Jr., George Wright, Armisted Hartwell, Hamlin Ledbettter, William James, Jr., & John Seward, Sr., Trustees for $1 the "lately erected House called & Known by the Rock Church

---

[117] Brunswick Co., Va., Deed Book 17:184

[118] Brunswick Co., Va., Deed Book 22:417; 22:418.

[119] Brunswick Co., Va. Tax List, Lower District, 1791, p. 28. He could be on the 1790 list, as it was illegible. However, he is not present in 1789.

[120] Knorr, Catherine L. Marriage Records and Ministers Returns of Brunswick County, Virginia, 1750-1810. (Pine Bluff, Ark.: NPD, 1953,) p. 109.

with the Land Annexed [one acre]...on the stage road leading from Petersburg to Warrenton..."[121] The deed goes on to indicate that the church is affiliated with "the Methodist Episcopal Church of the United States," and that control of the property rests with "the several conferences of the Ministers of the Methodist Episcopal Church in the said United States and no other persons to have and enjoy the free use & benefit of the said premises that they may therein Preach and expound God's Holy Word & provided always that the said persons Preach no other Doctrine than that contained in the Rev[d] John Wesley's Notes on the new Testament and his Volume of Sermons..." The indenture was signed by Samuel Wright and Sally Wright.

Samuel Wright appears in the 1810 Census for Brunswick Co., age 26-45, which is consistent with the estimated birth in 1770. He had a large household with his wife, one son 5-10 years old, one son under five, and three daughters under five. He also had 16 slaves.

The last deed involving Samuel Wright appears in 1811 when he made two indentures with Frederick Lanier.[122] *(Deeds not examined.)* He disappears from the tax lists after 1811, marking his remove to Ohio.

iii. LUCY[3] WRIGHT, m. WILLIAM OWENS 22 December 1806 Brunswick Co., Va., son of WILLIAM OWENS and MARY BATCHELOR; b. 9 March 1779 Brunswick Co., Va.; d. 26 December 1862 Xenia.

1825 Josias Wright of Madison Co., Illinois

Josias Wright sold 200 acres on the south side of the Meherrin River to Edmund Randle on 24 January 1778. This land was described as adjoining John Wright, George Wright, John Warren, Aron Smith, Steep branch, and Hays' Creek.[123] This indenture was signed by Josias Wright and witnessed by Richard Randle, John Lightfoot, James Randle, William Finch, and Josias Randle.

---

[121] Brunswick Co., Va., Deed Book 19:150.

[122] Brunswick Co., Va., Deed Book 21:265; 21:295.

[123] Brunswick Co., Va., Deed Book 13:122. Proved 25 May 1778.

In the very next indenture, William Finch purchased from John Randle, Richard Randle and Polly his wife, and Edmond Randle and Susannah, his wife, 235 acres in Meherrin Parish, Brunswick Co, described as adjoining Joseph Wright, Rocky Run, Long Branch, Richard Randle, John Randle and the main road.[124] On 22 April 1778, Edmond Randle and Susanna, his wife of Meherrin Parish, sold to Thomas Kimball of St. Andrew Parish the 200 acres of land he had bought earlier in the year from Josias Wright, described as being on the south side of the Meherrin River adjoining John Wright, George Wright, John Warren, Aaron Smith, Steep Branch, and Hays' Creek.[125]

Thomas Kirkpatrick made the pioneer improvement on the site of Edwardsville, and in the same part of the county, south and east of the present county seat. James Kirkpatrick, Frank Kirkpatrick, William Gillham, Charles Gillham, Thomas Good, George Barnbeck, George Kinder, John Robinson, Frank Roach, James Holliday, Bryant Mooney, Josias Randle, Thomas Randle, Jesse Bell, Josias Wright made early settlements…The Randle, Bell and Wright families left Georgia together in September, 1811, and reached Turkey Hill in St. Clair County on the 17th of October, and shortly afterward made their homes in Madison county. Josias Randle became the first clerk of the circuit court. Josias Wright settled the Shaeffer place two miles and a half southwest of Edwardsville….[126]

Josias Wright moved with his father-in-law and the other Randles to Montgomery Co., North Carolina, in 1779. He became an officer of North Carolina troops there in 1780. Josias Wright

---

[124] Brunswick Co., Va., Deed Book 13:123.

[125] Brunswick Co., Va., Deed Book 13:126.

[126] History of Madison County, Illinois. (Edwardsville, Ill.: W. R. Brink & Co., 1883,) p. 79. A biography of Josias Randle is on p. 359. It states he was born in Brunswick Co., Va., 1 October 1766, and became a ME minister. He moved to Georgia in 1790 and married Ann Thorn in 1795, and was an itinerating minister until 1810. They became disabused of slavery and moved to Illinois in September 1811, settling in the frontier of then St. Clair, and subsequently Madison Co., Illinois. He was appointed clerk when the area was still the territory of Illinois and was reappointed when statehood was granted in 1818. He died there 15 January 1824. Copy located online 8 March 2013 at
http://archive.org/stream/historyofmadison00brin#page/n7/mode/2up.

became a Methodist minister and in about 1799 they moved to Warren Co., Georgia. He left Warren County, Ga., 3 September 1811, arriving on 17 October 1811, when he bought the Shaeffer farm.

Genealogical Summary

1. JOSIAS WRIGHT was born 18 January 1746 in Brunswick Co., Va., and died 2 January 1825 in Madison Co., Illinois. He married APPHIA RANDLE 10 September 1778 Brunswick Co., Va., dau. of JOSIAS RANDLE and JANE PROCTOR. She was born 25 April 1761 in Brunswick Co., Va., and died July 1845 in Madison Co., Illinois.[127]

Children of JOSIAS WRIGHT and APPHIA RANDLE are:

    i. MARY[2] WRIGHT, b. 3 July 1779 Brunswick Co., Va.; m. JOHN BROOKS Montgomery Co., N. C., d. about 1813 Bedford Co., Tenn.

    ii. JANE[2] WRIGHT, b. 17 November 1781 Montgomery Co., N. C.[128]

    iii. RICHARD[2] WRIGHT, b. 3 May 1783 Montgomery Co., N. C.; m. MARY MOORE 4 January 1815 St. Clair Co., Ill.

    iv. ISHAM[2] WRIGHT, b. 2 March 1786 Montgomery Co., N. C.; m. ELIZABETH HARRISON 2 March 1815 Madison Co., Ill.

    v. JAMES B.[2] WRIGHT, b. 2 December 1788 Montgomery Co., N. C.; m. (1) MILICENT GREENWOOD 10 August 1813 Madison Co., Ill.; m. (2) ANN SCHUYLER.

    vi. JOHN WESLEY[2] WRIGHT, b. 7 July 1791 Montgomery Co., N. C.; d. 22 September 1875 Palmer, Ill.; m. (1) PRISCILLA SMITH 2 November 1822 Madison Co., Illinois.; m. (2) MATILDA RANDLE 22 January 1835 Madison Co., Ill.

    vii. TABITHA[2] WRIGHT, b. 5 November 1794 Montgomery Co., N. C.

---

[127] Nix-Judy Cemetery Pioneer Cemetery, Madison Co., Illinois. Additional data posted by Dennis Peterson. Located on http://www.findagrave.com, memorial #83441387. His marker is there, but he was probably buried Bethel Cemetery, Glen Carbon, Ill. Data on the children are from the memorial for Apphia Randle Wright.

[128] She may have died as a newborn. Eleanor. Randle Families.18 December 2010. Located at http://wc.rootsweb.ancestry.com, (db. randle99).

viii. NANCY RANDLE[2] WRIGHT, b. 13 July 1800 Warren Co., Ga.; d. after 1880 Christian Co., Ill.; m. HIRAM B. ROUNTREE 29 March 1818 Madison Co., Illinois; b. 22 December 1794 Rutherford Co., N. C.

ix. SAMUEL[2] WRIGHT, b. 25 January 1803 Warren Co., Ga.; m. LUCINDA MANVILLE 11 October 1827 St. Clair Co., Ill.

Joseph Wright

There is an unaccounted for entry for Joseph Wright in Lunenburg Co., Va., who may be the man later appearing in Brunswick Co., Va. On 11 August 1763 Richard Hanson's suit against Joseph Wright was dismissed, as the defendant was no longer resident in Lunenburg Co., Va.[129]

On 10 February 1780 Joseph Wright, Joseph Phelps and Sarah Phelps, his wife, sold to John Powell for £5000 "current money" a tract of land containing 100 acres bounded "Beginning at a corner black jack near the head of the Ready Branch Between the said Joseph Wright, John Powell, and John Lightfoot thence down the said line to a Corner Post Oak near a long Pine, between the said Powell and the land of Wm. Chapman, Dec'd, and an Entry of Land Entered for by the said Powell thence along the said Entry to a corner Red Oak Sapling thence along the said Enter to a Corner Post Oak on Phelps line, thence along the said Line to an Elbow or Corner, on a Red Oak Sapling the said Phelps Path that leads to the said Plantation, thence along the said Phelps Line about sixty yards into an old field, thence along Robert Davies Line to a post oak near the head of Rampaths thence along Lightfoots Line to a Corner black jack the Beginning..."[130]

This indenture was signed by Joseph Wright, and Joseph Phelps made his mark. The indenture was witnessed by James Meinhardt (?), Mark Jackson, and William Harris, who signed with a mark.

In 1783 Joseph Wright sold land to Absalom Bennett. (*Deed not examined.*) Joseph Wright was reimbursed by Meherrin Parish for keeping Benjamin Sexton for the church year 1785.

---

[129] Lunenburg Co., Va., Court Order Book 9:209, 11 August 1763. It was a busy session of court, as suits involving William Wright, John Wright, and Thomas Wright were also heard.

[130] Brunswick Co., Va., Deed Book 13:434.

(ended November "31st".) I find no record of Joseph Wright in the tax lists for Brunswick County from 1782 onward.

Chapter 4: Wright Families of Lunenburg County, Virginia

Untangling the Wright families of Mecklenburg County, Va. in the latter part of the eighteenth and first decade of the nineteenth centuries is complicated by changing political boundaries. Mecklenburg County was erected in 1765 from Lunenburg County, which in turn was erected in 1745 from Brunswick County. Consequently, I have tried to examine all three counties to identify groups of Wright families. Lunenburg County was formed in 1745 from the western portion of Brunswick County. Examination of the records has identified three different groups of Wrights, although one lone individual may be part of the first group, which I have termed the Wrights of Flatt Creek. Ironically, this group was located in an area that became Mecklenburg County in 1765, as the creek drains into the Meherrin River from the south.

1755 John Wright of Flatt Creek, Lunenburg Co., Virginia.

On 10 January 1748, John Wright patented 510 acres in two tracts: 224 acres on the upper side of Flatt Creek near Thomas Roberts, and 386 acres with no neighbors mentioned.[1] For convenience, he will be designated John Wright of Flatt Creek.[2]

The 1748 List of Tithes for Lunenburg Co., Virginia, shows John Wright with 4 tithes.[3] In 1749, he still has 4 tithes, one of whom is himself, and one is named as Thomas Wright.[4] This implies that Thomas has turned 21. In 1750, he has three tithes.[5] In 1752 he has four tithes including himself and John Shepherd.[6]

---

[1] Lunenburg County, Virginia Land Patents, 1746-1916. (Miami Beach: TLC Genealogy, 1990.) Va. Land Patent Book 28:462 and 28:463, 10 January 1748.

[2] On 10 September 1755, John Wright patented 400 acres on the head of Rocky Branch near Duke, John Patrick, Dortch, Roberts and his own lines. [Va. Land Patent Book 31:564.] This has to be the other John Wright, since John Wright of Flatt Creek was dead by May 1755.

[3] Bell, Landon C. Sunlight on the Southside. (Lists of Tithes: Lunenburg Co., Virginia, 1748-1783.) (Baltimore: Genealogical Publishing Co., 1974,) p. 67. Cited hereafter as Bell.

[4] Bell, p. 113.

[5] Bell, p. 143. He is on the list of William Howard, as he was in 1749.

[6] Bell, p. 193.

On 3 October 1750, John Wright of Lunenburg County made an indenture with his son, Laban[7] Wright, transferring all of his land, three slaves, George, Judy, and Peter, household furniture, etc., with the proviso that Laban is to "provide for me and my wife Jane a sufficient maintenance in the land and premises."[8] He also made provision of cattle to his daughters, Mary, Alice, Hannah, and Edea or Edloe. No witnesses to this deed were recorded and John Wright signed with his mark. In modern terms, John Wright has gifted his estate to his son, but retained a life interest in same.[9]

At the May Court 1755 Letters of Administration were granted to John Speed and Amy, widow of John Wright, and Laban Wright, orphan of John Wright asked for John Speed to be his guardian.[10] Laban had to be at least 14 years old in 1755 to be allowed to select his guardian, which yields a birth year of before 1741. Since his father was able to name him in the deed of 3 October 1750, he was probably close to his majority in 1755, so likely born about 1735. The inventory was reported 3 September 1755.

On 4 December 1759, the accounts of John Speed were audited showing the estate had a total value of £129.2.7. There was a balance owed the estate of £7.2.1.[11] The estate records include reporting payment of the poll tax and levy for 1754, and settling accounts with Thomas Wright and Amy Wright. The audit was signed by Henry Delony, Amos Timms, Jr., and Thomas Lark.

The 1759 Processioning report for Precinct 3, bounded by the Roanoke River, Miles Creek, Pennington's Old Road and Fox's Road, shows Laban Wright's land undergoing processioning by Philip Morgan and Thomas Roberts.[12] The same list shows

---

[7] Laban is also spelled Labin and Labon in the records. I will use Laban for consistency.

[8] Lunenburg Co., Va., Deed Book 2:138-9. Cited in Evans, June Banks. Lunenburg County Virginia, Deed Books 1 &2 (1746-1752). (New Orleans: Bryn Ffyliaid Publ., 1989,) p. 48. Cited hereafter as Evans.

[9] It is possible that John Wright, having amassed a considerable estate, wanted to keep it intact, and undivided. His "will" does provide for his daughters, though. Since he came to Flatt Creek (and the Lunenburg Co.) tithe list in 1750, then their lands would have been in the county from whence he came.

[10] Lunenburg Co., Va., Court Order Book 3:339, May Ct., 1755.

[11] Lunenburg Co., Va., Will Book 1:277.

[12] Evans, p. 142.

Laban Wright involved in the processioning of Philip Morgan's land. He clearly came into his majority before 1759, so he was born before 1738. As discussed above, he should have been born after 1736, so I will say he was born about 1737.

The List of Tithables for 1764, St. James Parish, which became Mecklenburg County in 1765, shows Laban Wright with three tithes and 460 acres, and Reuben Morgan with four tithes and 520 acres of land.[13]

The connection to Reuben Morgan is significant, as it leads to a clue as to the origins of John Wright of Flatt Creek. On 23 January 1777 Reuben Wright of Mecklenburg Co., Va., wrote his will, leaving his small estate to "my beloved sisters Mary Anne Rainey, Sally Morgan , Edith Morgan, Nancy Morgan, and Betsy Morgan" an equal share in £160 if it were collected by the time they reached age 21 or married. He also left a bay mare to his aunt, Elizabeth Morgan. He named as his executors, his father Reuben Morgan and Philip Morgan. The will was witnessed by John and George Baskerville, and proved in court April 14, 1777.[14] I think this indicates that Reuben Wright's father was dead and that his mother had remarried. However, there are some data that belie this.

Reuben Morgan's will was written 14 June 1781 and proved in court in Mecklenburg Co., Va. in July 1781.[15] He mentions his "beloved wife" Mary, to whom he left a small piece of land and three slaves. He divided his land among his children, and the descriptions make it clear that this tract was still next to the land originally patented by John Wright of Flatt Creek in 1749 and now owned by his son, Laban Wright.

Philip Morgan died 28 September 1826 in Washington Co. Kentucky, and wife died 24 July 1837. His executor, Jesse Peters, made application for a pension for him (R8314) based upon finding copies of two discharges for him. The application for pension was denied, but he did include a transcript of the family Bible record as part of the application.[16] The Bible record establishes that Reuben Morgan was the son of Philip Morgan and

---

[13] Evans, p. 151.

[14] Mecklenburg Co., Va., Will Book 1:223. Transcription by Carol York.

[15] Mecklenburg Co., Va., Will Book 1:367. Transcription by Carol York.

[16] Rejected Pension Application M804. Located on Ancestry.com, 30 December 2012. My thanks to Aaron Sugarman for calling this file to my attention.

his wife Mary, and was born 17 September 1724, location not specified. He married Mary Wright, date not specified, but about 1756 based on the age of the eldest child, daughter of John Wright and Jane. She was born 4 October 1728 and died 13 January 1819 at age 91. Their eldest son, Philip Morgan, was born 7 March 1758 and died 28 September 1826. He married Patty Puckett, daughter of Shippley A. Puckett and his wife, Mary. She was born 27 November 1759 and died 24 July 1837 at age 78. Shippley A. Puckett died 17 March 1783. Reuben W. Morgan, son of Reuben Morgan and Mary Wright, died January 1777.

An online source indicates Philip Morgan, the elder, was born about 1700 in Bristol Parish, Prince George Co., Va., and obtained a patent on 1000 acres of land in Brunswick Co., Va., in 1729.[17] He sold that tract on Island Creek 3 April 1735, and obtained a patent for another 1000 acres on the north side of the Roanoke River 16 June 1738. On 30 July 1756 he sold 120 acres of land on both sides of Miles Creek to Reuben Morgan for £50.[18] No further record of him was found.

Since Mary Wright, daughter of John and Jane Wright was born in 1728, is roughly contemporary with Laban Wright, who was born between 1734 and 1737, two other explanations seem possible. She could be a sister of 1755 John Wright, if we assume he was born somewhat later than I have estimated, and that both of them are children of yet another John Wright and his wife, Jane. On the other hand, she might be a daughter of John Wright and a first wife.

Genealogical Summary

1. JOHN[1] WRIGHT was born say 1695 in Virginia and died before May 1755 Lunenburg Co., Virginia. He married AMY _____.

Children of JOHN WRIGHT and AMY are:

i. MARY[2] WRIGHT, b. 4 October 1728; d. 13 January 1819; m. REUBEN MORGAN about 1756 Lunenburg Co., Va., son of PHILLIP MORGAN and MARY _____; b. 17 September 1724 Prince George Co., Va.; d. July 1781 Mecklenburg Co., Va.

---

[17] Hendricks, Timothy. Hendricks and Related Families. 7 March 2009. Located online at http://wc.rootsweb.ancestry.com, (db. henrictim.)
[18] Mecklenburg Co., Va., Deed Book 4:362, 3 June 1760.

104

ii. HANNAH[2] WRIGHT

iii. ALICE[2] WRIGHT

iv. EDEA[2] WRIGHT

v. THOMAS[2] WRIGHT, b. say 1727.

The tithe lists make it clear there were two men named Thomas Wright. In addition to the man living with John Wright around Flatt Creek, there was another living near the Mize family and Thomas Jarrett along Stony Creek. Since he was participating in his father's estate settlement as late as 1759, he had presumably relocated elsewhere. I have not been able to determine which Thomas Wright was this man.

2. vi. LABAN[2] WRIGHT, b. about 1737; d. after 1788 Mecklenburg Co., Va.

2. LABAN[2] WRIGHT was born say 1735 and died after 1788, probably in Mecklenburg Co., Va. He married (1) MARY _____. She died before 12 October 1771 Mecklenburg/Lunenburg Co., Va. He married (2) MILLEY.

On 11 October 1764 Laban Wright sold 150 acres of land, "part of 386 acres patent by John Wright 10 Jan 1748, Flatt Creek, adj. Haw Branch and Rock Branch, to Stephen Hatschel."[19] Mary, wife of Laban Wright, relinquished her dower right. This left Laban and Mary Wright with 224 acres on the upper side of Flatt Creek near Thomas Roberts in addition to the 236 acres of the first tract and the 400 acre tract from 1755, for a total of 860 acres.

On 19 May 1770 Stephen Hatchell sold 150 acres of land to Austin Wright of Mecklenburg Co., the tract being bounded by Flatt Creek, Robert Good, Ned's Branch, Laban Wright, and said Hatchell.[20] This man can be identified as 1829 Austin Wright of

---

[19] Ibid., p. 45.

[20] Mecklenburg Co., Va., Deed Book 2:484. Mecklenburg County, Virginia Deeds, 1765-1771. (Miami Beach: TLC Genealogy, 1990,) p. 106. Stephen Hatchell appeared with his father, William Hatchell in the 1752 tithe list, indicating a birth date before 1736. For reasons outlined later in this section, I think the tithe lists record the sons by name only when they are 21 or older, suggesting a birth date of 1730 or earlier. Stephen Hatchell spoke his nuncupative will 25 March 1781 and it was recorded 10 April 1781. His father's land was also on Flatt Creek, so his wife need not have been another sister of Laban

Mecklenburg Co., Va. (q.v.) Although it may be a coincidence, the fact that Austin Wright, son of 1783 Robert Wright of Brunswick Co., Va., bought this tract of land in the midst of Laban Wright's land, raises the possibility of a family connection with 1755 John Wright of Flatt Creek.

On 12 October 1771 Laban Wright sold a tract of land to Reuben Morgan containing about 400 acres, "where Laban Wright now lives," the tract being bounded by Morgan, Thomas Roberts, and John Hill.[21] The indenture was signed by Laban Wright, and "Milley" Wright released her dower rights.

In an indenture dated 7 November 1772,[22] Thomas Roberts made a gift of a tract of 183 acres on Flat Creek, adjoining Laban Wright, David Dortch, and John Roberts, upon Thomas' death. A deed dated 3 January 1778 leased the same 183 acres on Flatt Creek bounded by Laban Wright, John Roberts, and David Dortch, to James Blanton for the duration of Roberts' life and no longer.[23]

On 12 November 1777, Laban Wright witnessed the sale of 50 acres of land from John Roberts to William Nanney, the tract being bounded by the church road, Reuben Morgan, Laban Wright, and the dividing line between John and William Roberts.[24] (By implication, Thomas Roberts has died and William has come into possession of the 183 acre tract discussed above.)

On November 4, 1784 an indenture was made between Laban Wright of Mecklenburg County and Robert Turnbull of Dinwiddie County to sell a 460 acre tract of land for £460 Virginia money

> Beginning at William Robert's line on the aforesaid Creek down said creek as it meanders to Austin Wright's line thence the said Wright's line to Benjamin Morgan's line, thence the said Morgan's line to Benjamin Nanney's line,

---

Wright, although I had considered this possible. [Hatchell, Bill. Re: Stephen Hatchell 1702. 27 January 2005. Located at http://genforum.genealogy.com/hatchell/messages/111.html.]

[21] Mecklenburg Co., Va., Deed Book 3:461. Mecklenburg County, Virginia Deeds, 1771-1776. (TLC Genealogy, 1991,) p. 41.

[22] Mecklenburg Co., Va., Deed Book 3:486. Mecklenburg Co., Va., Deed Book 3:461. Mecklenburg County, Virginia Deeds, 1771-1776. (TLC Genealogy, 1991,) p. 43.

[23] Mecklenburg Co., Va., Deed Book 5:204. Mecklenburg County, Virginia Deeds, 1777-1779. (TLC Genealogy, 1994,) p. 34.

[24] Mecklenburg Co., Va., Deed Book 5:23. Mecklenburg County, Virginia Deeds, 1777-1779. (TLC Genealogy, 1994,) p. 37.

thence the said Nanney's line to William Roberts' line thence his line to Flat Creek at the beginning.

Signed   Laban Wright

Wife Willey released her dower rights.

Laban Wright appears on the Mecklenburg Co., Va., tax lists for 1784, 1785, 1786, and 1787, while Laban Wright, Jr., appears on the tax lists for 1787 and 1788, and again in 1792 Laban Wright, (almost surely "Junior" as he has no slaves, whereas Laban, Sr., had several.) The tax lists, plus the sale imply that Laban Wright died in Mecklenburg County, Virginia, about 1788, although I have not found public record of that fact.

Sadly, the court order books suggest the cause of the problem:

Laban Wright who stands presented by the grand jury for getting drunk having been duly summoned and not appearing though solemnly called. It is therefore considered by the Court that for the said Offense he forfeit & pay to the Churchwarden of Saint James Parish where the Offenses were committed five shillings or forty pounds of Tobacco to the use of the poor of the said Parish and that he pay the costs of this prosecution and may be taken.[25]

Laban Wright who stands presented by the Grand Jury for profane swearing two Oaths having been duly summoned and not appearing th° solemnly called. It is therefore considered by the Court that for the said Offense he forfeit and pay to the Churchwarden of Saint James Parish where the offense was committed ten shillings or one hundred pounds of Tobacco to the use of the poor of the said parish and that he pay the Costs of this prosecution and may be taken.[26]

Laban Wright, almost surely the son, was appointed constable in Mecklenburg Co., Va., on 9 March 1790.[27] One

[25] Mecklenburg Co., Va., Court Order Book 6:502. (May 1786)

[26] Mecklenburg Co., Va., Court Order Book 6:502. (May 1786)

[27] Mecklenburg Co., Va., Court Order Book 7:746.

possible clue, which will need to be followed is a note that Sally Roberts and Katie Vaughan were paid as witnesses for Christian W. Rainey, executor of William Rainey, deceased, as defendant in a suit brought by Laban Wright.[28] This suggests Laban Wright, Jr., was still in the vicinity, although not on the tax lists of Mecklenburg Co., Va., as late as 1800.

Child of LABAN WRIGHT and MARY is:

    i. LABAN[3] WRIGHT, b. about 1766 Mecklenburg Co., Va.
           Laban[3] Wright's birth year is calculated based on his appearance in his own right on the tax list. I have not located him after 1790.[29]
   ii. Others not identified.

After 1787 William Wright of Halifax County, Virginia
     William Wright had a 400 acre tract of land surveyed on Sandy Creek beginning at James Terry's corner on the creek in 1752.[30]

     William Wright was surety for the marriage bond between Robert Martin and Sarah Cunningham 10 February 1752 in Lunenburg Co., Va.

     "W" Wright was a witness 7 April 1752, along with Samuel Cobbs, Charles Irby, Hampton Wade, Clement Read, and Thomas Nash, to the sale of land from William Wynne and wife Frances, to Charles Barrett of Louisa County and John Lewis of New Kent County of two parcels of land.[31] One, containing 304 acres had been patented by William Wynne on 12 February 1742, the other, a tract of 400 acres, had been patented by him 20 August 1748. On 11 August 1752, "W" Wright, along with Thomas Nash, Paul Carrington, Joseph Williams, and John Cox, was witness to the sale of a 150 acre tract of land on the lower side of Little Roanoke River from Matthew Talbot to Clement Read, both of Lunenburg County, for £60.[32]

---

[28] Mecklenburg Co., Va., Court Order Book 10:184.
  [29] It is certainly possible that he is 1795 Laban Wright of Brunswick Co., Va., but for reasons outlined below, I have included him with the family of Wrights located on Stony Creek.
  [30] Edmunds, Pocahontas W. History of Halifax County. (npd) 2:211. Cited hereafter as Edmunds.
  [31] Lunenburg Co., Va., Deed Book 3:49.
  [32] Lunenburg Co., Va., Deed Book 3:115, 8 November 1752.

William Wright witnessed a deed of gift in 1755.

> To all whom these presents shall come greeting. Know ye that I Thomas Worthy of the Parish of Cumberland in the County of Lunenburg for diverse good causes and considerations whereunto moving but more especially for and in consideration of the natural love and affection which I have and bear unto my grandson Thomas Worthy, son of my son John Worthy, have given, granted confirmed and firmly made over to him....one bed and furniture, six plates, two dishes, six spoons, one iron pot, one bay mare, two heifers now with calf...signed Thomas Worthy
> Sealed & Delivered in the presence of William Wright and Frances Comer.[33]

William Wright was living in the part of Lunenburg Co., Virginia, that became Halifax County in 1752. At the first meeting of the vestry for Antrim Parish 24 April 1753, William Wright was the secretary.[34]

In 1762, George Currie sold a tract of land "next to the courthouse" to William Wright in 1758.[35] James Roberts sold William Wright land adjoining the town of Peytonsburg and the land of Mr. George Currie.[36] The tract was described as beginning in "a lower corner of Randolph Street to pointers on Currie's line. The tract was 3.1 acres, suggesting a "town lot." George Currie of Prince George Co., Va., sold an 80 acre tract of land for £50 to William Wright of Halifax County 26 February 1762, "whereon the courthouse of said county of Halifax now stands."[37]

William Wright was described as an adjoining neighbor of Henry Parish when he patented 131 acres of land on the south branches of the Meherrin River by 15 July 1760.[38]

William Wright appeared in the tax list of 1764 with one tithe, near John Wright and John Wright, his son, and again in the

[33] Lunenburg Co., Va., Deed Book 4:127-128, 3 June 1755.

[34] Chiarito, Marian. Vestry Book of Antrim Parish, Halifax County, Virginia, 1752-1811. (1983.) p.1.

[35] Edmunds, 2:14.

[36] Halifax Co., Va., Deed Book 3:244. Edmunds, 2:32.

[37] Halifax Co., Va., Deed Book 3:264, 26 February 1762. Edmunds, 2:32

[38] Virginia Land Patent Book 34:641.

tax list of 1772 on John Ragsdale's list along with Thomas "Rite", John Wright, Joseph Wright, and John Wright, Jr. It is not clear if these are the same or different men.

At the February 1760 Court, John Cox, orphan of William Cox, deceased, was apprenticed to William Wright.[39] In May 1763 Phebe, a Negro girl belonging to William Wright was adjudged to be nine years old.[40] On 3 March 1774 William Wright was a purchaser from the estate of William Irby.[41] William Wright, Ephraim Hill, and Thomas Brown witnessed the last will and testament of George Watkins 14 April 1782.[42]

Halifax County, Virginia, tax lists show William Wright last appeared on the list in 1787, suggesting he died about then. This is supported by finding a deed dated 4 March 1784 that reported that William Wright and his wife, Ann, had conveyed a 100 acre tract of land that was the home plantation to Ambrose Estes and John Wood, that was to be maintained as a life estate for Ann, then to go to their son Robert Wright upon Ann's death. However, all concerned, agreed that it was better to sell the land now to Robert Burchett and purchase another tract of land. The land was described as being bought from William Coventon, and bounded by William Thompson, Gent., Thomas Coventon, Thomas Blackstock, and Robert Eastham.[43]

Genealogical Summary

1. WILLIAM[1] WRIGHT was born before 1727 in Virginia and died about 1787 in Halifax Co., Virginia. He married ANN.

Children of WILLIAM WRIGHT and ANN are:

   i. BILLY[2] WRIGHT, b. before 1758 in Virginia; m. FANNY
   _____.

---

[39] Located at http://usgwarchives.net/va/halifax/court/orphans1.txt. Accessed 11 March 2013. This may well be the same Cox family as listed in the Lunenburg County deed.

[40] Located at http://usgwarchives.net/va/halifax/court/court3.txt. Accessed 11 March 2013.

[41] Halifax Co., Va., Will Book 1:23. 3 March 1774/20 April 1775. Accessed 11 March 2013 at http://usgwarchives.net/va/halifax/wills/willbk01.txt.

[42] Halifax Co., Va., Will Book 1:424-425, 14 April 1782/21 November 1782. Accessed 11 March 2013 at http://usgwarchives.net/va/halifax/wills/w3250001.txt.

[43] Halifax Co., Va., Deed Book 13:71, 4 March 1784/19 August 1784, cited in Halifax County, Virginia, Deeds, 1784-1790. (Miami Beach: TLC Genealogy, 1994,) p. 11.

He used the diminutive name repeatedly in public records. Billy Wright and Fanny Wright were witnesses when Ambrose Hunt sold a 100 acre tract of land on Buckskin Creek for £110 to Joseph Hunt 14 August 1779.[44]

Billy Wright purchased from Nathaniel Pass of North Carolina for £100, a 274 acre tract of land originally granted to Richard Brown, deceased, then to Richard Stanley, then to John Stanley, and then to pass. Witnesses were W. Wright, Elisha Lacy, and Evan Ragland.[45] Billy Wright sold 137 acres of this land to John Yates 17 December 1785 for £62.10sh.[46]

On 27 July 1789 Peter Moss of Surry Co., N. C., sold to Peter Mitchum of Halifax Co., Va., a tract of land on waters of Hico River bounded by William Wright.[47]

By January 1796 it appears that Billy Wright is no longer a land owner in Halifax County. On 4 September 1795 he witnessed the sale of a 265 acre tract of land on both side of Ellis' Creek from Ambrose Hunt to Thomas Scates for £100.[48] Ambrose Hunt of Fayette Co., Ky., gave a power of attorney to his brother, Joseph Hunt of Halifax County, to sell 134 acres of land on Ellis' Creek "whereon Billy Wright now lives" in an indenture recorded 25 January 1796.[49]

ii. THOMAS[2] WRIGHT, b. before 1764 Halifax Co., Va.

Thomas Wright appeared in his own right in the tax lists for 1785, implying that he was born before 1764.

iii. ROBERT[2] WRIGHT, b. after 1762 Halifax Co., Va.

[44] Halifax Co., Va., Deed Book 11:391, 14 August 1779/18 November 1779. Cited in Halifax County, Virginia, Deeds, 1778-1784, (Miami Beach: TLC Genealogy, 1992,) p. 53.

[45] Halifax Co., Va., Deed Book 11:396, 18 November 1779. Cited in Halifax County, Virginia, Deeds, 1778-1784, (Miami Beach: TLC Genealogy, 1992,) p. 54.

[46] Halifax Co., Va., Deed Book 13:357. Cited in Halifax County, Virginia, Deeds, 1784-1790. (Miami Beach: TLC Genealogy, 1994,) p. 40.

[47] Halifax Co., Va., Deed Book 14:624, 27 July 1789/23 June 1790, cited in Halifax County, Virginia, Deeds, 1784-1790. (Miami Beach: TLC Genealogy, 1994,) p. 152. The land was sold by John Mitchum to Stephen Hughes 7 December 1789 (DB 14:642), p. 154 in abstract book.

[48] Halifax Co., Va., Deed Book 16:518, 4 September 1795/25 January 1796. Cited in Halifax County, Virginia, Deeds, 1793-1796. (Miami Beach: TLC Genealogy, 1997,) p. 88.

[49] Halifax Co., Va., Deed Book 16:519, ibid.

Robert was still a minor in 1784 when the land he was to inherit after his mother's decease was sold.

Wrights of Stony Creek, Lunenburg County, Virginia

This group is the most numerous has proven difficult to keep separate, particularly given their close association in time and space as well as repetitive naming patterns. There were four men, likely brothers: Solomon, John, Thomas, and Joseph. In the discussion that follows, please keep in mind that the descendants of John and Joseph represent educated guesses, as I have found no probate records for either of these two men. Thomas did not leave a will, either, but his son, Parsons, did, and named bequests to his brothers and sisters.

It is helpful to discuss the associations between the Wright and Mize families and also to look at the geography in question, which is near the mouth of Stony Creek as it empties into the Meherrin River, just west of the intersection of the lines for Brunswick, Mecklenburg, and Lunenburg Counties.

Wright and Mize Connections Lunenburg Co., Virginia.

The 1748 tithe list shows Solomon Wright living near William Mize, James Mize, Jr., William Parker, and Thomas Jarrett, which locates him on Stony Creek. In 1749, Thomas "Right" and Solomon "Right" are listed just after James Mize, Sr., and Jeremiah Mize, which confirms the location on Stony Creek.[50] In 1750, the list of list of Hugh Lawson appear the names of Thomas Wright, John Wright and Solomon Wright with one tithe each.[51] They are listed near Thomas Jarrett, Stephen Mize and James Mize. All three men are listed again in 1751[52] and 1752[53] with the same neighbors.

June Banks Evans has published an analysis of several families living along Stony Creek, including the family of James Mize.[54] I will use her study as it sheds light on the Wrights living in this same area. Jeremiah Mize and James Mize purchased by

---

[50] Bell, p. 111. List of William Howard.
[51] Bell., p.144.
[52] Bell, pp. 171-172.
[53] Bell, p. 196.
[54] Evans, June Banks. Long Ago in Lunenburg on Stony Creek of the Meherrin. (New Orleans, Bryn Ffyliaid Publ., 1993.) Cited hereafter as Evans.

patent a tract of 118 acres on the north side of the Meherrin River along what was called Ruin Creek, which drained Little Creek on 28 September 1728.[55] On 4 December 1734 this tract was divided into two parcels each containing 59 acres. Jeremiah Mize took the lower half, adjoining the Meherrin River and up the little creek, and James Mize took the upper portion, along the river and up the Ruin Creek.[56] A later deed shows that Ruin Creek had been renamed as Stony Creek.[57] In the land processioning of 1763 and 1767 the land of Jeremiah Mize, probably the son of the original land owner, was shown as adjacent to Thomas Wright.[58]

The latter Jeremiah Mize sold the entire 59 acre tract to David Moss on 9 January 1775, at which time the land was described as following the line of Richard Boatman from the Meherrin River to the lines of Thomas Wright and George Steagall, and down the little [Aaron's] creek to the river. Moss sold this tract to William Denton 7 September 1781, when the tract was described as being bounded by the estate of Matthew Mathis, Thomas Wright, and George Steagall.[59]

James Mize subsequently patented 500 acres of land on both sides of Stony Creek on 22 September 1739, the same day that Thomas Jarratt patented 64 acres adjoining James Mize on the south (upper) side of the creek.[60]

Because of the association with the Mize family, we can be sure that the men named above, Solomon, Thomas, and John, were all located along Stony Creek.

On 7 March 1747/48, the Lunenburg County Court ordered Lewis Delony to establish a location for a bridge over the Meherrin River between the Fork and Mize's Ford.[61] William Williams was commissioned to build a bridge over the River at Mize's Ford that had been washed away in floods 2 October

---

[55] Ibid., p. 90, citing Va. Land Patent Book 14:81.

[56] Ibid., citing Brunswick Co., Va., Deed Book/Will Book 1:142-3.

[57] Ibid., p. 91, citing Lunenburg Co., Va., Deed Book 7:169.

[58] Ibid., p. 91.

[59] Ibid., citing 1) Lunenburg Co., Va., Deed Book 12:464; and 2) Lunenburg Co., Va., Deed Book 14:141.

[60] Ibid., p. 93, citing 1) Va. Land Patent Book 18:367; and 2) Va. Land Patent Book 18:384.

[61] Pawlett, Nathaniel M. and Boyd, Tyler J. Lunenburg County Road Orders 1746-1764, p. 17. Located at http://www.virginiadot.ort/vtre/main/online_reports/pdf/93-r17.pdf. Accessed 10 March 2013. Cited hereafter as Pawlett.

1750.[62] On 3 October 1752, Field Jefferson, Cornelius Cargill, and Richard Witton were ordered to build a bridge over the Meherrin River at Mize's Ford.[63] On 5 June 1753, the Court noted:[64]

It appearing to the Court by many years Experience that Maherrin River at a Place called Mizes foard in this County is a Very inconvenient Place to build a Bridge and that no bridge can be made there to stand, And that it is a very Convenient way for a Road to trade, It is therefore Ordered that the Banks of the said foard be Cut down, And that a Flat be built and kept at the Place to Carry over Tobacco &c And Henry Delony, George Baskervile & Hutchins Burton are appointed to let the same to Undertakers, to be Warrented Seven Years.

Apparently flooding continued to be a problem, as Henry Delony, John Speed, and Edmund Taylor were given the task of locating a bridge over the Meherrin near Mize's Ford 2 June 1762.[65] On 3 August 1762 John Wright was appointed surveyor of the Road from Mize's Ford to the Brunswick County line.[66] Lastly, on 13 December 1764:[67]

On the Motion of Wells Thompson for leave to turn the Road below his Plantation, Ordered that David Moss, John Wright and Thomas Wright being first sworn according to Law do view the said Road and the way the said Thompson Purposes to turn the same and report to Court of the Conveniencies and inconveniencies of the intended alteration.[68]

The key point is to note how close this area is to both the Brunswick and Mecklenburg county lines. The Wrights did not have to move far to cross over into another jurisdiction.

---

[62] Pawlett, p. 30.
[63] Pawlett, p. 53.
[64] Pawlett, p. 63.
[65] Pawlett, p. 150.
[66] Pawlett, p. 151.
[67] Pawlett, p. 173.
[68] The bend in the road over Dix Bridge indicated on the modern map probably reflects the difficulty noted in these orders.

The Wright and Mize families intermarried, as demonstrated by the last will and testament of James Mize, written 2 February 1761 and proved 7 April 1761 in Lunenburg Co., Va.[69]

In the Name of God Amen. I James Mize of the Parish of Cumberland in the county of Lunenburg, weak in body but of perfect mind and memory, Thanks be to Almighty God for the same and calling to mind the uncertainty of this Transitory life and that all flesh must yield to death when it Shall Please God to Call, so make this my Last Will and Testament, hereby revoking all other wills and Testaments heretofore made by me.

Imprimis: My soul I return to god that gave it expectation for Pardon and Remission of all my sins through the merits and mediation of Jesus Christ my Savior.

Item. My Body I commit to the Earth from whence it was Taken to be decently buried by my Excr hereinafter mentioned and for my Temporal Estate which it hat Pleased god to bestow on me I dispose of in manner following, viz:

Item. I give unto my loving son Stephen Mize Two Hundred Acres Land on which he now lives.

Item. I give to my loving son William Mize the plantation whereon I now live with my water mill and all other improvements containing 15 acres land more or less.

Item. I give unto my loving grandson Joseph Wright one feather bed and furniture after his mother's death.

Item. I give unto my loving and lawful wife Elizabeth Mize the rest and occupation of the Residue of my Estate During her Natural life and after her death to be Equally Divided amongst James Mize, Stephen Mize, William Mize, John Wright and Thomas Wright and as much as I have estate more than sufficient to pay my debts it may not be appraised or sold.

And I do hereby appoint my son Stephen Mize my Executor of this my last will and Testament in Witness whereof I have hereunto set my hand and affixed my seal

---

[69] Lunenburg Co., Va., Will Book 2:17-19. John Davis was security for Stephen Mize as executor. There is a note in the margin, not dated, that says "adm. granted to Parsons Wright"

the Second day of February One Thousand and Seven Hundred and Sixty One.

James (M) Mize

Signed, Sealed, and Delivered by the said James Mize as his last Will and Testament in the presence of John (⅃) Wright, William Mize, Thomas (+) Wright, and John Hight.

John Wright obtained a patent 10 September 1755 for 400 acres on the head of Rocky Branch near Duke, John Patrick, Dortch, Roberts and his own lines.[70]

On 12 May 1759 John Wright patented 200 acres of land described as being on both sides of little creek above Stony Creek, adjacent Dickerson and Mize.[71] On 10 October 1765 John Wright and Sarah Wright, his wife, sold to David Moss for £15 a tract of 200 acres patented by Wright on 12 May 1759 on both sides of the little creek above Stony Creek, adjacent Dickinson and Mize. This indenture was witnessed by George Carter, Thomas Wright, and Philip Russell.[72]

On 23 August 1760, James Mize sold to John Wright for £8 a tract of 60 acres on the north side of Stony Creek adjacent to Nathaniel Chambliss and Jeremiah Mize in an indenture that was witnessed by Thomas Jarratt and Joseph Wright.[73] He executed a similar deed with Thomas Wright, and both were entered 4 November 1760.[74]

On 8 September 1768 John Wright and Sarah Wright, his wife, sold to Thomas Wright for 5 shillings a tract of land containing 64 acres along Stony Creek, Jeremiah Mize, George Steagall, John Lantrope and Cedar Branch.[75]

On 10 August 1768, Thomas Wright and Hannah Wright, his wife, sold to John Wright for £15 a tract of land containing 50 acres, part of a patent by John Parker on the south side of Stony Creek, up the great meadow branch and down the creek.[76]

---

[70] Va. Land Patent Book 31:564.

[71] Va. Land Patent Book 34:262.

[72] Lunenburg Co., Va., Deed Book 10:234. Evans, pp. 32-33.

[73] Lunenburg Co., Va., Deed Book 6:245. Evans, p. 29.

[74] Lunenburg Co., Va., Deed Book 6:243, 1 September 1760/4 November 1760.

[75] Lunenburg Co., Va., Deed Book 11:193. Evans, pp. 30-31. Evans traces the deeds to establish that Lantorpe bought his land from James Mize. (p.99)

[76] Lunenburg Co., Va., Deed Book 11:192. Evans, pp. 30-31.

116

On 23 April 1779, John Wright, Senior, planter sold to William Keatt for £160 a tract of 50 acres "where sd. Wright lives" adjacent James Sturdivant, on Stony Creek, Thomas Jarratt, Jr., Nicholas Callahan, Edloe, and Wyatt Williams.[77] Sarah, wife of John Wright relinquished her dower rights.

The 1764 tithe list shows John Wright living on 260 acres with two polls, John and his son John Wright.[78] In 1769, John Wright is living on 50 acres of land with two polls, John and William Wright.[79] Thomas Wright is also present, but on a different list.[80]

In the 1772 tithe list names John Wright, John Wright, Jr., Joseph Wright, Thomas Wright (Rite), and William Wright.[81] These names appear on the list of John Ragsdale. In 1773, only one John Wright appears on the list of John Ragsdale.[82] In 1774 there is only one John Wright, Thomas Wright has two tithes, himself and Parsons, and Joseph Wright with one tithe. In 1776, John Wright appears in the household of John Patterson.[83] Joseph, Thomas and John Wright, along with one whose name was illegible are also there.

On 9 February 1790 Thomas Jarratt, Drury Allen, John Wray, John Wright & Nancy Wright sold to Joseph Wright of Lunenburg County for £200 a tract of 100 acres down Stony Creek adjacent to Stephen Mize, Arthur Turner, Parsons Wright, Julius Hight, and Thomas Jarratt.[84] Subsequently, on 17 November 1792 Thomas Jarrott, Joseph Wright, John Wright, Drury Allen, John Wray, and Nancy Wright (legatees of the estate of Thomas Jarrott, dec'd) sold to Luke Taylor for £60 a tract of land containing 117 acres in Lunenburg County on Stony Creek.[85] It is unclear which John Wright is the signer of these deeds.

On 8 November 1786 John Dizmang sold to John Wright "of Brunswick Co." for £40 a tract of 41½ acres obtained by grant to John Dizmang, that was located adjacent Parsons Wright, John

[77] Lunenburg Co., Va., Deed Book 13:218. Evans, pp. 46-47.
[78] Bell, p. 233. List of David Garland.
[79] Bell, p. 276. List of Charles Hamlin.
[80] Bell, p. 273. List of Everard Dowsing.
[81] Bell, pp. 306-307.
[82] Bell., p. 322.
[83] Bell., p. 380.
[84] Lunenburg Co., Va., Deed Book 15:503. Evans, p. 52.
[85] Lunenburg Co., Va., Deed Book 16:346. Evans, p. 55.

Connell, and Thomas Wright.[86] The indenture was signed by John Dizmang and Elizabeth Dizmang's marks, and witnessed by William Fisher, John Mize, Adah Jarrett, Drury Allen, John Mize, and Parsons Wright.

On 16 October 1793 John Wright sold to Emmanuel Callis for £25 a tract of 40½ acres adjacent said Callis, Luke Taylor, and James Callis. The indenture was signed by the mark of John Wright and witnessed by Clement Reed, Thomas Edmunds, John Orgain, William Fisher, and Ben Fisher.[87]

On 30 November 1793 John Wright sold to Julius Hite a tract of 40½ acres described as adjacent Parsons Wright, Thomas Wright, John Mize, and said Hite.[88] This indenture was also signed by John Wright's mark, and was witnessed by James Dizmang, Parsons Wright, David Wright, Joel Moore, and Thomas Wright., the latter signing by mark. (Other deeds make it probable that all of the Wrights singed by mark.)

The deeds seem to show two men named John Wright.[89] The first, who sold land to Emmanuel Callis, is probably the man who, with his sisters and brothers-in-law disposed of property inherited from Thomas Jarrett, Senior. The other, John Wright of Brunswick County, sold his land to Julius Hite, who bought up the land being sold by the other members of this family on Stony Creek. What the deeds do not tell us is the relationship of these two men.

1782 Solomon Wright of Brunswick Co., Va.

Solomon Wright makes his first appearance in the Lunenburg Co., Va., Tithe Lists for 1750 with one tithe.[90] He is also on the lists for 1751 and 1752, but not for 1764.[91] Solomon Wright witnessed the will of Edmund Huling 18 Feb 1772 and proved 24 February 1772 in Brunswick County, Virginia. He signed with a mark.

On 4 August 1750 John Parker of Cumberland Parish, Lunenburg County, Va., sold to Solomon Wright of Brunswick

---

[86] Lunenburg Co., Va., Deed Book 14:427. Evans, p. 49.

[87] Lunenburg Co., Va., Deed Book 16:451. Evans, pp. 71-72.

[88] Lunenburg Co., Va., Deed Book 16:452. Evans, pp. 71-72.

[89] It is possible, of course, that there is only one man, but the different witnesses makes me think there are two.

[90] Bell, p. 144. Much of the data is from Carol York, personal communication 2004.

[91] Bell, p. 171; p. 196; p. 233.

Co., Va., for £20 5sh a tract of 200 acres on the upper side of Stony Creek down the south side of the creek from William Bailey's lower corner.[92] The deed was witnessed by Isaac Johnson and John Howell.

On 13 May 1767 Solomon Wright of Brunswick Co. sold to Thomas Wright of Lunenburg Co. for £11 10s a tract of 100 acres, described as the upper part of 400 acres patented by John Parker, on the south or upper side of the creek, from Thomas Moody's lower corner, adjacent John Edloe.[93] The indenture was signed "R" by Solomon Wright, and witnessed by John Hight (Hite); and Thomas and Joseph Wright, both of whom signed by mark.

On the same day Solomon Wright sold to Thomas Jarrott, Jr., for £11 10s a tract of 100 acres on the south or upper side of Stony Creek, adjacent John Green, Hix, Thomas Wright.[94] This indenture had the same signature and witnesses as the previous deed.

I have found no deeds in Brunswick County involving Solomon Wright.[95]

Solomon Wright served as a private in the Virginia line in the early days of the Revolutionary War, as attested by his son, Bolling Wright, in his pension application. (see below).

Upon the attachment by William Davis against the estate of George Oldham who has privately removed himself…The Sheriff has attached all of his estate in the hands of Silvanus Stokes, Charles Oldham, and Solomon Right and summoned them as garnishees…[Solomon Wright had 19 shillings, one leather apron, and one chisel belonging to George Oldham that were garnisheed.][96]

William Davis was born about 1719 and married about 1738 Mary Marriott, daughter of William and Sarah (Collier) Marriott of Surry Co., Va.[97] They had 15 children, the penultimate

---

[92] Lunenburg Co., Va., Deed Book 6:197. Evans, p. 26.

[93] Lunenburg Co., Va., Deed Book 11:13. Evans, p. 14.

[94] Lunenburg Co., Va., Deed Book 11:15/.Ibid.

[95] I did find an assertion that Solomon Wright purchased land in Brunswick Co. in 1760. (http://genforum.genealogy.com/wright/messages/6124.html.) Deed not located.

[96] Brunswick Co., Va., Court Order Book 10:19, [28 October 1765.]

[97] Evans, June Banks. Anthony Evans of Colonial Southside Virginia. 1983.

being Silvia Davis, who married Sterling Wright 1788 Mecklenburg Co., Va. One of their sons, Isham Davis and his wife Charlotte of Halifax Co., N.C. on November 1, 1791 sold for £200 a 200 acre tract of land to his brother Marriott Davis. The deed was witnessed by Sterling Wright, John Hervey and Thomas Rose.[98] This deed establishes a connection between the Davis and Wright families in both Brunswick Co., Va., and Halifax Co., N. C., so the following contract for apprenticeship involves the widow and son of Solomon Wright of Brunswick Co., Va.

> This indenture made the first day of June one thousand seven hundred and ninety five...that Lucy Wright, of the said county, has put and placed my son Isaac Wright, an orphan of Solomon Wright, deceased, aged seventeen years, an apprentice to Thomas Carroll of the said county to dwell, reside and serve until he the said apprentice shall arrive to the age of twenty one years...to instruct him in the art and calling of a house carpenter.[99]

Lucy Wright appears in the Mecklenburg Co., Va., tax lists for 1782 on Capt. William Starling's list along with Bolling Wright,[100] a known son of Solomon[2] Wright. They are listed together in 1783[101] and 1784.[102]

Bolling Wright is listed in 1786,[103] although Lucy is not, then in 1787, Lucy Wright appears along with James Wright, who made his first appearance on the tax list of 1785.[104]

Genealogical Summary

1. SOLOMON[1] WRIGHT was born before 1729 in Virginia and died about 1782 in Brunswick Co., Virginia. He married LUCY _____

---

[98] Halifax Co., N. C., Deed Book 17:384. See also DB 17:778; DB 17:820; DB 18:842.

[99] Halifax Co., N. C., Deed Book 17:825. (Carol York's transcription. She notes that the deed was recopied later in the nineteenth century and "seventeen" was transcribed "an even ten." However, she found evidence that Isaac was on the tax list for Halifax Co., in 1800, which is consistent with a transcription error, since he would have been about 22 if the indenture said "seventeen."

[100] Mecklenburg Co., Va., Tax List 1782, p.16.

[101] Mecklenburg Co., Va., Tax List 1783, p. 26

[102] Mecklenburg Co., Va., Tax List 1784, p. 17.

[103] Mecklenburg Co., Va., Tax List 1786, p. 38.

[104] Mecklenburg Co., Va., Tax List 1785, p. 36.

about 1758 in Brunswick Co., Va. She died before 1800, probably in Halifax Co., N. C.

Children of SOLOMON WRIGHT and LUCY are:

    i. BOLLING[2] WRIGHT, b. 12 May 1759 Brunswick Co., Va.; d. 12 January 1841 Walton Co., Ga.; m. MILLY SAUNDERS 4 August 1787, (marriage bond 30 July 1787) daughter of JOHN SAUNDERS; b. 18 May 1772 Mecklenburg Co., Va.; d. after 1849 Jackson Co., Ga.

        The 1782 tax list listed Lucy Wright with no polls and Bolling Wright with 1 poll.[105] The 1783 list shows Lucy and Bolling Wright in the same household with one poll.[106]

        The 1784 Tax List is much more complete and shows Lucy Wright, with no polls[107] The 1785 list does not show either Bolling or Lucy Wright, but does show James Wright with one poll.[108] The 1786 list again shows Bolling Wright and adds Sterling Wright, with one poll and essentially no property.[109] Bolling Wright was listed for Brunswick Co., Va., in 1787, with his tax charged to Arthur Winkfield.[110]

        Bolling Wright married Milly Saunders 30 July 1787 in Mecklenburg Co., Va., with John Feagins as bondsman, and consent of her father, John Saunders. Bolling Wright was born before 1762, as he is on the tax list in 1782 in his own right. He would have been at least 25 when he married Milly Saunders.

        Bolling Wright was born 12 May 1759 in Brunswick County, VA, a son of Solomon Wright.[111] He was a Revolutionary War soldier and served four tours of duty with the 2nd Virginia Militia. In a

---

[105] Mecklenburg Co., Va. Tax List, Lower District, 1782, p. 16.

[106] Mecklenburg Co., Va. Tax List, Lower District, 1783, p. 26.

[107] Mecklenburg Co., Va. Tax List, Lower District, 1784, p. 17.

[108] Mecklenburg Co., Va. Tax List, Lower District, 1785, p. 9; p. 36.

[109] Mecklenburg Co., Va. Tax List, Lower District, 1786, p. 38.

[110] Schreiner-Yantis, N. and Love, Florene S. The 1787 Census of Virginia. (Springfield, Va.: Genealogical Books in Print, 1987.) Cited hereafter as Schreiner-Yantis. There are no land transactions for Bolling Wright in the Mecklenburg Co. deed books, and he does not appear on the census or tax lists in Mecklenburg, Lunenburg, or Brunswick counties in Virginia nor Warren or Franklin counties in North Carolina.

[111] Revolutionary War pension application (W5183), abstracted by Carol York.

deposition made in 1834 when he applied for a pension, he stated that he had been a resident of Fairfield County, SC, for some 45 years, having left Virginia five or six years after the peace of 1783. Listed as his neighbors who could testify as to his character and truthfulness were David R. Coleman, Thomas Lyles, Jacob Feaster, Robert Coleman, Andrew Feaster, John Feaster, Samuel Fant and Isaac Means.

"...When called into service he was living in Brunswick County, VA...Solomon Wright, father of Bolling, served as a private on this tour...He was living in Mecklenburg County when this and the following tours were served. He was called this time during the month of December and served under Capt. Oliver. Arthur Fox was first lieutenant...Wright kept no written record of his service at the time, and now (1834) due to his age and consequent loss of memory is unable to state months or years in which the service was rendered. But he can clearly remember the tours and the length of time served in each tour. He served 11 months as a private soldier."

In October 1788[112] their first child, Elizabeth was born. Their next surviving child, William, was born eight years later. Bolling and Millie became the parents of six more children: Jones, Uriah, Mary (Polly), Lucinda, Nancy and David. All of the children were given their mother's maiden name (Sanders.) Erdington's "History of Fairfield" states that of the eight children, William and Uriah were the most notable. William was "a Baptist preacher of the old school." Uriah was a home doctor, and his services were in great demand in three counties. He was called by almost all "Doctor Wright..."

In January 1840 Bolling Wright sold his land (185 acres) to Uriah Wright and 55 acres to Meredith Meador...[and]... moved to Jackson County, Ga...He died Jan. 12, 1841, at Jug Tavern (now Winder), Ga."

---

[112] Quoted by Brooks, Brian. Shedd, Dobbs, Dunn, Belton, Parks, Teague, Barber, Beck. 23 May 2002. Located at http://worldconnect.rootsweb.com, (db bbrooks).

Children of BOLLING WRIGHT and MILLIE SAUNDERS are:[113]

1. ELIZABETH[3] WRIGHT, b. 28 October 1788 Fairfield Co., S.C.
2. WILLIAM SANDERS[3] WRIGHT, b. 15 January 1796 Fairfield Co., S.C.; m. GEMIMA MOBLEY.
3. JONES[3] WRIGHT, b. 21 April 1798 Fairfield Co., S.C.
4. URIAH[3] WRIGHT, b. 31 May 1800 Fairfield Co., S. C.; d. 10 August 1872 Fairfield Co., S.C.; m. PINCKNEY ACKLAND SMITH 12 January 12 1822 Fairfield Co., S.C., daughter of JOHN SMITH; b. 27 February 1805; d. 9 October 1866 Fairfield Co., S.C.
5. LUCINDA[3] LINDSAY WRIGHT, b. 23 October 1801 Fairfield Co., S.C.; m. DAVID C. MOBLEY.
6. MARY[3] WRIGHT, b. 3 August 1802 Fairfield Co., S. C.; m. SION HILL.
7. NANCY[3] SANDERS WRIGHT, b. 2 November 1805 Fairfield Co., S.C.
8. DAVID[3] WRIGHT, b. 14 July 1809 Fairfield Co., S.C.; m. ELIZABETH ANN BEDDINGFIELD 11 February 1841 Walton Co., Ga.

   David Wright is in the 1850 Census for Walton Co., Ga., on p. 6 with[114] David Wright was listed as a ferryman in the 1870 Census for Walton Co., Ga.

ii. JAMES[2] WRIGHT, b. about 1763 Brunswick Co., d. after 1813; m. SARAH EASTER 28 December 1794 Mecklenburg Co., Va.

James Wright appears on the tax lists in Mecklenburg Co., Virginia, in 1785.[115] He appears fairly persistently through 1806. James Wright married

---

[113] Ibid., updated 7 February 2004. Additional data from Gail Llewellyn, personal communication.

[114] 1850 Census Walton Co., Ga., p. 6, with wife Eliza, 35, and children Mary S., 8, Amanda J., 6, Solomon B., 3, and Josiah C., 1. Courtesy of Margaret Alverson who descended from Josiah C. Wright, b. 2 Jan 1850 in Big Creek, Gwinnett Co., Ga., died 15 March 1929 in Woodville, Oklahoma. He married Emma Octavia Strickland 29 December 1872 in Gwinnett Co., Ga. She was born 27 August 1852 and died 8 March 1926.

[115] Mecklenburg Co., Va. Tax List, Lower District, 1787, p. 36. He is not close to Laban and Austin on the lists. He was born in 1764 or earlier.

Sarah Easter on 28 December 1794 in Mecklenburg Co., Va., as noted previously.

James Wright won a judgment for £170 against Peter Jones, Jr., and Martha Alexander, administrators of the estate of Robert Alexander on 17 March 1787.[116] Interest on the debt was computed from 25 December 1784. James Wright was ordered to pay Jesse Wright 350 pounds of tobacco for six days' attendance at court and twice coming and returning 25 miles as a witness for James Wright in the above suit.[117]

Peter Jones in turn sued James Wright "in chancery" and a commission was authorized to take the deposition of Jesse Wright of Warren Co., N. C. on 10 December 1787.[118]

James Wright was ordered to serve on a road crew 10 April 1787 which included John Bevill, John Oliver, Jefre Brown, John Easter, William Rowlett, Lewis Roffe, Hannah Clark, Benjamin Stone, Daniel Hutt, William Hudson, James Chavous, Edward Beville, & John Puryear; James Beville, surveyor.[119]

James Wright and others gave evidence that led to the indictment of James Coleman for hog stealing on 10 February 1789.[120]

On 13 July 1798 James Wright purchased land from John Beville.[121] On 14 January 1800 James Wright sold land to William Rowlett.[122] On 13 October 1806 James Wright sold land to Charles Thompson.[123] On 8 December 1806 James Wright purchased land from

---

[116] Mecklenburg Co., Va., Court Order Book 6:683.

[117] Mecklenburg Co., Va., Court Order Book 6:686.

[118] Mecklenburg Co., Va., Court Order Book 7:135. The action was sent for arbitration by a panel composed of William Stanley, William Johnson, and Roger Gregory. [Court Order Book 7:144, Feb. 11, 1788.] The case was dismissed with James Wright ordered to pay Peter Jones' costs only. [Court Order Book 7:190, May 13, 1788.]

[119] Mecklenburg Co., Va., Court Order Book 7:2.

[120] Mecklenburg Co., Va., Court Order Book 7:335.

[121] Mecklenburg Co., Va., Deed Book 7:433.

[122] Mecklenburg Co., Va., Deed Book 10:237.

[123] Mecklenburg Co., Va., Deed Book 13:99.

John Simmons.[124] On 17 July 1815 James Wright purchased land from William Bennett.[125]

Isham Davis sold 57 acres on the Cumberland River in Wilson Co., Tenn., to James Wright on 9 April 1817.[126] This may be the same man, since the Wright and Davis families had a long association.

iii. STERLING[2] WRIGHT, b. about 1763 Brunswick Co., Va.; d. after 1820; m. (1) SILVIA DAVIS 4 July 1788 Mecklenburg Co., Va., daughter of HENRY DAVIS and MARY MARRIOTT; b. about 1765 Brunswick Co., Va.; d. about 1803; m. (2) SALLY HILL 3 October 1804 Brunswick Co., Va.

Sterling Wright made his first appearance on the tax lists in 1786 with one poll.[127] In 1787, Randolph Davis was charged with the tax due on Sterling Wright.[128] He appears on the Mecklenburg Co. Tax Lists again in 1788[129] and then disappears from these lists, but does appear in Brunswick Co., Va., in 1805. Sterling Wright married Siviah or Silvia Davis 4 Jul 1788 in Mecklenburg Co., Virginia, although the marriage was also recorded in Brunswick Co., Virginia.[130]

He is present in Halifax Co., N. C. on the 1790 census one male over 16, six males under 16, and two females. Since he had been married to Silvia Davis for only two years, these data suggest he has other children in the household, perhaps including his youngest brother Isaac. (see above.) This supposition is supported by the data from subsequent censuses. He is also on the tax rolls of Halifax Co., N.C. in 1800, along with his youngest brother, Isaac, and also in 1801.

Sterling Wright is in Halifax Co., North Carolina, in the 1800 census age 26-45, Silvia, 16-25, with one son

---

[124] Mecklenburg Co., Va., Deed Book 13:137.

[125] Mecklenburg Co., Va., Deed Book 15:493.

[126] Partlow, Thomas E. Wilson County, Tennessee Deed Books C-M (1793-1829). (Easley, S.C.: Southern Historical Press, 1984,) p. 170.

[127] Mecklenburg Co., Va. Tax List, Lower District, 1786, p. 38.

[128] Schreiner-Yantis

[129] Mecklenburg Co., Va. Tax List, Lower District, 1788, p. 31.

[130] Elliott, p. 136; Knorr, Catherine L. Marriage Records and Ministers Returns of Brunswick County, Virginia, 1750-1810. (Pine Bluff, Ark.: NPD, 1953,) p. 109.

and four daughters under ten years old.[131] He was thus born after 1755 and before 1774. From the tax list, he was born before 1765. Assuming he was at least 25 when he married, this would yield a year of birth of 1763, which is consistent with the other estimates. Sterling Wright is in the 1810 Census for Brunswick Co., Va., over age 45, with two sons under five, one son 10-16, and one daughter 10-16, and was still present in St. Andrew's Parish, Brunswick County in 1820.[132]

Sterling Wright appears in the upper district of Brunswick Co., Va., in 1805. In 1811 he bought land from Charles Hill.[133] In 1815 he sold land to Green Hill,[134] and again in 1819.[135] He also sold land to John Judd in 1822,[136] and to James Wright, probably the son of 1810 John Wright, in 1824.[137]

Sterling Wright died in Brunswick Co., Va., before 1830. Sarah Wright, age 30-39, is living in the Meherrin District, with one son 5-9, and one 15-19, one daughter 5-9, and one 10-14.[138] On the same page is Silas M. Wright, 20-30, with his wife, also 20-30, but no children. The Census also shows John Wright, 20-30 with his wife, 15-19, and two sons under five.[139] Also shown are "Letty", presumably Letitia, 40-50, with women 15-19, and 20-30, and two boys, one 5-9, and one 10-14, and Susan, also 40-50, with one daughter 5-9, and Willie, 20-30, with a wife of the same age, and one son and one daughter, both under five. The following page shows what appears to be Silas M. Wright, Jr., under 5, with his mother, 15-19 years old, Laxton, 20-30 with a wife of similar age plus two sons and one daughter, all under five, and William, 20-30, with a wife of similar age and one son under five.[140]

---

[131] 1800 Census Halifax Co., N. C., Halifax, p. 350.
[132] 1820 Census Brunswick Co., Va., p. 29, [14011-20010, plus 2 slaves.]
[133] Brunswick Co., Va., Deed Book 21:242.
[134] Brunswick Co., Va., Deed Book 22:475.
[135] Brunswick Co., Va., Deed Book 24:271.
[136] Brunswick Co., Va., Deed Book 25:294, 25:381.
[137] Brunswick Co., Va., Deed Book 26:310.
[138] 1830 Census Brunswick Co., Va., Meherrin Dist., p. 250.
[139] 1830 Census Brunswick Co., Va., Meherrin Dist., p. 251.
[140] 1830 Census Brunswick Co., Va., Meherrin Dist., p. 252.

Laxton Wright seems to be Lewis L. Wright, who was born in 1800 Brunswick Co., Va., and died there 24 December 1882. His father was listed as "S." Wright and his mother as "D." Wright, and wife was noted as Sally.[141] Silas M. Wright was born 1806 in Brunswick Co., Va., and died 20 December 1881.[142] He certainly appears old enough to be the male shown in Sterling Wright's household in 1820, and would be a son of Sterling and Silvia Davis Wright.

Child of STERLING WRIGHT and SILVIA DAVIS is:

1. LEWIS[3] LAXTON WRIGHT, b. 1800 Brunswick Co., Va.; d. 24 December 1882 Brunswick Co., Va.; m. (1) REBECCA MOORE, b. about 1796 Va.; d. about 1864 Brunswick Co., Va.;[143] m. (2) SALLY ANN BRASWELL 19 October 1864 Brunswick Co., Va.

Children of LEWIS WRIGHT and REBECCA MOORE are:[144]

a. ARAMINTA[4] WRIGHT, b. 1826 Brunswick Co., Va.; d. 24 December 1863 Brunswick Co., Va.; m. SAMUEL WRAY 4 April 1848 Brunswick Co., Va., son of SAMUEL WRAY and TABITHA WRAY; b. 17 February 1819 Brunswick Co., Va.; d. 7 March 1903 Brunswick Co., Va.[145]

b. HENRY G.[4] WRIGHT, b. 1829 Brunswick Co., Va.

c. ROBERT[4] WRIGHT, b. 1831 Brunswick Co., Va.

---

[141] Virginia Deaths and Burial Index, 1853-1917. Online database at Ancestry.com, accessed 1 June 2013.

[142] He and his wife, Candis R. Wray, along with four children are buried in Alstrop's Mill Cemetery, Brodnax, Brunswick Co., Va. Located at http://www.findagrave.com, #95845443. Some online sources say he is a son of Letty.

[143] Phillips Family Tree. http://trees.ancestry.com/tree/25422354/person/1651489073. Rebecca is shown in the 1850 Census. This file also provided the marriage information for Sally.

[144] 1850 Census Brunswick Co., Va., Southern Dist., p. 321B, #95/95.

[145] Wray Family Bible Record, 1819-1968, http://image.lva.virginia.gov /Bible/31572/index.html Bible Record Image. Accessed 1 June 2013.

d. JAMES H.[4] WRIGHT, b. 1833 Brunswick Co., Va.

e. JOHN L.[4] WRIGHT, b. 1834 Brunswick Co., Va.

f. ELIZABETH[4] WRIGHT, b. 1836 Brunswick Co., Va.

g. CELIA A.[4] WRIGHT, b. 1838 Brunwick Co., Va.

h. CATHERINE[4] WRIGHT, b. 1840 Brunswick Co., Va.

iv. CLAIBORNE[2] WRIGHT, b. about 1768 Brunswick Co., Va.; d. before 13 October 1836 Camden Co., Ga. ; m. PATSY NANNEY 29 December 1792 Mecklenburg Co., Va.

Claiborne Wright made his first appearance on the Mecklenburg Co., Va. Tax lists in 1787, with no polls and one male under 21.[146] He does not appear again until 1791, when he is taxed for one poll.[147] This yields an estimated year of birth as 1768.

Claiborne Wright married Patsy Nanney on 29 December 1792 in Mecklenburg County, Virginia, with Hughberry Nanney as bondsman.[148]

Claiborne Wright is on the tax lists for the rest of the decade.[149] In 1800 he was taxed for one poll, one horse, and an ordinary license.[150] He appears again in 1801, and then disappears from the Mecklenburg Co., Va., tax lists.[151]

Claiborne Wright probably removed to Camden Co., Georgia as evidenced by a bond made 26 November 1836 involving Margaret Wright, widow of Claiborne Wright, and his children, Susannah Wright Morrison, Abner Wright, Thomas Wright, Margaret Wright Mott, Nancy Wright, and Allen Hinton to pay

---

[146] Mecklenburg Co., Va. Tax List, Lower District, 1787, p. 38.

[147] Mecklenburg Co., Va. Tax List, Lower District, 1791, p. 14.

[148] Elliott, p. 135. The ceremony was conducted by John Loyd. The Nanney family appears on deeds involving 1778 Laban Wright.

[149] Mecklenburg Co., Va. Tax List, Lower District, 1792, p. 31; 1793, p. 35; 1794, p. 29; 1795, p. 35; 1796, p. 31; 1797, p. 41; 1798, p. 50; 1799, p. 67.

[150] Mecklenburg Co., Va. Tax List, Lower District, 1800, p. 26.

[151] Mecklenburg Co., Va. Tax List, Lower District, 1801, p. 42. There is no record of Claiborne Wright in the land deeds of Mecklenburg Co., Va.

the debts of the estate of Claiborne Wright in exchange for distribution of his personal property to them.[152] Margaret Wright and Thomas Wright signed an administrators' bond at Jefferson, Camden Co., Ga., 13 October 1836.

The land grants of Camden Co., Ga., show Claiborne Wright was granted 250 acres in 1818 [Grant Book L-5, p. 867]; 100 acres in 1822 [Grant Book Q-5, p. 574]; 100 acres in 1829 [Grant Book R-5, p. 71]; and 150 acres in 1833 [Grant Book R-5, p. 21].

These grants establish Claiborne Wright in Camden Co., Ga., after 1818, but do not show where he went in 1802. Of course, the deeds do not show that Claiborne Wright of Camden Co., Ga., is the same as Claiborne Wright of Mecklenburg Co., Va. It seems likely Thomas, Margaret, and Sarah Ann had Margaret for their mother, while the others could be from the first marriage.

Children of CLAIBORNE WRIGHT are:[153]

1. THOMAS TESTONE[3] WRIGHT, b. about 1815 in Jacksonville, Duval Co., Fla.; d. 30 August 1861 Clay Co., Fla.; m. MARY EUBANK 12 November 1837 Duval Co., Fla., daughter of WILLIAM EUBANK and SARAH ELIZABETH BROWARD; b. 29 February 1816 Jacksonville, Duval Co., Fla.; d. 16 December 1900 Duval Station, Duval Co., Fla.

2. SUSANNAH[3] WRIGHT, m. GEORGE MORRISON 4 September 1823.

3. ALAFRED AGNES[3] WRIGHT, m. PETER REDDICK 4 January 1827.

4. ABNER HARRELL[3] WRIGHT, m. ELIZABETH ANN PAXTON 29 December 1836 Camden Co., Ga.

---

[152] Cited in Jackson, Jan. Walker, Haddock, Vanzant, Eubank, Broward, Swearingen, Minor, Johnson, Roddenbury, & Gay. 25 Aug 2002. http://worldconnect.rootsweb.com, (db janjaxw).

[153] Jackson, Jan. North FL/South GA Families. 9 March 2004. http://worldconnect.rootsweb.com. (db janjax).

She was b. about 1818 in Camden Co., Ga., d. 25 May 1848 Camden Co., Ga.

5. MARGARET E.[3] WRIGHT, b. 1817 Camden Co., Ga.; m. RICHARD S. MOTT 10 March 1836 Camden Co., Ga.

6. NANCY[3] WRIGHT, d. 1841; m. OWEN KING MIZELL, son of PERRY STALLINGS MIZELL and CHARLOTTE ALBRITTON.

7. SARAH ANN[3] WRIGHT, b. 1816 Camden Co., Ga.; m. ALLEN HINTON.

v. ANDERSON[2] WRIGHT, b. about 1770 Brunswick Co., Va., d. 28 August 1830 Warren Co., N. C.; m. (1) PHOEBE MALONE WATSON 30 May 1793 Mecklenburg Co., Va., daughter of BURWELL WATSON and MARTHA; she d. 1794 Mecklenburg Co., Va.; m. (2) ELIZABETH LANGFORD 7 December 1794 Mecklenburg Co., Va.; b. born about 1770 and d. before 1840 Warren Co. N. C.

Data on this man were provided by Carol York.[154] Anderson Wright makes his first appearance on the tax lists of Mecklenburg Co. in 1792.[155] Anderson Wright has one poll in 1792, and has a poll under 21 noted on the list of 1794,[156] but not thereafter until he disappears in 1798.[157]

Anderson Wright married Phebe Malone Watson 30 May 1793 in Mecklenburg Co., Va., with William Poole, Jr., as bondsman.[158] The ceremony was conducted by John Loyd.

---

[154] Carol York, personal communication, 26 Jan 2004. "Exact dates for marriages and marriage bonds, unless specifically cited, refer to the official marriage records of the relevant county. Several Bible records have been used; copies were obtained from the Warren County Courthouse for the Hundley Bibles. The Wright-Bell Bible references are from a transcript made by me from a Bible in the possession of Grace Bell Butler of Portsmouth, VA, in 1970; she has since died, and I do not know the present owner of the Bible. In 1966, Wright research was done by Kate Creech for Richard Allen Wright; this research was abstracted and sent to me by Linda Crader. I have used Kate Creech's materials for the descendants of John H. Wright; for the most part I have not been able to see the Bible records or tombstones mentioned myself. Estimated dates of birth are based on the censuses, as are the listings of children unless otherwise noted."

[155] Mecklenburg Co., Va. Tax List, Lower District, 1792, p. 29; p. 30.

[156] The poll under 21 in the 1794 is clearly not a son, but could be a brother or brother-in-law.

[157] Mecklenburg Co., Va. Tax List, Lower District, 1794, p. 29; 1795, p. 36; 1797, p. 40.

[158] Elliott, p. 135.

Anderson Wright applied for letters of administration for Phoebe Wright on September 8, 1794, Mecklenburg Co., Va., with Samuel Holmes, Jr., as his security.[159] Her parentage is established by the following suit in chancery filed in Mecklenburg Co., Va., on 10 November 1794.

"Thomas Watson, James Watson, also Susannah Watson, Charlotte Watson Rebecca Watson, which said Susannah, Charlotte and Rebecca are infants and orphans of Burwell Watson dec'd by William Starling their Guardian, also Anderson Wright Admr. of Phebe Wright dec'd who was one of the children of the said Burwell Watson dec'd.

Against Martha Watson Admrx. of Burwell Watson dec'd.

Comrs. Lewis Parham, Anthony Bennett, Samuel Holmes Jr., William Poole to set off widow's dower and hire out negro Charles, etc."[160]

Anderson Wright married Elizabeth Langford 11 December 1794 in Mecklenburg Co., Va., with James Watson as bondsman.[161] The ceremony was conducted by John Loyd. James Watson is probably a brother or other close relative of Phebe Watson, and John Loyd performed both ceremonies.

Anderson Wright is listed on the tax rolls of Hawtree District, Warren Co., N. C., in 1798 and 1799.[162] Anderson Wright is in the 1800 census for Warren County, North Carolina, aged 26-45, with one son under five, and four daughters, two under five and two 5-10 years old. He is still there in the 1820 census, age greater than 45, with one son 5-10, one son 16-26, and two daughters 5-10 years of age. The tax lists of Mecklenburg County suggest he was born before 1771. The 1800 census shows he was born after 1755 and

---

[159] Mecklenburg Co., Va., Court Order Book 8:344.
[160] Mecklenburg Co., Va., Court Order Book 8:363. [10 Nov. 1794.]
[161] Elliott, p. 135.
[162] Warren Co., N. C., Tax List 1798, p. 354 (spelled Rat); 1799, p. 383.

before 1774. The 1820 Census shows he was born before 1775. It seems likely, then that he was born around 1770.

On 27 February 1797 John Langford of Warren Co., NC, sold to Anderson Wright of Mecklenburg Co., VA, for £48 an 80 acre tract of land located I Warren Co., N. C. "bounded by a corner hickory on Jesse Bell's line, Worrell's line, Paine's line, Norsworthy's line." The indenture was witnessed by M.T. Egarton and Drury Thompson.[163] Presumably John Langford was a relative of his second wife.

On 12 June 1802 Anderson Wright sold to Joseph Shearin for £74 an 80 acre tract of land "on Hawtree Creek, Wm. Worrel's line, Pickerell's Spring Branch, Jesse Bell's line, James Pain's line. This indenture was witnessed by Robt. H. Jones, Charles Wortham.[164] The same day William Wortham sold to Anderson Wright for £93 a 150 acre tract of land bounded by "William Duke's line, Robert Caller's line, Robert Wortham's line." Witnesses to this indenture were Robert H. Jones and Charles Wortham.[165]

The will of Green Duke written 14 February 1811 in Warren Co., N. C., mentions lands "adj. to Charles Marshall, Anderson Wright, Edward Wortham, Mrs. Tanner, Mrs. Colleer, William Hogwood, Mrs. Marshall, William Watson, Col. Benja. Hawkins, on ES new road through the purchase patent, across Fishing Cr. bridge, across top of the mountain and the Ridge path and through the ninety six old field."[166]

Anderson Wright appears on several tax lists from 1811-1815 on this 150 acre tract with one poll.[167]

---

[163] Warren Co., N. C. Deed Book 14:464.

[164] Warren Co., N. C., Deed Book 18:37. "It appears that this deed was registered the 18th of January 1803 in a book said to be destroyed by fire the same is again registered the 17th day of August 1807."

[165] Warren Co., N. C., Deed Book 18:190. Registered 19 Jan. 1803, re-registered 21 April 1808..

[166] Warren Co., N. C., Will Book 16:31.[May Ct. 1811] Cited in Kerr, Mary Hinton. Warren Co., NC, Records, Vol. III, Abstracts of Will Books, 1779-1814. (1969,) p. 194.

[167] Warren Co., N. C., Tax List 1811 Capt. Green's district [Warren WB 16, p. 135]; 1812 Warrenton District, [Warren WB 17, p. 126]; 1813 Smith's Creek District [Warren

On 27 January 1819 Lewis Y. Christmas sold to Anderson Wright for $2079 a 294 acre tract "on both sides of the road leading from Warrenton by Marshall's tavern, Yellowwood Branch, Powers corner, Green's road, Warrenton Road, Meeting House Road, Twitty now Jones' corner, Falkener line, Christmas, "reserving the acre around the Meeting House and the Meeting House spring to the Baptist Society..." Witnesses were Peter A. Davis and Stephen Davis.[168]

One possible clue to the ancestry of Anderson Wright is that on 27 February 1801 James (Jones?) Wright, age 16, was apprenticed to Anderson Wright.[169] Wit. Robert R. Johnson. James could be either a younger brother or a nephew, since Anderson was about 33 years old at this time.

Anderson Wright was active in the Baptist Church of Christ at Tanner's meeting house.[170] His death on 28 August 1830 was recorded in a family Bible.[171]

On 11 October 1830 Drury Harris and Lucy, his wife, sold to Drury S. Wright for $50 the undivided portion or share of the real estate which may descend to the above named Lucy Harris as one of the heirs at law of the late Anderson Wright. This deed was witnessed by John H. Wright.[172] On 22 November 1830 Elizabeth Wright, widow of Anderson Wright, relinquished her right of administration on his estate "to my son Jno. Wright." The same day Administration Bond of $4000

WB 17, p. 312]; 1814 Smith's Creek District [Warren WB 18, p. 213]. In the 1815 list this land was valued at $525.

[168] Warren Co., N. C., Deed Book 21:175.

[169] Warren Co., N. C., Will Book 11:60.

[170] 25 Jan. 1828. Proceedings of the Baptist Church of Christ at Tanner's Meeting House: Met at Bro. Wright's; 12 July 1828. (Ditto). Brother A. Wright, Senr., prayed; 13 Sept.1828. (Ditto) Delegates to the Association included M. Collins, John Daniel, and A. Wright, Sr. 20 April 1829. (Tanner's minutes). Meeting adjourned by a prayer by Brother A. Wright, Sr. (a number of these follow) 9 Jan. 1830. A. Wright Senr. and John White were appointed a committee to wait upon Mrs. White for the purpose of getting information on a charge preferred against a negro woman belonging to her. Febry. 1830. "...the woman was guilty of abusive language to her mistress and harboring a runaway...Jenny belonging to Mrs. White was excommunicated from this church."13 March 1830. Mrs. Elizabeth Lewis received as a candidate for baptism. [These Church minutes are on LDS Film #986,272, Item 4]

[171] Hundley Bible; copy on file at the Warren Co., NC, Courthouse

[172] Warren Co., N. C., Deed Book 26:82.

for John H. Wright on the estate of Anderson Wright was made with Thomas Wright, Drury S. Wright, Anderson Wright, and John W. White as his securities.[173]

The family clearly made an effort to keep Anderson Wright's real estate holding together as witnessed by the following indentures.

On 20 September 1832 Thomas Wright of Nash Co., N. C. sold to John W. White for $84 all his right in tract of land on which the late Anderson Wright lived, containing 296 acres. This was witnessed by Thos. Bragg, Jr. and Wm. H. Hundley.[174]

On 16 October 1832 John H. Wright sold to John W. White for $25 all his right to a tract on which the late Anderson Wright lived and died, containing 296 acres. This was witnessed by Lewis Turner and George Newman.[175]

On 17 April 1833 William A. Hundley and Elizabeth his wife sold to Drury S. Wright for $20 "all our right in the real estate of Anderson Wright dec'd, being about 50 acres." This deed was witnessed by Jno. W. White.[176]

Children of ANDERSON WRIGHT and ELIZABETH LANGFORD are:

    1.   JOHN H.[3] WRIGHT, b. about 1795; died 1878 Granville Co., N. C.; m. SOPHIA L.

        John H. Wright was witness to the deed in which his sister Lucy relinquished her right to the land of their father to Drury S. Wright.[177] He also served as administrator of his father's estate, but sold his interest in 1832 to his brother in law, John White. He appears to leave the Warren Co., N. C. records after this time.

        Children of JOHN H. WRIGHT and SOPHIA L. are:

---

[173] Loose estate papers of Anderson Wright from NC Archives. All of the sons signed their name to the bond.

[174] Warren Co., N. C., Deed Book 26:297.

[175] Warren Co., N. C., Deed Book 26:280.

[176] Warren Co., N. C., Deed Book 26:353.

[177] Warren Co., N. C., Deed Book 26:82.

a. JOHN LUNDY[4] WRIGHT, b. 7 June 1833 Granville Co., N. C.; m. MILDRED N. FULLER 20 January 1868 daughter of ISAIAH FULLER and MARY H. CLARK; b. 7 Aug. 1843.[178]

b. GEORGE WASHINGTON WRIGHT, b. 8 June 1837, m. FRANCES COLLINS 7 Nov. 1865; d. 8 Mar. 1930, bur. Poplar Creek Church Cemetery, Granville Co.

c. MARY E. WRIGHT, m. ALBERT ELLINGTON 1851.

d. SOPHIA C. KELLY WRIGHT, m. RICHARD B. CALLIS 18 Dec. 1865.

e. HARRIET E. WRIGHT, m. ALBERT BULLOCH.

f. DRUCILLA H. WRIGHT.

g. ANDREW JACKSON WRIGHT, m. SALLIE BRAME.[179]

h. WILLIAM H. WRIGHT, d. 1874. Had at least two children.

2. THOMAS[3] WRIGHT, b. 1795-1800; m. FRANCES M. WHEELESS 14 April 1829 Halifax Co., N. C.

On 1 March 1820 a Bastardy Bond was posted by Thomas Wright for the child of Polly Evans with Anderson Wright and William Andrews his securities.[180] Thomas Wright was "of Nash Co., N. C." 20 September 1832 when he sold his interest in his father's estate to his brother-in-law John White.[181]

Tuesday the 14 April 1829. "Miss Frances M. Wheless of Halifax County N. Carolina was

---

[178] Children: Lundy Ruffin Wright, Sr. b. 26 Feb. 1870; d. 1944, Reading, PA; m. Agnes Dozier Morse, b. 9 Nov. 1877 in Norfolk, VA, d. Jan. 1933, Kingston, PA. (Their children: Lundy Ruffin Wright, Jr., b. 30 Aug. 1902, Newport News, VA, m. 18 April 1924 to Loretta Rachel Williams, b. 5 Dec. 1901, d. 18 April 192? &Richard Allen Wright, b. 19 July 1932, m. 17 Dec. 1955 to Maureen Rose Kielty.); Benjamin Fuller Wright, b. 26 July 1871; Robert H. Wright (Robin), b. 26 June 1873; Mary A. Wright, b. 5 Oct. 1888.

[179] Children: HeHil Dakota Wright, b. 8 June 1875, d. 5 Sept. 1895; Harry Wright, b. 1878; m. Martha Parham, living 11 Jan. 1966; Lena Wright, b. 1876; m. Mr. Wilborne, living 1966 in Middlesex, NC, (Nash Co.) and had Wright family Bible; Mary Wright, m. Mr. Dunn, living with Lena in 1966; Jake Wright, living in 1966 in Middlesex.

[180] Warren Co., N. C., Will Book 22:259.

[181] Warren Co., N. C., Deed Book 26:280

135

married to Mr. Thomas Wright of Warren County N. Carolina." [182]

He may be the same Thomas L. Wright who married Martha A. Power(s), Warren Co. marriage bond dated 24 Dec. 1832 with Bennett H. Stammire as bondsman.

3. DRURY STITH[3] WRIGHT, b. 1801; d. 28 May 1850 Warren Co., N. C.;[183] m. SARAH ANN SHEARIN 26 September 1831 daughter of DANIEL SHEARIN and ELIZABETH RODWELL; b. 31 January 1814 Warren Co., N. C.;[184] d. 6 June 1868 Warren Co., N. C.[185]

On 27 November 1834 William Evans, Orphan and a "free boy of color now 15" was bound to "Drewry" S. Wright to learn agriculture.[186]

In March 1834, "Rec'd as a candidate for baptism Drury S. Wright and his wife Sarah Wright." He must have been a satisfactory candidate as he was selected as deacon in May 1835. [187]

On 2 February 1835 Jno. W. White and William A. Hundley sold to Drury S. Wright for $75 each, "our right in the negroes Lucy and her child Maria, now in the possession of Elizabeth Wright," witnessed by John Wortham.[188] Within the week Anderson Wright sold to Drury S. Wright for $139 his right "in the negroes Lucy and her child Maria, now in the possession of his mother Elizabeth Wright" and for $64, part of the above sum, his right in the parcel of land on which the late Anderson Wright lived and died, adjoining the lands of Peter R. Davis, Thos. E.

Date given in Hundley Bible; copy on file at the Warren Co., NC, Courthouse.

[183] Bible Record of Drury Stith Wright.

[184] Bible Record of Daniel Shearin

[185] Bible Record of Drury Stith Wright.

[186] Warren Co., N. C., Will Book 35:33.

[187] Proceedings of the Baptist Church of Christ at Tanner's Meeting House. [These Church minutes are on LDS Film #986,272, Item 4] Cited hereafter as Proceedings.

[188] Warren Co., N. C., Deed Book 26:467.

Green and others, containing about 296 acres. This deed was witnessed by John W. White. [189]

Drury S. Wright was apparently still adjusting his boundary lines when he recorded on 23 July 1835 a sale to John W. White for $64 of a 26 acre tract "bounded by the dower line in the meeting house path leading from Green's mill, old purchase pattern road, adj. Peter R. Davis." [190]

Children of DRURY WRIGHT and SARAH SHEARIN:

a. VIRGINIA ANN WRIGHT, b. 20 May 1832, Warren Co., N. C.; d. 8 Nov. 1873 Warren Co., N. C.; m. DANIEL RIGGAN 15 Nov. 1854 Warren Co., N. C.

b. JAMES A. WRIGHT, b. 31 May 1833; d. before 1840.

c. WORTHAM P. WRIGHT, b. 5 Dec. 1835, d. before 1840.

d. HARRIET M. WRIGHT, b. 10 Aug. 1838, m. WILLIAM H. EDMONDS 28 July 1859 Warren Co., N. C.

e. WILLIAM D. WRIGHT, b. 15 Oct. 1840.

f. DRURY STITH WRIGHT, JR., b. 2 April 1842[191]

g. LUCY BROWN WRIGHT, b. 9 Sept. 1845 Warren Co., N. C.;, d. 4 April 1916 Warrenton, Warren Co., N. C.; m. WILLIAM S. BELL 29 Sept. 1865 Warren Co., N.C.; b. 30 November 1836 Mecklenburg Co., Va.; d. 26 October 1888, Warren Co., N. C. [192]

---

[189] Warren Co., N. C., Deed Book 26:464. [6 Feb. 1835.]

[190] Wit: Anderson Wright. Ms. York did not record the deed book citation.

[191] There was a Drury S. Wright who enlisted, 5 July 1861 in Halifax County N. C., Co. A, 14th Infantry Regiment.

[192] Children of Lucy Wright and William Bell are: Robert E.L. Bell, b. 3 Aug. 1866, d. Oct. 1931; m. 1 Nov. 1888 to Minnie Mae ___; Stith Wright Bell, b. 15 March 1869, d. 30 April 1959; Sallie Elizabeth Bell, b. 3 June 1872, d. 16 May 1916, in Portsmouth, VA; m. 27 Dec. 1892 Donald Franklin Morris; Willie Henry Bell, b. 10 May 1875, d. 28 Dec. 1935; Charlotte Ann Bell, b. 16 Nov. 1878, d. 14 Jan. 1953; John Shearin Bell, b. 22 July 1881, d. (various dates) m. 6 Dec. 1917 to Johnnie Helen Matthews; Lucy Ann Alfrida Bell, b. 8 March 1885, d. 9 Aug. 1865; m. 15 Feb. 1906 to Samuel Hawkins Weldon; William O.

He was a corporal, CSA, Inf. Co. B, 30th Regiment NC Troops. He had married (1) Martha J. Felts, 24 Dec. 1857. Information on this family is from the Wright-Bell Bible.

    h. WILLABY H. WRIGHT, b. 6 April 1848, d. before 1850.

    i. A. WRIGHT, b. 12 April 1850.

4. LUCY B. WRIGHT, b. 1800-1810, m DRURY HARRIS 9 June 1823.

5. ELIZABETH A. WRIGHT, b. 15 April 1804 Warren Co., N. C.[193]; d. 27 Feb 1837; m (1) 14 June 1821 FREEMAN LEWIS; d. before 29 August 1826 Warren Co., N. C.; m (2) WILLIAM A. HUNDLEY 26 July 1831 Warren Co., N. C.

Anderson Wright applied for letters of administration on the estate of Freeman Lewis, deceased, with Robert A. Jones and Abner Steed for $1000 on August 29, 1826.[194] On September 8, 1826, Elizabeth A. Lewis, widow of Freeman Lewis, dec'd; received one year's support for herself and her two children, James, four years old, and George, two years old.[195]

Mrs. Elizabeth Lewis was received as a candidate for baptism 13 March 1830.[196]

Children of ELIZABETH WRIGHT and FREEMAN LEWIS:

    a. JAMES J. LEWIS, b. 13 Aug. 1822

    b. GEORGE F. LEWIS, b. 9 July 1824

Children of ELIZABETH WRIGHT and WILLIAM HUNDLEY:

    c. JOHN A. HUNDLEY, b. 30 Apr. 1832

    d. NANCY ANN A.L. HUNDLEY, b. 16 Oct. 1834

Bell, b. 2 Sept. 1889, d. an infant. Children of William S. Bell and Martha J. Felts are: Harriet Cora Bell, b. 29 Sept. 1858; m. Mr. Dowling; Walter Thomas Bell, b. 15 Feb. 1860.

[193] Date given in Hundley Bible; copy on file at the Warren Co., NC, Courthouse.

[194] Warren Co., N. C. Will Book 30:8.

[195] Warren Co., N. C., Will Book 30:90. Anderson Wright was appointed guardian for James and George Lewis at the November Court 1828. Drury S. Wright was appointed guardian for James and George Lewis at the November Court 1830.

[196] Proceedings.

6. MINERVA H. WRIGHT, b. 17 June 1806 Warren Co., N. C; d. 26 June 1878 Warren Co., N. C.; m. JOHN W. WHITE 12 July 1828 Warren Co., N. C.; b. 31 May 1804 Warren Co., N. C.; d. 16 May 1862 Warren Co., N. C.

Children of MINERVA WRIGHT and JOHN WHITE are:

    a. MARY E. WHITE, b. 1831 Warren Co., N. C.
    b. MARTHA A. WHITE, b. 1834 Warren Co., N. C.
    c. WILLIAM A. WHITE, b. 1835 Warren Co., N. C.

7. ANDERSON WRIGHT, b. about 1808; m. 6 June 1831 ELIZABETH SHEARIN daughter of DANIEL SHEARIN and ELIZABETH RODWELL.

A committee was appointed to enquire into a report that is in circulation against Bro. Anderson Wright and make report to our next conference.[197] "A letter from the arm of the church at Gardner's requesting aid to settle a difficulty betwixt Sister Nichols and Brother A. Wright Junr. was rec'd. and a committee of brethren consisting of Mr. Collins, Guilford Tally and Henry Foot were appointed."[198] A charge of adultery brought against Anderson Wright by Philemon Jenkins. He did not deny the charge and did not attend his trial.[199]

Anderson Wright sold his interest in his father's slaves held by his mother to his brother.[200]

On 14 Oct. 1850 Anderson Wright and Elizabeth his wife sold to John R. Shearin for $600 a tract of 163¼ acres adjoining the land of Charles Myrick, the said John R., and others, being the land willed to the said Elizabeth by her father the late Daniel Shearin, bounded also by

---

[197] 7 July 1832. Proceedings.
[198] 6 Feb. 1835. Proceedings.
[199] August 1840. Proceedings.
[200] Warren Co., N. C., Deed Book 26:464.

Daniel and John Hardy's corner, Jesse Myrick's corner.[201]

On 16 Aug. 1866 a mortgage from Anderson M. Wright of Halifax Co., NC, to John R. Shearin of Warren was made to secure a debt of $1500, on tract of 545 acres, "bounded on the west by the lands of William Stokes and L.B. Shearin, on the south by those of John Williams and John Hardy, East by those of D.W. Bullock and John Adams, and North by those of Jones Lee and J.W. Shearin. Wit: Lafayette B. Myrick."[202]

Children of ANDERSON WRIGHT and ELIZABETH SHEARIN are:

   a. THOMAS D. WRIGHT, b. 1834
   b. NATHANIEL M. WRIGHT, b. 1837
   c. MARY A. WRIGHT, b. 1839 (not in 1860 census)
   d. SARAH E. WRIGHT, b. 1843; m. JOHN E. LAUGHTER 21 Jan. 1867.
   e. JOHN A. WRIGHT, b. 1846
   f. MARTHA E. WRIGHT, b. 1849, m. JOHN H. SHERMAN 22 Jan. 1866.

vi. ISAAC[2] WRIGHT, b. 1776 Brunswick Co., Va.; d. December 1849 Wilson Co., Tenn.; m. ELIZABETH HULM before 1803 Halifax Co., N. C., daughter of JOHN HULM and ANN.

Isaac Wright was 17 when his apprenticeship was signed in 1795 (see above) and he appears on the 1800 tax list for Halifax Co., N. C. in his own right, establishing that he was at least 21 years old.[203]

John Hulm of Halifax Co., N. C. wrote his will 8 April 1789 and it was proved at the May Court 1789. He left his estate to his wife, Ann Hulm, and mentions his daughter, Sarah Wood, and his minor children,

---

[201] Warren Co., N. C., Deed Book 31:17.
[202] Halifax Co., N. C., Deed Book 35:346; corrected Deed Book 37:71.
[203] He and Sterling Wright were in District 12 in both 1800 and 1802.

Thomas John Hulm, Robert Hulm, and Elizabeth Hulm.[204]

Ann Hulm of Halifax Co., N. C. wrote her will 19 January 1803 and it was proved at the February Court 1805. She left legacies to her daughter, Sarah Wood, and sons John and Hamblen Hulm, son Robert Hulm, and her land to her daughter Elizabeth Wright. She named as her executor her son-in-law Isaac Wright.[205]

On 16 November 1805 Isaac (x) Wright and his wife, Elizabeth (x) Wright, sold to Thomas Harvey, Sr., for $300 a 150 acre tract of land bounded by James Wright, Henry Bulley, Thomas Harvey, Sr., and Joshua Brinkley.[206]

On 25 June 1806 Isham Davis of Wilson Co., Tenn., sold to Dancy Flewellen of Halifax Co., N. C., for $10 and 10 acre tract of land on Fishing Creek adjoining Harvey, his own line and Matthews. This deed was witnessed by Marriott Davis and Robert Davis.[207]

Given the close connection between the Davis and Wright families, it seemed logical to examine the records of Wilson Co., Tenn. Isaac Wright is listed on the 1850 Mortality Schedule for Wilson Co., Tenn., as having died in November 1849 at the age of 73.[208] He was shown as being born in North Carolina. This raises the possibility that Solomon Wright was also moving back and forth between Brunswick Co., Va., and Halifax Co., N. C. The records of Halifax Co. will need to be searched looking for evidence of this possibility.

At the December 1849 term of court for Wilson Co., Tenn., commissioners were appointed to set aside a year's allotment for Elizabeth Wright, widow of Isaac Wright, dec'd.[209] The estate sale account was rendered

---

[204] Halifax Co., N. C., Will Book 3:164.

[205] Halifax Co., N. C., Will Book 3:438.

[206] Halifax Co., N. C., Deed Book 20:370. Thomas Harvey, Sr., died in Halifax Co., N. C., in February 1806, and he mentions in his will the land that he bought of Isaac Wright. [Halifax Co., N. C., Will Book 3:448.]

[207] Halifax Co., N. C., Deed Book 20:511.

[208] The 1850 Mortality Schedule for Wilson Co., Tenn.

[209] Wilson Co., Tenn., Wills and Inventories (1848-1853):194.

by Isaac B. Wright, administrator, and showed purchases by Jno. W. Wright, widow Roach, J. B. Oldham, Jas. G. Wright, and Solomon Bass.

Deeds of interest include the purchase by Isaac Wright of 60 acres on Spencer's Creek from James Campbell of Kentucky 20 September 1817.[210] On 6 March 1823 Isaac Wright purchased another 78 acres on Spencer's Creek from Lucy Downy.[211]

Isham Davis sold 57 acres on the Cumberland River to James Wright on 9 April 1817.[212] Marriott Davis sold to his daughter Martha H. Parrish a 90 acre tract of land on 23 June 1823,[213] and sold to James Johnson a tract on Spencer's Creek on 21 May 1825.[214] These deeds seem to establish that Isaac Wright and Isham Davis were in the same part of Wilson Co., and further supports the notion that Isaac Wright is also from Halifax Co., N. C. Isham Davis died before 31 October 1835, when Henry Davis and other petitioned to sell his property.[215]

Elizabeth Wright, age 65 and born in North Carolina is living with Brown Wright in the 4th Civil District of Wilson Co., Tenn., in the 1850 census.[216] Also in the household were Emily Roach and her six sons.

Children of ISAAC WRIGHT and ELIZABETH HULM are:

1. JOHN RUFFIN[3] WRIGHT, b. 25 January 1808, Halifax Co., N. C.; d., 25 October 1837 Chariton Co., Mo.; m. SARAH (EAGAN) MAYO 4 October 1829 Wilson Co., Tenn., daughter of WILLIAM

---

[210] Partlow, Thomas E. Wilson County, Tennessee Deed Books C-M (1793-1829). (Easley, S.C.: Southern Historical Press, 1984,) p. 104. Cited hereafter as Partlow.

[211] Partlow, p. 170.

[212] Partlow, p. 170. It is not certain, but I believe this is probably James Wright of Mecklenburg Co., Va., as he is not present in Mecklenburg Co., Va., on the 1820 Census.

[213] Partlow, p. 174.

[214] Partlow, p. 191.

[215] Partlow, p. 256. There is also a reference in the Wilson Co., Tenn., Circuit Court Records in which John D. Hallum, orphan of John Hallum, petitioned to have Isham Davis removed as his guardian as he was "now near eighty" and too old to perform the duties. [Partlow, p. 23.]

[216] 1850 Census Wilson Co., Tenn., p. 347, family 482.

EAGAN and MARGARET MOTHERAL; b. 15 October 1806 Wilson Co., Tenn.

John R. Wright and his wife Sarah were mentioned as guardians for Mary and William Mayo, only children of William Mayo who died in 1826, leaving as his widow Sarah, now Sarah Wright. The marriage records show Sally Eagan and William J. Mayo obtained a marriage bond in Wilson Co., Tenn., on 8 September 1824.

In June 1841 Margaret Eagan, Sarah Wright, Anderson Wright and his wife Sina, Barnaby Eagan, and Samuel Eagan of Randolph Co., Mo., sold a 141 acre tract in Wilson Co., Tenn., to Benjamin Estes.[217]

The Wilson Co., Tenn., Circuit Court Minutes show that on 17 December 1816 Peggy Eagan was appointed guardian for Sally, Sincey, Barnaby, Samuel, and William Eagan, minor heirs of William Eagan, deceased, with Samuel Motheral and Robert Neal, security.[218]

The last will and testament of Sarah Motheral mentions her daughter, Margaret Eagan.[219]

Sarah Wright, 43, b. in Tenn., is listed in the 1850 Census for Chariton Co., Mo., is listed as head of household, along with her children, Isaac, 19; John, 16; b. TN, and Samuel, 12, and Sinah, 16, b. Mo.[220] This indicates that John R. Wright moved to Missouri between 1834 and 1838. From the obituary for his brother, Anderson Wright, it seems most likely that they moved in 1836.[221]

The date of birth and middle name for John R. Wright and the middle initial for

---

[217] Partlow, p. 223.

[218] Wilson Co., Tenn., Circuit Court Minutes (1816-1819):59.

[219] Wilson Co., Tenn., Wills and Inventories (1848-1853):244.

[220] 1850 Census Chariton Co., Mo., Buffalo Lick township, p. 183, family 243.

[221] Birth dates listed are Isaac Newton Wright, b. January 8, 1831; John Wright, b. 1834; Sinah Elizabeth Wright, b. Feb. 1, 1835, all in Wilson Co., Tenn., and Samuel Anderson Wright, b. Feb. 12, 1837 in Chariton Co., Mo.

Anderson C. Wright were obtained from an Internet file. [222]

2. ANDERSON C.[3] WRIGHT, b. 8 December 1805 Halifax Co., N. C.; d. 19 September 1843 Chariton Co., Mo.; m. SINA EAGAN 5 December 1827 Wilson Co., Tenn., daughter of WILLIAM EAGAN and MARGARET MOTHERAL; b. 17 November 1808 Wilson Co., Tenn., and d. 1854 Chariton Co., Mo.

The obituary of the Rev. Anderson Wright was published in *The Western Christian Advocate* on 16 October 1843.[223] It mentions his birth and death dates, and that he was the son of Isaac and Elizabeth Wright and that he married Sina Eagan in 1828. He moved with his parents from North Carolina to Wilson Co., Tenn., and he moved with his wife and three children to Chariton Co., Mo., in the fall of 1836.

Anderson Wright bought 50 acres of land on Spencer's Creek, Wilson Co., Tenn. from Henry Holmes on September 22, 1829.[224] On October 5, 1836 Anderson Wright sold 50 acres on Spencer's Creek, Wilson Co., Tenn., to Minor Carswell.[225] "John W. Wright, farmer...his father Anderson Wright, was a native of Tennessee and was for many years a prominent farmer and stock dealer of Wilson Co., that state. His mother, former Miss Lina Eagan, was also of the same state and while John W. was still in his infancy, in 1836, the family removed to Missouri and made their home in Chariton County. Here they lived until their deaths, the father's in 1843 and the mother's in 1854. Of the family of three, two are living: John W and Margaret a younger sister.

---

[222] Schmehl, Linda. Ancestors of Linda Herring and Kenneth Schmehl. 11 Mar. 2004. Located on http://worldconnect.rootsweb.com (db. choctaw_lady).

[223] Waters, Margaret R., et. al.: Abstracts of Obituaries in The Western Christian Advocate, 1834-1850. (1988), p. 150.

[224] Partlow, p.3.

[225] Partlow, p. 163. He also granted an easement, probably the bank of the creek to Matthew Hunt on October 8, 1836.

144

John W. Wright was born in Wilson County, Tennessee May 31st, 1835 but was reared in Chariton County...November 1, 1854 he was married to Miss Mary, daughter of Howard C. Dunn, Esquire.[226] William T. Dunn of Wayland Township married in 1856 Miss Sarah W., daughter of Anderson Wright."[227]

3. ELIZABETH^3 WRIGHT, b. 1812 Wilson Co., Tenn.; m. ALEXANDER ROACH 1 July 1828 Wilson Co., Tenn.

>Elizabeth Roach, age 38, born in Tennessee, is listed with her mother, along with her children, all surname Roach, James G., 22; Samuel, 18; Thomas, 15; Finis E., 13; John A, 9; and William, 7. It is reasonable to conclude that Alexander Roach died about 1843 in Wilson Co., Tenn.

4. BROWN^3 WRIGHT

>Brown Wright is head of household that includes his mother, Elizabeth Wright, his younger brother James G. Wright, his sister, Elizabeth Roach, and her children in the 1850 Census. He has not been traced further. His age was obscured in the text.

5. JAMES G.^{3} WRIGHT, b. 1828 Wilson Co., Tenn.

>See note above. He has also not been traced further.

6. daughters:

>There are two marriages in Wilson Co., Tenn., which may involve daughters of Isaac Wright and Anne Hulm, although no data has been found yet to confirm this. The first is between Lucy Wright and Henry Hulm, 11 September 1823. The other is between Charlotte E. Wright and John W. Hulm, 21 December 1833.

vii. daughters of Solomon and Lucy as yet unidentified.

---

[226] History of Howard and Chariton Counties, Missouri. (St. Louis: National Historical Co., 1883,) p. 1122f.

[227] Ibid., p. 1173f.

1804 Thomas Wright of Lunenburg Co., Virginia

On 1 September 1760 James Mize sold to Thomas Wright "for love & affection" a tract of 34 acres, which was described as part of a tract survey by Mize and his brother Jeremiah Mize, which lay on the north side of Meherrin River.[228] This indenture was also witnessed by Thomas Jarratt, Joseph Wright, and by John Hight [Hite].

James Mize wrote his will 2 February 1761 and it was proved 7 April 1761 in Lunenburg Co., Va. He named his wife, Elizabeth, sons Stephen, William, and James Mize, and grandson Joseph Wright. The will does not specify whether Thomas or John was the father of this grandson. The will was witnessed by John Wright, William Mize, Thomas Wright, and John Hite.[229]

On 10 June 1764, Thomas Wright, planter, and Hannah Wright, his wife, sold to George Carter of Brunswick Co., planter, for 5 shillings a tract of land containing 34 acres (by force of statute for transferring uses into possessions,) the land having been part of land given by James Mize, deceased, to said Wright 1 September 1760.[230]

On 13 May 1767 Solomon Wright "of Brunswick County" sold to Thomas Wright for £11 10s. a tract of land containing 100 acres, which was the upper part of the tract of 400 acres obtained by patent of John Parker on the south, or upper, side of Stony Creek, from Thomas Moody's lower corner on the creek to John Edlow, down branch, and up the creek.

On 10 August 1768, Thomas Wright and Hannah Wright, his wife, sold to John Wright for £15 a tract of land containing 50 acres, part of a patent by John Parker on the south side of Stony Creek, up the great meadow branch and down the creek.[231] On the same date, they sold for £15 a tract of 50 acres, described as part of the patent of John Parker on the south side of Stony Creek, adjacent to John Green, John Wright, and his own line, up a small branch that runs out of the great Meadow Branch, and to the property of John Green.[232]

---

[228] Lunenburg Co., Va., Deed Book 6:243. Evans, p. 29.
[229] Lunenburg Co., Va., Will Book 2:17. Accessed 22 April 2009 at http://ftp.rootsweb.ancestry.com/pub/usgenweb/va/lunenburg/wills/willbk02.txt.
[230] Lunenburg Co., Va., Deed Book 10:222. Evans, p 31.
[231] Lunenburg Co., Va., Deed Book 11:192. Evans, pp. 30-31.
[232] Lunenburg Co., Va., Deed Book 11:195. Evans, pp. 30-31.

On 18 July 1788 Thomas Wright sold to Frank Pace Connell for £25 a 60 acre tract up the mouth of a small branch on Stony Creek adjoining the widow Matthews, Denton, Steagall, and Hudson.[233] This deed was signed by mark, and recorded 8 April 1790. This deed indicates that Hannah (Mize) Wright died before 1790.

On 17 January 1801 Thomas Wright sold to Allen Steagall for £20 a tract of 100 acres on Stony Creek, "where said Steagall now lives." Thomas Wright died in Lunenburg Co., Virginia 1804.[234]

From the tithe lists, it appears that Thomas was born say 1727 and he was the father of Parsons Wright, and John Wright. From Parsons' will we know he also had James Wright, David Wright, Henry Wright, Rosa Wright, Amy (Wright) Shell, and Chastity (Wright) Scott.

Hannah appears to have still been living in 1810 when the last of the land of John Wright was sold by son David.[235]

The tithe lists suggest that John Wright and his sons moved to Mecklenburg Co., Va., before the personal property tax lists were collected beginning in 1782. Review of these lists for Lunenburg Co., Va., from 1782-1812 showed a number of items. First, all were enumerated in the Lower District. The 1782 list shows Joseph Wright, Thomas Wright with Parsons Wright in the household, James Wright, and John Wright.[236] The 1783 list shows John Wright, Joseph Wright, James Wright, Parsons Wright, and Thomas Wright, with Thomas, jr., and "J." Wright.[237] The 1784 list shows James Wright with Laban and David Wright, Joseph Wright, Parsons Wright, and John Wright.[238] By 1785, the list was down to Joseph, John, Parsons, and Thomas Wright.

The estate of Thomas Wright was taxed 10 April 1804.[239] He had two tithes living in the household that year, and one in the year following. His estate was appraised 8 May 1804 at

---

[233] Lunenburg Co., Va., Deed Book 16:10. Evans, p. 2.

[234] Lunenburg Co., Va., Will Book 6:89A and 154A.

[235] Lunenburg Co., Va., Deed Book 22:148. Evans, p. 46.

[236] Lunenburg Co., Va., Personal Property Tax List, Lower District, p. 21 (Joseph) and 22.

[237] Lunenburg Co., Va., Personal Property Tax List, Lower District, p. 25.

[238] Lunenburg Co., Va., Personal Property Tax List, Lower District, p. 27, and 28, (John).

[239] Lunenburg Co., Va., Personal Property Tax List, Lower District, p. 36. Joseph and Parsons are the only others listed.

$418.15.[240] A second appraisal was recorded 5 May 1806 at $439.70.[241]

Hannah Wright was head of household in 1810, but had one male over 45, and one male 26-45, as well as another woman over 45 living with her.[242]

The will of Parsons Wright establishes a list of his brothers and sisters living in 1818, which can be combined with the tax and tithe lists to establish the children of Thomas Wright and Hannah Mize.

Genealogical Summary

1. THOMAS[1] WRIGHT was born say 1725 and died April 1804 in Lunenburg Co., Virginia. He married HANNAH MIZE, daughter of JAMES MIZE, about 1760 Lunenburg Co., Virginia. She died after 1810 in Lunenburg Co., Va.

Children of THOMAS WRIGHT and HANNAH MIZE are:

> i. PARSONS[2] WRIGHT, b. about 1753 Lunenburg Co., Va.; d. 1818 Putnam Co., Ga.; m. MARY _____.
>
> The tithe list for 1774 shows Parsons Wright listed with Thomas Wright as head of household. This means Parsons was born about 1752-53, as the 1772 list does not show him.[243]
>
> Parsons Wright was listed as a private in Capt. James Johnson's Company, 6th Virginia Regiment, Lt. Col. James Hendricks, commanding, from 2 February 1776-31 May 1777, and again from 1 April to 1 May 1777.[244]
>
> On 29 January 1785 Shepherd Mize and Sarah Mize sold to Parsons Wright for £60 an 81 acre tract of land by grant to Shepherd and Sarah Mize, adjacent Arthur Turner, Drury Allen, Mary Mize, Thomas Wright, and

---

[240] Lunenburg Co., Va., Will Book 6:89A-90. Appraisal was done by Benjamin Montgomery, Arthur Turner and Joseph Wright. It was recorded 13 September 1804.

[241] Lunenburg Co., Va., Will Book 6:154A-155. Appraisal was done by John Blackwell, Julius Hite, and Benjamin Montgomery, and was entered 12 June 1806.

[242] 1810 Census Lunenburg Co., Va., p. 364. Perhaps one of the males is Henry Wright, about whom I have not found anything.

[243] Bell, p. 345.

[244] Bell, p.

Betty Dizmang.[245] This deed was witnessed by James Wright, who signed by mark.

On 8 October 1790 Shadrack Witt of Lunenburg Co., Va., sold to Parsons Wright for £50 a 40.5 acre tract bounded by the little creek, Thomas Wright, Parsons Wright, and Moses Dobyns.[246] The deed was witnessed by William Fisher, James Dizmang, and Moses Dobyns.

On 21 January 1791 Parsons Wright sold to Julius Hite for £18 a 40 acre tract of land adjacent to Emanuel Callis, Joseph Wright, Stephen Mize, and his own land.[247] This deed was signed by Parson Wright's mark.

Parsons Wright, over 45, Hannah, also over 45, have a boy 16-26, and a girl, 10-16, living with them in the 1810 Census for Lunenburg Co., Va.[248]

On 11 November 1813 Parsons Wright and Mary Wright, his wife, sold to Julius Hite for $400 a tract of 121½acres adjacent the little creek and Hite's own lands.[249] The clerk did not note Parsons signed by mark, although it was noted that Mary did.

Parsons Wright may have actually left Virginia before this indenture was executed, as he does not appear on the tax rolls of Lunenburg County after 1811, when he appears with John Wright, probably his brother. The other known brothers left in 1810. There are no men named Wright in Lunenburg Co., Va., after 1811 until the mid 1850's.

The Last Will and Testament of Parsons Wright[250]

In the Name of God, Amen. I, Parsons Wright, of the State of Georgia and the County of Putnam considering the uncertainty of Life that the body must return and the Soul to God who gives it, being at this time in Perfect health and memory do make and

---

[245] Lunenburg Co., Va., Deed Book 14:299. Evans, p. 37.

[246] Lunenburg Co., Va., Deed Book 16:121, 8 October 1790/14 April 1791.

[247] Lunenburg Co., Va., Deed Book 16:115. Evans, p. 19.

[248] 1810 Census Lunenburg Co., Va., p. 364. The will suggests these were not their children, but perhaps children of his sister, Betty Dizmang.

[249] Lunenburg Co., Va., Deed Book 23:143. Evans, p. 21.

[250] Putnam County, Georgia, Will Book A:104-105.

constitute this my Last will & testament in manner and form following, Viz. After paying my just debts first I given an bequeath to my beloved wife, Mary Wright, at my decease all my property to hold as long as she lives and at her death to Susan Messervey Mize, daughter of James & Elizabeth. And if the said Susan Messervey Mize dies before my wife, Mary Wright, then all the property shall go to the heirs of sd. James and Elizabeth Mize. Except two dollars to each of my brothers and sisters, to wit, John Wright, James Wright, David Wright, Henry Wright, Rosa Wright, Amy Shell, and Chastity Scott. I do hereby appoint Mary Wright and James Mize to be executors of my last will and Testament and hereby revoking all former wills by me made heretofore, in witness I have set my hand and seal this 19th day 1818.

Witnesss: his
    Benjamin King   Parsons X Wright
    Rhoda Mize   mark
    Shepherd Mize

Georgia, Putnam County) Presented in open court 28 Sept 1818 by Shepherd Mize, Rhoda Mize. Teste: Coleman Pendelton.

iii. JOHN[2] WRIGHT, b. about 1756 Lunenburg Co., Va.; d. after 27 October 1834 Jasper Co., Ga.; m. _____ JARRETT.

The land deeds are difficult to assign in that this John appears certain to have had both an uncle and a first cousin named John, all living in proximity. Nonetheless, I suspect this man is the one mentioned when John Dizmang of Lunenburg Co., Va., sold to John Wright of Brunswick Co., Va., for £40 a 41 acre tract of land adjoined by Parsons Wright, John Connell, and Thomas Wright.[251] Witnesses were William Fisher, John Mize, Adah Jarrett, Drury Allen, and Parsons Wright. Likewise, he may be the man meant when Adda Jarrett of Mecklenburg Co., Va., sold to John Wright of Lunenburg Co., Va., for £30 a 40.5 acre tract of land bounded by Thomas Jarrett, James Callis, and

---

[251] Lunenburg Co., Va., Deed Book 14:427, 8 November 1786/12 April 1787.

Emmanuel Callis.[252] Polly, wife of Ada, relinquished her dower rights.

John Wright of Lunenburg Co., Va., sold to Emanuel Callis for £25 a 40.5 acre tract of land bounded by Emanuel Callis, Luke Taylor, and James Callis.[253] This deed was witnessed by Clement Reed, Thomas Edmunds, John Orgain, William Fisher, Ben Fisher, and Parsons Wright. This is the same tract he bought from Adah Jarrett.

John Wright sold another 40.5 acre tract to Julius Hite of Lunenburg Co., Va., for £35 a tract bounded by Parsons Wright, Thomas Wright, John Mize, and Hite.[254] This deed was witnessed by James Dizmang, Parsons Wright, David Wright, Joel Moore, and Thomas Wright. This seems to be the Dizmang tract.

The land deeds showing John Wright disposing of the land inherited from Thomas Jarrett, Sr., indicate his wife was a Jarrett. Unfortunately, her first name was not recorded in the deeds nor in his application.

This is probably the John Wright, over age 45, living in Lunenburg Co., Va., with two boys under 10, one girl under 10, one 10-16, one 16-26, and his wife, over 45.[255] It is not clear who these children are.

John Wright, age over 45, and a woman of similar age, is living in Monticello, Jasper Co., Ga., in the 1820 Census.[256] In 1830, he was 60-69 years of age, as was his wife, and they had a five year old girl, one male 20-30, and two women 20-30, living in the household.[257]

John Wright filed an application for a Revolutionary War pension (R11,893) on 27 October 1834 in Jasper County, Ga. At the time of his

---

[252] Lunenburg Co., Va., Deed Book 15:526, 6 March 1790/8 April 1790.

[253] Lunenburg Co., Va., Deed Book 16:451, 16 October 1793/10 April 1794.

[254] Lunenburg Co., Va., Deed Book 16:452, 30 November 1793/10 April 1794.

[255] 1810 Census Lunenburg Co., Va., p. 364.

[256] 1820 Census Jasper Co., Ga., Monticello, p. 190. Also living in Monticello are Joseph, p. 190, 200010-00100; and William, p. 188, 220010-00010. These seem good candidates to be sons of John Wright.

[257] 1830 Census, Jasper Co., Ga., p. 368. William Wright, p. 372, was 30-39 years old, as was his wife, and they had one daughter, 5-9. Also listed was "CWC" who is Charles Wright, also age 30-39, with his wife of same age, one boy under 5, one 5-9, and one girl under 5, plus one slave, (p. 370.)

application, he stated he was 78 years of age, and had entered into service in the 2nd Virginia Regiment, Continental Line, in the fall of 1780 in Lunenburg Co., Va., Col. Greene and Capt. Overton. He stated that he participated in the battle of Guilford C. H., N. C., and was wounded at the battle of Camden, and later participated in the battle of Eutaw Springs. He mustered out at Salisbury, N. C., in 1782. He did not provide witnesses or other documentation, and his daughter, Sarah Junior,[258] petitioned for payment through her attorney, William Williams, in Randolph Co., Alabama, 24 July 1854. The documents provide no information about his date of death.

iv. THOMAS^2 WRIGHT, b. before 1762 Lunenburg Co., Va.

He may be the Thomas Wright listed as a private in Capt. James Johnson's company, 6th Virginia Regiment, Lt. Col. James Hendricks, commanding, from 2 February 1776-31 May 1777,[259] since his grandfather was likely too old. He was also listed in Capt. John Stokes' company, 2nd Virginia Regiment, Col. Christian Fiberger, commanding, in November 1778 and May 1778.[260]

v. JAMES^2 WRIGHT, b. before 1762 Lunenburg Co., Va.

James Wright married Lucy Shell, daughter of William Shell and Amelia Ellis, but his date of birth is recorded as 1745, which is too early to be this man, who was not 21 when the last tithe list was published. However, he appears in his own right in 1782, and at a time when Parsons Wright was still living at home.

---

[258] Sarah Ann Wright married Sylvester Junior 27 February 1835 in Baldwin Co., Ga. Silvester was listed in the 1830 census for Henry Co., Ga., p. 245, with himself 20-29 and a woman of same age, presumably a first wife. Next door is Anthony Junior, 60-69, with one boy 10-16, and his wife also 60-69. Anthony Junior married Obedience Cockerham 17 January 1781 in Halifax Co., Va., according to online sources. He certainly was living in Morgan, Rutherford Co., N. C., in 1800, p. 121, [120010-50010]. Also listed in Rutherford Co., was John Right, (p. 140), 000100-10100. Anthony Junior applied for a Revolutionary War pension from Jasper Co., Ga., 3 October 1838. (R 5789, viewed online at Ancestry.com, 17 March 2013.) He states he enlisted in the Continental line from Halifax Co., Va., in 1776, and served until the end of the war, although apparently was also in the local milita for a time. His claim was denied.

[259] Bell, p. 218, 219.

[260] Bell, p. 234, p. 235.

152

On 29 January 1785 Shepherd Mize and Sarah Mize sold to Parsons Wright for £60 an 81 acre tract of land by grant to Shepherd and Sarah Mize, adjacent Arthur Turner, Drury Allen, Mary Mize, Thomas Wright, and Betty Dizmang.[261] This deed was witnessed by James Wright, who signed by mark.

He may be the "J" Wright enumerated with Thomas Wright in 1783, and may be the James listed with Laban and David in 1784. James Wright is mentioned again in 1787, but not thereafter.

vi. CHARLES[2] WRIGHT, b. about 1771 Lunenburg Co., Va.

Charles Wright appeared on the tax lists for 1792 and 1793 Lunenburg Co., Va., which suggests a birth year of 1771. Charles Wright married Nancy Wright 22 December 1791 in Lunenburg Co., Va.

vii. DAVID[2] WRIGHT, m. NANCY WRIGHT 28 December 1797 Mecklenburg Co., Va., daughter of JOHN WRIGHT and MARY _____.

David Wright of Lunenburg Co., Va., married Nancy Wright 28 December 1797 in Mecklenburg Co., Va., with Roderick Wright as his surety.[262] The connection to Roderick Wright is the reason I have listed her as a sister to 1832 John Wright of Clarke Co., Ga.

On 19 December 1810, David Wright and his wife, "Jincy," and Hannah Wright sold to Julius Hite for £80 a tract of 110 acres adjacent to Parsons Wright on the little creek, Hite, Fisher, the ridge path, and Turner.[263] The indenture was signed by David Wright and by Hannah Wright's mark, and witnessed by Parsons Wright.

David Wright appears in the personal property tax list with James and Laban in 1784, and by himself in 1787 and 1789, but it is not certain this is the same man. He appears in 1805-1807, and from the deeds, is almost surely this man.

---

[261] Lunenburg Co., Va., Deed Book 14:299. Evans, p. 37.
[262] Elliott, p. 135.
[263] Lunenburg Co., Va., Deed Book 22:148. Evans, p. 46.

David Wright appears on the 1810 Census for Lunenburg Co., Va., age 26-45, with one girl under 10 and his wife of the same age.

viii. HENRY[2] WRIGHT.

I have found no evidence for Henry in the tax lists, although Hannah was taxed with one tithe, who may be this man. If so, he was born between 1784 and 1788.

ix. ROSA[2] WRIGHT.

x. AMY[2] WRIGHT; b. 1755 Lunenburg Co., Va.; d. 20 September 1830 Newberry Co., S. C.; m. WILLIAM SHELL son of WILLIAM SHELL and AMELIA ELLIS; b. 9 September 1759 Surry Co., Va.; d. 1822 Newberry Co., S. C.

Students of the Shell family agree that William Shell, Jr., married a woman named Amy, although her last name is not known to them. I have made this connection based upon the statement in Parsons Wright's will that his sister was Amy Shell.

She is probably buried in Abrams-Shell Cemetery, Whitmire, Newberry Co., S.C. His death date is estimated, as there is no headstone.

xi. CHASTITY[2] WRIGHT, m. _____ SCOTT.

The overseers of the poor of Lunenburg Co., Va., were ordered to bind out Randall Wright to John Christian according to law 14 April 1790.[264] The overseers were ordered to bind out Randolph Wright, son of Chastity Wright, to Thrower Truman according to law 11 April 1799.[265]

xii. DOLLY[2] WRIGHT, m. JAMES DIZMANG 2 January 1790 Lunenburg Co., Va.

Parsons Wright was bondsman for this marriage, indicating a family relationship. He was also listed as bondsman in the marriage of James Dizmang to Sally Huling 25 September 1794 in Lunenburg Co., Va., indicating Dolly (Wright) Dizmang had died. This is probably why she was not listed in his will. I have

---

[264] Lunenburg Co., Va., Court Order Book 17:8, 14 April 1790.
[265] Lunenburg Co., Va., Court Order Book 18:9, 11 April 1799.

found very little information about this family despite the unusual surname.

A Note on Procedures Used

The tithe lists establish that John Wright had at least two sons: John and William. There is reasonable evidence that both of these men migrated to then Wilkes, later Lincoln Co., Ga., after the Revolutionary War. The records in Lincoln Co., Ga., show a relationship between 1827 William Wright of Lincoln Co., Ga., and 1818 Sugar Wright of Lincoln Co., Ga., who also appears in the lists of soldiers who served in the units from Lunenburg Co., Va., who were present at Valley Forge. William Wright and after 1827 John Wright of Lincoln Co., Ga., also can be associated with each other and with 1820 Jarrett Wright of Lincoln Co., Ga. and 1836 Nathan Wright of Lincoln Co., Ga. Nathan Wright can be associated with 1838 Job Wright of Mecklenburg Co., N. C.

I have assumed that these men are all brothers. However, the intermarriage between two children of 1827 William Wright of Lincoln Co., Ga., and two children of 1836 Nathan Wright of Lincoln Co., Ga., raises questions about this assumption. It is possible that Nathan and Job Wright are actually sons of after 1788 Laban Wright of Mecklenburg Co., Va.

After 1810 Joseph Wright of Lunenburg Co., Va., is the father of 1835 Jarrett Wright of Allen Co., Ky., who can be associated with another Joseph Wright present in Allen Co., Ky., around 1820, and with 1849 John Wright of Allen Co., Ky. This John is thought by his descendants to have married Mary Brewer of Brunswick Co., Virginia. This John can be associated with 1795 Laban Wright of Brunswick Co., Va., 1793 James Wright of Brunswick Co., Va., and a Reuben Wright. Jarrett Wright and families lived in Warren Co., Ky., in the part that became Allen Co., Ky., in 1815.[266].

After 1784 John Wright of Mecklenburg Co., Virginia

Given the number of men named John Wright it is difficult to be certain at various times which John Wright is being

---

[266] 1825 Josias Wright of Madison Co., Illinois, who was from Brunswick Co., Va., was also in Allen Co., Ky., but he is probably from an unrelated group of Wright families. This illustrates the limitations of the association as a method to group these people and should be borne in mind by anyone reading this discussion

mentioned in the records. John Wright was listed as a tithe in 1750, so was at least 21. This gives an estimated birth year of 1729 or earlier. Using a similar argument, he has at least one son, John, Jr., named in the tithe list of 1764, which indicates he was born before 1743, and certainly before 1748. Since the James Mize family was present on Stony Creek from about 1732 onward, it would indicate contact between the families prior to the tithe and land deeds. Yet, the last will and testament of James Mize, proved 7 April 1761 certainly indicates that John and Thomas Wright were sons-in-law.[267] However, he also mentions his grandson, Joseph, who is probably the eldest son of John Wright, given that there is only one Joseph Wright in the Lunenburg Co., Va., tax lists.

John Wright patented 400 acres of land on the head of Rocky Branch adj. Duke, John Patrick, Roberts, and his own lines 10 September 1755.[268]

On 12 May 1759 John Wright patented 200 acres of land described as being on both sides of little creek above Stony Creek, adjacent Dickerson and Mize.[269] On 10 October 1765 John Wright and Sarah Wright, his wife, sold to David Moss for £15 a tract of 200 acres patented by Wright on 12 May 1759 on both sides of the little creek above Stony Creek, adjacent Dickinson and Mize. This indenture was witnessed by George Carter, Thomas Wright, and Philip Russell.[270]

On 23 August 1760, James Mize sold to John Wright for £8 a tract of 60 acres on the north side of Stony Creek adjacent to Nathaniel Chambliss and Jeremiah Mize in an indenture that was witnessed by Thomas Jarratt and Joseph Wright.[271] On 8 September 1768 John Wright and Sarah Wright, his wife, sold to Thomas Wright for 5 shillings a tract of land containing 64 acres along Stony Creek, Jeremiah Mize, George Steagall, John Lantrope and Cedar Branch.[272]

On 10 August 1768, Thomas Wright and Hannah Wright, his wife, sold to John Wright for £15 a tract of land containing 50

---

[267] Lunenburg Co., Va., Will Book 2:17, 2 February 1761/7 April 1761.

[268] Va. Land Patent Book 31:564.

[269] Va. Land Patent Book 34:262.

[270] Lunenburg Co., Va., Deed Book 10:234. Evans, pp. 32-33.

[271] Lunenburg Co., Va., Deed Book 6:245. Evans, p. 29.

[272] Lunenburg Co., Va., Deed Book 11:193. Evans, pp. 30-31. Evans traces the deeds to establish that Lantorpe bought his land from James Mize. (p.99)

acres, part of a patent by John Parker on the south side of Stony Creek, up the great meadow branch and down the creek.[273]

On 23 April 1779, John Wright, Senior, planter sold to William Keatt for £160 a tract of 50 acres "where sd. Wright lives" adjacent James Sturdivant, on Stony Creek, Thomas Jarratt, Jr., Nicholas Callahan, Edloe, and Wyatt Williams.[274] Sarah, wife of John Wright relinquished her dower rights.

The tithe lists show John Wright and Sarah had at least two sons: John Wright and William Wright. William Wright appears on the tithe list of 1769 having 50 acres of land with two tithes, and John Wright with no acreage. I think this is probably the two sons of this John Wright, as the father had been recorded with 260 acres of land. The tithe list of 1772 lists John Wright, Sr., and John Wright, Jr., as well as Joseph Wright, Thomas Wright, and William Wright. In 1774, though, there is only one man named John Wright listed. Although not certain, I think this is probably John Wright, son of Thomas Wright, who appears regularly on the personal property tax lists.

In conclusion, John Wright left Lunenburg Co., Va., before 1774, and probably moved to Mecklenburg Co., Va. On 10 May 1779 John Wright bought from William Wilson "of Halifax County" for £180 a tract of 50 acres of land "on the drafts of Buffalo Creek[275] bounded as followeth: Beginning at a white oak sapling on David Chandlers line thence on his line to a corner red oak on John Buller's line thence along his line to a pine, thence a new line to a hickory corner and then a new line to the beginning..."[276]

On 8 November 1784 John Wright sold to David Chandler, Jr., for £50 a tract of 50 acres of land on the south side of the Dan River on one of the branches of Great Buffalo Creek bounded "Beginning at a corner small hickory on David Chandler Senr.'s line thence nearly west on John Butler's line, to pointers on a corner lightwood, not on the said Butler's land and Zachariah Overbee's line, thence nearly east on said Overbee's and William Wilkerson's lines to a corner white oak on said David Chandler,

[273] Lunenburg Co., Va., Deed Book 11:192. Evans, pp. 30-31.

[274] Lunenburg Co., Va., Deed Book 13:218. Evans, pp. 46-47.

[275] Buffalo Creek is in the far western part of Mecklenburg County adjacent to the Halifax County line.

[276] Mecklenburg Co., Va., Deed Book 5:419.

157

Senr's line, thence nearly south along said Chandler's line to the beginning...."[277] John Wright signed this indenture with his mark. Sarah Wright released her dower right to this land by private inquiry at the same time.[278]

Genealogical Summary

1. JOHN[1] WRIGHT was born say 1720 and died after 1784 in Mecklenburg Co., Virginia. He married SARAH MIZE, daughter of JAMES MIZE in Lunenburg Co., Va., say 1740 in Lunenburg Co., Va.

Children of JOHN WRIGHT and SARAH MIZE are:

i. JOHN[2] WRIGHT, b. say 1743 Brunswick Co., Va.; d. after 1820 Lincoln Co., Ga.

I have considered the possibility this is the same John Wright as after 1834 John Wright of Jasper Co., Ga. I chose to list that man as the son of Thomas Wright because he served in the militia from Lunenburg Co., Va., in 1780.[279] He may be the John Wright on the Halifax Co., Va., tax list of 1787 with five white souls living near John Mize and Nathan Wright on the list of John P. Smith.[280]

Lincoln County was erected in 1796 from Wilkes County, so early records are in the former county. William Wright bought 200 acres of land on Soap Creek from John Troy and wife Mary, of Washington Co., Ga., adjacent Daniel Burnett and Robert Walton on 14 October 1786.[281] John Wright bought 271 acres on Little Kettle Creek, part of an original grant of 1784 to

---

[277] Mecklenburg Co., Va., Deed Book 6:424.

[278] I have found no further record for them in Mecklenburg Co., Va., and have found nothing in Halifax Co., Va., that can be tied to them with any certainty, although I do think some of his sons may have passed through there briefly.

[279] By 1780 the family of John Wright, the father, was established in Mecklenburg Co., Va. This conclusion is based on the deeds discussed above, but also from the data recorded by the descendants of William Wright, who is his brother.

[280] John Wright listed on the tax lists for Halifax Co., Va., in the years 1785, 1786 and 1787. There is also a "Betty" Wright listed in 1782 and 1790. Could she be the Elizabeth noted under the discussion about William?

[281] Wilkes Co., Ga., Deed Book HH:355, 14 October 1786. Located online 17 March 2013 at http://giddeon.com/wilkes/early-records-of-ga-vol2/104-125.shtml.

George Lumpkin, from John H. Foster on 19 May 1791.[282] He purchased another 21 acres, location not named, from Buckner Harris on 4 October 1791.[283] John Wright, of Kettle Creek, Wilkes Co., Ga., had two draws in the 1803 Georgia Land Lottery.[284]

John Wright, over age 45, with his wife and three slaves, but no children, was living next to Nathan Wright in Lincoln Co., Ga., in the 1820 census.[285] He was listed as a revolutionary soldier and a fortunate drawer in the 1827 Georgia Land Lottery.[286]

He does not appear in the 1830 Census and is presumed to have died in Lincoln Co., Ga.[287]

ii. WILLIAM[2] WRIGHT, b. before 1743 Lunenburg Co., Va.; d. after 13 January 1827 Lincoln Co., Ga.; m. DRUCILLA GRIFFIN possibly daughter of RICHARD GRIFFIN and MARY.

In 1787 William Wright was listed in Mecklenburg Co., Va., with the tax being charged to John Holmes. William Wright appears again in 1792[288] and appears in the tax lists until 1805.[289] However, this is probably the son of 1819 Reuben Wright, who died in about 1824, probably in Mecklenburg Co., Va.

Others indicate he served in Capt. Elijah Graves' company from Mecklenburg Co., Va., during the

---

[282] Wilkes Co., Ga., Deed Book GG:508, 19 May 1791. Located online 17 March 2013 at
http://giddeon.com/wilkes/early-records-of-ga-vol2/071-104.shtml.

[283] Wilkes Co., Ga., Deed Book GG:527, 4 October 1791. Located online 17 March 2013 at
http://giddeon.com/wilkes/early-records-of-ga-vol2/071-104.shtml.

[284] Located online at http://www.giddeon.com/wilkes/books/early-records-of-ga-vol1/299-320.shtml. Accessed 17 March 2013.

[285] 1820 Census Lincoln Co., Ga., p. 165. John [000001-00001-3]; Nathan [001201-12010-3].

[286] Ancestry.com. *Georgia Land Lottery, 1827* [database on-line]. Provo, UT, USA: The Generations Network, Inc., 1997.

[287] There is another John Wright who wrote his will 6 January 1818 and proved 23 January 1818. (Lincoln Co., Ga., Will Book D:74.) He names his sister, Elizabeth Taylor, brother Peter Twitty's children, brother George Wright, sister Polly Twitty, sister Nancy Twitty, and names his friend John Sims and brother Peter Twitty as executors. Witnesses were James LeSeuer, William Mosby, and Richard White?

[288] Mecklenburg Co., Va., Tax List 1792 A:30.

[289] Mecklenburg Co., Va., Tax List 1794 A:28; 1798 A:49; 1800 A:24; 1802 B:40; 1804 B:52; 1805 A:52.

Revolutionary War, and that he married Drucilla Griffin about 1773, as the eldest child was born 17 February 1774.[290] A student of this family indicates that he had moved from Mecklenburg Co., Va., to Granville Co., N. C., after the Revolution, but sold his land there in 1785, and appeared on Soap Creek in then Wilkes, now Lincoln Co., Ga., in 1786.[291] William Wright and Lydia his wife, sold to Thomas Brown 200 acres on a branch of Rocky Creek on the north side 6 August 1789.[292] It is unclear if this is a different William Wright or if his wife Drucilla's name was corrupted.

The 1810 tax list for Lincoln Co., Ga., shows William Wright "for Elizabeth Wright" taxed on 300 acres of land adjacent Stovall on Soap Creek, Lincoln Co., and for 202½ acres "N106/13th WC".[293] Nathan Wright was taxed on 297 acres on Soap Creek adjacent Tatum, while William Wright, Jr., paid a poll tax, as did "Sugar" Wright. The latter is particularly interesting, since "Sugar" Wright was listed as a private in the Lunenburg Co., Va., militia along with Thomas and Parsons Wright.

Sugar Wright wrote his will 28 November 1817 and gave $50 to his beloved brother, William, then left the remainder of his estate to be divided between brothers William and Isaac Wright.[294]

William Wright is listed in the 1820 Census, as is William, Jr.[295] He wrote his will 16 January 1827 and it was proved there 7 May 1827.[296] He described himself

---

[290] See for example Rogers, David. Rogers-Randall. 24 June 2012. Located at htttp://wc.rootsweb.ancestry.com, (db. gilest).

[291] Dorris, Calvin. Re: Wright Family of Lincoln Co., Ga. 14 January 2012. Located at http://genforum.genealogy.com/wright/messages/24018.html. See also the land deed from 1786 cited under John Wright.

[292] Wilkes Co., Ga., Deed Book HH:100, 6 August 1789. Located online 17 March 2013 at http://giddeon.com/wilkes/early-records-of-ga-vol2/104-125.shtml.

[293] Located online at http://files.usgwarchives.net/ga/lincoln/taxlists/1810tax.html. Accessed 17 March 2013.

[294] Lincoln Co., Ga., Will Book D:70, 28 November 1817/6 December 1817. Witnesses were Wm. E. Hughes, Wiley E. Tatum, and William Greer. The will was recorded 21 January 1818.

[295] 1820 Census Lincoln Co., Ga., p. 162, [001201-12010-3]; William, Jr., is on p. 163, [000110-60100.]

[296] Lincoln Co., Ga., Will Book D:193.

as being of an "advanced age" and directed that his property and two slaves be under the control of his wife Drucilla for her lifetime use, and then to be bequeathed to his daughter Lucy Stovall, wife of Drury Stovall. He mentioned his son William Wright, Jr., and the heirs of Mary Barnett, formerly Mary Stovall. He finally listed 11 children as residual legatees. He named Sally Wright, wife of Lewis Wright, Elizabeth Wright, William Wright, Jr., Richard Wright, John Wright, Reuben Wright, David Wright, Amelia Wright, Samuel Wright, Nathan Wright, and Benjamin Wright. Sons Samuel and Benjamin Wright were named executors. Subscribing witnesses were Peter Laman, Ezekiel Laman, and Nathan (x) Wright.

Children of WILLIAM WRIGHT and DRUCILLA GRIFFIN are:[297]

1. MARY[3] WRIGHT, b. 17 February 1774 Mecklenburg Co., Va.; d. 23 November 1864 Giles Co., Tenn.[298]; m. (1) DAVID JOSEPH STOVALL son of JOSIAH STOVALL and MARY HICKS; b. about 1772 Granville Co., N. C.; d. 6 June 1808 Lincoln Co., Ga.; m. (2) _____ BARNETT.

2. ELIZABETH[3] WRIGHT, b. 11 March 1777 Halifax Co., Va.; d. 10 June 1846 Lincoln Co., Ga.; m. WILLIAM CAVE.

3. LUCY[3] WRIGHT, b. about 1780; d. before 1870 Marion Co., Miss.; m. DRURY STOVALL, son of JOSIAH STOVALL and MARY HICKS; b. about 1771 Granville Co., N. C.; d. 1 November 1858 Columbus, Marion Co., Miss.

4. SARAH[3] WRIGHT, b. 17 March 1774 Virginia; d. after 1850 Morgan Co., Ala.; m. LEWIS WRIGHT

---

[297] Tyer, Ed. Tyer, Hughes, Rhodes, Wright, and others. 25 February 2011. Located online at http://wc.rootsweb.ancestry.com, (db. edltyer). This has been supplemented by Dorris, Calvin. Wright Family of Lincoln Co., Ga. 28 September 2004. http://genforum.genealogy.com/wright/messages/17976.html

[298] Buried in Bee Spring Cemetery, Giles Co., Tenn. http://www.findagrave.com, #12261662.

1802 Lincoln Co., Ga.; b. 1772; d. before 1 December 1849 Morgan Co., Ala.

5. RICHARD[3] WRIGHT.

6. WILLIAM[3] WRIGHT m. SARAH WRIGHT 2 December 1810 Lincoln Co., Ga., dau. of NATHAN WRIGHT and ELIZABETH COCKERHAM.

7. JOHN[3] WRIGHT, m. ELIZABETH WALKER 1820 Lincoln Co., Ga.; d. 19 December 1845 Lincoln Co., Ga.

8. SAMUEL[3] WRIGHT, d. before 5 December 1848 Lincoln Co., Ga.; m. AGNES SAMUEL 10 September 1816 Lincoln Co., Ga., dau. of BENJAMIN SAMUEL and AGNES SANDERS; b. 27 September 1792 Lincoln Co., Ga.; d. 28 December 1841 Lincoln Co., Ga.

9. REUBEN[3] WRIGHT.

10. DAVID[3] WRIGHT.

11. NATHAN[3] WRIGHT, d. about 1870 Lincoln Co., Ga.; m. NANCY BURDETT 5 October 1825 Wilkes Co., Ga., dau. of JOHN BURDETT and DEBORAH PRATHER; d. about 1895 Little Hope, Wood Co., Texas.

12. BENJAMIN[3] WRIGHT, m. JANE SAMUEL 17 September 1829 Lincoln Co., Ga., dau. of BENJAMIN SAMUEL and AGNES SANDERS; b. 12 January 1795 Lincoln Co., Ga.; d. 7 August 1873.

13. AMELIA[3] WRIGHT, m. BENJAMIN HOLMES 8 February 1830 Lincoln Co., Ga.

iv. NATHAN[2] WRIGHT, b. 7 November 1760 Lunenburg Co., Va.; d. 17 March 1836 Lincoln Co., Ga.; m. (1) ELIZABETH COCKERHAM 20 September 1782 Mecklenburg Co., Va.; m. (2) MARY FULTON 17 February 1792 Wilkes Co., Ga.

Nathan Wright appears on the substitute Census tax list for Halifax Co., Va., with two white souls listed just below John Mize with four white persons and one dwelling, along with John Wright with five white souls and an outbuilding, but no dwelling house on the list of Jno. P. Smith.[299] He was listed only for the year 1785.

Nathan Wright married Elizabeth Cockerham 20 September 1782 in Mecklenburg Co., Va. Nathan Wright bought a 50 acre tract of land for £30 from Benjamin Cockerham on 9 October 1786.[300] The tract was described as being on the waters of the south side of the Dan River, bounded by William Hills, Joseph Randolph, and Benjamin Cockerham. The deed was signed by the mark "B" and witnessed by Luke Wiles, Benjamin (+) Cockerham, Peter (+) Crawford, and Owen Franklin. On 8 October 1787 he sold the land to Francis Lewis for £45.[301] The tract was then described as 50 acres on the south side of the Dan River on Irish Creek adjacent Benjamin Cockerham, Joseph Randolph, and William Hills. He signed with a distinctive mark, but witnesses were not listed. The connection to the Cockerham family raises the possibility of a connection between 1838 Job Wright and Nathan Wright, but does not prove it.[302] Their time in Mecklenburg Co., Va., was brief, and there was little, if any time, for overlapping activities. Students of Job Wright think he was from Southampton Co., Va., so I have kept him separate.

Nathan Wright applied for a pension in October 1832 from Lincoln Co., Ga.[303]

State of Georgia
Lincoln County
On the 23d day of October 1832 personally appeared in open court before William H. Crawford the

---

[299] 1790 Substitute Census of Virginia. Located online

[300] Mecklenburg Co., Va., Deed Book 7:64. *Deed not examined.*

[301] Mecklenburg Co., Va., Deed Book 7:195. *Deed not examined.*

[302] Another source reports that Nathan and Elizabeth (Cockerham) Wright went to Edgefield Co., S. C., and then to Wilkes Co., Ga., where Elizabeth died about 20 August 1791.(http://genforum.genealogy.com/Cockerham/messages/285.htm and /179.htm. There is a Benjamin Cockerham who died Morgan Co., Ga., 1815-1818 who may be the father.

[303] Revolutionary War Pension Application S32083. Transcription published by Ed Tyer. [Tyer, Ed. Tyer, Hughes, Rhodes, Wright, and others. 25 February 2011. http://wc.rootsweb.ancestry.com, (db. edltyer).] Pension file viewed online at Ancestry.com with minor corrections made to the transcription. The file establishes his birth date as 7 November 1760 in Lunenburg Co., Va. The file also records a notation that he died 17 March 1836.

presiding judge thereof being the Superior Court of the said county and state now sitting, Nathan Wright a resident of said county of Lincoln, aged seventy two years of age the seventh day of November next according to the register kept of the family record and accounts from the older children from whom he derived his birth record. Born in the county of Lunenburg, state of Virginia, who being first duly sworn according to law, Nathan by oath makes the following declaration in order to obtain the benefit of the Act of Congress passed the 7th of June 1832.

That he entered the service of the United States under the following named officers and served as herein stated.

A call was made for a quota of the Militia in the county of Mecklenburg Va. for a three months tour of duty. In this call out, George Stovall was drafted. Soon after, another call was made on the Militia for eighteen months anew and according to the recollection of deponent, a squad of 12 to 20 , the exact number he don't recollect, furnished a man and those who had him drafted for a three month tour, not being called out, had the opportunity of enlisting for eighteen months, thereby clearing the squad to which they were attached and this was done previous to his marching. Deponent substituted in the place of said George Stovall and immediately was ordered to meet the recruits at Mecklenburg Court House Va. And from there marched under charge of Sgt. Moody Burt with the other recruits to Petersburg in Va. where he joined with the Army within a few days. While on evening parade, a Colonel Parker turned out and called on the Army for volunteers to march immediately to the south who soon formed a regiment which was commanded by Col. Parker. Deponent having himself volunteered and was attached to a company under Benjamin Tolliver, Col. Parker's regiment, and the regiment immediately took up the line of march from Petersburg Va. by Hillsboro and Saulsbury No. Carolina, Camden and the Ridge So. Carolina to Augusta Georgia. Soon after, the regiment again moved down to Buckhead Spirit Creek and on to the Ogechee quieting the disaffected and checking the fears from the Indians. Remaining but a short time at either place and again retraced to Augusta, remaining but a short time there. Again, marched to Spirit Creek where the regiment remained a few weeks and moved to Buckhead again and on to Ogechee and from there marched to Savannah which was at that time in the possesion of the British and united with other troops. He believes Gen'l Lincoln was in command besieging the place in all which deponent was continually with the regiment and was in the attack made on the breastworks at Savannah which terminated unsuccessfully to the American troops and they withdrew. Parker's regiment returned to Augusta where they remained a considerable time, much of the winter.

Sometime in February after the siege of Savannah, Parker's regiment was ordered to march to Charleston, So. Carolina, deponent with them, where they remained as deponent now believes until last of April or the first of May. The British made an attack on the city and took possession thereof. In that attack Col. Parker was killed in the 'Half Moon Battery'. Deponent with others were made prisoners. In this detention he remained until the 28th of June at night, when an opportunity offered and deponent with one William Espy deserted from the British and made their way through South Carolina to Orangeburg. Near that place they were retaken by the British. In that deplorable situation measures were made to take them immediately off to Charleston and from there on board a prison ship. While under these threats, an officer of the British Army who was in command, made overtures to deponent and Espy to enlist for six months with the British Army in which time difficulties would be over and a Sgt. Hawkins, who was one of Parker's regiment 'had enlisted' and made an opportunity to recommend that course with deponent and Espy which they done with a belief and the recommendation of the Sergeant they could have an opportunity the sooner to desert and go home. They were taken from Orangeburg to Augusta which was then in possession of the British. No opportunity to escape having afforded they remained for some time until taken down the Savannah river to guard boats which were bringing goods and etc. for the use of the troops. When near to Golphinton an opportunity offered and deponent with two other soldiers, Marshall and Taylor, deserted again and made their way to a detachment of American troops under the command of Maj. James Jackson near to Savannah river on the South Carolina side between Golphinton and Augusta. The dangers of traveling were so great we were recommended and determined to continue until a better opportunity offered of getting back to Virginia in a short time. Thereafter deponent availed himself of enlisting as a volunteer in Colonel Hammond's regiment in Capt Wm. Johnston's company Maj. Perdee's battalion in the detachment. He remained sometime, was at the siege of Augusta, was at the storming of Greasons Fort, from thence marching to various points and routes in South Carolina and eventually reached Cambridge So. Carolina and there met Gen'l. Greene in command, who gave deponent a discharge, altho he continued at the seige of Ninety-Six until it was raided, as the discharge was intended for deponents protection traveling home when an opportunity might offer to return home. Soon after this, Colonel Hammond's regiment marched through the upper part of South Carolina by Gen'l Pickens and on Sandy River he left the detachment being the safest route for a return. He started from there and arrived safe in Mecklenburg in Virginia and was absent from the time he went into service until he returned home a period of two years.

Soon after this, deponent married, removed to Georgia and has resided in that part of Georgia, Wilkes and Lincoln counties upwards of forty years.

Deponent further swears that he has no documentary testimony to prove his service, his discharge from Gen'l Greene he has long since lost. He is a very poor scholar, not capable of keeping accounts, consequently at a loss about dates which he could not keep for he is able to set them out correctly. Nor is he able to prove his actual service by any living witness which he can procure the testimony of at this time. He will be able to prove by standing as a revolutionary character, his standing in society, and the reasonableness of his claim by John Guice and Reverend John H. Walker and John Crosson, all revolutionary soldiers, all of whom will state their knowledge of deponent.

Deponent never received a pension nor was his name on the pension list roll of any agency in any state and he hereby relinquishes all but the present. Sworn to: 23 October 1832

Signed Nathan Wright (X His mark)

Sworn to before me the 23rd day of October 1832 in open court

Peter Lamar, Clerk.

Nathan Wright wrote his will 12 February 1836 in Lincoln Co., Ga.,[304] and he apparently died the next month if the pension file is correct.

Georgia

Lincoln County

In the name Of God Amen. I Nathan Wright Sr. of the county and state aforesaid being weak in body but of sound mind and memory do make and ordain this to be my last will and testament in the manner and form following.

1st. I commit my soul into the hands of God who gave it and wish my body to be buried in a decent and Christian like manner.

2nd. It is my wish and desire that after my death that all my just debts be paid.

3rd. I give and bequeath to my beloved wife Polly a certain Negroe man Jim during her natural life and then after her death to be equally divided between my three

---

[304] Transcript by Ed Tyer.

children, viz., Charlotte, Louisa and Nathan (Jr), also one bed, bedstead and furnature.

3rd. I give and bequeath to my daughter Charlotte a certain Negroe girl Mahaley.

4th. I give and bequeath Louisa a certain Negroe girl Milly and each of the above children, viz, Charlott, & Louisa one bed, stead and furnature.

5th. I give and bequeath unto my three children, viz, Charlott, Nathan and Louisa the whole of the Plantation whereon I live for their own proper use and benefit and for the support and maintenance of my beloved wife Polly her life time, that is with the exception of the part my son Meredith now lives on known as the John Wrights old place which tract of land I hereby give and bequeath to my son Meredith forever.

6th. I further give and bequeath unto my son Nathan one bed, bedstead & furnature.

7th. It is further my wish and desire that the balance of my property not here to fore disposed of shall be equally divided between my beloved wife and children viz, my wife Polly Wright, Aggy, Susan, Pleasant, Sally, Polly, David, Betsey, Charlotte, Nathan, Meredith, Matilda, Louisa and Pamelia share and share a like.

8th. I do hereby nominate and appoint my two sons Nathan Wright and Meredith Wright to be my lawful executors to this my last will & testament.

In witness hereof I have hereunto set my hand & seal this twelfth day of February in the year of our Lord one thousand eight hundred and thirty six.

Nathan Wright (his mark)

In presence of: Charles Latham, Thomas Simmons, Isham Mc Dowell, Peyton W. Sale

Children of NATHAN WRIGHT and ELIZABETH COCKERHAM are:

1. PLEASANT PRESLEY[3] WRIGHT, b. about 1785 Edgefield Dist., S. C.; d. about 1836 Putnam Co., Ga.; m. NANCY JONES 9 August 1812 Morgan Co., Ga.

2. AGNES[3] WRIGHT.

3. SUSANNAH[3] WRIGHT.
4. SARAH[3] WRIGHT, m. WILLIAM WRIGHT 2 December 1810 Lincoln Co., Ga.
5. MARY[3] WRIGHT, b. 20 August 1791 Wilkes Co., Ga.; d. 26 October 1873 Gordon Co., Ga.; m. WILLIAM BUCKNER JARRETT 18 November 1822 Lincoln Co., Ga., son of PETER JARRETT and SUSANNAH GRIFFIN; b. 17 February 1779 Abbeville Dist., S. C.; d. 8 November 1888 Gordon Co., Ga.

Children of NATHAN WRIGHT and MARY FULTON are:

6. DAVID FULTON[3] WRIGHT, SR., b. 10 December 1792 Wilkes Co., Ga.; d. 7 October 1867 Pine Level, Montgomery Co., Ala.; m. JEANETTE GOSS 11 January 1826 Newton Co., Ga., dau. of BENJAMIN GOSS, JR. and SUSANNAH DAVIS; b. 19 September 1807 Wilkes Co., Ga.; d. 26 November 1878 Montgomery Co., Ala.
7. ELIZABETH[3] WRIGHT, m. THOMAS JARRETT 1 July 1816 Lincoln Co., Ga.
8. CHARLOTTE[3] WRIGHT, b. about 1796; d. 27 February 1874 Lincoln Co., Ga.
9. NATHAN[3] WRIGHT, d. about 1870 Lincoln Co., Ga., d. s. p.
10. MATILDA[3] WRIGHT, b. 5 February 1805 Lincoln Co., Ga.; d. 25 October 1861 Montgomery Co., Ala.; m. ALLEN FRAZER 12 October 1830 Lincoln Co., Ga., son of ARTHUR FRAZER and MARY GOODRUM; b. 10 August 1807 Lincoln Co., Ga.; d. Montgomery Co., Ala.
11. MEREDITH W.[3] WRIGHT, b. about 1806 Lincoln Co., Ga.; d. 5 November 1860 Montgomery Co., Ala.; m. JANE M. FRAZER, dau. of ARTHUR FRAZER and MARY GOODRUM; b. about 1810 Lincoln Co., Ga.; d. about 1867 Montgomery Co., Ala.
12. LOUISA[3] WRIGHT, b. 21 June 1807 Lincoln Co., Ga.; d. 7 February 1867; m. LLEWELLYN EVANS,

JR., 9 December 1849 Lincoln Co., Ga., son of LLEWELLYN EVANS, SR. and MARY HARRIS; d. 7 June 1889 Montgomery Co., Ala.

13. PERMELIA ARMETICIA[3] WRIGHT, b. 29 November 1810 Lincoln Co., Ga.; d. 21 January 1849 Lincoln Co., Ga.; m. LLEWELLYN EVANS, JR., 14 December 1831 Lincoln Co.,. Ga.; son of LLEWELLYN EVANS, SR. and MARY HARRIS; d. 7 June 1889 Montgomery Co., Ala.; he m. (2) LOUISA WRIGHT; m. (3) EVALINE CONE 4 September 1867 Montgomery Co., Ala.

v. JOB[2] WRIGHT, b. 1757 Virginia; d. 1838 Rutherford Co., N. C.; m. SARAH NEWTON; d. 27 April 1811 Mecklenburg Co., Virginia.

The tax lists record the appearance of Job Wright in the upper district of Mecklenburg County in 1787.[305] He had one poll. On 8 October 1787 Job Wright bought land from Benjamin "Cocurum," probably Cockerham.[306] The tax list for 1789 does record the appearance of John Wright, "himself exempt" in the upper district along with Job Wright.[307] John Wright was also exempt in 1790,[308] but paid one poll in 1791,[309] so was almost certainly born in 1770/71. John is not listed after 1791, but Job Wright is on the tax list for the upper district almost continuously through 1814. In 1795 Job Wright has a second poll, a Thomas whose last name I could not decipher.[310]

Curiously, I also found Job Wright listed on the tax list for Halifax Co., Va., in 1787.

Benjamin Cockerham appears on the tithe list of Lunenburg Co., Va., as early as 1748, living near Drury Allen in what became Mecklenburg County in 1765.[311]

On 19 Jan 1818 Job Wright and Polly Wright sold land to James H. Newton.[312] Job Wright is not listed in

---

[305] Mecklenburg Co., Va. Tax List, Upper District, 1787, p. 37.
[306] Mecklenburg Co., Va., Deed Book 7:193.
[307] Mecklenburg Co., Va. Tax List, Upper District, 1789, p. 38-39.
[308] Mecklenburg Co., Va. Tax List, Upper District, 1790, p. 38.
[309] Mecklenburg Co., Va. Tax List, Upper District, 1791, p. 44.
[310] Mecklenburg Co., Va. Tax List, Upper District, 1795, p. 62.
[311] Bell, p. 66, District of Mr. Bacon.

the 1820 census, and there is no record of a will in Mecklenburg County, which suggests that he left the area in 1818. From the tax lists and deeds we can also assume that John Wright and Nathan Wright were brothers of Job Wright. Job Wright's marriage to "Polly" is not recorded.

The descendants of Job Wright have been published.[313] Job Wright married Sarah Newton, who died in Mecklenburg Co., Va., 27 April 1811. His eldest son, Newton Wright, removed to Rutherford Co., N. C. following service in the War of 1812, for which his wife filed a pension application, and was joined by his father, Job Wright, who died there in 1838. According to these authors, he was born in 1757, probably in Southampton Co., Va., based upon a receipt for donation of beef for public use dated October 1781.

"There is a monument in the Pleasant Grove church cemetery erected in his honor inscribed as follows: "Job Wright 1757-1838. Soldier in the Revolutionary War. Early Planter of what is now Cleveland County. Leader of men. Father of large, influential and useful family. Set good example of Christian Living." The Job Wright cemetery, where Job and his second wife, Polly Sparks and several other family members are buried, is located in #6 township about two miles north of Shelby, near the old Mc Brayer Mineral Springs."[314]

The John Wright who appears on the tax lists with Job Wright is likely a younger brother. His birth year can be estimated as 1770, since he turned 21 between the collection of the tax in 1790 and 1791. I have no information as to where he went, although North Carolina seems likely.

---

[312] Mecklenburg Co., Va., Deed Book 17:158.

[313] Wright, Theresa and Curtis, Joanna. Job Wright of Mecklenburg Co., Va. http://footprints.org/9-100125.htm and http://footprints.org/9-100136.htm.

[314] Ibid. They also mention they have a letter from a sister of Job Wright, Sally Griffin, who wrote him from Georgia in 1813, sending it through Mr. Flournoy. The letter implies a number of other family members. I cannot find they have posted the letter. Job Wright's tombstone is located at http://www.findagrave.com, #17771670.

Children of JOB WRIGHT and SARAH NEWTON are:

1. NEWTON[3] WRIGHT, b. 21 April 1792 Mecklenburg Co., Va.; d. 15 January 1849 Cleveland Co., N. C.;[315] m. SARAH FARMER 10 March 10 1802 Mecklenburg Co., Va., daughter of JAMES FARMER. She was born 10 March 1802 Mecklenburg Co., ,Va.; d. 8 February 1882 Cleveland Co., N. C.

   On 15 July 15 1813 Newton Wright volunteered for Poole's Company, 6th Regiment of Virginia Militia, commanded by Lt. Col. G. Green and Col. Sharp. He was discharged at Norfolk 17 October 1813 due to inability to perform his duties because of illness.[316] Newton Wright appears in the 1820 Census for Mecklenburg Co., Va., with no children.[317]

2. GEORGE[3] WRIGHT, b. before 1794 Mecklenburg Co., Va.; d. after 1838 Georgia.

3. JOHN[3] WRIGHT, b. 5 May 1794 Mecklenburg Co., Va.; d. 11 September 1851 Rutherford Co., N. C.; m. PEGGY BOSWELL 13 February 13 1822 Rutherford Co., N. C.[318]

4. MARY[3] WRIGHT, m. _____ JACKSON, d. Mecklenburg Co., Va.

vi. JARRETT[2] WRIGHT was born say 1766 in Lunenburg Co., Va.; d. before 16 November 1820 Lincoln Co., Ga.; m. TABITHA HOWELL 28 November 1791 Brunswick Co., Va.

   Jarrett Wright, John Wright, Laban Wright, Nancy Wright, and Sarah Wright appear together in the 1792 tax list for the lower district of Brunswick Co., Va.[319]

---

[315] Both are buried in Wright Family Cemetery, McBrayer Mineral Springs, Cleveland Co., N. C. http://findagrave.com, #52240135.

[316] Ibid.

[317] 1820 Census Mecklenburg Co., Va., p. 151A, 00010-00100, with one slave.

[318] This may well be the John Wright listed in the 1820 Census, Mecklenburg Co., Va., p. 163, 10010-00100.

[319] 1792 Tax List Lower District, Brunswick Co., Va., p. 27. I have previously noted that he might be a grandson of 1829 Austin Wright of Mecklenburg Co., Va.

In 1793 James Wright has been added, and John Wright is designated as "Jr."[320]

On 9 February 1790 Thomas Jarratt, Drury Allen, John Wray, John Wright & Nancy Wright sold to Joseph Wright of Lunenburg County for £200 a tract of 100 acres down Stony Creek adjacent to Stephen Mize, Arthur Turner, Parsons Wright, Julius Hight, and Thomas Jarratt.[321] Subsequently, on 17 November 1792 Thomas Jarrott, Joseph Wright, John Wright, Drury Allen, John Wray, and Nancy Wright (legatees of the estate of Thomas Jarrott, dec'd) sold to Luke Taylor for £60 a tract of land containing 117 acres in Lunenburg County on Stony Creek.[322] From these deeds I conclude that Nancy Wright was the daughter of Thomas Jarrett, and sister-in-law to Joseph Wright, John Wright, Drury Allen, and John Wray. I conclude that "Jarrott" Wright is son of Nancy Wright. The tax list also implies that Nancy has at least one son at home.

Jarrett Wright married Tabitha Howell 28 November 1791 in Brunswick Co., Virginia, with John Wright as bondsman. The ceremony was performed by Edward Dromgoole.[323] Jarrett Wright appeared on the tax lists from 1792 through 1796.

Jarrett Wright was listed as a tax defaulter in Wilkes Co., Ga., in 1799 and 1802.[324] Jarrett Wright was listed in Hancock County, Georgia, in the 1812 tax list. Jarrett Wright appears in Greene County, Georgia, in 1820.[325] He was over age 45, (born before 1775), as was Tabitha, and had one female under 10, two males under 10, two males 10-15, one 16-18, and one 18-26. Jarrett Wright's orphans were fortunate drawers in the 1832 Cherokee Land Lottery, and were in Capt. Cannon's district of Wilkinson County.

---

[320] 1793 Tax List Lower District, Brunswick Co., Va., p. 29.

[321] Lunenburg Co., Va., Deed Book 15:503. Evans, p. 52.

[322] Lunenburg Co., Va., Deed Book 16:346. Evans, p. 55.

[323] Knorr, p. 109.

[324] Avery, William. Avery & Watson Descendants. 1 March 2013. Located at http://wc.rootsweb.ancestry.com, (db. avery2). Cited hereafter as Avery.

[325] 1820 Census Greene Co., Ga., Capt. Slaughter's district, p. 211.

The will of Jarrett Wright was written 10 October 1820 and proved in Greene County, Georgia on 16 November 1820.[326] In the will he noted that he had already provided his daughter, Nancy Palmer, household and kitchen furniture and a feather bed. He left his son John a shotgun. He left four shoats to his son Reddick Pearce Wright. He left his daughter Lucy furniture and a featherbed. Daughter Maria received six chairs. He left a loom and the balance of his possessions to his wife, Tabitha. Tabitha Wright and John Oslin were appointed executors, and the will was witnessed by H. G. Slaughter, Reuben Brown, and Nathaniel Howell.

Children of JARRETT WRIGHT and TABITHA HOWELL are:

1. NANCY[3] WRIGHT, m. JAMES PALMER 21 July 1816 Greene Co., Ga.
2. MARIA[3] WRIGHT.
3. JOHN WESLEY[3] WRIGHT, d. 1869 Greene Co., Ga.; m. CELIA ROWLAND 11 January 1825 Greene Co., Ga., dau. of HIRAM ROWLAND and RHODA ATKINSON; b. 1805 Greene Co., Ga.
4. REDDICK PEARCE[3] WRIGHT, b. about 1813 Georgia; d. after 1880 Wood Co., Texas; m. (1) MIRIAM EUGENIA MALLORY 18 November 1832 Greene Co., Ga.; m. (2) MATILDA CHAPPELL 25 December 1837 Pike Co., Ga.; m. (3) SARAH A. (_____) FINCHER 23 January 1868 Elmore Co., Ala.

Reddick Wright, 37, Matilda Wright, 33, and the children, William 15, Mary A., 12, John F., 10, James A., 9, Malinda 6, Alexandria 4, Sarah A, 3, and Eugenia, newborn, are in Upson Co., Ga., in 1850.[327]

R. P. Wright, 52, Matilda, 38, James A. 18, Malinda A. 15, Alexander 13, Sarah A. E. 11, Eugenia 9, Frances 7, Benjamin H. 5, Margaret

---

[326] Greene Co., Ga., Will Book F:44. Cited by Avery.
[327] 1850 Census Upson Co., Ga., Militia District 86, p. 318B-319A, #480/480

3, and James A. Chappell, 37, are living in Coosa Co., Ala., in 1860.[328] Frances was born in Georgia and Benjamin was born in Alabama, so they presumably moved about 1855. On one side is J. S. Wright, 21, b. Georgia, and Georgia A., 5/12, and on the other is William L. Wright, 25 Ga., Julia A., 18 Ala., and Mary J., 1. These match with his sons John and William.[329]

5. LUCINDA[3] WRIGHT, m. JORDAN ROWLAND 12 July 1829 Greene Co., Ga., son of JORDAN ROWLAND and SARAH SWAN; b. 1814 Georgia;

Jordan and Lucy Rowland are present in the 1850 Census for Greene County, Ga., along with James 14, Littleberry 12, Reddick 10, William 8, and Nancy, 4.[330]

vii. SUGAR[2] WRIGHT, d. before 21 January 1818 Lincoln Co., Ga., d. s. p.

Sugar Wright served in Capt. James Johnson's company, 6th Virginia Regiment, that served from 2 February 1776 to 31 May 1777.[331] Thomas and Parsons Wright are also in the same company.

Sugar Wright was present in the 1810 tax list for Lincoln Co., Ga., in Capt. Mayes' district along with William Wright.[332] Sugar Wright wrote his will 28 November 1817 and gave $50 to his beloved brother, William, then left the remainder of his estate to be divided between brothers William and Isaac Wright.[333]

viii. ISAAC[2] WRIGHT, b. about 1780.

Isaac Wright appeared with 1 poll in the Lincoln Co., Ga., Tax List of 1806 in Capt. Smith's district,

---

[328] 1860 Census Coosa Co., Ala., Southern Division, p. 179, #1254/1275.

[329] W. T. Wright, 35 Ga., J. A., 33 Ala., J. A. f 12, and M. A. M., f 7, Ala., are in Wood Co., Texas in 1880. [Precinct 1, p. 519B, #273/273.] "L. A." Wright, 23 M, Ga., is living next door in the household of M. A. Gilliland (f). and this could be Alexander. He is listed as a farmer.

[330] 1850 Census Greene Co., Ga., Militia District 147, p. 86B, #214/214.

[331] Bell, p. 218.

[332] 1810 Tax List, Lincoln Co., Ga., located 9 May 2013 at http://files.usgwarchives.net/ga/lincoln/taxlists/1810indx.txt.

[333] Lincoln Co., Ga., Will Book D:70, 28 November 1817/6 December 1817. Witnesses were Wm. E. Hughes, Wiley E. Tatum, and William Greer. The will was recorded 21 January 1818.

along with William (1 poll), Nathan (222 and 150 acres), John (100 acres), Jack (1 poll), Charles (1 poll), John Griffin (165) acres, and William Wright (300 acres.)[334]

Isaac Wright was taxed for 100 acres on Mill Creek, Lincoln Co., Ga., in 1818, Capt. Stokes' list, along with John Wright and Nathan Wright.[335]

Isaac Wright, 26-45, appears in the 1820 Census for Lincoln Co., Ga.,[336] along with a wife and three sons.

After 1810 Joseph Wright of Lunenburg Co., Virginia

Joseph Wright was of age by 1760 when he witnessed the sale of land from James Mize to his two sons-in-law, John and Thomas Wright.[337]

Either Thomas or John Wright was the father of another Joseph Wright when James Mize wrote his will, mentioning his grandson Joseph. There is only one Joseph Wright listed in the extant tax lists, which I believe is the older man, since he appears to have lived on Stony Creek most of his life.

Joseph Wright appears on the tax lists consistently from their beginning in 1782 through 1810. He is not present after 1810. He is listed in Lunenburg Co., Va., in 1810 along with his wife, one boy under 10, two girls under 10, one 10-16, one 16-26, and one 26-45.[338]

On 9 February 1790 Thomas Jarratt, Drury Allen, John Wray, John Wright and Nancy Wright sold to Joseph Wright a tract of 100 acres described as "down Stony Creek to Stephen Mize, Arthur Turner, Parsons Wright, Julius Hight, Thomas Jarratt."[339] The indenture was signed by mark by Thomas Jarratt,

---

[334] Georgia Property Tax Digests 1799-1806. Online database located at Ancestry.com. Accessed 9 May 2013.

[335] 1818 Tax List, Lincoln Co., Ga. Online database located at Ancestry.com. Accessed 9 May 2013.

[336] 1820 Census Lincoln Co., Ga., p. 158. [21010-00010].

[337] This was indicate a birth year of before 1739, and the lack of a listing in 1754 would imply that he was born after 1733. Given that his first born is probably Jarrett Wright, born in 1758, I think he was born in the earlier part of that range, say 1735.

[338] 1810 Census Lunenburg Co., Va., p. 364.

[339] Lunenburg Co., Va., Deed Book 15:503. Evans, p. 52. A student of the Jarrett family identifies Thomas Jarrett, Sr., as father of Mary Jarrett, who married Benjamin Gist, Sarah Jarrett who married Thomas Wright, an unknown daughter who married John Wright, another unknown daughter who married John Wray, Nancy Wright, who married an unknown Wright, and Eleanor, who married Drury Allen. Donald. Henry Gerard/Jarrett

176

John Wray, and Nancy Wright, and apparently signed by Drury Allen and Nancy Wright. However, the latter point is apparently refuted by an indenture from the same parties dated 17 November 1792, when all signed by mark.[340] The land appears to be the estate of Thomas Jarrett, Senior, and the sellers are his heirs, suggesting that John Wright married a Miss Jarrett and Nancy Jarrett married a Mr. Wright.

On 1 September 1790 Arthur Turner sold 50 acres of land to Stephen Mize described as bounded by Thomas Wright, John Wright, Joseph Wright, and Parsons Wright.[341]

On 21 January 1791 Parsons Wright sold to Julius Hite for £18 a 40 acre tract of land adjacent to Emanuel Callis, Joseph Wright, Stephen Mize, and his own land.[342] On 17 November 1810 Joseph Wright and Sarah Wright, his wife, sold to Thomas Callis for £118 a 100 acre tract adjacent Benjamin Lewis, the estate of Emanuel Callis, dec'd, Jesse Turner, John Mize, Julius Hite.[343] Joseph and Sarah Wright both signed by mark. This deed is consistent with the tax lists suggesting he left Lunenburg Co., Va., about 1810, by which time he was at least 60 years old.

Sarah's maiden name is implied by the naming of her son, Jarrett, but also supported by the land deeds.[344]

Genealogical Summary

1. JOSEPH[2] WRIGHT was born about 1735 in Virginia and died after 1810, probably in Lunenburg Co., Va. He married SARAH JARRETT about 1757 in Lunenburg Co., Va.

Children of JOSEPH WRIGHT and SARAH JARRETT are:

  i. JARRETT[3] WRIGHT, b. 29 March 1758 Lunenburg Co., Va.; d. 20 December 1835 Allen Co., Ky.; m. ELIZABETH GRIFFIN; d. after 1843 Allen Co., Ky.[345]

Family. 29 August 2011. Located at http://wc.rootsweb.ancestry.com, (db. jarrdff). Cited hereafter as Donald.

[340] Lunenburg Co., Va., Deed Book 16:346. Evans, p. 55.

[341] Lunenburg Co., Va., Deed Book 16:98. Evans, p. 17.

[342] Lunenburg Co., Va., Deed Book 16:115. Evans, p. 19.

[343] Lunenburg Co., Va., Deed Book 22:174. Evans, p. 54.

[344] A detailed study of the Jarrett family reaches the same conclusions. [Donald.] He reports analysis of the various land deeds involving the Wright, Mize, and Jarrett families along Stony Creek.

[345] Simpson County was formed in 1819 from Allen, Logan and Warren Co., Ky. Allen County was formed 1815 from Barren and Warren Counties. Barren County was

Jarrett Wright was born 29 March 1758 Lunenburg County, Virginia, son of Joseph Wright.[346] He enlisted in the Virginia line from that county, and after the war moved to Halifax County, where he resided for seven years. He subsequently moved to Caswell County, Va., and then to Allen County, Kentucky, where he filed his application on 22 August 1832. Jarrett Wright died 20 December 1835.[347] He married Elizabeth Griffin in August 1781, [probably in Lunenburg or Halifax County, Virginia], and she applied for a pension in his name 13 August 1839 in Allen Co., Ky., age 80, and she was still living there in 1843.[348] Her application was supported by a joint affidavit of Harbert and Griffin Wright, and an affidavit by John Wright, aged 69 years and 3 months, (birth May 1770), whose relationship is not given.

The Halifax County, Virginia, tax lists show Jarrett Wright present in 1782, 1783, and 1784, so he must have moved there about 1777.

Jarrett Wright of Caswell County, N. C., purchased 307 acres on Double Creek of the South Hico River adjacent the claims of Jesse Jones, John Smith, and Aaron Christenberry from Nicholas Christenberry 4 January 1787.[349]

---

formed 1798 from Green and Warren County. Warren County was formed 1796 from Logan County. Green County was formed 1792 from Lincoln and Nelson County, and Lincoln County was formed 1780 from Kentucky Co., Va. All of these counties lie almost due west of Lunenburg County, Virginia, along the Kentucky/Tennessee border in the middle part of the state. There have been major record losses, so the use of Allen County is from the RW pension application, although the graves are located in Simpson County.

[346] Revolutionary War Pension Application W627, paid to his widow, Elizabeth.

[347] Buried in Smith Cemetery NE 3, Franklin, Simpson Co., Ky., http://www.findagrave.com, memorial #47644608.

[348] Buried in Smith Cemetery NE 3, Franklin, Simpson Co., Ky., http://www.findagrave.com, memorial #99223633.

[349] Caswell Co., N. C., Deed Book E:131. Cited in Kendall, Katherine K. Caswell County, North Carolina, Deed Books, 1777-1817. (Easley S. C.: Southern Historical Press, 1989,) p. 49. There are two other deeds of interest. (p. 101) [DB E:251] John Wright of Caswell to Richard Duty of Granville for £150, 181 acres on both sides of S. Hico adjacent Carter Lea, owen Lea. S/ Phebe Wright. 23 Oct 1787. Wit: Charles Bostick and George Duty; and (p. 118) [DB G:15-16] Richard Wright of Caswell to Reuben Parrott of same for £135 a 135 acre tract on E. side of S. Hico adj. Stanley Qualls, Charles Bostick, Derby Henley, James D. Henley. 15 November 1788. Wit: Charles Bostick, Richard Bostick, John Wright. The deeds imply a relationship between John Wright and Richard Wright, but I

178

Jarrett Wright sold 100 acres of land on Trammel's Fork or Drake Creek in Warren Co., Ky., to Joseph Roberts for $300 on 23 January 1807.[350] Jarrett Wright purchased 50 acres on the west side of Trammel's Fork of Drake's Creek for $120 from John Sherry on 26 May 1809.[351] This deed was witnessed by Joseph Wright.

Jarrett Wright is listed in the 1810 Census for Warren Co., Ky., age greater than 45, with three males and one female, plus Elizabeth, also over 45 years of age.[352] Also listed on the same page is a young man named Joseph Wright,[353] and John Wright.[354]

Allen County was created in 1815 from part of Warren County, including the area occupied by Jarrett Wright. In 1825, he was taxed on two tracts of land on Trammel's Fork, one for 150 acres, and one 200 acres.[355] He appeared on multiple tax lists thereafter, but it does not appear that he moved.

Jarrett "Right" is in Allen County, Ky., in 1830 with himself 60-69, one male 20-29, and his wife, also 60-69 along with seven slaves.[356] One student of this family reported that he died in Simpson Co., Ky., although he was buried in Allen County, and it is from his tombstone that the dates were identified. His son

---

cannot connect either to the John Wright who died 1849 Allen Co., Ky., who was born 1770 in Lunenburg Co., Va.

[350] Warren Co., Ky., Deed Book B2:362. Cited in Murray, Joyce M. Deed Abstracts of Warren County, Kentucky, 1797-1812, (Deed Books A1, B2, C3, D4, E5.) (Dallas Texas, 1985,) p. 30. Cited as Murray.

[351] Warren Co., Ky., Deed Book D4:172. Murray, p. 64.

[352] 1810 Census Warren Co., Ky., p. 268. [02101-10001].

[353] 1810 Census Warren Co., Ky., p. 268. [10100-00100].

[354] 1810 Census Warren Co., Ky., p. 268. [22010-21010]. There are a number of other individuals named Wright in this census, but none of the others appear proximate to Jarrett Wright in the lists. Jacob Wright can be excluded, as "Polly Wright, the first child of Jacob and Miriam (Held) Wright was born on 16 November 1797...The 1797 Tax Rolls of Warren County show that Jacob and his mother, Elizabeth, were placed on the rolls in July 1797. Elizabeth (Waters) Wright is the Widow Wright mentioned as one of the first four families living in Barren County...(established 1798, effective 1799.)" Jackson, Everts C. Item About the Wright Family. Traces of South Central Kentucky 14(1):58-59, 1986. Another source says they came from South Carolina without producing any documentation.

[355] Gardner, Jeanetta S. Allen County, Kentucky, Tax Records. (Collierville, TN: 1999,) p. 29.

[356] 1830 Census Allen Co., Ky., p. 47. Also in the family are one man 60-69, presumably a son, and his wife, 50-59, plus one male 5-9, and one 15-19, and one female 10-14, and two females 15-19.

Harbert was living there in 1840, so it is certainly possible that he was at his son's house when he died.

Children of JARRETT WRIGHT and ELIZABETH GRIFFIN are:

1. HARBERT[4] WRIGHT, m. ERWIN 30 January 1813 Warren Co., Ky.[357]
   Harbard Wright, age 50-59, is listed in the 1840 Census for Simpson Co., Ky., p. 190, along with what appears to be his wife, and a son/daughter with spouse and two young children.

2. GRIFFIN[4] WRIGHT, b. 3 May 1799 Caswell Co., N. C.; d. 13 October 1843 Allen Co., Ky.; m. (2) NANCY (V.) WILLIAMS 9 March 1837 Allen Co., Ky.; b. 31 October 1816; d. 8 June 1894 Allen Co., Ky.[358]

   Griffin Wright wrote his last will and testament 5 October 1843 and it was proved 11 December 1843. He left his estate to his wife Nancy and named his children in birth order as Joseph L. Wright, Frances E. Wright, and Lucinda J. Wright, William B. McElroy and wife Nancy Wright were named executors and witnesses were Reuben Sherry, Robert Harris, and William Russell.

   Joseph L. Wright was wounded at Shiloh in April 1862 and evacuated to Louisville, Ky., where he died. His mother went there, claimed the body and brought it home. The sheet she used as a shroud was preserved as a memorial.[359]

---

[357] Herbert Wright m. Erwin Graham 30 January 1813 Warren Co., Ky. Gorin, Sandra K. Warren County, Kentucky, Marriages 1797 through 1851. (Glasgow, KY: Gorin Genealogical Publ., 1999), pp. 201-202. She notes that consent was given for him by Jarrett Wright, so he was under 21, and consent for her was given by George Graham. Charles Wright was security.

[358] Buried Wright Cemetery, Trammell, Allen Co., Ky.; second wife is Nancy V. (Williams) Wright, b. 31 October 1816, d. 8 June 1894, buried same place. Their marriage license was granted 9 March 1837 and the ceremony was performed by Thomas Lyles, who performed ceremonies for a number of the children of John Wright and Mary Brewer. There is a son, Joseph L. Wright, b. 7 December 1837; d. 2 May 1862 as the third and final burial in this cemetery.

[359] Simpson County, Kentucky Families Past and Present. (Paducah: Turner Publ., Co., 1974,) pp. 416-417. Lucinda Jane Wright married William Ewing Dixon according to this family report.

Nancy V. Wright wrote her will in February 1894 and it was proved 11 June 1894 in Allen Co., Ky. She left her estate to her daughter, Lucinda J. Dixon, and also left $5.00 to Francis E. Butler.

3. CHARLES D. WRIGHT, b. 1791 Caswell Co., N. C.; d. 8 August 1860 Montgomery Co., Illinois; m. REBECCA LYNCH 29 May 1811 Warren Co., Ky.; b. 1790; d. 1843 Montgomery Co., Illinois.[360]

ii. JOHN[3] WRIGHT was born May 1770 Lunenburg Co., Va., and died before 18 May 1849 Allen Co., Ky.; m. MARY BREWER 12 October 1796 Brunswick Co., Va.

John Wright deposed that he was born about May 1770 in Lunenburg Co., Virginia, when he provided a witness for the pension claim of Jarrett Wright. John Wright married "Polly" Brewer 12 October 1796 in Brunswick Co., Va., with Willis Brewer as his security and Reuben Wright as his witness.[361] John Wright usually appears on the tax lists as "Junior" to distinguish him from 1810 John Wright of Brunswick Co., Va. This label first appears in 1793, and recurs in 1794 (p. 29); 1795 (p. 26); and 1796 (p. 28). In 1796 he is shown with one slave and two horses.

John Wright received an original patent for land in Warren County, Kentucky 21 September 1798.[362] As noted, he was listed a few persons down from Jarrett and Joseph Wright in the 1810 Census. His land also went into Allen Co., Ky., when it was created in 1815. In 1825 he was taxed on 100 acres of land on Difficult Creek, obtained by patent, and 100 acres purchased from W. Duncan.[363] There must have been some uncertainty about the name of the waterway, though, as

---

[360] Buried Mulberry Grove Cemetery, Montgomery Co., Illinois. http://www.findagrave.com, #98421047.

[361] Knorr, p. 109.

[362] Gorin, Sandra K. Warren County, Ky., Survey Book 1, 1797-1814. Glasgow, KY: Gorin Genealogical Publ, 1993, p. 29. The tract was described as 120 acres, certificate #2311 on Spring Creek.

[363] Gardner, Jeanetta S. Allen County, Kentucky, Tax Records. (Collierville, TN: 1999,) p. 29.

in 1826 he was taxed for 200 acres on Middle Fork,[364] and in 1829 the 200 acres was on Bays Fork.[365]

A similar conclusion was reached by Mildred Mackey, who responded to an online post about this family in 2005.[366] She showed children before 1805 as being born in Virginia. She assumed Lunenburg Co., Va., but the land deeds suggest Brunswick Co., and the children born after 1805 being born in Allen Co., Ky. John Wright wrote his will in Allen Co., Ky., 13 February 1844 and it was proved 18 May 1849.[367] He mentions a wife, but does not name her. He left his property in life estate to her, with son William to inherit after her death. He left the balance of his estate to be divided amongst his children: Philip Wright, James K. Wright, Nancy Barnes, Jesse Wright, Sally Wright, Temperance Sherry, Matilda Taylor, Washington W. Wright, Wesley Wright, and William Wright. He named his sons Philip and Washington Wright as executors. Witnesses were Benjamin Jackson and Samuel Jackson.

Children of JOHN WRIGHT and MARY BREWER are:[368]

1. CYNTHIA[4] WRIGHT, b. 20 October 1805 Brunswick Co., Va.; d. 18 January 1867 Nashville, Washington Co., Illinois; m. HARTWELL MOORE 14 February 1822 Allen Co., Ky., son of WILSON MOORE; b. 21 March 1796 Virginia; d. 20 April 1865 Washington Co., Illinois.[369]

---

[364] Ibid., p. 58.

[365] Ibid., p. 88.

[366] Mackey, Mildred. 6 May 2005. http://genforum.genealogy.com/wright/messages/18673.html. She descends from Jesse L. Wright and Catherine Morris.

[367] Allen Co., Ky., Will Books. (WPA transcription without location identification).

[368] Early Allen County Marriage Records 1815-1889. Accessed online 7 March 2013 at http://www.rootsweb.ancestry.com/~kyallen/marriage_records.html. These confirmed the information obtained from Mildred Mackey.

[369] Dates are from Leitner, Mary K. Owner.7 December 2008.Located at http://wc.rootsweb.ancestry.com, (db. mkleitner). Children all born in Bowling Green, Warren Co., Ky.

Hartwell Moore and Lucinda, along with their children, all born in Kentucky, are living in Washington Co., Illinois, in 1850.[370]

2. PHILLIP[4] WRIGHT, b. about 1795 Brunswick Co., Va.; m. SUSAN JACKSON 27 April 1818 Allen Co., Ky., dau. of JORDAN JACKSON and NANCY WRIGHT.

3. JAMES KENSON[4] WRIGHT, b. about 1799 Brunswick Co., Va.; m. (1) MALINDA TODD 14 January 1822 Allen Co., Ky.; m. (2) ELIZABETH DOUGLAS 9 January 1843 Allen Co., Ky.

4. L.[4] WRIGHT, b. 1801; d.s.p.

5. NANCY[4] WRIGHT, b. 6 September 1800 Brunswick Co., Va.; d. 15 April 1878; m. NATHANIEL BARNES 2 November 1824 Allen Co., Ky.; b. 3 April 1803 Brunswick Co., Va.; d. 14 May 1869 Washington Co., Illinois.[371]

Nathaniel Barnes and Nancy along with their children are living in Washington Co., Illinois, in 1850.[372] The oldest child listed was Stephen H., 21, born in Illinois. They are seven households away from Hartwell Moore and Cynthia (Wright) Moore, Nancy Wright's sister.

6. JESSE L.[4] WRIGHT, b. 1803 Brunswick Co., Va.; m. CATHERINE MORRIS 5 May 1829 Allen Co., Ky.

7. SALLY[4] WRIGHT, b. 1808 Allen Co., Ky.; d. s. p.

8. TEMPERANCE[4] WRIGHT, b. 10 March 1810 Allen Co., Ky.; d. 18 February 1888 Allen Co., Ky.; m. REUBEN SHERRY 26 October 1829 Allen Co., Ky., son of JOHN SHERRY and WINNIFRED HORTON; b. 10 December 1818 North Carolina; d. 7 July 1873 Allen Co., Ky.[373]

---

[370] 1850 Census Washington Co., Ill., District 20, p. 155B, #836/836.

[371] Date from Lucinda. Birds of a Feather. 15 February 2013. Located at http://wc.rootsweb.ancestry.com, (db mlb2).

[372] 1850 Census Washington Co., Illinois, District 20, p. 155A, #829/829.

[373] Buried in cemetery located on the farm of Spence Davis, Allen Co., Ky. Accessed 6 March 2013 at http://www.allencountyky.com/database/death/cemetery/spencedavis.html.

9. MATILDA[4] WRIGHT, b. 1812 Allen Co., Ky.; m. WILLIAM TAYLOR 15 December 1840 Allen Co., Ky.; b. 1824 Monroe Co., Ky.; d. 26 January 1915 Allen Co., Ky.[374]

10. WASHINGTON[4] WRIGHT, b. 16 February 1814 Allen Co., Ky.; d. 4 August 1890 Montgomery Co., Ill.; m. (1) LOUISA WILLOUGHBY 24 December 1835 Allen Co., Ky., divorced before 1848; m. (2) ELIZABETH ALDERSON 8 March 1848, dau. of WILLIAM ALDERSON and MARY ORR.[375]

11. WESLEY[4] WRIGHT, m. (1) MYSANATH DODSON 3 November 1837 Allen Co., Ky.; m. (2) MARY MCMURRAY 20 July 1840 Allen Co., Ky.

12. WILLIAM J.[4] WRIGHT, b. 15 December 1817 Allen Co., Ky.; d. 24 August 1874 Simpson Co., Ky.; m. NANCY DIXON 27 December 1836 Allen Co., Ky., dau. of WILLIAM DIXON and MARTHA ANN JACKSON; b. 10 April 1818 Allen Co., Ky.; d. 26 July 1893 Simpson Co., Ky.[376]

iii. LABAN[3] WRIGHT, b. before 1769 Lunenburg Co., Va.; d. before 27 July 1795 Brunswick Co., Va.

Laban Wright in the 1792 tax list is surely "Labin" Wright, whose will was written 29 May 1795 and probated 27 July 1795.[377] He left his mother, who is not named, "my sow & six pigs, all my cattle, 2 chairs, my cotton, my bed, my bees, my hat"; to his brother John, "3 sows & shoats, my shoe boots, my mixed coat"; and to his brother Reuben "1 chest, my greatcoat, my close body coat, my bridle & saddle, my shoes & buckles, a couple of jackets." He instructed his

---

[374] He is probably the William Taylor 28, married to M. Taylor, 38, along with their children in the 1850 Census for Allen Co., Ky. [1850 Census Allen Co., Ky., p. 185A, #1209/1221.] His death certificate states that he was 89 years old and born in Monroe Co., Ky. [Kentucky Death Records 1852-1953. Viewed online at ancestry.com 6 March 2013.] He was buried at New Bethel Cemetery, Allen Co., Ky.

[375] Woodside Cemetery, Montgomery Co., Illinois.

[376] Dates are from tombstones in Salem Methodist Church Cemetery, Simpson Co., Ky. Cited by Glaze, Roxie. My Family. 11 June 2004. http://wc.rootsweb.ancestry.com, (db. :2897365). Note that Jarrett Wright is also buried in Simpson Co., Ky.

[377] Brunswick Co., Virginia, Will Book 5:624.

administrators to sell his horse to pay his debts. He does not mention any land and also forgot to name an administrator. He signed the will with an "X". The will was witnessed by Thomas Richardson[378], John Rodgers and Henry (x) Brewer. Administration was granted to John Wright, with Thomas Richardson as his security.

Mary Wright applied for letters of administration on the estate of James Wright with Laban Wright and John Wright as her securities and posted £1000 bond on 22 April 1793 in Brunswick Co., Va.[379] Edward Dromgoole,[380] William Warwick, Owen Myrick, and James Randle were appointed to appraise the estate.[381] From the estate record, it seems likely that there is a brother named Reuben Wright.

    iv.   REUBEN[3] WRIGHT. [382]

    v.   JAMES[3] WRIGHT, d. before 22 April 1793 Brunswick Co., Va.; m. MARY. She died 1793 Brunswick Co., Va.

Mary Wright applied for letters of administration on the estate of James Wright with Laban Wright and

---

[378] Another possible connection between the families is the fact that John Wright, possibly John (Taylor) Wright, served as administrator of the estate of Charles Gordon, whose account of estate was filed by Anne Richardson. (WB 4:451, 25 September 1775.)

[379] Brunswick Co., Va., Court Order Book 16:89, 22 April 1793.

[380] Edward Dromgoole's family papers are stored in the Southern Historical Collection of the Louis Rounds Wilson Special Collections Library at the University of North Carolina. An introduction to the papers says "Edward Dromgoole was an Irish immigrant who settled in Maryland, ca. 1770; became a Methodist minister, ca. 1772; and, after 1777, was a minister, merchant, and planter in Brunswick County, Va. Also represented are his sons Edward Dromgoole, Jr. (1788-1840), Methodist minister, physician, and planter of Brunswick County and Northampton County, N.C., and George Coke Dromgoole (1797-1847), lawyer, Virginia legislator, militia general, and Democratic U.S. representative. The collection includes chiefly correspondence and other papers, mainly 1840-1848, of Edward Dromgoole and sons Edward, Jr., and George. Pre-1807 papers are mainly letters from other Methodist ministers pertaining to the state of religion in Maryland and Virginia. Included is a letter, 17 September 1783, from John Wesley. From 1807 to 1830, there are family letters concerning religion, land holdings, and plantation business. Included is correspondence from friends who had moved to Ohio with family and regional news, descriptions of the financial prospects there, and exhortations to the Dromgooles to migrate. Accessed 7 February 2013 at http://www.lib.unc.edu/mss/inv/d/Dromgoole,Edward.html.

[381] Brunswick Co., Va., Court Order Book 16:90, 22 April 1793.

[382] Reuben Wright appears in conjunction with the will of Laban Wright and the marriage of John Wright. He may be the Reuben Wright described by Diane Etheridge. She reports that he was born in 1779 and died 1856 in Hancock Co., Indiana. He married Joanna Gilbert 1798 in Sussex Co., Va. Her most recent post on this subject is located at http://genforum.genealogy.com/wright/messages/24397.html.

John Wright as her securities and posted £1000 bond on 22 April 1793 in Brunswick Co., Va.[383] Edward Dromgoole, William Warwick, Owen Myrick, and James Randle were appointed to appraise the estate.[384]

vi. DAVID[3] WRIGHT, d. before 1790 Lunenburg Co., Va.; m. NANCY JARRETT Lunenburg Co., Va.[385]

viii. JOSEPH[3] WRIGHT, b. about 1788 Lunenburg Co., Va.; m. ELIZABETH McCLURE 30 April 1818 Allen Co., Ky., dau. of MOSES McCLURE; b. about 1800 Kentucky.[386]

Joseph Wright appears next to Jarrett Wright in the 1810 Census for Warren Co., Ky. He is married, with one male under 10. He was over 21 in 1809, but under 26 in 1810, giving him an estimated birth year of 1785-1788. His marriage to Elizabeth McClure is recorded in Allen Co., Ky.[387]

Unassigned Wrights of Lunenburg Co., Va.

Robert Wright married Sally Wright 5 March 1805 in Lunenburg Co., Va.

On 12 July 1809 Robert Wright sold to William Hite for £20 a tract of 20 acres adjacent Mize, Turner, and the ridge path. The deed was signed by the mark of Robert Wright.[388]

Robert J. Floyd and Millie Wright were married 6 November 1802 in Lunenburg Co., Va.

James Wright bought a tract of land from John Barnard 9 November 1769 in Lunenburg Co., Va.[389] This is probably 1825 James Wright of Newberry Dist., S. C.

[383] Brunswick Co., Va., Court Order Book 16:89, 22 April 1793.

[384] Brunswick Co., Va., Court Order Book 16:90, 22 April 1793.

[385] The deeds cited earlier establish Nancy Wright as a daughter of Thomas Jarrett. I think her husband was David, mostly because he appears only once in the tax lists.

[386] Foley, James and Foley, Marcia. Moses McClure Lineage. 5 October 2005. http://www.marciesalaskaweb.com/Genealogy/moses_mcclure_lineage.htm. 11 May 2013.

[387] Dodd, Jordan. Kentucky Marriages, 1802-1850. Accessed 27 April 2013 at Ancestry.com

[388] Lunenburg Co., Va., Deed Book 22:44. Evans, p. 14.

[389] Lunenburg Co., Va., Deed Book 11:313, 9 Nov 1769.

Chapter 5: Ancestry of John (Fox) Wright

The documentary data show 1832 John Wright of Clarke Co., Ga., is the son of John (Taylor) Wright, who was related to the Wrights of Waqua Creek, Brunswick Co., Va. These men appeared in Brunswick Co., Va., before 1762, but did not purchase land until 1777. Reuben Wright, a son of 1783 Robert Wright of Brunswick Co., Va., was noted as "of King William Co., Va." when he purchased land on Waqua Creek. King William Co., Va., is a burned record county, and review of the extant information available at the Library of Virginia in March 2006 confirmed the documentary trail was at a dead end,.

I submitted a sample for Y-DNA analysis as part of the Wright Surname Study.[1] My results were a 25/25 match for two men descended from after 1771 John Wright of Goochland Co., Va., "the carpenter," and 24/25 match with three men descended from 1767 Francis Wright of Amherst Co., Va., and a 24/25 match with two bases removed for one man also descended from 1767 Francis Wright.[2]

All of these men have been studied extensively by Robert N. Grant of Menlo Park, California.[3] The discussion that follows has been taken from his work.

1698 John Wright, bricklayer, of Lancaster Co., Virginia

John Wright first appears on the tithe list 10 November 1675 "at Mr. Champions, so he was born before 10 November 1659, and quite possibly before 10 November 1654. He does not appear in his own right until 1686, which implies that he had married and established his own household sometime in the intervening 11 years.

John Wright had difficulty getting paid for his work, as he was involved in a series of suits, sometimes as plaintiff, sometimes as defendant. John Wright, bricklayer, appeared in the court

---

[1] Family Tree DNA. Data are located at http://www.wright-dna.org.

[2] All of the variation in these 25 markers was as DYS 389ii, with my DNA showing 32 repeats, those of 1767 Francis Wright of Amherst showing 31 and 30 repeats respectively. These results over 14 generations are considered to be virtually identical and imply the last common ancestor should be found with 99% probability.

[3] See reference in the Preface.

records 10 October 1688 in a suit against Abraham Correll.[4] On 13 February 1688/89 John Wright, bricklayer, was sued by Mr. Jeremiah Packquet for 462 pounds of tobacco, and attachment was granted.[5] When Mr. Packquet did not appear, the case was dismissed with John Wright being granted his court costs 10 April 1689.[6] John Wright was again granted his court costs as a result of Robert Bennett not appearing to prosecute his case 10 July 1689.[7] Wright then sued Robert Bennett for 675 pounds of tobacco and received a judgment 8 Jan 1689/90.[8]

Jeremiah Packquet sued John Wright again 9 April 1690 for 462 pounds of tobacco, but Wright claimed this was not a lawful debt.[9] John Skelson appeared in the next court, 11 June 1690, and testified for Jeremiah Packquet, and Wright was ordered to pay the sum plus court costs.[10] John Wright also prosecuted a suit against John Morris on 9 April 1690 for payment of 990 pounds of tobacco. Since Morris did not appear, judgment was granted the plaintiff.[11] On 12 November 1690, John Wright, bricklayer, sued David Flaker for 506 pounds of tobacco.[12]

John Wright does not appear again until 12 March 1695/96, when he sued Morris Brazil's estate for 18 days work that had not been paid.[13] On 9 September 1696, he sued Henry Boatman for the work he had done.[14]

John Wright died before 11 August 1698 when William Janua, Administrator of the estate settled accounts with Thomas Buckley.[15] John Wright's suit against Mary Pullen was dismissed 12 January 1698/99 because of his death.[16] William Jannua, in his role as administrator, recorded a settlement of a suit against William More on 8 January 1698/99, [17] and presented a writ in

---

[4] Lancaster Co., Va., Court Order Book 3:92.
[5] Lancaster Co., Va., Court Order Book 3:100.
[6] Lancaster Co., Va., Court Order Book 3:103.
[7] Lancaster Co., Va., Court Order Book 3:106.
[8] Lancaster Co., Va., Court Order Book 3:116.
[9] Lancaster Co., Va., Court Order Book 3:120.
[10] Lancaster Co., Va., Court Order Book 3:124.
[11] Lancaster Co., Va., Court Order Book 3:122.
[12] Lancaster Co., Va., Court Order Book 3:141.
[13] Lancaster Co., Va., Court Order Book 3:339.
[14] Lancaster Co., Va., Court Order Book 3:362.
[15] Lancaster Co., Va., Court Order Book 4:46.
[16] Lancaster Co., Va., Court Order Book 4:59.
[17] Lancaster Co., Va., Court Order Book 4:62.

chancery against William Man 13 July 1699, [18] which resulted in the following award, recorded 12 October 1699. [19]

Lancaster County Court 12th of October 1699

To all to whome these present writing indented of Award shall come, Robert Carter of Lancaster County sendeth Greeting; Whereas divers controversies and suites have been had moved and depending between William Jannua, Administrator of Johnaran Wright deceast of ye one part and William Man of ye other part, both partys of ye aforesaid County, for touching and concerning ye goods and chattles and Estate of ye sd Wright in ye hands of William Man and for all causes suits and demands whatsoever yt have or may arrise concerning ye premises for ye appeasing whereof either of ye partys have elected and chosen me, Robert Carter, to be Arbitrator indifferently between them and to yt end have bound themselves either to other by Obligation in ye sum of twenty pounds sterling to stand and abide ye premises. Now Know ye yt I Robert Carter takeing upon me ye charge of ye award and intending yt a finall end shall be had and continued from henceforth between ye partys touching ye premises doe make and declare yt my award in manner following, that is to say, I doe award unto William Jannua in lieu and full satisfaction of all causes suits and demands whatsoever yt William Jannua as Administrator aforesaid hath may might or ought to have against William Man of touching or concerning all or any of ye premises ye sum of thirteen hundred pounds of good sound merchantable tobacco in cask convenient in ye aforesaid County. In Witness whereof I have hereunto sett my hand and seale this seventh day of 8br 1699

Robert

Carter
Recorded ultimo die 8br 1699
p Jos: Tayloe, Cl."

---

[18] Lancaster Co., Va., Court Order Book 4:71.
[19] Lancaster Co., Va., Court Order Book 4:90.

The tithe list for 12 November 1691 shows John Wright with two tithes.[20] Although a tithe was any white male over 16 years of age and any slave, male or female, over age 16, it seems unlikely from the foregoing court orders, that 1698 John Wright, bricklayer, was a member of the slaveholding class, but he could have had an indentured servant.

The tithe list of 15 December 1692 shows John Wright with only one tithe, and Mr. Mottrom Wright with seven.[21] The list of 5 December 1695 shows John Wright with three tithes and Mr. Mottrom Wright with 12.[22] The list of 11 November 1697 shows Samuel Wright with three tithes, two men named John Wright, one having only one tithe, the other having two, Francis Wright with one tithe, and Mottrom Wright with 18.[23] The tithe list for 10 November 1698 shows Samuel Wright with three tithes, Mottrom Wright with 22, Francis Wright and John Wright with one each.[24]

The tithe list for Christ Church Parish, 9 November 1699, shows Samuel Wright with three, John Wright, plasterer with two, Arthur Wright with one, and Mr. Mottrom Wright with 27.[25] The list for Christ Church Parish, 14 January 1700/01, shows Samuel Wright with three, Mottrom Wright with 27, John Wright one, Francis Wright, one, and John Wright, "planter", one.[26] The list for 10 December 1701 shows Arthur Wright, one, John Wright, planter, one, John Wright, two, Samuel Wright, one, and Richard Wright, 24.[27] The Christ Church Parish List of 12 November 1702 shows Charles Wright, two, John Wright, one, John Wright, two, Samuel Wright, four. Arthur Wright, with three tithables is now in St. Mary's White Chapel Parish.[28]

The Christ Church Parish tithe list of 11 November 1703 shows John Wright with one, then Charles Wright, one, John Wright, one, and Francis Wright, one, all adjacent, then another John Wright with two tithes. Arthur Wright is in St. Mary's White Chapel Parish with one tithe.[29] The list of 8 November 1704 shows

---

[20] Lancaster Co., Va., Court Order Book 3:187.
[21] Lancaster Co., Va., Court Order Book 3:332.
[22] Lancaster Co., Va., Court Order Book 3:332.
[23] Lancaster Co., Va., Court Order Book 4:32.
[24] Lancaster Co., Va., Court Order Book 4:49.
[25] Lancaster Co., Va., Court Order Book 4:93.
[26] Lancaster Co., Va., Court Order Book 4:127.
[27] Lancaster Co., Va., Court Order Book 4:153.
[28] Lancaster Co., Va., Court Order Book 5:12.
[29] Lancaster Co., Va., Court Order Book 5:54.

Charles and Francis Wright adjacent each other with one tithe, John Wright with one, John Wright, plaisterer, one, and Arthur Wright, two tithes.[30] On 13 December 1705, Arthur Wright had two tithes, Charles and Francis Wright, again adjacent, had one each, and John Wright had two tithes.[31]

It is uncertain if the reference to John Wright, planter, in the above lists, should, in fact be read as John Wright, plaisterer.[32] Since the first mention of "Planter" John was in January 1701, it is quite possible this is a reference to 1730 John Wright of Prince William Co., Va., son of 1713 Francis Wright of Westmoreland Co., Va., and nephew of 1700 Mottrom Wright of London, England, who was the "cousin" who inherited land in Lancaster Co., Va. However, a suit was recorded 9 December 1703, when "John Wright, plaisterer, with will of Mottrom Wright, deceased, annexed" obtained a judgment against John Wright for 800 pounds of tobacco.[33]

On 14 June 1699 Duncan Brown, servant to John Wright, "plaisterer," 17 years of age, was bound for seven years service.[34] Alice Stretchley, as executrix for the estate of John Stretchley, deceased, was involved in an ongoing suit against John Wright, "plaisterer," beginning in October 1699.[35] John Wright, plaisterer, was attached for 1500 pounds of tobacco when he failed to appear to answer the suit of James Haines 16 February 1699/1700.[36] As was typical, John Wright appeared to answer the suit on 13 March 1699/1700, when James Haines was identified as a blacksmith, and the amount was reduced to 772 pounds plus costs.[37] On 9 July 1702 Hugh Ladner obtained a judgment against John Wright, plaisterer, for 525 pounds of tobacco.[38]

John Wright appears to have had one son, John Wright, who was a plaisterer. There is evidence, though, that John Wright,

---

[30] Lancaster Co., Va., Court Order Book 5:108.

[31] Lancaster Co., Va., Court Order Book 5:138.

[32] The term "plaisterer" is still in use in England, and refers to a decorative plasterer, one who made the more elaborate pieces commonly used in decoration of upper class houses.

[33] Lancaster Co., Va., Court Order Book 5:63.

[34] Lancaster Co., Va., Court Order Book 4:66.

[35] Lancaster Co., Va., Court Order Book 4:89, [12 October 1699]; 4:94, [9 November 1699]; 4:144, [10 July 1701.]

[36] Lancaster Co., Va., Court Order Book 4:107.

[37] Lancaster Co., Va., Court Order Book 4:107.

[38] Lancaster Co., Va., Court Order Book 4:175.

plaisterer died before 12 May 1719 in Lancaster Co., Va., leaving only daughters. On that date Thomas Flint and his wife, Elizabeth, sold a tract of land that had been given by John Wright to his daughters, Elizabeth Wright and Mary Wright before his death.[39] This deed does not preclude the existence of sons, but there is no evidence for them, either. The simplest solution is that this line "daughtered out."

1690 Francis Wright of Lancaster Co., Virginia

Francis Wright[40] appears in the Lancaster Co., Va., records 11 January 1670/71, when Will Frizell was ordered to deliver all the cattle due to Mary Wright as orphan of Charles Hill.[41] From these records it seems that Francis Wright was of legal age, but also that he had recently married Mary Hill, daughter of Charles Hill. Mary Hill had not been of age in her own right when her father died before 11 September 1661.[42] This all indicates Francis Wright was born before 1650, and probably closer to 1645.

Francis Wright appeared in the tithe lists in 1671 when he was on the land of Will Frizell,[43] which argues a birth year of before 1650, and as noted, John Wright first appeared residing at Mr. Champion's in 1675.[44]

Francis Wright served as a constable in 1679, when he was ordered to obtain the tithe list.[45] He was discharged from his service 10 March 1679/80.[46] He appeared in tithe lists 1688.

On 13 August 1690 letters of administration were granted to Mary Wright, widow of Francis Wright, deceased. William Edmonds, Henry Boatman, Thomas Hubbard, and John Wright were ordered to appraise the estate. Mr. Jeremiah Packquet and Thomas Thompson were securities.[47] Mary Wright arranged for marriage to William Lawrence shortly thereafter, for on 26

[39] Lancaster Co., Va., Deed Book 11:119.
[40] Grant, Robert N. 1690 Francis Wright of Lancaster County, his wife Mary (Hill) (Wright) (Lawrence) Meredith and his Descendants. (Menlo Park, CA: 17 December 2012.)
[41] Lancaster Co., Va., Court Order Book (1660-1680), p. 177.
[42] Lancaster Co., Va., Court Order Book (1656-1666), p. 152.
[43] Lancaster Co., Va., Court Order Book (1666-1680), p. 212.
[44] Lancaster Co., Va., Court Order Book (1666-1680), p. 337.
[45] Lancaster Co., Va., Court Order Book (1666-1680), p. 477, 3 June 1679.
[46] Lancaster Co., Va., Court Order Book (1666-1680), p. 526.
[47] Lancaster Co., Va., Court Order Book (1686-1696), p. 136.

September 1690, Mary Wright, widow and relict of Francis Wright, stated that she had inherited 300 acres of land from her father, Charles Hill, and, as legatee, transferred ownership of the tract, located on the easternmost bank of Corotoman River, to her "contracted husband" William Lawrence.[48] Mary Lawrence filed her inventory of the estate of Francis Wright on 10 June 1691, with the appraisal dated 30 August 1690.[49] Total value was £14.15 plus cattle and two horses.

Francis Wright and Mary Hill had four children documented in court records. On 12 January 1698/99 Mary Lawrence, as administratrix of the estate of her late husband, and William Lawrence, were ordered to give Francis Wright his inheritance, with similar orders issued for Charles Wright, Mary Wright, and John Wright.[50] William Lawrence appears to have died shortly after this order as on 9 March 1698/99 Charles Wright brought suit against Mary Lawrence as administratrix of William Lawrence, although the suit was continued by consent.[51] This suggests he had not received his due from his mother before William Lawrence died, and he filed suit to establish his prior claim on his-step father's estate. The suit was dismissed 13 July 1699.[52]

John Wright petitioned the court to appoint Mary Lawrence as his guardian 14 September 1699.[53] This establishes that he was at least 14 years old, but not yet 21, so was born between 15 September 1678 and 13 September 1685. John Wright filed receipt for his share of his father's estate 14 June 1705, by which time he would have been 21 years old.[54] This establishes his date of birth as before 13 June 1684. Since it seems unlikely he would have waited a long time for his legacy, I think this means he was born in late 1683 or early 1684.

Mary Lawrence, *nee* Hill, contracted one final marriage, this to William Meredith after 11 November 1706. On that date she conveyed a 50 acres tract of land to Joseph Tayloe for either

[48] Lancaster Co., Va., Deed Book 7:33.
[49] Lancaster Co., Va., Will Book 8:13B.
[50] Lancaster Co., Va., Court Order Book 4:59.
[51] Lancaster Co., Va., Court Order Book 4:65.
[52] Lancaster Co., Va., Court Order Book 4:69.
[53] Lancaster Co., Va., Court Order Book 4:79.
[54] Lancaster Co., Va., Court Order Book 5:126.

99 years or the natural life of William Meredith.[55] The deed specifically mentions an intended marriage between Mary Lawrence and William Meredith that was pending.

John Wright, son of 1690 Francis Wright is of particular interest to our line, as he is probably the father of John Wright, Goochland County carpenter, who has a living descendant who is a match for my Y-DNA. Detailed description of the descent of the other three children is contained in Mr. Grant's work.

1730 John Wright of Goochland Co., Virginia

On 8 March 1706/07 John Wright witnessed the sale of a 50 acre tract of land from Francis Wright to Charles Wright, the land having been part of the estate of Charles Hill and inherited from Francis Wright, deceased.[56] He was again a witness on 10 June 1707 when Francis Wright sold a 100 acre tract of land to Francis Edwards.[57]

William Meredith gave his grandson, Meredith Wright, a young filly, and Charles Wright gave a two year old heifer to Meredith Wright.[58] Meredith Wright is 1735 Meredith Wright of Goochland Co., Va., a known son of 1730 John Wright and his wife Elizabeth. (*vide infra.*) This record indicates that John Wright's wife, Elizabeth, was a daughter of William Meredith, the third husband of his mother, Mary Hill. This latter point has not been fully established, however.

Francis Wright and his wife Anne conveyed a 50 acre tract of land to John Wright, carpenter, by deed of lease and release 11 and 12 January 1713/14.[59] The deeds were witnessed by Charles Wright. The description of the land shows this was a parcel likely drawn from the original 300 acres of Charles Hill. On 8 January 1713/14 John Wright purchased a 50 acre tract of land from Peter and Elizabeth Kilgore, which had previously been owned by Ralph Briggs.[60] Ralph Briggs had married John's sister, Mary Wright, as established by data analyzed by Mr. Grant, so this land, too, was still in the original tract.

---

[55] Lancaster Co., Va., Deed Book 9:186.
[56] Lancaster Co., Va., Deed Book 9:225.
[57] Lancaster Co., Va., Deed Book 9:230.
[58] Lancaster Co., Va., Deed Book 9:324.
[59] Lancaster Co., Va., Deed Book 9:458, 459.
[60] Lancaster Co., Va., Deed Book 9:461.

John Wright was a witness to the sale of a 50 acre tract of land from Francis Wright and wife, Anne, to Ralph Briggs on 15 December 1713.[61] On 6 November 1714 John Wright, carpenter, and Elizabeth, his wife, conveyed a 50 acre tract of land in trust to Joseph Tayloe establishing a life interest in the tract for Nicholas Terkelson and his wife, Ann.[62] The land was described as having been originally granted to Elias Edmonds, inherited by his son, William Edmonds, and sold by William Edmonds to Alexander Reed. Reed died, leaving the land to his daughter, Anne Reed. When Anne died intestate, the land was passed to her son Peter Kilgore. The land was described as on the west side of Corotoman River, where the original Hill tract was described as on the "easternmost" branch of the river.

On 10 December 1718 John Wright witnessed the sale of a 70 acre tract of land from Charles Wright, Frances Wright and wife Anne, and Ralph Briggs to William Ranken, the land being specifically noted as part of the land inherited by Francis Wright from his mother, sold to Charles Wright, and then sold to Ralph Briggs.[63] None of these people appear further in the records of Lancaster Co., Va.

John Wright was appointed guardian for Lydia Briggs 7 January 1722/23 in Henrico Co., Va.[64] Ralph Briggs was dead by 7 January 1722/23, for on that date George Briggs relinquished his right to letters of administration on the estate of Ralph Briggs in favor of Robert Hughes, and then chose Robert Hughes as his guardian.[65] Ralph Briggs probably married Mary Wright, sister of John Wright, so Lydia Briggs was his niece. It certainly seems to link John Wright of Goochland County to John Wright of Lancaster County.

Goochland County was formed from Henrico County 1 January 1727. John Wright of Henrico County witnessed the last will and testament of William Runals 4 August 1725 that was probated in Goochland County 16 June 1730, suggesting John Wright was already in the part of Henrico that became Goochland County.[66]

---

[61] Lancaster Co., Va., Deed Book 9:477.
[62] Lancaster Co., Va., Deed Book 9:516.
[63] Lancaster Co., Va., Deed Book 11:110.
[64] Henrico Co., Va., Court Minute Book (1719-1724):226.
[65] Henrico Co., Va., Court Minute Book (1719-1724):225 and 226.
[66] Goochland Co., Va., Deed Book 1:194.

John Wright patented a 333 acre tract of land in Goochland Co., Va., 28 September 1728.[67] The land was described a lying south of the James River in Henrico County adjacent Robert Hughes being "the lower Corner on the River of the Muddy Creek Survey." Muddy Creek now serves as the border between Cumberland and Powhatan Counties.

The will of John Wright was dated 14 March 1729/30 and was proved in Goochland County 16 June 1730.[68] He instructed his wife to sell his land on Muddy Creek if she could get £35 current money for it, and if successful, she was to use the money to purchase another tract that could be parceled out to his four sons, all of whom were under age: Meredith, William, John, and Francis. If the land could not be sold, the current tract was to be divided so Meredith had the upper tract, William the next, John the next, and Francis the last. Elizabeth was to live on the land of Meredith Wright. He made a bequest of a one year old heifer to Lydia Briggs, gave his best feather bed and furniture to his wife, and directed the residue be divided among his wife and children. The will was witnessed by Edward Scott, John Williams, and John Burgis.

Elizabeth Wright presented the will and obtained security for her letters of administration on the estate of her husband 16 June 1730.[69] Elizabeth Wright, Joseph Woodson and John Fleming agreed to be securities on the estate. Court records suggest that Elizabeth had problems defending her land from encroachment, and the usual problems of debts to be settled. She did manage to sell the land patented by John Wright as directed by him in the will.

In a deed of lease and release dated 1 and 3 November 1733 and recorded 19 February and 19 March 1733/34, Elizabeth Wright as executrix for John Wright's estate deeded the entire 333 acre tract on Muddy Creek to John Nichols for £60.[70] The deeds were witnessed by John Pleasants, a Quaker, Mary Burgess, Jeremiah and Margaret Mather, and signed by the mark of Elizabeth Wright.

[67] Virginia Land Patent Book 14:8.

[68] Goochland Co., Va., Deed Book 1:193.

[69] Goochland Co., Va., Court Order Book 1:257, and loose papers (bond).

[70] Goochland Co., Va., Deed Book 1:457, 458. The proof was also recorded in Goochland Co., Va., Court Order Book 3:223, February Ct., 1733/34; and 3:228, March Ct., 1733/34.

Sadly, Elizabeth Wright was summoned by the court meeting in July 1735 to take administration of the estate of Meredith Wright.[71] She returned the inventory 20 January 1735/36 showing a total estate of £1.15.6,[72] and petitioned for closure of the estate in March 1735/36.[73] Clearly, Meredith Wright was of age at the time of his death, so was born sometime between 4 March 1708/09 and July 1714. The tithe list for 1735 shows William Wright as a tithe for the first time, suggesting he was born in 1714. Since Meredith seems to have been the eldest, this suggests he was born between 1709 and 1713. However, as noted previously, he was born before 19 August 1710, when William Meredith recorded his gift to his grandson Meredith Wright. We can be confident then he was born between 4 March 1708/09 and 19 August 1710, and died probably June 1735 at about age 25.

The 1736 Tithe list includes Elizabeth Wright in the district described as being between Deep Creek and Fine Creek, which are all on the south side of the James River. This area became Southam Parish, Goochland Co., Va., in 1744. John Wright first appeared on the tithe list for Southam Parish in 1746, and Francis Wright first appeared in 1748. This suggests they were born about 1725 and 1727 respectively. Southam Parish became Cumberland County in 1749. The only further record of John Wright, son of 1730 John Wright, was recorded 26 February 1753, when Thomas Pleasants filed for collection of debts from John Wright, Frank Wright, Peter Booker, and George Wright.[74] From other work, Mr. Grant can affirm that there are no more records for John Wright until 1759, and those records can be related to the activities of 1770 John Wright of Cumberland Co., Va., who was a son of 1769 George Wright of Essex Co., Virginia.

John Wright, Goochland County Carpenter

John Wright[75] first appears in the records of Goochland Co., Va., on 10 April 1739 when he purchased 358 acres of land from Robert Mimms for £45.[76] The land was described as "on the

---

[71] Goochland Co., Va., Court Order Book 3:276.

[72] Goochland Co., Va., Will Book 2:163.

[73] Goochland Co., Va., Court Order Book 4:44.

[74] Cumberland Co., Va., Court Order Book 1752-1758:59.

[75] Grant, Robert N. Sorting Some of the Wrights of Southern Virginia, Part II: John Wright (Goochland County Carpenter.) (Menlo Park, CA, 2004, three CDs).

[76] Goochland Co., Va., Deed Book 3:213, 15 May 1739.

waters of Lickinghole Creek" and were originally obtained by patent to Mimms 31 October 1726.[77] Robert Mimms signed with his mark ("R") and the indenture was witnessed by Rob. Walton, John Mimms, John McFarland, and David A. Mimms. This deed implies that John Wright was born before 1722.

John "Right" and his wife Judith sold 179 acres of this land to Stephen Clement 25 September 1741 for £22.10.[78] The tract was described as being in St. James Parish lying on the upper fork and south side of Lickinghole Creek adjacent Mimms. Clearly, this is one half of the tract he bought in 1739.

John Wright appears on the 1746 tithe list for St. James Northam Parish, Goochland Co., Va., with two tithes—himself and Jenny. The 1747 tithe list also shows another John Wright, this one in Southam Parish, south of the James River, and probably a son of 1730 John Wright of Goochland Co., Va.

On 17 September 1747, both John Wright and his wife Judith appeared as witnesses for John Laine in his suit against Ashford Hughes.[79]

The land of John Wright was processioned on 12 April 1748, establishing that his abutting neighbors were John Pleasants, John Mullins, and John Mimms, and that their adjoining neighbors included Philip Ryan, William McCormick, Charles Toney, John Mann and Arthur Hopkins.[80] The tithe list for the same year showed John Wright, carpenter, with three tithes: himself, Jeffry, and Jany, who is likely the same as Jenny previously listed.

John Wright appears in his role as a carpenter in several entries in the Vestry Book. On 27 Jan 1748 he was paid for taking down "a pair of stairs." On 5 December 1749, Tarlton Fleming, Arthur Payne, and John Hopkins were ordered to view the "work done by John Wright on the Glebe House..." and on 6 March 1749/50, he was paid for "Horseblocks and putting putty on the windows at St. John's Church."

On 19 November 1751 John Wright sold a 60 acre tract to Robert Pleasants for £20, the land "lying on the North side of

---

[77] The original patent is Patent Book 13:9. The original patent described the land as on the north side of the James River and the waters of Lickinghole Creek. The location north of the river is important for keeping this man separate from another John Wright present south of the James.

[78] Goochland Co., Va., Deed Book 3:491, 17 November 1741.

[79] Goochland Co., Va., Court Order Book 6:389.

[80] St. James Northam Parish Vestry Book 1744-1850, Goochland Co., Virginia.

James River...bounded on the east by the land of John Pleasants, on the South by the South branch of Lickinghole Creek, on the West by the Whittle Creek, and on the North by the Land of Phil. Ryan."[81] The deed was witnessed by John Thaxton, Wm. Harding, and Wm. Allen. This reduced his holding to 119 acres of land.

The 1752 Tithe List for Goochland County shows John Wright, his son John Wright, and Jenne. This list, combined with the list for 1748 establishes that John Wright, Jr., was born between 10 June 1732 and 11 June 1736. Since it is likely that John Wright, carpenter, was at least 18 years old when his son was born, this pushes his birth year to before 1719. These three also appear in the Tithe Lists for 1754 and 1755.

The Douglas Register shows that John Wright and Judah Easley on Lickinhole [Creek] had a daughter, Betty, born February 1756 and baptized 21 March 1756. John Wright and Judith Barns had a son named Benjamin, b. 22 March 1759 and baptized 29 April 1759.

The Tithe List for 1757 shows that John Wright and John Wright, Jr., have separate households, indicating a marriage has likely taken place. Mr. Grant notes this is consistent with the marriage of 1814 John Wright of Bedford Co., Va., to Mary Pace in 1756. John Wright is listed only once in 1759, but in 1760 John Wright and James Wright are listed together, while John Wright, Jr., appears in his own right. This appearance indicates James Wright was likely born between 10 June 1743 and 11 June 1744. The 1763 Tithe List marks the first appearance of William Wright, Jr. (sic) in the household of John Wright. This John Wright was taxed with 120 acres, as predicted from the deed records, and indicates that William Wright was born between 10 June 1745 and 11 June 1747. The 1765 Tithe list shows that William Wright moved into his brother John Wright's household sometime the year previous, but in 1766 he is back with his father, and his brother Francis makes his first appearance, indicating he was born between 10 June 1749 and 11 June 1750.

On 7 May 1767 John Wright executed a mortgage on his remaining 119 acres of land with George Kippen & Co., of Glasgow, to secure a debt of £106.9.8.3.[82] The land was described

---

[81] Goochland Co., Va., Deed Book 6:178, 19 November 1751.
[82] Goochland Co., Va., Deed Book 9:116, 15 December 1767.

as part of the tract bought of Robert Mimms on Lickinghole Creek, adjacent Robert Pleasant, John Mullins, James Clement, and William Wright.

John Wright and John Wright, Jr., continued to appear on the tithe lists, but in 1769 Roderick Wright appeared in the household along with William Wright, indicating he was born between 10 June 1752 and 11 June 1753. John Wright, Jr., though, was not present in 1769, and is consistent with his move from Goochland to Bedford Co., Va., in 1768.

In 1770 Roderick Wright was still living with his father, although William Wright was no longer listed. On 23 August 1770, George Kippen & Co., filed suit to foreclose on the mortgage undertaken by John Wright. On 24 April 1772 the court ordered publication of a summons to John Wright to answer the complaint.[83] An order to foreclose was obtained in July 1772.[84]

The 1773 Tithe List showed Francis Wright with an extra tithe, Roderick Wright in the household of Maj. Josias Payne and William Wright, Jr. This suggests that John Wright died in 1772.

Conclusions

I have used {←} to indicate where Y-DNA evidence indicates the ancestors of John (Taylor) Wright of Brunswick Co., Va., must descend from the early Wrights of Lancaster Co., Va. The most likely place seems to be through 1690 Francis Wright of Lancaster Co., Va.

1. UNKNOWN[1] WRIGHT[85]

Children of UNKNOWN WRIGHT

2.   i.   FRANCIS[2] WRIGHT.
3.   ii. JOHN[2] WRIGHT

2. FRANCIS[2] WRIGHT, b. say 1645; d. before 13 August 1690 Lancaster Co., Va.; m. MARY HILL about 1671 daughter of

---

[83] Goochland Co., Va., Loose Court Papers.

[84] Goochland Co., Va., Court Order Book 12:212.

[85] Although early Lancaster Co., Va., records date from 1652 and appear reasonably intact, there is insufficient data to identify the progenitor of this line. It is not even certain that Francis and John Wright were brothers, although I have chosen to show them that way, given the data outlined above.

CHARLES HILL and AUDREY ____; m. (2) WILLIAM LAWRENCE October 1690 Lancaster Co., Va.; m. (3) WILLIAM MEREDITH about 1706 Lancaster Co., Va.

Children of FRANCIS WRIGHT and MARY HILL are:

    i. FRANCIS[3] WRIGHT, b. say 1675 Lancaster Co., Va.; d. after 1719 King William Co., Va.; m. ANNE.

        Children of FRANCIS WRIGHT and ANNE are:

        1. FRANCIS[4] WRIGHT, d. 1767 Amherst Co., Va.

        2. ←

    ii. CHARLES[3] WRIGHT, b. say 1680 Lancaster Co., Va., d. after 1719 King William Co., Va. ←

    iii. MARY[3] WRIGHT, b. Lancaster Co., Va.; d. before January 1722/23 Henrico Co., Va.; m. RALPH BRIGGS; d. before January 1722/23 Henrico Co., Va.

    iv. JOHN[3] WRIGHT, b. say December 1683 Lancaster Co., Va.; d. 1730 Goochland Co., Va.; m. ELIZABETH MEREDITH say 1709 Lancaster Co., Va.

        Children of JOHN WRIGHT and ELIZABETH MEREDITH are:

        1. MEREDITH[4] WRIGHT, b. before 11 July 1710 Lancaster Co., Va.; d. before July 1735 Goochland Co., Virginia.

        2. WILLIAM[4] WRIGHT, b. say 1715 Lancaster Co., Va.; 1782 Goochland Co., Va.

        3. JOHN[4] WRIGHT, b. say 1718 Lancaster Co., Va.; d. 1772 Goochland Co., Va.; m. JUDITH BARNES.

        4. FRANCIS[4] WRIGHT, b. say 1722 Henrico Co., Va.

3. JOHN[2] WRIGHT, (bricklayer,) b. say 1655; d. 1698 Lancaster Co., Va.

Children of JOHN WRIGHT

    i. JOHN[3] WRIGHT, plaisterer, d. before 1719 Lancaster Co., Va.

        Children of JOHN WRIGHT:

1. ELIZABETH[4] WRIGHT, m. THOMAS FLINT by 1719 Lancaster Co., Va.
2. MARY[4] WRIGHT.
3. ←

Chapter 6: Ancestry of Sarah Fox

1771 Richard Fox of Mecklenburg Co., Virginia

The ancestry of 1771 (year of death) Richard Fox of Mecklenburg Co., Virginia (place of death) is disputed. Richard was a grandson of Henry[1] Fox, the immigrant, and his wife, Anne West, of King and Queen Co., Virginia, but there is dispute as to whether Richard was the son of Henry's proven son Thomas, or Henry, who was unborn when his father wrote his will.[1] Henry[2] Fox was present in Brunswick County at an early date,[2] but there is no clear record of his death and little is no of him with certainty.

Richard Fox married about 1728 Hannah Williamson, daughter of 1732 John Williamson of Surry Co., Virginia.[3] On 2 December 1742, "Hollum Sturdivant and Elizabeth of Surry Co., John Rottenbury & Susannah of same, Henry Ledbetter and Edith of Brunswick Co., Richard (R) Fox and Hannah, alias Joanna (X) Fox, and Sarah Mabry to George Mabry of St. Andrew's Parish in Brunswick Co.," sold for "£30 280 ac. patented by John Williamson 18 Feb 1722 and left to his daughters upon his death, the land being on the south side of Nottoway River joining the n. side of Rocky Run." [4]

Richard Fox rented 550 acres on the south side of the Roanoke River 1 September 1736.[5] He later patented land on the Roanoke River, in what was then Lunenburg, and is now Mecklenburg County, Virginia.[6]

---

[1] See also Fox Family. William & Mary Q J 20:262-266, 1912.

[2] Cf. Brunswick Co., Court Order Book 1:8, 12, 18, 21, 22, 24. [Brunswick County, Virginia Court Orders, 1732-1737. (Miami Beach: TLC Genealogy, 1992.)]

[3] She is named in his will, dated 30 January 1731 as Hannah Fox, so she clearly married prior to that date. Also named were daughter Elizabeth, wife of Hollum Sturdivant, Susannah wife of John Rottenbury, Edith Williamson, and son Cuthbert Williamson under age. Cited in Holtzclaw, B. C. Kendrick of Gloucester Co., Va., and North Carolina. In Boddie, John B. Historical Southern Families, Vol. 1. (Baltimore, Genealogical Publishing Co., 1967,) p. 42. Cited hereafter as Boddie.

[4] Brunswick Co., Va., Deed Book (henceforth DB) 2:204. Bradley, Stephen E. Brunswick County, Virginia Deed Books, Vol. 1: 1732-1745. (Lawrenceville, Va.: 1997,) p. 69. [Hereafter cited as Bradley.]

[5] Brunswick Co., Va., DB/WB 1:296. Bradley, p. 69.

[6] Richard Fox received a patent for 400 acres "on Keith's branch" on 15 December 1749, and a total of 630 acres in two tracts (on both sides of the Roanoke River) on 16 August 1756. [Lunenburg County, Virginia Land Patents, 1746-1916. (Miami Beach: TLC Genealogy, 1990.)]

His will was written 4 January 1771, and proved 10 January 1771, Mecklenburg County, Virginia. His will does not name his son William[4] Fox, who had been provided for in a deed of gift for 400 acres recorded June 10, 1765.

"To all whom these Presents shall come, Greeting, Know ye that I, Richard Fox of Mecklenburg Co., for and in consideration of the natural love which I have and bear to my beloved son, William Fox, hath given and granted, and by these presents do freely, clearly, and absolutely give and grant unto the said William Fox, his Heirs and Assigns forever, one track of land containing four hundred acres, be the same more or less, lying and being in the County aforesaid..."[7]

Last Will and Testament of Richard Fox. [8]

In the name of God, Amen, I Richard Fox of the County of Mecklenburg in the Colony of Virginia being weak in body but sound in mind and memory praised be Almighty God for the same do make and ordain this my last will and testament in the manner and form following viz: First and principally I recommend my Soul into the hands of Almighty God my Maker hoping through the meritorious death of Jesus Christ my Savior to receive all pardon of all my sins and as for my body to be buried at the discretion of my Executors hereafter nominated, and calling to mind what worldly estate it hath pleased Almighty God to help me with, I give and dispose in manner and form following.

I give and bequeath to my grandchildren Amy Burchett, James Burchett and Joseph Burchett, John Burchett, Mary Ann Burchett and Isaac Burchett my Negro woman Anaca and all her present and future increase to be equally divided amongst them after the

---

[7] Mecklenburg Co., Va., DB 1:49. Cited by McFarlane, Jim. Ancestors of Angus Duncan McFarlane. 31 May 2003. Located at http://worldconnect.rootsweb.com (db mcfarlane).

[8] Mecklenburg Co., Va., WB 1:94. Cited by Oberlies, Denise. Denise's Research Files. 30 Aug 2003. Located on http://worldconnect.Rootsweb.com (db :2648461). Cited hereafter as Oberlies.

death of their father Joseph Burchett. I desire he may have the use of them all during his life.

Item: I give and devise to my son Jacob Fox my mill and one acre of land on the South side of Mill Creek at the end of the dam and also all the land I bought of George King and John King Rossser that lays on the North Side of the Mill Creek to him and his heirs forever.

Item: I give and devise to my son Richard Fox all the tract of land that I now live on with the Ferry and all other conveniences of the same to him and his heirs and assigns forever together with two cows and calves to him and his assigns forever.

Item: I give and devise to my son Isham Fox all the land that I now own on the South side of Mill Creek except the acre I give to my son Jacob Fox to him and his heirs and assigns forever, together with two cows and calves to him and his heirs forever, also I give to my son Isham Fox all that tract or parcel of land I bought of Shipiallen Puckett after the death of my daughter Sarah Price, to him and his heirs forever.

Item: I give to my daughter Nancy Fox the use of my Negro boy Abram and my Negro girl Phebee to be and continue in the hands of my wife during her life and after death for my daughter Nancy to go in care of John Kendrick and Amy his wife, also I give to my daughter Nancy one featherbed and furniture and two cows and calves to be and continue with her Mother during her life and after her death to go to John Kendrick for the use of my daughter, and if my said daughter Nancy should died without heirs lawfully begotten of her body my will and desire is that the said Negro's Abram and Phebee go to John Kendrick and his wife, and their heirs forever.

Item: I give and bequeath to my daughter Hannah my Negro girl Anaca and a good bed and furniture together with two cows and calves to her and her heirs forever.

Item: I give to my son Richard Fox one Negro named Kitt and a good bed and furniture to him and his heirs and assigns forever. My will and desire is that the land I bought of James Dozer to be sold to defray the charges in buying the said land.

Item: I give to my daughter Ann Fox my Negro girl Molly together with a good bed and furniture and two cows and calves to her and her heirs forever.

Item: I give to my son Isham Fox my Negro girl Paul [sic] together with one good bed and furniture two cows and calves to him his heirs and assigns forever.

Item: I give to my son Isham Fox that land that I bought of Hutchens Burton to him and his heirs forever.

Item: I give to my beloved wife all the rest of my estate during her life and after her decease my will and desire is that all that part I give my wife the use of during her life to be equally divided amongst my children except Nancy who I don't allot to have any part of my estate.

Item: My will and desire further is that if any of my children die before they come of age or have lawful issue that his or their part shall be equally divided amongst my surviving children.

Lastly I nominate and appoint my son Jacob Fox and John Kendrick Executors of this my last will and testament, Revoking and disannulling all former wills and ratifying and confirming this and no other to be my last will And testament. In witness whereof I have hereto set my hand and seal this fourth day of January One Thousand Seven Hundred and Seventy One.

Signed, Sealed and Delivered by the said Richard Fox and said to be his last will and testament.

Alex Morrison   S/Richard Fox
Wm. C. Morrison (by his mark)
Elizabeth Davis (by her mark)

Genealogical Summary

1. RICHARD[3] (HENRY[2], HENRY[1]) FOX was born about 1705 King William Co., Va., and died before 10 January 1771 Mecklenburg Co., Va. He married HANNAH WILLIAMSON about 1728 in Surry Co., Va., daughter of JOHN WILLIAMSON. She was born about 23 November 1714 and died about 1776 in Mecklenburg Co., Virginia.

Children of RICHARD FOX and HANNAH WILLIAMSON are:[9]

2. i. JACOB[4] FOX, b. about 1730 in Surry Co., Va.; d. after 22 March 1807 Franklin Co., N. C.; m. ELIZABETH LARK; b. 18 October 1750 Mecklenburg Co., Va.; d. 6 July 1843, Lawrence Co., Miss. [10]

3. ii. WILLIAM[4] FOX, b. 13 February 1731/32 Surry Co., Va.; d. 1783 Mecklenburg Co., Va.; m. MARY KENDRICK before 1761 Brunswick Co., Va., daughter of WILLIAM KENDRICK and SARAH JANE JONES; b. 12 April 1738 Isle of Wight Co., Va.; d. before 9 November 1795 Mecklenburg Co., Va.

4. iii. RICHARD[4] FOX, b. 1734 Surry Co., Va.; He died before 1820 Franklin Co., N. C. He married (1) unknown about 1760. He married (2) MARY RAINEY 22 March 1775 Mecklenburg Co., Va.; d. 1795 Mecklenburg Co., Va.

iv. ANN[4] FOX, b. 1740, Virginia; m. JACOB KENDRICK 1756, Brunswick Co., Va., son of WILLIAM KENDRICK and SARAH JANE JONES; b. about 1730; d. 1794 Culpeper Co., Va.

Jacob Kendrick is said to be the father of Benoni Kendrick. According to "Colonial Caroline" Jacob Kendrick was a bricklayer and resided in Caroline County, VA in the early 1700…Jacob had five known children: Nancy, Daniel, Benjamin, William and Benoni, the latter four sons all fought in the Revolution. Anna Fox is reputed to be their undocumented mother. Benoni Kendrick married Mary Warner in 1789 in Culpeper County, VA where the Kendrick clan moved earlier. From Culpeper County they moved west to Kentucky settling in Paris, Bourbon County. The Kendricks followed the Baptist faith and were early members of Cooper's Run Baptist Church, Battle Creek Baptist Church, and Silas Creek Baptist Church. [11]

---

[9] The children are considered in detail because of the overlap with the Wright connections outlined in Chapter Two.

[10] Jackson-Jimenez, Lisa. Jackson, Fox, Nash, Prewitt, etc. 12 Nov 2003. Located at http://worldconnect.rootsweb.com (db :2718937).

[11] Oberlies. Children of Ann Fox and Jacob Kendrick are: Sarah; Elizabeth; Daniel, Benjamin, William (b. 29 December 1757 Culpeper Co., Va.); Benoni; Millie; Jacob; and Reuben.

v. AMY[4] FOX, b. 1740; m. JOHN KENDRICK 1760 Brunswick Co., Va., son of WILLIAM KENDRICK and SARAH JANE JONES; b. 21 July 1735 Gloucester Co., Va.; d. 1 July 1811 Mecklenburg Co., Va.

On 4 September 1759, Richard Fox made a deed of gift to his son-in-law John Kendrick, in Lunenburg County, Virginia.[12]

John Kendrick was appointed First Lieutenant in Capt. James Lewis' Company 13 October 1777.[13] The land-tax records of Mecklenburg refer to him as Captain Kendrick in 1782, 1787, and 1789.

He wrote his will 10 October 1807, died on 1 July 1811, and the will was probated 15 July 1811.[14] He mentions wife Amy, daughter Molly Cunningham, deceased, and her children Keziah, Jacob, Rebecca Jones, George and Sally K. Baird and "my grandson" John Cunningham; children of son William, deceased, not named; daughters Sarah Patrick, Keziah Stevens, son John, daughter Betsy Price, son James, daughter Obedience Dinkins, daughter Lucy Dinkins, grandsons Greenberry and Asa Stevens and John Stevens.[15]

vi. SARAH[4] FOX, b. 1742; d. before 4 January 1771; m. JOSEPH PRICE.

vii. HANNAH[4] FOX, b. 1744; m. DAVID TOWNES; d. before 28 August 1794 Warren Co., N. C.

On 28 August 1794 Richard[4] Fox took out a bond for £1000 as administrator of the estate of David Towns, deceased.[16] The inventory was recorded the same day.[17] On 17 February 1801, Richard Fox "of

---

[12] Lunenburg Co., Va., Deed Book 5:545.

[13] Mecklenburg Co., Va., Court Order Book 4:374. Oath Order Book 4:403, 11 May 1778.

[14] Mecklenburg Co., Va., Will Book 7:115.

[15] Oberlies. Children: Sarah, b. about 1761; m. John Patrick 29 Sept 1779, Mecklenburg Co., Va.; Elizabeth, m. John Price 10 October 1787 Warren Co., N. C.; Keziah, m. John Stevens 11 January 1791 Warren Co., N. C.; John, d. 1823 Mecklenburg; William, d. 1807 Mecklenburg; James, d. 1811 Mecklenburg, m. Elizabeth Wright Mecklenburg 12 December 1797, dau. of 1829 Austin Wright of Mecklenburg, and Sarah Lark; Obediece, m. John Osborne and Joshua Dinkins; Lucy, m. James Dinkins 5 January 1796 Warren Co., N. C.; and Bennett, d. 1807 Mecklenburg.

[16] Warren Co., N. C., WB 7:153. 28 Aug. 1794; Aug. Ct .1794.

[17] Warren Co., N. C., WB 7:165. 28 Aug. 1794; Aug. Ct. 1794.

Mecklenburg Co., Va." gave Hannah Towns, widow of David Towns, the slave he had received for management of the estate. After her death, the slave was to pass to "my near kinsmen" heirs of David Towns, excepting Polly Sale, wife of William Sale, including Susanna, Nancy, Edmund, Sally, Betsy and David Towns.[18] Final settlement of the estate was made in November 1802 when the report showed receipts from the sale and rental of the plantation for five years and payment to Hannah Towns for the board of Edmund, David, Betsy and Sally Towns, to Brooks Neal for schooling, to William Sale for Polly Towns, to Richard Neal for Nancy Towns and Susanna Towns, and to Ebenezer McGowan for E. Towns and for the estate of D. Towns.[19]

viii. MARY[4] FOX, b. 1746; m. SAMUEL JONES

ix.. LUCY[4] FOX, b. 28 November 1747 Brunswick Co., Va.; d. 12 February 1831; m. LUKE MATHEWS 26 January 1766 Mecklenburg Co., Va.; b. 15 March 1739; d. 7 April 1788 Brunswick Co., Va.[20]

x. ISHAM[4] FOX, b. about 1750; d. before 1770 Brunswick Co., Va.

On 7 February 1777[21] "William Fox, Jacob Fox, Richard Fox, Anne Fox, and John Kindrick and Amy his wife, of Mecklenburg Co., Joseph Price & Sarah his wife and David Towns & Hannah his wife of the County of Bute, NC, Samuel Jones and Mary his wife of the Province of Georgia and Luke Matthews & Lucy his wife of the County of Brunswick in VA aforesaid (which said William, Jacob, Richard, Anne, Amy,

---

[18] Warren Co., N. C., WB 11:67. 17 Feb. 1801; Feb. Ct. 1801.

[19] Warren Co., N. C., WB 12:9. Nov. Ct., 1802.

[20] Mathews Family Bible. Original in the Tennessee State Archives. Cited by Harlow Chandler. 23 Dec 1999. http://genforum.genealogy.com/matthews/messages/1453.html. Children: Angelina, b. 28 June 1767; Hannah, b. 25 September 1768; Elizabeth, b. 14 May 1772; Lucy, b. 27 October 1774; John, b. 9 March 1777; Luke, b. 22 August 1779; Isham, b. 7 April 1782; Nancy, b. 11 October 1785; and Drury, b. 4 September 1788.

[21] Mecklenburg Co., Va., Deed Book 5:122, 10 Nov. 1777. the land was described as being "on both sides of Smith's Creek, containing 200 acres." Description mentions Ballard's formerly Fowler's corner red oak on the west side of the creek; Kirk's formerly Robertson's line Davis's, formerly King's corner. The deed was signed by Jacob Fox, Richard Fox, John Kindrick, Amy Kindrick, Joseph Price, Sarah Price, and Anna Fox.

Sarah, Hannah, Mary, Lucy are devisees of Richard Fox late of the County of Mecklenburg aforesaid, deceased) of the one part," made an indenture with "William Davis, Gentleman, of the other Part. Whereas the said Richard Fox, deceased, did by his last will and Testament, duly proved and recorded in the County Court of Mecklenburg aforesaid, give and devises unto his son Isham Fox amongst other tracts of land, the land he the said Richard Fox bought of Hutchens Button?, but which said tract was conveyed to the said Richard Fox by Robert Wooding by deed recorded in the County Court of Mecklenburg aforesaid 12 Oct 1766, and further the said Richard Fox did by his said last will and Testament direct that if any of his children should die before they came of age or had lawful issue, his or their parts would be equally (divided) amongst all his children as by the said Will will more fully appear and the said Isham Fox having died under the age of twenty-one years, and without lawful issue, the devisees aforesaid became possessed of the said tract of land aforesaid, with others under the clause aforesaid of the said Richard Fox's will..."

xi. NANCY[4] FOX, b. about 1751(?); m. JOSEPH BURCHETT; d, before November 1795 Warren Co., N. C.; m. (2) MARTHA WILSON.

Nancy Fox had evidently fallen into disfavor with her father, as he specifically excluded her from the residue of his estate, even in the event of the death of siblings. Joseph Burchett was listed as one of Richard Fox' tithes 1750 Lunenburg County. Nancy Fox died about 1770 and he married (2) Martha Wilson.

The will of Joseph Burchett names wife Martha, and her children, Elizabeth, Sarah, Edward, Ezekiel, and Daniel Burchett. He also names his son James, daughter Amy Beckhannum/(Buchanan?), son Isaac, deceased son Joseph, daughter Aggy Nants, husband of Frederick Nants, and son-in-law James Paschall.[22]

---

[22] Warren Co., N. C., WB 8:168, November Ct., 1795. Oberlies.

2. JACOB[4] FOX was born about 1730 in Surry Co., Va., and died after 22 March 1807 in Franklin Co., N. C. He married ELIZABETH LARK, daughter of ROBERT LARK and MARY. She was born 18 October 1750 in Mecklenburg Co., Va., and died 6 July 1843 in Lawrence Co., Miss.[23]

Jacob[4] Fox is present on the "Census" (substitute tax lists) in Mecklenburg Co., Va. in 1787 and in 1800. His wife's name is established by the her father's will.

The last will and testament of Robert Lark was written 8 February 1793 and proved 10 June 1793. He mentions his daughter, Elizabeth Fox, wife of Jacob Fox, daughter Sarah Wright, daughter Joyce Taylor, daughter Anne Collier, and son Samuel Lark.[24]

On 13 July 1795, suit was filed by Frederick Collier and Ann, his wife, against Samuel Lark, Jacob Fox and Elizabeth, his wife, Augustine Wright and Sarah, his wife, John Holmes, Walter Leigh, and Joshua Smith. Notation was made that Jacob Fox and Elizabeth, Walter Leigh, and Joshua Smith were not inhabitants of the Commonwealth of Virginia.[25] This suit establishes that Frederick Collier's wife was Ann Lark, and that Augustine Wright's wife was Sarah Lark.

Children of Jacob Fox and Elizabeth Lark are:[26]

> i . ROBERT[5] FOX, b. about 1782 Mecklenburg Co., Va.
> Robert Fox of Mecklenburg Co., Va., made a deed to Isham Fox of Franklin Co., N. C., 22 December 1800, which was witnessed by Lark Fox and Jacob Fox.[27]
> On 13 August 1806 Robert Fox, as assignee of Samuel Lark, Jr., was awarded a judgment against Edmund and Benjamin Wall for £102.13. In the usual formula, he was awarded costs, plus 6% interest from

---

[23] Jackson-Jimenez.

[24] Mecklenburg Co., Va., Will Book 3:163.

[25] Mecklenburg Co., Va., Court Order Book 8:475. See also Mecklenburg Co., Va., Court Order Book 8:223. [10 Feb 1794.] The suit was abated 13 May 1799 on the death of the plaintiffs. [Mecklenburg Co., Va., Court Order Book 10:170.]

[26] The names of the children are from Boddie, pp. 53-55.

[27] Franklin Co., N. C., Deed Book 3:91. Watson, p. 40.

the date the note was due, but the note would be paid in full if half the principal were paid.[28]

Robert[5] Fox is the only member of the family still present in Mecklenburg Co., Va., at the time the tax lists were made in March-April 1810.

ii. LARK[5] FOX, b. 1782 Mecklenburg Co., Va.; m. ELIZABETH GHOLSON 19 February 1805 Mecklenburg Co., Va.

Lark Fox bought land in Franklin Co., N. C., 26 October 1803 in a deed witnessed by Isham Fox.[29] Lark Fox made a bill of sale to Jacob Minor Goodloe of Wake Co., N. C. on 11 September 1805 in Franklin Co., N. C., which was witnessed by Jacob Fox.[30] Lark Fox appears on the 1810 Census in Franklin Co., N. C.

On 5 September 1828 Lark Fox and wife Elizabeth Fox made a bill of sale to William Gholson of Brunswick Co., Va., for her interest in certain slaves she inherited from her father Thomas Gholson who were now in the possession of his widow Jane for her lifetime.[31]

iii. ISHAM[5] FOX, b. 1784 Mecklenburg Co., Va.; d. before 1834 Franklin Co., N. C.; m. MARY.

Isham Fox appears on the 1810 Census for Franklin Co., N. C. Isham Fox bought a Negro sold as the property of Richard Wright on 12 May 1820.[32]

On 29 January 1834 Burrell Fox made a deed to Jacob Fox for the tract of land allotted to him in the lands of Isham Fox, deceased.[33] On 8 January 1835 Jacob Fox sold the two lots of land allotted to Jacob and Burrell Fox in the division of the lands of Isham Fox, deceased.[34]

iv. RICHARD[5] FOX, b. 25 November 1786 Mecklenburg Co., Va.; d. 17 October 1853 Lawrence Co., Miss.; m. MARY

---

[28] Mecklenburg Co., Va., Court Order Book 13:295.

[29] Franklin Co., N. C., Deed Book 11:250. Watson, p. 35.

[30] Franklin Co., N. C., Deed Book 13:103. Watson, p. 55.

[31] Franklin Co., N. C., Deed Book 25:106. Watson, p. 180.

[32] Franklin Co., N. C., Deed Book 20:35. Watson, p. 134. This may be 1865 Richard Wright of Decatur Co., Ga.

[33] Franklin Co., N. C., Deed Book 26:206. Watson, p. 206.

[34] Franklin Co., N. C., Deed Book 27:106. Watson, p. 211.

S. THOMAS, b. 1 March 1794, Louisburg, Franklin Co., N. C.; d. 25 June 1859 Lawrence Co., Miss.

Richard Fox gave a deed of trust on 29 March 1820 for land on which Elizabeth Fox had a life estate and on which she then resided, 9 March 1821.[35] The same issue was noted in the deed book on 12 September 1821.[36] In April 1833 Stephen Sparks made a deed of gift to Robert Fox, son of Richard Fox.[37]

On 16 March 1843 Mrs. Mary Fox, wife of Richard Fox, a legatee under the will of Samuel Thomas, deceased, was about to remove to Mississippi with her husband and family. John E. Thomas had purchased the remainder in the estate after the expiration of her life interest. Mrs. Mary Fox was the mother of William A. Fox. This note was witnessed by Thomas K. Thomas.[38] William A. Fox made a deed to John E. Thomas witnessed by Thomas K. Thomas on 1 March 1843.[39] Mary Fox, sister of Samuel Thomas, deceased, relinquished her life estate in the land where her late brother had lately resided.[40]

v. ARTHUR[5] FOX, b. 19 August 1788 Mecklenburg Co., Va.; d. 9 January 1852 Lawrence Co., Miss.; m. PATIENCE ANN JEFFREYS HUNT, daughter of JOHN HUNT and MARY JEFFREYS. She was b. 9 November 1789 Franklin Co., N. C.; d. 16 April 1851 Lawrence Co., Miss.

Arthur Fox (carpenter) made a deed to Robert Fox of Mecklenburg Co., Va. on 4 March 1812 witnessed by Richard Fox and Lark Fox.[41]

3. WILLIAM[4] (RICHARD[3], HENRY[2], HENRY[1]) FOX was born 13 February 1731/32 in Surry Co., Va., and died before November 1783 in Mecklenburg Co., Va. He married MARY KENDRICK

[35] Franklin Co., N. C., Deed Book 19:125. Watson, p. 130.
[36] Franklin Co., N. C., Deed Book 20:24. Watson, p. 133.
[37] Franklin Co., N. C., Deed Book 26:520. Watson, p. 203. This is probably land left by Isham[4] Fox to Elizabeth Lark, Richard's mother.
[38] Franklin Co., N. C., Deed Book 28:443. Watson p. 249.
[39] Franklin Co., N. C., Deed Book 28:444. Watson, p. 250
[40] Franklin Co., N. C., Deed Book 28:445. Watson, p. 250.
[41] Franklin Co., N. C., Deed Book 16:35. Watson, p. 83.

before 1761, daughter of WILLIAM KENDRICK and SARAH JANE JONES. She was born 12 April 1738 in Isle of Wight Co., Va., and died before 9 November 1795 in Mecklenburg Co., Virginia.

Last Will and Testament of William Fox[42]

In the name of God, Amen, I William Fox of the County of Mecklenburg, County and State of Virginia being sick and weak of body but of sound and perfect Sence and Memory blessed by Almighty God for the same and calling to mind the uncertainty of life and that it is appointed for all men once to die do make and ordain this my last Will and Testament in manner and form following, that is to say first and principally I recommend my soul to Almighty God the giver thereof in full hopes of my Resurrection through the Merits of Jesus Christ my Saviour and my body to be buried in a Christian like and decent manner at the Discretion of my Executors hereafter Mentioned and as for what worldly estate it hath pleased Almighty God to bless me with in this life, I give and dispose in manner and form following:

Item: I give and devise to my son Arthur Fox my Bay colt called Liberty and my Sorrell Filley to him and his heirs forever.

Item: I give and devise to my son Richard Fox my Filley named Betty Fine and my Pocotate to him and his heirs forever.

Item: I give and devise to my son William Fox my great Bay mare and her future increase to him and his heirs forever.

Item: I give and devise to my son Henry Fox my Sorell Colt to him and his heirs forever.

Item: I give and devise to my daughter Mary Kendrick Fox one good feather bed and furniture to her and her heirs forever.

Item: I give and devise to my son Benjamin Fox twenty pounds specie to him and his heirs forever.

---

[42] Mecklenburg Co., Va., WB 2:36 [4 Sep 1783] Cited by Peggy. 20 Apr 2000. http://boards.ancestry.com/mbexec?htx=messages&r=rw&p=surnames.fox&m=2566html.

Item: I give to my daughter Sally Jones Fox one good feather bed and furniture to her and her heirs forever.

Item: I give and devise to my daughter Johanna Fox one good feather bed and furniture to her and her heirs forever.

Item: I give and devise to my daughter Priscilla Fox one good feather bed and furniture to her and her heirs forever.

Item: I give and devise to my daughter Betsy Fox one good feather bed and furniture to her and her heirs forever.
Item: I give and bequeath to my beloved wife Mary Fox the use of my plantation and land also the use of Jack, Sucka, and Chainey and all the rest of my estate both real and personal during her life except she marries then for her to have only her third and my desire and will is that after my wife's death except as aforesaid all that part that I give my wife the use of during her life to be equally divided amongst my surviving children.

My will and further desire is that if any of my Surviving children should have died before they come of age or without Lawful issue that his or their part to be equally divided amongst all my surviving children and lastly my will is that my beloved wife Mary Fox and my friend John Kendrick be my sole executors of this my last will and Testament hereby revoking and Disannuling all other former Wills and Testaments by me heretofore made and Declaring this and only this to be my last as witness my hand and seal this 4th day of December in the year of our Lord One Thousand Seven Hundred and Eighty Three. Signed and sealed in the presence of us

John Kendrick   s/ William Fox (LS)
James Blanton
Lucas Sullivant

Last Will and Testament of Mary Fox[43]

In the name of God, Amen, I Mary Fox of Mecklenburg County, Virginia do appoint and ordain this writing to be my last will and Testament revoking all others heretofore made. Imprimis: I give to my son Henry Fox and to his heirs forever all that tract of land I bought of Benjamin Pennington except a corner which runs into the tract I now live on supposed to be five acres laid off by a marked line which I desire may be sold with my husbands land and the money be divided as is directed by his will. Now the above legacy to my son Henry is considered and intended by me as full discharge of any and all dues and debts I do now owe him upon hand or other ways and if he should fail to grant immediate and sufficient discharges I will and desire that so much of the land given to him as will answer the purpose, may be sold to pay any claim he may bring against my estate.

Item: I give to my daughter Mary Kindrick Fox and her heirs forever a Negro girl named Aggy.

Item: I lend in trust to my son Henry Fox for the use of my daughter Sally Jones Nowell and to no other purpose whatsoever so long as she shall live a Negro boy named Nicholas and at her death I give the said Nicholas to her son William and if William should die before his mother, I desire the said Nicholas may be sold and the money equally divided among my surviving children of my said daughter.

Item: I give to my daughter Jo-Hannah Fox and to her heirs forever a Negro girl named Fanny Bailey and a saddle and bridle.

Item: I give to my daughter Priscilla Fox and her heirs forever a Negro girl named Courtney Bailey, a mare called Spinnett and a saddle and bridle.

Item: I give to my daughter Betsey Fox and to her heirs forever one Negro boy named Burwell and a woman

---

[43] Mecklenburg Co., Va., WB 3:311-312 [9 Oct 1795] This transcription was posted on the FOX-L list serve on the Rootsweb site on 9 Apr 2000. This will is also on file for the Kentucky Court of Appeals; DB A-B1-B2, vol. 4, p. 208, recorded 12 October 1826.

named Doll, (but none of her future increase) and my saddle and bridle.

Item: I give to my grandson Arthur Fox and to his heirs forever a Negro boy named Randolph.

Item: I will and desire that the future increase of my Negro woman Doll be equally divided amongst my daughters Mary Kendrick Fox, Joe-Hannah Fox, Priscilla Fox and Betsey Fox, notwithstanding the above restriction in respect to the future increase of Doll, I still intend her certain proportion agreeable to this clause.

Item: My will and desire is that my Negro boy Robin be sold to the highest bidder upon twelve months credit and out of the money arising from this sale I give to my daughters Joe-Hannah and Betsey twelve pounds each.

Lastly I appoint my sons Henry Fox, Richard Fox, William Davis, James Harwell and John Davis, Jr., Executors of this my last will and testament in witness whereof I have hereunto set my hand and affixed my seal this 9th day of October 1795.

Signed, Sealed and Published in presence of

S/ Mary Fox (Seal)

John Wright

Samuel Lambert

Isham (X his mark) Lambert

Stephen Mabry

At a Court of Quarterly Session held for Mecklenburg County the 9th day of November 1795 this will was proved by the oath of John Wright and Samuel Lambert witnesses thereto and ordered to be recorded and at a court held for the same County the 14th day of December 1795 on the motion of Henry Fox and Richard Fox, two of the Executors therein named who made oath thereto and together with Nathaniel Ingles and James B. Davis their securities entered into and acknowledged their bond in penalty of two thousand pounds conditioned as the law directs certificate was granted them for obtaining a probate thereof in due form. Liberty being reserved for the other Executors therein named to be in the probated when they shall see fit. Teste: William Baskerville, CC

Children of William Fox and Mary Kendrick are:

  i. ARTHUR[5] FOX, b. 27 February 1761 Mecklenburg Co., Va.;
     d. after 19 September 1793 Mason Co., Ky.; m. MARY
     YOUNG. [44]

 ii. RICHARD[5] FOX, b. 2 March 1764 Mecklenburg Co., Va.; d.
     10 January 1833; m. MARY BLANTON; b. 20 October
     1772 Mecklenburg Co., Va. [45]

iii. WILLIAM[5] FOX, b. 2 March 1764 Mecklenburg Co., Va.

 iv. HENRY[5] FOX, b. about 1766 Mecklenburg Co., Va.; m. (1)
     SARAH WOODSON b. 25 January 1765 Edgecombe Co.,
     N. C.; d. Warren Co., Ky.; m. (2) SARAH PARKE b. 1783
     Mecklenburg Co., Va.[46]

     Henry Fox was a witness for the Commonwealth
     against Nelson Cole 10 December 1792. Also paid 25
     pounds of tobacco for their day at court in this case
     were Edward Pennington, Thomas Roberts and Laban
     Wright.[47] Henry Fox was awarded £15.16.6 in a case
     against Uriah Hawkins and Jesse Taylor on 13 August
     1806.[48]

  v. MARY KENDRICK[5] FOX, b. about 1768 Mecklenburg Co.,
     Va.

     Mary Kendrick Fox was resident of Mason Co.,
     Kentucky when she applied for adjustment in her share
     of her father's estate.

 vi. BENJAMIN[5] FOX b. 1770 Mecklenburg Co., Va.; m.
     MARTHA NOWELL 9 June 1792, Mecklenburg Co., Va.

     Georgia, Putnam County) This Indenture made this
     twenty fourth day of July Eighteen hundred and
     seventeen between Adam Harden of the one part and
     Benjamin A. Fox of the other part, both of the State and
     County aforesaid...for the sum of five hundred
     dollars....one half of a certain tract of land lying and
     being in the county and state aforesaid and in the third
     district of originally Baldwin County, but now in the

---

[44] Boddie, pp. 53-55.
[45] Oberlies.
[46] Jackson-Jimenez. Holtzclaw, pp. 53-55. This source says the first wife's last name
was Kendrick.
[47] Mecklenburg Co., Va., Court Order Book 8:87.
[48] Mecklenburg Co., Va., Court Order Book 13:294.

County of Putnam aforesaid known in the form of said land plat held by number (121) one hundred twenty one drawn by Job Tidwell..." Signed by Adam Harden.[49]

"Georgia, Putnam County) This indenture made this 29th day of December Eighteen hundred and seventeen between Benjamin A. Fox of the State and County aforesaid of the one part and Osborn Williams of the State aforesaid and County of Hancock of the other part, Witnesseth that the said Benjamin A. Fox for and in consideration of nine hundred dollars to him in hand paid ...one half of a certain square of land lying and being in the County and State aforesaid and in the Third District of originally Baldwin, but now Putnam County known in the plan of said district by the number of one hundred and twenty one drawn by and granted to Job Tidwell and bounded by...[bounded] East by Goodrich Jones' line which land last mentioned is the other half of the square of land, which square contains 202½ acres more or less, the conveyed premises containing 101¼ acres more or less..." Signed by "Benj. A. Fox"; witnesses Hadley Varner and illegible.[50]

Benjamin A. Fox was present on the 1815 tax list for Putnam Co., Ga., along with Richard W. Fox. This is Richard[5] (Richard[4], Richard[3]) Fox. Benjamin A. Fox appears on the Morgan Co., Ga., tax lists for 1819, 1820, 1822, and 1825 along with Richard W. Fox,[51] probably Richard W.[6] Fox, son of Richard[5] Fox.

Benjamin A. Fox appears in Troup Co., Ga., 1830.[52]

vii. SALLY JONES[5] FOX, b. about 1772 Mecklenburg Co., Va.; d. before 9 October 1804 Mecklenburg Co., Va.; m. THOMAS NOWELL

Henry Fox, Benjamin Fox, and Mary K. Fox, Joanna Fox, Priscilla Fox, and Betsey Fox, "which said Joanna, Priscilla, and Betsey are infants under 21," by Samuel Hopkins, Jr., "their next friend," and Thomas

---

[49] Putnam Co., Ga., Deed Book H:245. 13 August 1819
[50] Putnam Co., Ga., Deed Book H:302-303. 6 February 1821.
[51] Morgan Co., Ga., Tax Lists located on http:www.usgenbweb.org.
[52] 1830 Census Troup Co., Ga., p. 55, [He was listed as being 30-40 years old as was his wife, with one male under 5, one 5-10, one 10-15, one 15-20, one 20-30, and two girls under five, one 5-10, and one 15-20. There were 16 slaves.]

219

Nowell and Holley Joshua, his wife, sued Richard[4] Fox and John Kendrick as the surviving executors of William Fox for a suit in chancery regarding their inheritance 9 Oct 1804.[53] Since William Fox died in 1783, all of his children would have reached their majority by the time of this suit, so I think the reference is to the fact they were underage in 1783. The form of the suit indicates that Sally Jones Fox is dead, as her husband has married Holley Joshua.

viii. JOHANNA[5] FOX, b. about 1774 Mecklenburg Co., Va.; m. SAMUEL HOLMES, Jr. 13 December 1796, Mecklenburg Co., Va.

ix. PRISCILLA[5] FOX, b. about 1776 Mecklenburg Co., Va.; m. WILLIAMS

x. BETSEY[5] FOX, b. about 1778 Mecklenburg Co., Va.; d. 13 before July 1801, Mecklenburg Co., Va.

"On the motion of Henry Fox, with William Davis, Sr., & Roger Gregory as his securities, a certificate of administration for the estate of Betsy Fox is granted...William Holmes, Pennington Holmes, John Davis, and Edward Delony or any three of them...to appraise"[54]

4. RICHARD[4] FOX was born 1734 Surry Co., Va. He died before 1820 Franklin Co., N. C. He married (1) unknown about 1760. He married (2) MARY (DAVIS) RAINEY March 22, 1775 Mecklenburg Co., Va., widow of JAMES RAINEY.

Richard[4] Fox inherited the the tract patented by his father south of the Roanoke River, as shown by the 1782 "Census" of Mecklenburg County, which shows Richard[4] Fox by himself in the district surveyed by William Davis, which ran south of the River from the Brunswick Co., Virginia line. His brothers, William[4] and Jacob[4] Fox were in the district surveyed by Lewis Parham, which ran north of the Roanoke, again from the Brunswick County line.[55]

---

[53] Mecklenburg Co., Va., Court Order Book 12:253.

[54] Mecklenburg Co., Va., Court Order Book 11:21. [July 13, 1801]

[55] Elliott, Katherine B. Early Settlers of Mecklenburg County, Virginia, Vol. 2. (Easley SC: Southern Historical Press, 1983,) pp. 204, 208-209. Cited hereafter as Elliott.

There are four men named Richard Fox living in Mecklenburg County. The first is Richard[4] Fox. He is shown in the 1800 tax list to have a son, also named Richard,[56] who was over 21, hence born before 1779, who will be called Richard[5] Fox. The third person is Richard[5] (Jacob[4], Richard[3]) Fox, a nephew of Richard[4] Fox by his eldest brother, who was born 1786, and so turned 21 in 1807. The available evidence suggests this family had moved to Franklin Co., N. C., about 1800, so this man should not appear in the Mecklenburg County records as an adult. Lastly, there is Richard[5] (William[4], Richard[3]) Fox, another nephew of Richard[4] Fox, by his next oldest brother William. This Richard Fox was born in 1764, and so would be expected to appear in the Mecklenburg County records after 1785, so for convenience I will designate him as Richard[5] (William) Fox, in distinction to his first cousin Richard[5] (Richard) Fox.

There are two marriages recorded for Richard Fox in the Mecklenburg Co., Va., records. The first bond was obtained by Richard Fox on 22 March 1775 to marry Mary Rainey, with William Davis as his security.[57] This is surely Richard[4] Fox, as Richard[5] (William) and Richard[5] (Richard) would have been too young. Mary Rainey was the relict of James Rainey, and was probably Mary Davis.[58] I have found no evidence of children from the first marriage.

There is a second marriage bond this time obtained by Richard Fox on 4 October 1792 to marry Nancy Wright with Solomon Patillo as security.[59] While this could be either Richard[5] (Richard) Fox or Richard[5] (William) Fox, the former is more likely for several reasons.

First, the connections between Solomon Patillo and the Fox family were through Richard[4] Fox. Anna Harwell, sister of Grief Harwell, and as will be shown later, probably son-in-law of Richard[4] Fox married as her second husband, Augustine Patillo in

[56] Elliott, p. 188. Henry Fox is the only other man named Fox who shows up on this list, (p. 187).

[57] Nottingham, Stratton. The Marriage License Bonds of Mecklenburg County, Virginia, from 1765 to 1810. (Onancock, Va.:,1928,) p. 19. Accessed at ancestry.com. Cited hereafter as Nottingham.

[58] Mary Rainey applied for letters of administration on the estate of James Rainey, deceased, on 8 November 1773.[58] None of the children of Francis[5] Rainey are of the right age to be Mary Rainey, and I think she is almost surely Mary Davis, relict of James F. Rainey, deceased.

[59] Nottingham, p. 19.

Warren Co., N. C., where he died in 1794. The Patillo and Harwell families were inter-connected, as shown by the estate sale of John Pettway conducted by Sterling Harwell 12 January 1796.[60] This included bonds and notes due from Solomon Patillo, and purchases from Richard Fox, John Wright, and Captain William Davis.[61] Lastly, Kendrick family researchers show the name of Richard[5] (William) Fox wife as Mary Blanton.[62]

If we accept that this marriage bond is for Richard[5] (Richard) Fox then we need to push back his date of birth, to as early as 1761. Mary Rainey, then, was likely the second wife of Richard[4] Fox. There is indirect evidence that Richard[5] Fox was not the only child of a putative first marriage. Harwell researchers have been reasonably sure that Grief Harwell's wife Anna or Ann was Ann Fox. She is generally thought to be the daughter of 1771 Richard Fox and his wife Hannah Williamson. However, the available evidence suggests Ann[4] Fox was born about 1740 and married Jacob Kendrick and moved to Caroline and then Culpeper Co., Va. Furthermore, Grief Harwell was thought to have been born around 1753, and had his children from 1782 to about 1796. This suggests to me a marriage about 1780 to a woman born about 1760, who would have been 36, rather than 56 at the time of Hannah's birth. The close association of Richard[4] Fox and Grief Harwell in the affairs of Mecklenburg County from about 1790 to 1810 suggests a family relationship, but I believe it more likely he is the father-in-law. Ann Fox, wife of Grief Harwell, was born say 1760-1762 to Richard[4] Fox and his unknown first wife, and was a granddaughter of 1771 Richard Fox and Hannah Williamson.

There are other marriage bonds of interest. Two clearly involve daughters of Richard[4] Fox and Mary Rainey. The first is between Mary Fox and Moses Lunsford obtained 28 June 1796 with the consent of Richard, father of Mary. This ceremony was performed by John Loyd, who was certified to perform marriages as a Methodist minister in Mecklenburg County on 10 October 1791.[63] Since parental consent was required, we can be sure that

---

[60] Warren Co., N. C., WB 8:333.
[61] Kerr, Mary Hinton. Warren County North Carolina Will Book 8. http://rootsweb.com/~ncwarren/will8.html.
[62] Boddie, pp. 53-55.
[62] Oberlies.
[63] Mecklenburg Co., Va., Court Order Book 7:644.

Mary Fox was born after 1775, so her mother would have been Mary Rainey.

The other bond was obtained by John Wright on 3 October 1797 to marry Sarah Fox with William Taylor (Speed) as his security. Again consent was obtained from her father Richard Fox. His release is on file in the marriage records, and shows that he signed the consent with his full name, (as did John Wright.) Again, we can be sure Sarah was born after 1777, so her mother would also be Mary Rainey.

There are two marriage bonds that are uncertain. The first was obtained 9 December 1801 between James Taylor and Priscilla Fox, with Josiah Floyd as security. This is probably Priscilla[5] (William[4], Richard[3]) Fox, although there is some information that she married a man named Williams. The second was obtained on 3 March 1799 for a marriage between Abner Ragland[64] and Nancy Fox, with Richard Fox acting as security.[65] This ceremony was performed by Ebenezer McGowan, who was also a Methodist minister. Since there are no other known children of the three sons of 1771 Richard Fox named Nancy who would be getting married at this time, I believe she should be included as a third daughter of Richard[4] Fox and Mary Rainey. The Richard Fox who acted as security could be either Richard[5] (Richard) Fox or Richard[5] (William) Fox. If the former, it is another indication that Nancy was also a daughter of Richard[4] Fox and Mary (Davis) Rainey.

Richard[4] Fox sold a tract of land to James Blanton on 10 March 1777.[66] In 1791, the town of St Tammany was laid out on fifty acres on the Roanoke River owned by James Blanton. The town was established to serve as a warehouse for tobacco inspection.. Grief Harwell, Richard Fox, and Stephen Mabry (who was Grief's brother-in-law, a brother to Jordan and Joshua Mabry,) were the first inspectors appointed. Grief Harwell and

---

[64] Donald Simpson, Jr., says Abner Ragland was from Hanover Co., Va., born about 1777 and died in Putnam Co., Ga., leaving sons Reuben, Richard, Williamson, Edward and John and daughters Polly and Nancy. [John Barber connections. 13 Dec 2002. Located on http://worldconnect.rootsweb.com (db :2339872).] For reasons discussed under Richard[5] Fox's entry, I think he may have gone to Putnam County, Ga., and died there before 1830, which also supports the notion that Nancy is another daughter of Richard[4] Fox.

[65] Nottingham, p. 19. Thomas Fox is bondsman, but I have not located anyone of that name so far.

[66] Mecklenburg Co., Va., DB 5:20. (Deed not examined.)

Richard Fox would be reappointed every year up until 1807 for this position. Between 9 February 1795 and September 1800 Richard Fox was involved in seven transactions with the Commonwealth of Virginia.[67]

In 1801, the warehouse was constructed at St Tammany under the name of Samuel Lambert & Company with Samuel Lambert, Grief Harwell and Richard Fox as business partners.[68]

Richard Fox's financial affairs began a downward spiral in 1803, as witnessed by the following extracts from the County Court Minutes.

On 10 November 1803, Ebenezer McGowan filed a suit *in fiere facias* against Richard Fox and John Wright (Fox), which was not contested. A judgment was rendered for the plaintiff in the amount of £596.19.71/2d. As was the pattern at that time, the judgment could be satisfied by paying one half of the debt, or £295.18.3 "and three farthings," plus costs an annual interest rate of 6% from 5 October 1803.[69] This judgment was appealed to the next district court to be held at Brunswick. (records not found.)

On 7 January 1804 Pleasant Allen & Co. obtained a judgment against Richard Fox and John Wright for defaulting on a bond in the amount of £86.13.2. This judgment would also be satisfied by payment of half the debt plus costs and 6% annual interest from 20 November 1803.[70]

Richard Fox entered a Deed Poll of Trust with Presley Hinton on 9 July 1804.[71] Ebenezer McGowan filed suit against Walter Pennington and Richard Fox on 12 August 1804, and the defendants were ordered to pay or go to jail. The same day Grief Harwell, acting as administrator for John Davis filed suit against John Wright and Richard Fox, although there was a dispute as to whether the debt had already been paid or not.

On 10 March 1806, Edward Davis brought suit against John Wright, Richard Fox, and Lewis Wright in fiere facias and obtained a judgment in the amount of £67.7.3.[72] The same day the

---

[67] Mecklenburg Co., Va., DB 8:493; 9:151; 9:336; 10:70; 10:227; and 10:384. (Deeds not examined) There are additional transactions up until 1808, when they stop.

[68] Bracey, Susan L. Life By the Roaring Roanoke: A History of Mecklenburg County, Virginia. (Mecklenburg Bicentennial Committee, 1977,) pp. 117-118.

[69] Mecklenburg Co., Va., Court Order Book 12:58.

[70] Mecklenburg Co., Va., Court Order Book 12:97.

[71] Mecklenburg Co., Va., Court Order Book 12:194; cf. also DB 12:282.

[72] Mecklenburg Co., Va., Court Order Book 13:102.

case of Edward Delony against John Wright (Fox) was heard, and a judgment against John Wright for non-performance of the assumption was levied for £7.6 plus costs.[73]

On 14 April 1806 a deed poll of trust between Richard Fox and Samuel Lambert of the first part and Grief Harwell of the second part was recorded.[74] This likely refers to Richard[4], *(William[3])* Fox rather than Richard[3] *(Richard[2])* Fox, since Samuel Holmes would have been a brother in law to the former.

On 12 May 1806 William Wright was granted a judgment against Grief Harwell as executor of John Davis, deceased, for £77.7.1.[75] The next day Grief Harwell, acting as executor of John Davis, deceased, had his case against John Wright and Richard Fox for debt heard and obtained a judgment of £13 Virginia money, the debt to be satisfied by the payment of £6.10 plus costs, and 6% interest from 16 November 1803.[76] The same day Grief Harwell was ordered to pay Richard Fox $3.18 for six days as a witness in his suit against William Wright.[77] Ebenezer McGowan, as assignee of John Wright was awarded £40.2 in a suit against Richard Fox and Walter Pennington.[78]

Finally, again on 13 May 1806 Richard Fox, as the assignee of Samuel Lark in his suit against Edmund Wall and Samuel Simmons was awarded a judgment for £40.[79] In this case, I suspect this is Richard[5] (William) Fox rather than Richard[4] Fox, because of the latter's association with the Lark family. This suspicion is heightened by the suit of Robert Fox, assignee of Samuel Lark, Jr., against Edmund and Benjamin Wall in which he obtained a judgment for £102.13.0.[80]

On 8 September 1806, Richard Fox and Jacob Bugg were security in the amount of $5000 for John Wright's application for letters of administration for the estate of Roderick Wright. Smith Collier, Daniel Taylor, Elijah Rideout and Stephen Mabry were appointed to appraise the estate.[81] The same day Richard Fox with

---

[73] Mecklenburg Co., Va., Court Order Book 13:103.
[74] Mecklenburg Co., Va., Court Order Book 13:145.
[75] Mecklenburg Co., Va., Court Order Book 13:175.
[76] Mecklenburg Co., Va., Court Order Book 13:185.
[77] Mecklenburg Co., Va., Court Order Book 13:186.
[78] Mecklenburg Co., Va., Court Order Book 13:191.
[79] Mecklenburg Co., Va., Court Order Book 13:187.
[80] Mecklenburg Co., Va., Court Order Book 13:295.
[81] Mecklenburg Co., Va., Court Order Book 13:303.

Grief Harwell and Ebenezer McGowan as his securities for a $5000 bond, received a certificate for letters of administration of the estate of Moses Lunsford.[82] Richard Fox appears several times in his capacity as administrator of Moses Lunsford.

On 13 October 1806 Grief Harwell, again in his capacity as administrator for John Davis, deceased, was awarded a judgment for £21.9.6 against John Wright, Richard Fox, and Isham Fox, the penalty of the bond they had made.

On 14 September 1807 Richard Fox and Grief Harwell were appointed inspectors of tobacco at St. Tammany one last time.[83]

Further evidence of economic hard times are the suits of Samuel Lambert, Grief Harwell, and Richard Fox, doing business as Samuel Lambert & Co., against William Blanton and Judson Burnett,[84] and William Baskerville against Richard Fox and Henry Watson in which judgment against the defendant Fox in a suit *fiere facias* for £211.8.6 was obtained.[85] Finally a deed poll of trust between John Wright of the first part, Richard Fox of the second part, and Evan Evans of the third part was entered 12 Sep. 1808.[86]

All of these financial losses, which are enormous compared to the usual suits in the records, led the nearly 75 year old Richard[4] Fox to throw in the towel, by selling his land to William Baskerville in a deed recorded 11 June 1810.[87]

Richard Fox does not appear in the 1810 tax list for Mecklenburg Co., Va., and I have found no evidence of his death in the court records through 1816 when his son-in-law Grief Harwell died. I have not found him in either Warren or Franklin Co., N. C., after that date, either.

Children of RICHARD FOX and unknown wife are:

    i.   ANN[5] FOX b. say 1760, Mecklenburg Co., Va.; d. after 12 October 1816; m. GRIEF HARWELL about 1780 Mecklenburg Co., Va., son of JAMES HARWELL and ELIZABETH PEPPER. He was b. about 1749 in Brunswick

---

[82] Mecklenburg Co., Va., Court Order Book 13:301.
[83] Mecklenburg Co., Va., Court Order Book 14:215.
[84] Mecklenburg Co., Va., Court Order Book 14:96. [11 May 1807]
[85] Mecklenburg Co., Va., Court Order Book 14:299. [14 Jan 1808]
[86] Mecklenburg Co., Va., Court Order Book 14:454.
[87] Mecklenburg Co., Va., Court Order Book 15:224. cf. DB 14:292. (not examined.)

Co., Va., and d. before May 15, 1816 Mecklenburg Co., Virginia.

"In 1777, during the American Revolution, he was commissioned as a first lieutenant in the local county militia, the Brunswick Blues.[88] The extent of his military service or any records dealing with the same or unknown to me at this time (if any exist). He's listed along with his cousin Buckner Harwell and Paul Harwell as being compensated in 1785 for supplying the army with beef and clothing—another way that he was involved besides being a soldier. In November 1781, he was added to the list as a fit person for the commission of the peace. In December of that year he was given a commission of the Peace and Oyer along with thirteen others. In 1787 Grief was commissioned as Captain in the Brunswick militia. Also in 1787, he was one of seven sworn as a Brunswick County Deputy Sheriff. The next year 1788, he was appointed under sheriff of Brunswick County. In 1794, he was appointed General Justice of the Brunswick court.

Obviously Grief was doing very well in Brunswick. It would appear that he was well-known and perhaps well-liked, and that he had his nose in a lot of different activities. So why did he move to Mecklenburg? Obviously he had land interests there as a result of his father's will but before his made his move to Mecklenburg he appears to have sold most of his Mecklenburg land. Some of the other more plausible reasons in my opinion are: (1) his brother James moved there and his wife Anne's family (the Foxes) was there, (2) speculation in regard to St. Tammany, the new town that was being planned and built on the banks of the Roanoke, (3) maybe he just thought it was time for a career change.

The year 1807, the last year that Grief was appointed as a tobacco inspector, seems to signal Grief's retirement from public life. His appearance in

---

[88] Harvell, Roger. Charles and Bob and the Reunion. 2 Mar 2003. Located on http://genforum.genealogy.com/harwell/messages/1443.html.

the records show a marked decrease after 1807. Why? Maybe it was just time to slow down or was it something else? In reading between the lines of Grief's will, I now see some significant inferences and omissions which I did not when I first read the will. Grief wrote his will in 1809 but he didn't die until seven years later. I get the feeling that something rather drastic moved Grief to write his will a bit prematurely. It may be that he was sick and was prompted to think "I better write this while I'm still alive" OR maybe it was because of a tragedy. I'm inclined to think it was the latter. Grief Harwell's will always gave Michael and I the idea that something is not as it sounds. For some time it provided a false lead (at least to us) as to who my ancestor Samuel Harwell's father was. Samuel is mentioned in the will as a grandson but Samuel's father is not mentioned. However I think Samuel's father was very much in Grief's thoughts. In fact, if my feelings are correct this unmentioned son may be the very reason Grief wrote his will in 1809. He named his wife Ann, his son Thomas, his daughter Hannah, and his two grandsons Samuel and Grief Harwell. Originally we thought the two grandsons were sons of Thomas, later we discovered that Grief had another son, James T. Harwell, a son that perhaps an anguished father could not bear to refer to as "deceased". This I think was the tragedy that compelled Grief to write his will. This unmentioned son would prove to be my ancestor. In the following years Grief continued to sell and buy properties but other than that, appears to have retreated somewhat from public life. In 1816, on April the 25th, he sold a hundred and thirty eight acres of land, on May the 15th, the same year, his will was presented in court. Sometime during that short span of time Grief died."

Children of GRIEF HARWELL and ANN FOX are:

1. THOMAS[4] HARWELL, b. about 1782, Brunswick Co., Va.; d. 1854, Shelby Co., Tenn.; m. (1) MARTHA SMITH October 3, 1804, Warren Co., N. C.; d. about 1841 Shelby Co., Tenn.; m. (2)

ELIZABETH EDDINS 20 January 1848 Shelby Co., Tenn.

2. JAMES[4] T. HARWELL, b. about 1784 Brunswick Co., Va.; d. 1807 Warren Co., N. C.; m. MARY NANCE 20 March 1804, Warren Co., N. C.; d. about 1810 Warren Co., N. C.

3. HANNAH[4] HARWELL, b. about 1796 Mecklenburg Co., Va.; d. about 1866 Rutherford Co., Tenn.; m. (1) ALLEN RAINEY 22 October 1817, Mecklenburg Co., Va. He died 1831 Rutherford Co., Tenn.; m. (2) JOHN GAMBLE, before 1840, Rutherford Co., Tenn. (d. s. p.)

5. ii. RICHARD W.[5] FOX b. about 1765 Mecklenburg Co., Va.; d. 15 March 1828 Putnam Co., Ga.; m. (1) NANCY WRIGHT 4 October 1792, Mecklenburg Co., Va.; m. (2) WILMOUTH WRIGHT, b. about 1790 in Virginia; d. 1865 Talbot Co., Ga.

Children of RICHARD FOX and MARY RAINEY are:

iii. MARY[5] FOX, b. about 1776 Mecklenburg Co., Va..; m. MOSES LUNSFORD 28 June 1796 Mecklenburg Co., Va.; d. before 8 September 1806 Mecklenburg Co., Va.

On the motion of Richard Fox who made Oath according to law & together with Grief Harwell and Ebenezer McGowan his securities entered into and acknowledged their bond in the penalty of five thousand dollars conditioned as the law directs, certificate is granted him for obtaining letters of administration for the estate of Moses Lunsford, dec'd., in due form...Ordered that William Davis, Amasa Palmer, Jacob Bugg and Thomas Palmer or any three (appraise the estate of Moses Lunsford, dec'd.)[89]

Thomas Dent won a judgment against Richard Fox as administrator of the estate of Moses Lunsford for £17.6.11 on 16 March 1808.[90] On 10 July 1809 Richard Fox relinquished his role as administrator.

---

[89] Mecklenburg Co., Va., Court Order Book 13:301.

[90] Mecklenburg Co., Va., Court Order Book 14:343. The judgment had been set aside March 9, 1807. (OB 14:46) In this action Thomas Dent was assignee for the firm of Ferrell, Delony, and Abernathy.

"On the motion of Richard Fox administrator of Moses Lunsford, deceased, It is ordered that Grief Harwell, Amasa Palmer, Thomas Palmer, and Joshua Davis or any three of them do examine, state, and settle the account of the administration of the said decedents estate and report thereof to the Court."[91] The estate was finally settled 13 March 1810.[92]

iv. SARAH[5] FOX, b. about 1776 Mecklenburg Co., Va.; d. about 1810 Mecklenburg Co., Va.; m. JOHN WRIGHT 27 October 1797 Mecklenburg Co., Va. He was b. about 1764 Brunswick Co., Va.; d. before 10 October 1832 Clarke Co., Ga. (See Chapter Seven.)

v. NANCY[5] FOX, b. about 1779 Mecklenburg Co., Va.; m. ABNER RAGLAND 3 March 1799 Mecklenburg Co., Va.; b. about 1777 Hanover Co., Va.; d. Putnam Co., Ga. (see Chapter One.)

5. RICHARD W.[5] FOX was born about 1765 in Mecklenburg Co., Va. and died 15 March 1828 in Putnam Co., Ga. He married (1) NANCY WRIGHT 4 October 1792 in Mecklenburg Co., Va. She died about 1810 Putnam Co., Ga. He married (2) WILMOUTH WRIGHT, born about 1790 in Virginia and died 1865 in Talbot Co., Ga.

Richard Fox is present in the household of his father in the 1800 Tax List for the lower district of Mecklenburg Co., Va. His activities in Georgia were reviewed earlier.[93] I have not yet found where Richard Fox purchased land. He may have given these lands to his two sons from his first marriage: Richard W. Fox and Benjamin A. Fox. (see below.)

Wilmouth Fox is shown as head of household in the 1830 Census for Putnam Co., Ga., (p. 209) with one son under five, one five to ten, and three daughters, one 5-10, one 10-15, and one 15-20. She was listed as aged 30-40. Given that she had one daughter 15-20 years of age, and was probably at least 20 years old when

[91] Mecklenburg Co., Va., Court Order Book 15:6.
[92] Mecklenburg Co., Va., Court Order Book 15:161.
[93] See pp. 12-14.

she had that child, she must have been closer to 40, and so born about 1790.

In 1840 Wilmouth Fox is in Talbot Co., Ga., with two males between the ages of 15 and 20 and two females between the ages of 20 and 30, plus two slaves.

Wilmouth Fox was a fortunate drawer in the 1838 land lottery, where she qualified as a widow of a Revolutionary War soldier. She qualified for a tract of land in Walker Co., Ga., and one in Murray County, Ga.[94]

In the 1850 Census for Talbot Co., Ga., Wilmouth Fox has Harriet Fox living with her and is living near Elizabeth (Fox) Athon, wife of Nathaniel Athon, blacksmith, and their three children. In the 1860 census Wilmouth Fox is living in the household of Nathaniel Athon, who is now described as a blacksmith and a Methodist minister. She is said to be 70 years old, born in Virginia, again leading to an estimated birth year of about 1790.

From these census records, we can establish the names of two of the daughters of Richard W. Fox and Wilmouth Wright: Harriet and Elizabeth. The third, and probably the eldest was Johanna Williamson Fox. She left letters which give her mother's maiden surname as Wright, and record their deaths.[95]

The probate file gives the names of Quintana Fox and Charles James Fox as minor children. I am not certain if Quintana was a boy or a girl, but from the census records, I would have to infer that these are the two sons of Richard and Wilmouth (Wright) Fox.

Child of RICHARD W. FOX and NANCY WRIGHT is:

> i. RICHARD W.[6] FOX, b. about 1795 Mecklenburg Co., Va.; m. FRANCES C. WEST, daughter of WILLIAM WEST and ALICE LAWRENCE in Morgan Co., Ga.

Children of RICHARD W. FOX and WILMOUTH WRIGHT are: [96]

> ii. CAROLINE[6] FOX
> iii. IRENE[6] FOX

---

[94]Smith, James F. Cherokee Land Lottery. Cited by John Fox, 23 Feb 2004.

[95] Baumgardner.

[96] Baumgardner, Walker. Walker Baumgardner Family. 16 Nov 2002. Located on http://worldconnect.rootsweb.com. (db wbaumgar).

iv. WILMOUTH[6] FOX

v. ELIZABETH CAROLINE[6] FOX, b. 16 December 1809 Putnam Co., Ga.; d. 10 July 1892 Pike Co., Ala.; m. NATHANIEL ATHON 24 April 1829 Putnam Co., Ga.

vi. JOANNAH W.[6] FOX, b. May 1812 Putnam Co., Ga.; d. 19 March 1885 Wilkinson Co., Ga.; m. JEREMIAH WALKER 12 April 1829 Henry Co., Ga., son of ELISHA WALKER and ELIZABETH BOWERS; b. about 1792 Washington Co., Ga.; d. 29 July 1875 Wilkinson Co., Ga.

vii. HARRIET[6] FOX was born about 1816, Putnam Co., Ga.

viii. QUINTANA[6] FOX, b. about 1820, Putnam Co., Ga.; m. THOMAS MOSS, b. about 1821 SC.

ix. THOMAS[6] FOX, b. about 1823 Putnam Co., Ga.

x. CHARLES JAMES[6] FOX , b. about 1826 Putnam Co., Ga.

1777 William Kendrick of Bute Co., North Carolina[97]

1. WILLIAM[2] (*JOHN[1]*) KENDRICK was born 1704 in King William Co., Virginia and died 1 July 1777 in Bute Co., North Carolina. He married (1) MARY BURWELL. He married (2) SARAH JANE JONES about 1726 in King William Co., Virginia, the daughter of ROBERT JONES and REBECCA WEST. She was born in July 1714 perhaps in Suffolk Co., Virginia, and died in February 1796 in Edgecombe Co., North Carolina.

William[2] Kendrick was born in 1704 and his wife, Sarah Jones, was born in 1715 according to the family Bible record of their grandson, Richard Fox, now in the possession of Mrs. Rose Freeman Ferrell of Anson, Texas, a descendant. It is probable that a deed in Hanover Co., Va., dated 21 May 1730 from Henry Fox of King William Co., and Joseph Fox of Hanover Co., to William Kendrick of King William Co. for 400 acres on which Joseph Fox lived at the time refers to William[2] Kendrick.[98] By 1735 William[2] Kendrick had moved to Isle of Wight, Co., Va., where he witnessed a deed on 18 Feb 1735 from William Bowers to Edward Morgan. On 20 Nov 1744 he proved his right for importation of three persons into North Carolina.[99]

[97] Boddie, pp. 34-39

[98] Hanover Co., Va. Records 1733-35 p. 208.

[99] North Carolina Colonial Land Records IV, 705, p. 446.

William[2] Kendrick's brother in law, Edward Jones, died Granville Co, NC in 1750. William Kendrick was deeded 200 acres in Granville Co. from the estate of Edward Jones 2 Sep 1751.[100]

Sarah was probably the daughter of Rebecca West who on 21 Nov 1719 made a deed of gift to her four children: Edward Jones, Obedience Jones, James Jones, "when he is 20, he being 11 years old in February next"), and Sarah Jones "she being 5 years old last July."[101]

William[2] Kendrick appears in numerous deeds in Granville Co. His land fell into Bute Co. (later Warren Co.) and he died there in 1777. His will, dated 12 Jan 1776 and probated at the May Court 1777 in Bute Co. mentions children John, James, Mary, Sarah, Rebecca, and Martha, grandson Benjamin Thornton, son Jones, son Isham.[102]

Children of WILLIAM KENDRICK and SARAH JONES are:

i. JACOB[3] KENDRICK, b. about 1730; d. 1794 Culpeper Co., Va.; m. ANNE[4] FOX 1756, daughter of RICHARD[3] FOX and HANNAH WILLIAMSON.

Probate: 17 February 1794 Culpeper County, Virginia. Value of estate 52 pounds. Occupation: Bricklayer Caroline County, Virginia.

In Culpeper County, Virginia, 21 June 1750, Jacob Kendrick purchased 240 acres on the north side of Potato run in the Great Fork of the Rappahannock for 20 pounds. In Louisa County, Virginia 14 September 1767, Jacob Kendrick bought 500 acres for 40 pounds. On 6 February 1752 in Culpeper County, Jacob Kendrick sold about 50 acres for five shillings. On 5 September 1792 Culpeper County, Virginia, Jacob Kendrick sold 150 acres, the residue of his land. Sold land 1 August 1785 in Louisa County, Virginia. On 18 April 1765 in Culpeper County, Jacob Kendrick leased 192 acres to grow tobacco, apples and peaches. On 11 May 1791 he leased 195 acres in Culpeper County, Virginia,.

---

[100] Granville Co., N. C., Deed Book A:540.
[101] Isle of Wight Co., Va., Great Book:311.
[102] Warren Co., N. C., Will Book 2:119.

Jacob Kendrick is said to be the father of Benoni Kendrick. According to "Colonial Caroline" Jacob Kendrick was a bricklayer and resided in Caroline County, VA in the early 1700...Jacob had five known children: Nancy, Daniel, Benjamin, William and Benoni, the latter four sons all fought in the Revolution. Anna Fox is reputed to be their undocumented mother. Benoni Kendrick married Mary Warner in 1789 in Culpeper County, VA where the Kendrick clan moved earlier. From Culpeper County they moved west to Kentucky settling in Paris, Bourbon County. The Kendricks followed the Baptist faith and were early members of Cooper's Run Baptist Church, Battle Creek Baptist Church, and Silas Creek Baptist Church.[103]

   ii. BURWELL[3] KENDRICK, b. 1731; d. 1777 Edgecombe Co., N.C.

2. iii. JAMES[3] KENDRICK, b. about 1733; d. 1805 Ga.; m. SUSANNAH ROBERSON about 1755, daughter of ISRAEL ROBERSON and SARAH.

   iv. JOHN[3] KENDRICK, b. 21 July 1735 Gloucester Co., Va.; d. 16 December 1811 Mecklenburg Co., Va.; m. AMY[4] FOX 1760 Lunenburg Co., Va., daughter of RICHARD[3] FOX and HANNAH WILLIAMSON.[104]

   v. MARY[3] KENDRICK, b. 12 April 1738 Isle of Wight Co., Va.; d. before 9 November 1795 Mecklenburg Co., Va.; m. WILLIAM[4] FOX, son of RICHARD[3] FOX and HANNAH WILLIAMSON.[105]

   vi. BENJAMIN[3] KENDRICK, b. 1739 Granville Co., N.C.

   vii. REBECCA[3] KENDRICK, b. 1741 N.C.; m. _____ NICHOLSON.

  viii. SARAH[3] KENDRICK, b. 1744 in N. C.; d. before 1793; m. _____ THORNTON.

   ix. MARTIN[3] KENDRICK, b. 1747 in Edgecombe Co., N. C.; before 1800; m. SUSANNAH THOMPSON, b. November 16, 1749 Surry Co., Va.

   x. MARTHA[3] KENDRICK, b. 7 January 1746/7 Edgecombe Co., N. C.; d. 14 February 1831 Randolph Co., N. C.; m.

---

[103] Oberlies.
[104] See p. 208.
[105] See pp. 213-220.

WILLIAM WOOD 28 May 1764; b. about 1737; d. 26
April 1804 Randolph Co., N. C.

xi. JONES[3] KENDRICK, b. about 1750 in N. C.; d. before 5
February 1818 Maury Co., Tenn.; m. MARGARET.

xii. ISHAM[3] KENDRICK, b. about 1755 in N. C.; d. 17 March
1818 Spartanburg, S.C.; m. (1) ELIZABETH TUCKER 31
October 1781 Warren Co., N. C.; m. (2) ELIZABETH
DUNCAN 17 April 1788 Warren Co., N. C.; b. about 1770
Va.; d. about 1852 Georgia.

Isham Kendrick was a Revolutionary War soldier
for North Carolina as shown by the Revolutionary
Accounts at Raleigh.[106]

Revolutionary War Pension Claim R5862, shows
Isham married Elizabeth Duncan 17 April 1788 in
Warren Co., N.C.; and died 17 March 1818 in
Spartanburg, S.C. When his widow applied for pension
4 July 1850, she was 79 years of age and living in
Cherokee County, Georgia. She had previously lived at
Greenville and Spartanburg districts in S. C. The widow
stated that Isham, while residing in Warren County,
N.C. had served as a private for about 12 months with
North Carolina Troops, a part of the time in Capt.
Sterling Clark's Company and under Major Charles
Davis and that he was in the battles of Cowpens and
Hillsborough. The claim was not allowed as the widow
failed to furnish proofs according to the law. Reference
is made in the pension claim to a son Alston Kendrick

2. JAMES[3] KENDRICK was born about 1733 in Virginia and died
in 1805 in Georgia. He married SUSANNAH ROBERSON about
1755 in North Carolina, daughter of ISRAEL ROBERSON and
SARAH.

He and his brother John were old enough to be in the
Granville County Militia, 8 October 1754 in the Great Muster for

[106] N.C. Rev. Accts. Book 4, page 104, folio 1; book 5, page 8, folio 2; book 8, page
97, folio 3; book 11, page 15, folio 3; book B, page 62; book 4, page 51, folio 2, page 54,
folio 2;

the French and Indian War.[107] The tax-lists of Granville County show him as tithable in 1755, in William Kendrick's family.

He was given a deed of gift for land in Granville County, N. C. on 4 Mar. 1758,[108] and deeded it back to his father in 1762.[109] He had land grants in Chatham Country from 1778-1782 totaling over 1500 acres[110] and appears in numerous deeds in Chatham County from 1772-1784.

James[3] Kendrick moved to Georgia about 1784 and is shown in Wilkes Co., Ga., on the 1785 tax list. Children John[4], Burwell[4] and James[4] all moved to Ga., son William[4] did not go until about 1791 from Chatham Co., N. C. James[3] died in GA before 1805.

Children of JAMES KENDRICK and SUSANNAH ROBERSON are:

3. i. JOHN[4] KENDRICK, b. about 1756 in N.C.; d. 14 December 1802 Washington Co., Ga.; m. MARTHA MONTGOMERY 1797 Richmond Co., Ga. She was b. 1756 Chatham Co., N.C.; d. before 6 May 1822 Putnam Co., Ga.
   ii. WILLIAM[4] KENDRICK, b. about 1758 in Granville Co., N. C.
   iii. BURWELL[4] KENDRICK, b. about 1760 in Granville Co., N. C.
   iv. JAMES[4] KENDRICK, b. about 1765 in Granville Co., N. C.
   v. BENJAMIN[4] KENDRICK, b. about 1768 in Granville Co., N. C.
   vi. MARTIN[4] KENDRICK, b. about 1772 in Chatham Co., N. C.
   vii. JONES[4] KENDRICK, b. about 1778 in Chatham Co., N. C.
   viii. SARAH[4] KENDRICK

3. JOHN[4] KENDRICK was born about 1756, probably in Granville Co., N. C. and died 14 December 1802 Washington Co., Georgia. He married MARTHA MONTGOMERY 1787 Richmond Co., Ga. She was born 1757 in Chatham Co., North Carolina and died between 6 March 1822 and 6 May 1822 Putnam Co., Ga.

[107] N.C. Col. and State Records, 22: 373.
[108] Granville Co., N. C., Deed Book C:440.
[109] Granville Co., N. C., Deed Book E:86.
[110] N.C. Grant Books 30:49, 30:63, 30:156, 36:452, 48:11.

John[4] Kendrick was a Lieutenant in the Revolutionary troops under Gen. Butler and on 30 September 1781 in a skirmish with the British and Tories at Brown Marsh, was wounded in the breast very severely. The wound incapacitated him to such a degree that he appealed for assistance, first to the Auditors of Hillsborough District and later to the Legislature of North Carolina. The County Court of Chatham Co.. endorsed the petition, and he was finally granted a pension by the State of North Carolina.[111] John Kendrick also testified in 1784 to the innocence of Col. Alston in the death of Thomas Taylor, a Tory.[112] The following payments to John Kendrick from the North Carolina Revolutionary Accounts at Raleigh also show his Revolutionary services, one of them mentioning that he was from Chatham Co., another being endorsed by him at "Lt. John Kendrick," and two others indicating that the claim or pension had been transferred as an obligation to the Federal Government...[113]

John[4] Kendrick is a proved son of James[3] Kendrick and Susannah Roberson, since he is mentioned in George Roberson's will in 1761 as "my sister Susannah Kendrick's son, John Kendrick. His widow and children moved to Putnam Co., Ga. I knew personally there Mr. David Lawrence, a grandson of Meredith Kendrick, son of John[4], and he knew of the kinship to the families of James[4], Martin[4], and Benjamin[4] Kendrick who resided in Putnam, and talked to me of them long before this genealogy had been perfected."[114]

The Last Will and Testament of Martha Kendrick[115]

Georgia, Putnam County) I Martha Kendrick in perfect mind and memory in the presence of Almighty God do make this my last will and testament. I do give and bequeath unto my beloved daughter Betty A. Kendrick my bay mare.

---

[111] North Carolina Colonial and State Records 18:122; 126; 173-4; 351; 420; 19:526; 528; 697; 20:192; 199; 236; 317; 418-19; 525. The petition was made first about 1784 and was granted finally in 1787.

[112] North Carolina Colonial and State Records 17:399; 20:73.

[113] Date of death contained in Death Dates of Revolutionary War Officer Pensioners in the South. Ga. Gen. Soc. Q 16:240,1980. Cited by Oakes, Elaine. Oakes/Brunson. 29 Nov 2003. Located on http://worldconnect.rootsweb.com (db eoakes).

[114] Boddie, p. 45.

[115] Putnam Co., Ga., Will Book B:2.

I give and bequeath unto my four grandchildren, John W. Carter, William B. Carter, Walton T. Carter, and Robert M. Carter fifty dollars in cash to be equally divided between them. I bequeath unto my son-in-law Lewis Wright five dollars in cash.

I do further give and bequeath my real and personal Estate and all debt due me at this ___ after paying all my just debts the balance of my property to be equally divided into five equal parts (as follows:)

I do give and bequeath unto my four grandchildren, John W. Carter, William B. Carter, Walton J. Carter, and Robert M. Carter one fifth of my estate to by Equally divided between them.

I do given and bequeath the balance of my Estate unto John Monk, Meredith Kendrick, Priscilla Goode and Betty A. Kendrick to be equally divided between them.

And do further nominate and appoint John Monk and Meredith Kendrick my lawful executors. This 6th day of March 1822. Martha (x) Kendrick
Signed in the presence of
Harvey Kendrick
Richard Wright
Silas Monk.
Georgia, Putnam Co.)The within will was duly proven in open court by Harvey Kendrick and Richard Wright subscribing witnesses to the same this 6th day of May 1822. Coleman Pendleton, C. C. A.

Children of JOHN KENDRICK and MARTHA MONTGOMERY are:

   i. MEREDITH[5] KENDRICK, b. about 1790
  ii. MARY[5] KENDRICK, b. 1789, d. after 1844 Putnam Co., Ga.; m. (1) JOHN CARTER about 1804 Georgia; b. 7 May 1786 Greene Co., Ga.; d. 31 May 1820 Putnam Co., Ga.[116] m. (2) LEWIS WRIGHT 1820 Putnam Co., Ga.[117]

---

[116] Hill, Gerry. 27 Feb 2005. She cites a Bible record made by his father, Josiah Carter, a copy of which is at the GA State Archives. Also obituaries on the Augusta *Chronicle* for 4 August 1820 and the Savannah *Reporter* for 5 September 1820. http://genforum.genealogy.com/wright/messages/18463.html.

[117] The marriage is proved by the will of Martha Kendrick from 1822. In the 1820 census he has eight men in his household. Given a marriage in 1806, it raises the possibility

Children of MARY KENDRICK and JOHN CARTER are:[118]

    1. WILLIAM BENNETT[6] CARTER, b. about 1805 in Georgia
    2. WALTON THOMAS[6] CARTER, b. 24 October 1811 Putnam Co., Ga.
    3. JOHN W.[6] CARTER, b. about 1812 Putnam Co., Ga.
    4. ROBERT MILTON[6] CARTER, b. 18 February 1813 Putnam Co., Ga.

  iii. BETTY A.[5] KENDRICK,
  iv. PRISCILLA[5] KENDRICK,
  v. SALINE[5] KENDRICK.

1804 Francis Rainey of Brunswick Co., Virginia[119]

1. FRANCIS[5] (FRANCIS[4], ROGER[3], WILLIAM[2], FRANCIS BARTHOLOMEW[1]) RAINEY was born 12 October 1733 in Prince George Co., Virginia, and died before February 1804 in Brunswick Co., Va. He married (1) ELIZABETH ANN ROTTENBERRY about 1751 Dinwiddie Co., Va., daughter of JOHN ROTTENBERRY and SUSANNAH WILLIAMSON.[120] She was born about 1733 in Surry Co., Virginia, and died March 9, 1779 in Mecklenburg Co., Virginia. He married (2) JUDITH LAMBERT January 7, 1797 Mecklenburg Co., Virginia.

His first appearance in Lunenburg (now Mecklenburg) County, Virginia was 24 April 1758 when John Rottenberry of Lunenburg Co. sold to Francis Rainey of Bath Parish, Dinwiddie Co. for £30 a tract of 100 acres, part of a 400 acre tract granted to Henry Rottenberry on 16 August 1756, located on the north side of

---

that he has the four sons of Mary Carter in his household by the time of the census in late 1820.

[118] Tuggle, Joseph. Jtuggle. 1 June 2002. http://worldconnect.rootsweb.com (db :2116249).

[119] Carol York, personal communication, 1 February 2004. The ancestry of Francis Rainey is from Raney, Don. Raney GEDCOM. 8 Dec 2001. (db don_raney); Hoffman, Bruce. Hoffman and Day Ancestry Family Tree. 28 Jan 2004. (db :2777137). http://worldonnect.rootsweb.com. As always in early Virginia genealogy, there is controversy and a lack of solid documentation.

[120] Susannah Williamson's sister, Hannah, was the wife of 1771 Richard Fox of Mecklenburg Co., Va.

the Roanoke River and the east side of Great Creek. This indenture was witnessed by Jon. Ezell, Jr., Eph. Mabry, and Wm. Bartlett.[121]

On 10 April 1762 Francis Rainey, John Rottenberry and Benjamin Harrison, Jr., witnessed the sale for £29 of 400 acres of land on Mill Branch from James and Lurney Sheffield of Brunswick Co., Va., to William Bartlett of Lunenburg Co., Va.[122]

Francis Rainey continued to be active in land transactions after the area became Mecklenburg County in 1765 as witnessed by the following deeds. "9 May 1767. John Lankford to Francis Rainey. For £10, 200 A Great Branch, Stephen Jones, Rottenberry, patent to John Lankford on 7 July 1763; Wit: Joshua Mabry, Sr, Jordan Mabry, Stephen Mabry.[123] 6 April 1769. Francis Rainey. 400 A on Great Creek, adj. Malone, Lankford et al.[124] 7 December 1771. William Bartlett and Elizabeth his wife to Francis Rainey. For £30, 100 A, south side of the North fork of Great Cr., John Bozman. Wit: Daniel Thomas, James Blanton, Samuel Rotenbery."[125]

By the end of 1771 Francis Rainey had amassed a tract of 1200 acres in Mecklenburg Co., Virginia. He sold 600 acres to his sons Frederick and Buckner Rainey in 1778 and 1779. "3 February 1778. Francis Rainey to his son Frederick Rainey. For 5 sh., 100 A Great Br., Spring Br. Wit: John Brown, Stephen Mabry, John Neal.[126] 7 February 1789. Francis Rainy to Williamson Rainy. For £10, 300 A on Great Cr. at mouth of Persimmon Br., Mabry's line, Isham Nance's line, Hargroves branch, Mark Jackson's line, Licking Br. Wit: Nelson Cole, Lucas Sullivant, William Fox.[127] 7 February 1789. Francis Raney to Buckner Raney. For £10, 300 A. New corner in Mark Jackson's line, Ellis Carrell's line, John Lambert's line, Thomas Booth's line, the Creek, mouth of the Licking Br. Wit: Nelson Cole, Lucas Sullivant, William Fox.[128] 7 February 1789. Francis Raney to Frederick Raney. For £10, 200

---

[121] Lunenburg Co., Va., Deed Book 5:229.

[122] Lunenburg Co., Va., Deed Book 8:189.

[123] Mecklenburg Co., Va., Deed Book 1:383.

[124] Va. Land Patent Book. 38:662. Cited in Elliott, Katherine B. Early Settlers of Mecklenburg Co., Va.

[125] Mecklenburg Co., Va., Deed Book 3:267.

[126] Mecklenburg Co., Va., Deed Book 5:177.

[127] Mecklenburg Co., Va., Deed Book 7:387.

[128] Mecklenburg Co., Va., Deed Book 7:389.

A, Thomas Booth's line, Stephen Jones' line, sd. Francis Raney's s line. Wit: Nelson Cole, Lucas Sullivant, William Fox.[129]

There are also deeds of interest which show the neighbors, including several who subsequently intermarried with the Rainey family. "7 October 1772. John Langford to Isham Nance. For £175, tract on Great Cr., 400 A bounded by William Cleaton, Francis Rainey. Wit: Thomas Winfield, William Malone, Thomas Malone.[130] 8 March 1773. Henry Langford to James Hargrove. For 10, 200 A, east fork of Great Cr., William Cleaton Sr., John Nipper, part of land where Langford lives. Wit: Lewis Parham, Isham Malone, William Poythress.[131] 5 April 1774. George Langford and Judith his wife of Bute, NC, to Stephen Mabry. For 112/10, 293 A on upper side of West fork of Great Cr., b. Persimmon Branch, Isham Nance, John Cleaton, Frederick Rainey, Francis Rainey. Part is part of tract patented to Henry Rottenberry, & other part patented by John Langford; land whereon George Langford formerly lived. Wit: Joshua Mabry, William Davis, Richard Fox, Reps Mabry."[132]

Elizabeth Rottenberry, wife of Francis Rainey died 9 March 1779 according to a family history. His second marriage, to Judith Lambert is of record in Mecklenburg Co., Va., 7 January 1797. On 12 May 1800 Francis Rainey and his wife Judith sold a tract of land to Frederick Rainey, presumably the remainder of his 600 acre "home place." Witnesses were Grief Harwell and Samuel Lambert and subsequently Richard Fox.[133] These three were also business partners. On 13 October Thomas Lambert and wife Judith, William Lambert, James Lambert, Jabez Lambert, Lucretia Lambert, Sarah Lambert, John Mize and Lavender his wife, Francis Rainy and Judith his wife, Jeremiah George and Mary his wife" sold land to Lewis Williams.[134]

The Will of Francis Rainey of Brunswick Co., Va.[135]

Francis Rainey of Brunswick being sick...To the heirs of my son James Rainey dec'd in right of their father one

---

[129] Mecklenburg Co., Va., Deed Book 7:392.

[130] Mecklenburg Co., Va., Deed Book 3:555.

[131] Mecklenburg Co., Va., Deed Book 3:553.

[132] Mecklenburg Co., Va., Deed Book 4:325.

[133] Mecklenburg Co., Va., Court Order Book 10:341. [p. 394: third witness, Richard Fox]

[134] Mecklenburg Co., Va., Court Order Book 10:440.

[135] Brunswick Co., Va., Will Book 7:2-4. [Feb. Court 1804.]

dollar & whatsoever I have heretofore given him or them. To the children of my son Frederick Rainey dec'd ...To my son Buckner Rainey...To my son Williamson Rainey...To my daughter Cresey Malone...To my daughter Sarah Sturdivant.....To my daughter Dicy Sturdivant....To the children of my dec'd. daughter Celor Jackson....To my beloved wife Judith Rainey during widowhood tract whereon I now live...204 acres, also 5 Negroes, Daniel, Jacob, Peter, Linda and Grace...all estate kept together provided she does not intermarry before my son Isaac Rainey becomes of age...Son Isaac Rainey and daughter, Betsy L. Rainey. If both should die without issue Judith to have estate for life, and then divided between all children, including those deceased, to wit: James, Frederick & Druscilla. Ex. friends Grief Harwell and James Harwell. Wit: James Petillo, James Baugh, William Shell.

Children by Elizabeth are:

i. JAMES F.[6] RAINEY, b. about 1751 Dinwiddie Co., Va.; d. 8 November 1773 Mecklenburg Co., Va.; m. MARY DAVIS 1772 Mecklenburg Co., Va.

Mary Rainey applied for letters of administration on the estate of James Rainey, deceased, on 8 November 1773.[136] Mary Rainey married Richard Fox 22 March 1775. None of the children of Francis[5] Rainey are of the right age to be Mary Rainey, and I think she is almost surely Mary Davis, relict of James F. Rainey, deceased. I have found no mention of children for James Rainey.

There are three mentions of a James Rainey who is otherwise not accounted for. In the first, the estate of John Jeffries paid money to "James Rainey for schooling children."[137] However, the date for this is problematic, in that James, son of James 6 would have been only ten or so. In April 1789 he was deposed in the suit of James Hasten v. George Minor.[138] The third is a record of his death before 11 December 1809, when no

---

[136] Mecklenburg Co., Va. Court Order Book 4:134.
[137] Mecklenburg Co., Va., Will Book 2:23. [9 Dec. 1782].
[138] Mecklenburg Co., Va., Court Order Book 7: 375. [April 1789]

one would come forward to administer his "small" estate.[139] Schoolteachers weren't well paid in those days, either.

ii. FREDERICK[6] RAINEY, b. about 1752 Dinwiddie Co., Va.; d. before 10 October 1803 Mecklenburg Co., Va.; m. MARY ANN MORGAN 10 March 1775 Mecklenburg Co., Va., daughter of REUBEN MORGAN and MARY ANN.

Frederick[6] Rainey is estimated to have been born about 1752, but he must surely have been born before 31 October 1751, for on 31 October 1772 he is shown purchasing a 165 acre tract of land for £25 from Drury Murphy and his wife, Lucy. The land was described as "William Murphey's Spring Br., Blanton's line, Jones, Davis; pat. to Drury Murphey 3 Aug 1771." The deed was witnessed by Joshua Mabry, Stephen Mabry and William Bartlett.[140]

On 14 December 1772 Joshua Mabry sold to Frederick Rainey another tract of 211 acres for £3, 19 shillings.[141] This purchase allowed Frederick Rainey to sell the original 165 acre Murphy tract to his uncle, William[5] Raney for £30 on 11 Sep 1773.[142] In those days, a 20% annual rate of return on an investment was unheard of.

Francis Rainey sold his son 100 acres of land on Spring Branch for the nominal 5 shillings in a deed dated 3 February 1778 that was witnessed by John Brown, Stephen Mabry and John Neal.[143] Francis Rainey made a further sale of 200 acres "on Thomas Booth's line, Stephen Jones' line," and his own line for £10 on 7 February 1789.[144]

In April 1789 Frederick Rainey and his wife, Maryann, apparently traded tracts of land with Stephen Mabry and his wife, Tabitha.

"Stephen Mabry and Tabitha his wife to Frederick Rainey. For £270, 284 acres on west fork of Great Cr.,

[139] Mecklenburg Co., Va., Court Order Book 15:102. [11 Dec. 1809].
[140] Mecklenburg Co., Va., Deed Book 3:480. [31 Oct. 1772.]
[141] Mecklenburg Co., Va., Deed Book 3:510. [14 Dec. 1772.]
[142] Mecklenburg Co., Va., Deed Book 4:151. [11 Sept. 1773.]
[143] Mecklenburg Co., Va., Deed Book 5:177. [3 Feb. 1778.]
[144] Mecklenburg Co., Va., Deed Book 7:392. [7 Feb. 1789.]

mouth of a large branch, Williamson Rainey's line, Isham Nance's line, Lewis Williams' line, Thomas Roberts, dec'd., sd. Frederick Rainey's line. Wit: Williamson Raney, Buckner Raney, Isham Nance."[145] Frederick Rainey and Maryann his wife to Stephen Mabry. For £200, 200 A, patent granted to Robert Brooks 30 Aug. 1763, William Rainey's line, James Blanton's line, Jarvis Lambert's line, Thomas Roberts' line, Samuel Good's line. Wit: John Loyd, Jesse Lambert, Delphia Walker."[146]

The price was essentially £1 per acre, with a slight discount on Stephen Mabry's land. Interestingly, each deed has its own set of witnesses. I suspect this 200 acre tract was the latter of the two he purchased from his father.

In sum, Frederick Rainey had his initial 211 acre tract, another 100 acre tract from his father, and the 274 acre Mabry tract, for a total of almost 600 acres, which represented a sizeable land holding for the time and place.[147]

Frederick[6] Rainey died before 10 October 1803 when his son, Smith[7] Rainey was summoned to appear in Court after his uncle, Williamson[6] Rainey attested under oath that he had delivered the will of Frederick Rainey, deceased, to Smith Rainey following Frederick's death.[148] The last will and testament of Frederick Rainey was produced in court 12 December 1803 and was proved by the oaths of James Meachum, Williamson Rainey, and Thomas Nance.[149] (Will not examined.) Smith Rainey applied for letters of administration on the estate of his father on 13 February 1804. Bond was posted for $10,000 with Buckner Rainey, Reuben M. Rainey and William Baskerville as securities. Francis Rainey and John Rainey, orphans of Frederick Rainey chose Smith Rainey as their Guardian,

---

[145] Mecklenburg Co., Va., Deed Book 7:402. [7 April 1789.]
[146] Mecklenburg Co., Va., Deed Book 7:403. [7 April 1789.]
[147] He may have had more acreage as there is a note of a Sheriff's sale to Frederick Rainey Mecklenburg Co., Va., Court Order Book 8:110. [8 April 1793.]
[148] Mecklenburg Co., Va., Court Order Book 12:44. [10 Oct 1803.]
[149] Mecklenburg Co., Va., Court Order Book 12:84. [12 Dec. 1803.]

and Smith Rainey was also appointed guardian for Philip Rainey who had not attained the age of choice. (14 years old.) Smith Rainey posted guardian bond for $15,000 with the same securities.[150]

The marriage bond of Frederick Rainey and Mary Ann Morgan is of record. In April 1777 the last will and testament of Reuben Wright was recorded in which he left his estate, valued at £160 to be divided equally among his "beloved sisters Mary Anne Rainey, Sally Morgan, Edith Morgan, Nancy Morgan, and Betsy Morgan." He left a bay mare to his aunt, Elizabeth Morgan and named as his executor his father Reuben Morgan and Philip Morgan.[151] The will was witnessed by John and George Baskerville.[152]

Reuben Morgan's will is also extant, being recorded in July 1781.[153] He names his wife, Mary, to whom he leaves three slaves and a small piece of land on the south side of Miles' Creek, "adjacent the meadow tract". His son, Philip is to have use of this land at his mother's discretion, but at her death, the land is to go to "my grandson Smith Rainey." He left the home plantation totaling 170 acres bounded by "Mr. Goode's line and the main road" to his son John. His son Philip received a 200 acre tract bounded by Howell Hargrove's line, Dockery's Creek, Miles' Creek, and Dortch's line." To his son Benjamin he left a 200 acre tract bounded by "Dockery's creek, Great Branch, Dortch's line, Hay Meadow Branch, Laban Wright's line, Rockey Br., and Wolf Pit Br." He also left Benjamin a slave named Adam. To his daughter Sarah King he left a tract of 150 acres bounded by "Great Branch, Dortch's line, Collier's line, MacLin's line, Church Road, Mr. Goode's church road, to Benjamin's

---

[150] Mecklenburg Co., Va., Court Order Book 12: 109. [13 Feb. 1804.]

[151] Mecklenburg Co., Va., Will Book 1:223.

[152] I read this will as saying that Reuben Morgan was his wife's second husband, and that she had Reuben Wright by her deceased first husband. Elsewhere I argue that this deceased first husband is a son of 1755 John Wright of Lunenburg Co., Va. (Flatt Creek). One tantalizing bit of information is that Bolling Wright was recorded in the household of Frederick Rainey on the personal property tax list for 1785.

[153] Mecklenburg Co., Va., Will Book 1:367.

line." He also left her a slave named Molly. He left Edith Rainey a tract of 150 acres bounded by "the fork of the road, Flatt Creek, Wright's line to my own line, to Benjamin's line," and a slave named Ned. His daughter Nancy Morgan also received a 150 acre tract bounded the "fork of Rocky Branch to Benjamin's line, to School House Branch," and a slave boy named Joe. His daughter Betsy Morgan received a 150 acre tract bounded by "Mr. Goode's line, School House Branch," and a slave girl named Lydia. His daughter, Mary Ann Rainey received a slave named James. Son Sterling Morgan, who was not of age, received at the death or re-marriage of his mother, Mary Morgan, the "land purchased of John Hill on Miles' Creek, Dockery's, Dortch's line, Philip Morgan's line, Benjamin's line, School House Branch, Betsey's line, John's line" for a total of 500 acres. He also received a slave named Absalom. Mary Morgan, wife, son-in-law Frederick Rainey, and son Philip Morgan were named executors. The will was witnessed by Lewis Parham, Nathaniel Moss, Mary Baskerville, and William Eastland. His total land holdings approach 1400 acres.

As might be expected, there were difficulties in settling the estate as witnessed by a suit filed by "John Allen and Nancy his wife, James King and Sally his wife, Williamson Rainey and Edith his wife, and Elizabeth Morgan by John Allen her next friend" against "Mary Morgan, Frederick Rainey and Philip Morgan Ex & of Reuben Morgan dec'd and Maryann Rainey wife of the said Frederick Rainey.[154] Reading of the order books suggests this was a common practice when there were large estates and perhaps a shortage of cash. This suit, like most of those read in the records, was resolved among the parties and the suit was discontinued.[155]

Elizabeth Morgan, orphan of Reuben Morgan chose Frederick Rainey as her guardian on 8 October 1786.[156]

---

[154] Mecklenburg Co., Va., Court Order Book 6:72. [June 1784.]

[155] Mecklenburg Co., Va., Court Order Book 6:197. [14 Feb. 1785.]

[156] Mecklenburg Co., Va., Court Order Book 6:607. [9 Oct. 1786.]

This implies that she was born in September 1772. Frederick Morgan chose Frederick Rainey as his guardian in September 1788,[157] which implies he was born in August 1774. The records also contain his guardian accounts.[158]

iii. LUCRETIA[6] RAINEY, b. about 1754 Dinwiddie Co., Va.; married _____ MALONE about 1782.

iv. DICEY[6] RAINEY, born 1755 in Mecklenburg County, Virginia,[159] and died 9 Feb 1846 in Randolph Co, N. C.; m. RANDOLPH STURDIVANT 27 May 1776 Mecklenburg Co., Va., son of MATTHEW STURDIVANT and SARAH OLIVER; born about 1750 Mecklenburg Co., Va.; d. 1816 Jackson Co., Tenn.

v. SARAH[6] RAINEY, b. about 1757 Dinwiddie Co., Va.; m. HENRY STURDIVANT about 1773 Mecklenburg Co., Va.

vi. BUCKNER[6] RAINEY, b., about 1759 Mecklenburg Co., Va.; d. about 1820 Bedford Co., Tenn.; m. (1) REBECCA HOLMES 12 Jun 1780 Mecklenburg Co., Va.; d. about 1801 Mecklenburg Co., Va. He m. (2) MARY ___ about 1801.

Samuel Lark was security on the marriage bond of Buckner Rainey to Rebecca Holmes obtained 12 June 1780. Rebecca Holmes was the orphan of Isaac Holmes, deceased and was not 21 when she chose Samuel Holmes, Jr., as her guardian the same date Buckner Rainey took out the marriage bond.[160] As a result of the

---

[157] Mecklenburg Co., Va., Court Order Book 7:290. [Sept. 1788.]

[158] Mecklenburg Co., Va., Court Order Book 7:99. [Sept. 1787] for Elizabeth Morgan; Court Order Book 7:442 [14 Sept. 1789] and Court Order Book 8:178. [9 Sept. 179 for Sterling Morgan. Children: Smith, m. Anne Standley 31 December 1796 Mecklenburg; Frederick, m. Catherine Cabiness 11 November 1813 Putnam Co., Ga.; Reuben Morgan, m. Catherine Thomas Cleaton 22 August 1811 Mecklenburg; John F., d. 5 September 1843 Meriwether Co., Ga., m. (2) Permilia Edwards 2 March 1809 Brunswick Co., Va., dau. of John Edwards and Elizabeth Rainey; Elizabeth Wright, d. 1852 Newton Co., Ga.; m. William James King 6 September 1815 Mecklenburg, son of James King

[159] Francis Rainey was security. For more on this couple, see Southside Virginian, Vol. VI, #2, April 1988, p. 87. Children: Randolph Henry, m. Mourning Lambert 5 January 1797 Mecklenburg; Henry; John L., b. 15 November 1793 Warren Co., N. C.; d. 3 August 1866 Worth Twp., Boone Co., Ia., m. Mary Green June 1817 Jackson Co., Tenn., b. 17 November 1792 Wake Co., N. C., d. 16 June 1889 Douglas Twp., Boone Co., Ia.; Rebecca, m. John Presnell 5 July 1808 Randolph Co., N. C., d. there 7 October 1847; Francis, d. 1816 Mecklenburg; Philip, b. 19 January 1794 Mecklenburg, d. there 19 May 1850, m. Ann Lewis Boyd 3 August 1824, b. 14 June 1807, d. 25 June 1871, Mecklenburg.

[160] Mecklenburg Co., Va., Court Order Book 5:50. [12 June 1780].

marriage, she was able to dismiss him as guardian, and he was excused from the requirement to make a guardian's account, at the same session.[161]

On 8 December 1794 Buckner Rainey and his wife Rebecca traded tracts of land with his brother Williamson Rainey and his wife Edith, with the net effect that Buckner was able to generate £82, 10 shillings cash.[162] "Buckner Rainey to Williamson Rainey. For £137/10, 275 A on Great Cr., mouth of Lick Br., Mark Lambert Jackson, Ellis Carroll, Thomas Booth. Rebecca, wife of Buckner Rainey, relinquished dower. Wit: Jordan Bennett, Lewis Williams, Ludwell Tanner. Williamson Rainey and Edith to Buckner Rainey. For 75, 150 A, Rocky Br. "fork of Church road from thence down the road towards Flatt Cr. to Roberts line" William Nanney, Robert Turnbull, Hay Meadow Br. Wit: Jordan Bennett, Lewis Williams, Ludwell Tanner."

The same day Benjamin Morgan sold a tract of 61½ acres for £40 to Buckner Rainey, the tract being bounded by "Robert Turnbull, Hay Meadow Br." Witnesses were Samuel Goode, Solomon Pettillo and Williamson Pettillo.[163] The final transaction, all of which seem to have been designed to consolidate the inheritances from Reuben Morgan with land already owned by members of the Rainey family was when Buckner Rainey and Rebecca, his wife, sold a 25 acre tract "bounded by Great Creek, sd. Ellis Carroll, Williamson Rainey, Booth's line, Lambert's line," for £12 to Ellis Carroll.[164]

One final note of interest, on 11 September 1809 Buckner Rainey was appointed surveyor from Goode's Mill along Julius' road to Collier's road in the room of Sterling Morgan. The male laboring tithables of Sterling Morgan, Mary Morgan, Benjamin Morgan,

---

[161] Mecklenburg Co., Va., Court Order Book 5:66.

[162] Mecklenburg Co., Va., Court Order Book 8:469. [8 Dec. 1794]; Mecklenburg Co., Va., Court Order Book 8:470. [8 Dec. 1794.]

[163] Mecklenburg Co., Va., Court Order Book 8:471. [8 Dec. 1794.]

[164] Mecklenburg Co., Va., Court Order Book 8:471. [8 Dec. 1794.]

Solomon Pettillo, John Creedle, Christopher Guy, and Samuel Goode at his fork plantation to attend.[165]

Buckner Rainey is said to have died in Bedford Co., TN, in 1820.[166]

vii. WILLIAMSON[6] RAINEY, b. 2 Nov 1760 Lunenburg Co., Va.; d. before 19 Apr 1847 Virginia;[167] m. EDITH WRIGHT MORGAN 23 Nov 1779 Mecklenburg Co., Va., daughter of REUBEN MORGAN and MARY ANN ____.

Francis Rainey was security for Williamson Rainey's bond to marry Edith Morgan 23 November 1779. Edith was underage as consent from her father, Reuben Morgan, was required.

On 14 February 1780 Williamson Rainey was appointed surveyor of the road from the Carolina line to Harrison's Ferry.[168]

Williamson Rainey acquired a 300 acre tract on "Great Creek at the mouth of Persimmon Branch, Mabry's line, Isham Nance's line, Hargrove's Branch, Mark Jackson's line, and Licking Branch" from his father on 7 February 1789.[169] In the 1789 Personal Property Tax List he paid for himself, three slaves, and Anderson Wright.

He was involved in the land swap in 1794 with his brother Buckner as described above.

Williamson Rainey's application for a pension for his service in the Revolution (R8563 VA) includes an affidavit given 23 October 1841 in Mecklenburg, which states that he was born in Mecklenburg county, VA, (i.e. Lunenburg), 2 Nov. 1760, and served with William Inscoe (age 85 in 1842), William Coleman, and Thomas Tanner. The rendezvous was at Mecklenburg

---

[165] Mecklenburg Co., Va., Court Order Book 15:53. [11 Sept. 1809.]

[166] The Drumright Family Tree, by Gracie Drumright Dowland, 1974, p. 61. This book names 5 of his children: Frances, m. William Cook 5 May 1803 Mecklenburg; Martha m. Nathaniel Crowder 25 November 1805 Mecklenburg; Elizabeth Holmes, m. Richard W. Drumwright 8 November 1821; Bozell; Buckner, m. Martha M. Nance 25 November 1828; Robert. [The latter was listed with Buckner Rainey on the 1800 Mecklenburg Personal Property Tax List.]

[167] Williamson Rainey's last will and testament was written 8 Jan 1846 and proved 19 April 1847. Mecklenburg Co., Va., Will Book 16:374.

[168] Mecklenburg Co., Va., Court Order Book 5:10. [14 Feb. 1780.]

[169] Mecklenburg Co., Va., Deed Book 7:387.

Courthouse, 1776 or 1777. A son, William Rainey, is mentioned.

Williamson Rainey seems to have been much involved with the affairs of the Methodist Church. The noted circuit rider minister, John Early, stayed once at his house after preaching at Calvary Church. (Rainey's house was north of Rt. 627 near Rt. 620.) Williamson's nephew Smith Rainey (son of Frederick) and his wife Ann deeded the land on which Sardis Church was built in 1812 to Lewis Williams, Williamson Rainey, Ebenezer McGowan, George Rogers, James Nolley, Samuel Holmes, and Lewis Griggs, as trustees.[170]

viii. DRUCILLA[6] RAINEY, b. 1763/1764 Lunenburg Co., Va.; d. about 1796 Mecklenburg Co., Va.; m. MARK LAMBERT JACKSON 8 Nov 1784 Mecklenburg Co., Va.; d. before 25 July 1826 Maury Co., Tenn.

Francis Rainey was security when Mark Lambert Jackson obtained a marriage bond to marry Drucilla Rainey November 8, 1784. He also served as security for John Lambert, who was chosen as guardian for Rainey Rottenberry, bastard of Anne Rottenberry, January 9, 1786. This implies that Rainey Rottenberry had been born in December 1774.[171]

Children of FRANCIS RAINEY and JUDITH LAMBERT are:

ix. BETSY L.[6] RAINEY, b. about 1798 Mecklenburg Co., Va.
x. ISAAC[6] RAINEY, b. about 1800 Mecklenburg Co., Va.

2. WILLIAM[5] RAINEY was born April 13, 1731 Prince George County, Va., and died before 15 March 1798 in Mecklenburg Co.,

---

[170] Bracey, Susan L. Life By the Roaring Roanoke: A History of Mecklenburg County, Virginia. (Mecklenburg Bicentennial Committee, 1977,) pp. 108-109. Children: Isham; Nancy, m. Isham Nance 8 August 1803 Mecklenburg; William m. Elizabeth Wright Rainey 19 June 1822; Bartlett, m. Matilda Bradley; Williamson, d. 1857 Mecklenburg, m. Martha Cook 22 December 1810 Mecklenburg; Mary Ann, m. Paschall Thomas 17 July 1815 Mecklenburg, d. 1872 Greensville Co., Va.; Allan, d. 1831 Rutherford Co., Tenn., m. Hannah Harwell 20 October 1817 Mecklenburg, dau. of Grief Harwell and Ann Fox; Elizabeth, m. John B. Kidd 16 February 1818 Mecklenburg; Sarah A., m. Robertson C. Thomas 24 December 1823 Mecklenburg; Rebecca, m. (1) Peter Bass 14 August 1823 Mecklenburg, m. (2) Richard King.

[171] Mecklenburg Co., Va., Court Order Book 6:449. [9 Jan. 1786.]

Virginia. He married (1) MARY MORRIS. He married (2) CHRISTIANA WILLIS.

William[5] Rainey appears in the records of Mecklenburg Co., Va. on 8 April 1780 when he bought a 180 acre tract of land "bounded by John Brown, Jr., the Pine Cosey Branch," from William Pennington "of Brunswick Co., Va." for £36.[172] This indenture was witnessed by Richard Grinnell, Elizabeth Holmes, Sack Pennington, Richard Meanly, Peter Winfield, Anna Pennington, and Jesse Oslin. He sold this land to John Hubbard on 14 February 1791, for £ 160. The tract was described as 180 acres bounded by "Brown's corner, Malone's corner, and Cosway Branch." [173] There is no record of dower release, which implies that his wife was dead.

The existing court records show a man who was apparently hard to get along with, as he was involved in numerous suits, including some that included physical violence.[174] In documents dated 1795 until his death he is often referred to as William Rainey (guy) presumably to distinguish him from Williamson Rainey, his nephew. Some of the suits are probably related to debt, others remain uncertain.[175]

On 13 July 1795 he was excused from paying the county and poor levies due to age and infirmity.[176] This makes it

---

[172] Mecklenburg Co., Va., Court Order Book 6:150. [8 April 1780.]

[173] Mecklenburg Co., Va., Court Order Book 8:8. [14 Feb. 1791].

[174] Mecklenburg Co., Va., Court Order Book 5:522 [8 March 1784] William Raney v. Jacob Watson. Trespass, Assault and Battery. (dismissed); Court Order Book 7:498 [10 May 1790] William Rainey v. Henry Pennington. Trespass, Assault and Battery; Court Order Book 7:479 [9 Mar. 1790] William Rainey v. Isaac Malone, Junr. Trespass, Assault and Battery; Court Order Book 8:69 [12 Nov. 1792.] William Rainey v. Henry Pennington. Trespass, A & B. Plt. not prosecuting, suit dismissed; Court Order Book 8:253 [12 Mar. 1794] William Rainey v. Claiborne Wright In Trespass, Assault and Battery. Claiborne Wright v. William Rainey. In Case (for Slander); Court Order Book 9:30 [15 March 1796] Claiborne Wright v. William Rainey (guy) In case for Slander; William Rainey (guy) v. Claiborne Wright, Trespass, Assault and Battery.

[175] Mecklenburg Co., Va., Court Order Book 7:567 [14 March 1791] Alexander Boyd Ex. Of Richard Swepson dec'd. v. William Rainey and Anthony Bennett. Jordan Bennett sec.; Court Order Book 8:121 [13 May 1793] John MacRae v. Stephen Mabry and William Rainey (guy) Court Order Book 8:192 [11 Nov. 1793] Anthony Bennett v. William Rainey. Frederick Collier, sec.; Court Order Book 8:510 [9 Nov. 1795] William Rainey(guy) v. Lewis King, Debt; Court Order Book 8:517 10 Nov. 1795. William Rainey v. Thomas Cypress. Court Order Book 9:232 [13 March 1797] William Rainey summoned for a breach of the peace v. John Gober. Peace bond with Frederick Collier and Jones Taylor his securities.

[176] Mecklenburg Co., Va., Court Order Book 8:472. [13 July 1795.]

reasonable to suppose that he is the William Rainey born in Prince George Co., Va., and brother to 1804 Francis Rainey of Brunswick Co., Va. There are a series of notations from 1797 indicating he was trying to settle his debts.[177] The court actions only stopped with William Rainey's death.[178]

The last will and testament of William Rainey was written 27 September 1790 and proved 10 September 1798 in Mecklenburg Co., Va.[179] He names his wife, Christian Willis Rainey, to whom he left a life interest in his estate, with the residue to go to William Cook upon her death. He named his wife as executor along with William Taylor. The will was witnessed by James Standley, Sr., and Anthony Bennett. When the will was proved, the signature of Anthony Bennett was attested to by Jordan Bennett, since Anthony Bennett was "now in Kentucky."

In September 1798 Samuel Lambert, William Cook, and Christiana Rainey made an indenture to Henry Walker.[180] On 9 December 1799 Christian W. Rainey, executor of William Rainey, deceased, was ordered to pay Sally Roberts and Katie Vaughan as witness for her in the suit filed by Laban Wright.[181] On 14 July 1800 Samuel Lambert, William Cook, and Christian Rainey made an indenture to Henry Walker.[182] Finally, on 12 May 1801 Christian Willis Rainey, executrix of William Rainey (guy) deceased, sued William Baskerville, executor of Frederick Collier, deceased, and was awarded £23, 2 shillings.[183] Her witnesses were John Webb, Samuel Lark, Highberry Nanney, and William Roberts. This document is also important in that it firmly connects 1798 William Rainey of Mecklenburg Co., Va., with the man excused from paying taxes due to age in 1795.

---

[177] Mecklenburg Co., Va., Court Order Book 9:53 [11 April 1796] Stephen Mabry and Tabitha his wife to William Rainey (quy); Court Order Book 9:237 [10 April 1797] Bill of sale William Rainey to Joel Lambert, oath of Richard Fox; Court Order Book 9:333 [11 Sept. 1797] William Rainey (quy) to John Davis, Junr.; Court Order Book 9:340 [9 Oct. 1797] William Rainey (quy) to Joel Lambert; Court Order Book 9:391 [12 Feb. 1798] William Rainey (quy) to Samuel Lambert. Wit: Stephen Mabry, Richard Fox, and Moses Lunsford.

[178] Mecklenburg Co., Va., Court Order Book 9:420. [15 Mar. 1798.]

[179] Mecklenburg Co., Va., Will Book 4,:39. [10 Sept. 1798.]

[180] Mecklenburg Co., Va., Court Order Book 10:35. [Sept. 1798.]

[181] Mecklenburg Co., Va., Court Order Book 10:184. [9 Dec. 1799.]

[182] Mecklenburg Co., Va., Court Order Book 10:394. [14 July 1800]

[183] Mecklenburg Co., Va., Court Order Book 10:592. [12 May 1801.]

Chapter 7: Descendants of John Wright and Sarah Fox

1. JOHN[2] (JOHN[1]) WRIGHT was born about 1764 Brunswick Co., Virginia, and died before 22 October 1832 Clarke Co., Georgia. He married (1) SARAH[5] FOX 27 October 1797 Mecklenburg Co., Va., daughter of RICHARD[4] FOX and MARY (DAVIS) RAINEY. She was born about 1776 Mecklenburg Co., Virginia and died about 1812 Mecklenburg Co., Virginia. He married (2) LUCY GARLAND[5] ANDREW, daughter of JOHN[4] ANDREW and MARY OVERTON[6] COSBY 10 May 1830 Clarke Co., Ga. She was born 25 August 1799 Elbert Co., Ga., and died 8 July 1870 in Campbell Co., Georgia.

John Wright's date of birth is estimated from his appearance in the personal property tax lists of Brunswick Co., Va., associated with his father, John (Taylor) Wright. I have outlined the data concerning John Wright from Virginia in Chapter 1.

The marriage of Puritha Wright to Boykin Bass occurred in Franklin Co., N.C. on 27 September 1822. He died in 1827 and she moved to Putnam Co., Georgia in 1836. (see her entry) It seems certain that John Wright was living in Franklin Co., N. C., in 1822. Unfortunately, the 1820 Census for Franklin Co, N. C. did not survive.

The earliest entry found in Franklin Co., NC, was in 1816, when John Wright was taxed on 52 acres of land, one male and one female in Capt. Davis' district. In 1818, John Wright was taxed on 160 acres of land and one white poll in Capt. Farmer's district. In 1820 John "Write" paid one white poll in Capt. Davis' district.[1] John Wright was not found on the tax lists for 1813, 1814, or 1815 in Franklin County. The lists for 1821 and 1822 are not extant, and there is no John Wright found in 1823 to 1828. There is no evidence that anyone named John Wright bought or sold property in Franklin County between 1793 and 1844. However, John Wright was mentioned as a renter of part of the

---

[1] Franklin County, N. C., Tax List, 1816, p. 353; Franklin County, N. C., Tax List 1818, p. 412; Franklin Co., N. C., Tax List 1820, p. 473.

estate of Benjamin Perry, who died in Franklin Co., N. C., and whose estate was divided in September 1815.[2]

Fortunately, he is the only Wright in the northern part of the county. There are only two others on the tax lists for these years: 1816 Griffin Wright of Franklin Co., N. C., and his sons George, Gideon, Jeptha, Stephen, and Thomas D. Wright.[3] There is no evidence of any connection of these men to John Wright.

Examination of the tax records of Warren County, N. C., were also examined, and show John Wright appearing in the Shocco District in 1813,[4] and the Hawtree District in 1814.[5] The fact that he is in two different districts in successive years is consistent with the notion that he was renting land. Since there is no overlap, and no one else named John Wright in these records,[6] it seems reasonable to conclude these tax lists all reflect the presence of one man, the father of Puritha (Wright) Bass.

John Wright married Pamelia Brantley in Warren Co., N. C., on December 17, 1812.[7] This appears to be the first appearance of this man in the Warren County, N.C. records. John Wright was also the bondsman on December 19, 1812 for the marriage of Hannah Wright and Jason Terry. This bond was witnessed by William Green, C.C.C.[8]

---

[2] Franklin Co., N. C., Will Book F:368. I examined the file at the North Carolina Archives in Raleigh, and these documents failed to show anything about John Wright. They did show that Perry's land lay on both sides of Shocco Creek, the dividing line between Warren and Franklin Counties. There was a chancery suit filed over the division, which was not settled in state court in 1825, but the final settlement of the estate did not occur until 1837.

[3] Data courtesy of Robert N. Grant.

[4] Warren Co., N. C., Will Book 17:302.

[5] Warren Co., N. C., Will Book 18:227.

[6] There are a father and son John Wright, Sr., and John Wright, Jr., who appear in the Warren County records. However, John Wright, Jr., appears to have removed to Sumner Co., Tennessee by 1809, and his father had died by this time, as there is a record in Will Book 15:309, dated October 30, 1809, showing the legatees of John Wright, deceased, including a power of attorney from John Wright, Jr., now of Sumner County, Tenn.. See Kerr, Mary Hinton. Warren County, North Carolina Records, Vol. III, (1779-1814). (Warrenton, N. C., 1969.)

[7] Holcomb, Brent Howard. Marriages of Bute and Warren Counties, North Carolina, 1764-1868. (Baltimore: Genealogical Publ. Co., 1991,) p. 185. Bondsman was Henry G. Williams and witness was Jno. H. Green. To date, I have not found any further useful information about this woman or her family. In May 2006, I obtained a copy of the original bond from the N. C. State Archive. Unfortunately, the bond was signed only by the bondsman, not by John Wright, so it is not certain this is "our" John Wright.

[8] Holcomb, Brent Howard. Marriages of Bute and Warren Counties, North Carolina, 1764-1868. (Baltimore: Genealogical Publ. Co., 1991,) p. 162.

I have not been able to find certain evidence of John Wright's whereabouts from 1822 to 1830. He married Lucy Garland Andrew, daughter of John Andrew and Mary Overton Cosby in Clarke Co., Ga., on 10 May 1830 in a service performed by her older brother, James Osgood Andrew, Methodist minister and future Methodist bishop.[9] It is worth noting that this was the first marriage for Lucy Garland Andrew, who was then almost 31 years old.

Examination of the Clarke Co., Ga., tax records shows John Wright, Sr., John L. Wright and John C. Wright present in 1830.[10] John C., John L., and a John G. Wright were present in 1831. John L. and John G. Wright were defaulters in 1832. John Wright, Sr., appears only in 1830 and John C. Wright is not listed in 1832. John C. Wright is known to be young, and was the son of William Wright. He has been identified as the husband of Lucy Andrew in an IGI file from the LDS Records, but this is clearly an error, given the information in Puritha's letter. Although not certain, it appears probable that John Wright, Sr., is the man who married Lucy Andrew. In this case, the "Senior" would simply denote that he was older than the other men named John Wright. There are no records in the deed books for Clarke Co. showing John Wright. There is no indication of John Wright, Sr., in the records of Clarke Co., Georgia prior to 1830.[11]

John Wright and Lucy Andrew had one son, John Andrew Wright, born 9 October 1831.[12] John Wright then wrote his wrote his will 9 July 1832 and it was proved in Clarke Co., Ga., by his widow, Lucy Wright, on 22 October 1832.[13]

Clark County, Georgia
I, John Wright, of the County & State above written being weak of body but of sound and disposing mind and memory do make constitute & ordain This to be my last will and Testament.

---

[9] Clarke Co., Ga., Marriage Book B:155.

[10] Clarke Co., Ga., Tax Digests, 1822-1832, Ga. Department of Archives and History.

[11] Clarke Co., Ga., Tax Digests, 1822-1832, Ga. Department of Archives and History. The Grantor Index for Clarke County, Ga., shows 1841-Estate of John G. Wright to Richard Richardson.

[12] Family records.

[13] Clarke Co., Ga., Will Book B:111.

Item 1st. I will & bequeath to my beloved wife Lucy Wright & my Son John Wright all of my property which I have none in my possession, consisting of my Household & Kitchen furniture, my Stock, farming utensils & together with all the money due me.

Item 2nd. I will & bequeath to my beloved wife Lucy Wright and my Son John Wright all of the right, title and interest which I have in the Georgia Land Lottery for which I (unreadable) given in.

In testimony whereof I have hereunto Set my hand and Seal 9th July AD 1832-

/s/ John Wright   (Seal)

Signed & Seal by the testator John Wright in our presence who have hereunto

Signed our names in the presence of each other as witnessed

Thos. E Williamson)
James Brown   )
Martin S Davenport)

Georgia Clarke County Court

Personally appeared in open Court

Thomas E Williamson and Martin S Davenport, two of the Subscribing witnesses to the foregoing will, who on oath Saith that they Saw John Wright the Testator Sign the Same and heard him acknowledge the Same to be his last Will and Testament, that he was of Sound and disposing mind & memory at the time of so doing & that they Saw James Brown, the other witness Sign the Same.

Sworn to in open Court   Thos E Williamson
this 22nd Oct 1832   Martin S Davenport
_____Joseph Ligon C. C. P.

Children were described by Puritha Wright, (cf. pp. 1-3.) Confirmatory information was obtained from a copy of a letter from John E. Ellis, a descendant of Richard Wright, (cf. pp. 18-20).[14]

Children of JOHN WRIGHT and SARAH FOX are:

2. i. RICHARD W.[3] WRIGHT, b. 1799 Mecklenburg Co., Virginia; d. before 6 November 1865, Decatur Co., Ga.; m. MARY ANN HARRISON about 1824 Putnam Co., Ga., daughter of NATHANIEL HARRISON; b. 1799 in Georgia; d. before 10 July 1884 Faceville, Decatur Co., Ga.

3. ii. PURITHA[3] WRIGHT, b. 1802 Mecklenburg Co., Virginia; d. about 1855 Putnam Co., Ga.; m. BOYKIN BASS 27 September 1822 Franklin Co., N. C., son of JACOB BASS and ANN ____; b. 1800 Franklin Co., N. C.; d. before December 1827 Franklin Co., N. C.

4. iii. ISHAM BROOKS[3] WRIGHT, b. 1809 Mecklenburg Co., Virginia; d. 19 February 1890 Putnam Co., Ga.; m. EMILY BARKSDALE 17 January 1831 Putnam Co., Ga., daughter of NATHAN BARKSDALE; b. Hancock Co., Georgia; d. 8 May 1897 Putnam Co., Ga.

5. iv. FRANCES[3] WRIGHT, b. say 1807 Mecklenburg Co., Virginia; d. about 1842 Muscogee Co., Ga.; m. WILLIAM BARKSDALE 19 August 1830 Putnam Co., Ga.; son of NATHAN BARKSDALE; b. 1807 Hancock Co., Ga.; d. after 1880 Chambers Co., Ala.

6. v. MARY[3] WRIGHT, b. 1803 Mecklenburg Co., Va.; d. after 1870 Fort Bend Co., Texas; m. JOHN GOSWICK (GOSSETT) 15 December 1827 Franklin Co., Texas; b. 1809 Franklin Co., N. C.; d. after 1860 Fort Bend Co., Texas.

Child of JOHN WRIGHT and LUCY GARLAND ANDREW is:

vi. JOHN ANDREW[3] WRIGHT, b. 9 October 1831 Clarke Co., Ga.; d. 16 January 1859 Monticello, Drew Co., Ark.; m. (1) SARAH J. CAMP 29 September 1854 Campbell Co.,

---

[14] Mr. Ellis mentioned a son Samuel, not mentioned by Puritha. There is a Samuel Wright, 26-44, with one male under 10, two girls under 10, two women 16-25, and one 26-44 in Capt Mahone's District, Putnam Co., Ga., in 1820, [p. 109.] He may be the same man listed in 1830 in Jones County with one son under 5, one 5-9, himself 30-39, and one male 70-79, along with a wife also 30-39, and one girl each in the under 5, 5-9, 10-15, and 16-20 group. [p. 475.] I have not found anything to suggest a linkage with our John Wright or his family in the census data.

Ga., daughter of LANGLEY BILLUPS CAMP and CHRISTIAN MCCLURE; b. 1835 Campbell Co., Ga.; d. 8 January 1855 Campbell Co., Ga.; m. (2) THYRZA FRANCES FLEMING 7 February 1856 Campbell Co., Ga., daughter of JOHN FLEMING and FRANCES BAILEY, b. 28 November 1829 Abbeville Dist, S. C.; d. 12 September 1907 Troup Co., Ga.[15]

2. RICHARD W.[3] WRIGHT was born 1799 in Virginia, and died before 6 November 1865 in Decatur Co., Ga. He married MARY ANN HARRISON, daughter of NATHANIEL HARRISON about 1824 in Putnam Co., Ga. She was born in 1799 and died before 10 July 1884 in Faceville, Decatur Co., Ga.

Richard W. Wright was born in Virginia from 1793-1799, based upon his report in the census. He was a militia captain in the 1830 Census for Putnam County, Georgia, and was also present there in 1840 and 1850. He is listed in Decatur County, Georgia in 1860. Review of the records of Decatur County, Ga., showed that Matthew M. McAllilley was appointed administrator of the estate of Richard W. Wright on November 6, 1865, and notes that he died intestate.[16]

The record of his marriage to Mary Ann Harrison has also not been located. Her last name was derived from the will of Nathaniel Harrison, dated 1 March 1845, and probated in Putnam Co., Ga., 6 May 1845, which specifically names her, and gives her portion to her husband Richard Wright.[17]

Nathaniel Harrison was born 16 December 1770 and died 5 April 1845 in Putnam Co., Ga.[18] His wife, Martha K. Harrison, was born 12 September 1776 and died 9 May 1858 in Putnam Co., Ga. Nathaniel Harrison's son, Alexander Brown Harrison, was born 19 October 1801, and died 10 February 1863 in Putnam Co., Ga. His wife, Lucy Wright Claiborne, daughter of Sarah Brooking

---

[15] Chapter 8.

[16] Decatur Co., Ga., Court of Ordinary Minutes, Book B:612.

[17] Putnam Co., Ga., Will Book B.

[18] Tombstone data from Harrison Family Cemetery, surveyed by Millicent Arnold. http://ftp.rootsweb.com/pub/usgenweb/ga/Putnam/cemeteries/harrison162gcm.txt. Accessed 7 July 2007. The cemetery is located on Crooked Creek Road, which is near where Isham Wright and his wife are buried.

and James Claiborne, was born 21 February 1808 and died 20 February 1863 in Putnam Co., Ga.

Mary Ann Harrison's first name was confirmed from the two census reports. Her death was reported as "recently" in the Decatur Co., Ga., newspaper, when she was identified as in her 85th year and the widow of Richard Wright.[19]

Richard Wright witnessed the will of Martha Kendrick in Putnam Co., on Mar. 6, 1822. Richard W. Wright signed a notice published 3 October 1829 as "T. C.," which in the context of the announcement is probably "town constable."[20] Richard W. Wright was Sheriff of Putnam County from 1840-1842. Richard W. Wright, along with Gabriel Harrison, applied for letters of administration for the estate of Edmund Butts 6 June 1843. He was a Methodist and a Whig as late as 1849.[21] On 4 October 1847 he was listed as a sponsor of a concert scheduled for Friday, 5 November 1847 at Wesley Chapel, and on 5 June 1849, he signed (with others) as a sponsor of a rally for the Whig Party meeting scheduled for Putnam County.[22]

Richard W. Wright (and Isham B. Wright) were fortunate drawers in the 1832 Cherokee Land Lottery as orphans of John Wright.[Cherokee Land Lottery, 1832: Isham B. Wright, Mil. Dist. 307, Lot 346, Dist. 16, sec. 2; Richard W. Wright, Mil. Dist. 374, Lot 1097, Dist. 2, sec. 4.[23]

Richard W. Wright bought 97 ¾ acres of land, part of lot #203 in the 3rd district of what was Baldwin County, now Putnam, lying on Turkey Creek, from Warren West on 12 September 1825.[24] The land adjoined Samuel Smith, John Murphy, Bushrod Johnston, and Henry Hurt. Elizabeth West relinquished her dower rights to this land. The deed was witnessed by Anderson Harwell and Nathaniel Harrison, J. P. In 1827 50 acres of this parcel were taxed as land of the second quality, the remainder as third quality, while in 1826 it was all taxed as land of the second quality.

---

[19] Decatur Co., Ga., Newspaper Clippings, Vol. II (1876-1885). Cited by Marialis Hamlett, personal communication 13 March 2004.

[20] Evans, Ted. Georgia Newspaper Clippings, Putnam Co. Extracts. (Savannah, Ga.: 1998.)

[21] The Southern Recorder, Milledgeville, Ga., 6 June 1843; cited in Evans, Ted. Georgia Newspaper Clippings, Putnam Co. Extracts. (Savannah, Ga.: 1998.)

[22] Ibid.

[23] See also Putnam Co., Georgia, Court Records, p. 46.

[24] Putnam Co., Ga., Deed Book N:451.

On 26 July 1834, Richard W. Wright bought 202½ acres in the 386th District, known as the Askew tract, from John P. Walker for $450.[25] This tract adjoined Richard W. Wright's land on the northeast and southeast, James C. Burt on the southwest, William Akins on the northeast and John P. Walker on the northwest. This deed was witnessed by A. B. Harrison and Nathaniel Harrison, J. P.

Review of the tax lists makes it clear that the Richard Wright present in Putnam County in 1820 was subsequently known as Richard J. Wright. Richard J. and Richard W. Wright were near neighbors, were in the same militia district, and Richard J., listed as Richard I., is the one who married Martha Burt, daughter of James C. Burt. Bushrod Johnston's sister was married to the John Wright who died in Putnam Co., 1827, according to an online file identified by Kathryn Wright Myers in 2001. Presently, we have not been able to find where Richard W. Wright was from 1820, by which time he should have been at least 21, and possibly 27 years old, and we do not know where he acquired the money to buy his land as we have not found any evidence that his father owned land from 1813 onward.

The marriages of the children are taken from Decatur Co., Ga., Marriage Book A.

Children of RICHARD WRIGHT and MARY HARRISON are:[26]

    i. ALEXANDER HARRISON[4] WRIGHT, b. 1826 Putnam Co., Ga., d. 24 June 1864, Ft. Delaware, Del.; m. SARAH ANN ARNOLD 15 June 1846 Putnam Co., Ga., daughter of WILLIAM ARNOLD.[27] She was born about 1826 in Georgia.

        Alexander Wright, 24, is living right next door to Richard W. Wright.[28] In fact, the census taker marked the last names as ditto. The name of his wife comes

---

[25] Putnam Co., Ga., Deed Book O:190.

[26] 1850 Census Putnam Co., Ga., Dist. 70, p. 298, #307/307. "Richard W. Right."

[27] Putnam Co., Ga., Will Book C: , LWT of William Arnold, written 6 January 1860 lists among his legatees a daughter, Sarah Ann Wright, wife of Alexander H. Wright. Interestingly, Wiley W. Arnold married Amanda F. Wright on 3 July 1838. She could possibly be the eldest daughter of Richard W. Wright and Mary Harrison, if she married as a teenager. No data presently on either William or Wiley W. Arnold. It is also possible that Amanda F. is the Frances Wright who was sister to Richard W. Wright, and who "died in Harris" in the 1840's. Wiley Arnold has not been looked for in the 1850 Census.

[28] 1850 Census Putnam Co., Ga., Dist. 70, p. 298, #308/308.

from this census, as does the name of his first born child.

It is probable that he is A. H. Wright of Webster Co., Ga., in 1860, 33, born in Ga., merchant, with wife Sarah A., also 33, born in Ga. The children listed do not include Gabriel, so he probably died young. Children listed are Mary G., 5, Wesley A., 4, and Sarah A., 10/12. (Sept. 1859.)[29]

Alexander Harrison Wright enlisted in Co. F., 44th Regt., Ga. Volunteer Infantry as a private on 13 May 1862, Putnam Co., Ga. He was elected as the junior 2nd Lt. on 13 May 1863. He was captured at the battle of Spotsylvania C. H., Va., on 10 May 1864 and died "of chronic diarrhea" at Fort Delaware, Delaware, 24 June 1864.[30]

Sarah Wright, age 50, is head of household in Floyd Co., Ga., in 1870.[31] Her children include "Mollie" 17, John W., 14, working the farm, Sarah 10, and Fredrick, 7. All the children were born in Georgia.

Children of ALEXANDER WRIGHT and SARAH ARNOLD are:

1. GABRIEL H [5] WRIGHT, b. May 1850 Putnam Co., Ga.; died before 1860.
2. MARY G.[5] WRIGHT, b. 29 July 1854 Putnam Co., Ga.; d. 24 December 1934; m. JOHN HAYWORD ELLIS son of JAMES M. ELLIS and MARY E. IVY; b. about 1849; d. 20 June 1932.[32]
3. WESLEY A.[5] WRIGHT, b. about 1856 in Georgia

---

[29] 1860 Census Webster Co., Ga., Southern Dist., p. 426, #215/215.

[30] Harper Johnson, Carolyn L. Muster Roll of Company F, 44th Regiment, Georgia Volunteer Infantry, Army of Northern Virginia, CSA. Putnam Co., Ga., Putnam Vols. http://ftp.rootsweb.com/pub/usgenweb/ga/putnam/military/civilwar/rosters/cof44reg.txt. Accessed 5 November 2005.

[31] 1870 Census Floyd Co., Ga., Div. 141, p. 299B, #794.

[32] Johnson, Bruce D., op cit. He lists a son form this marriage, James Fred Ellis, b. 28 February 1874 Habersham Co., Ga.; d. 7 Sep 1954 Phoenix, Maricopa Co., Ariz. Ancestry.com indicates he was living in Coal Mountain, Forsyth Co., Ga., in 1880, in Justice Precinct 6, Bexar Co., Texas, in 1900, Atlanta Ward 2, Fulton Co., Ga., in 1910, and in Phoenix in 1930 and 1940. He also indicates a marriage to Martha Ellen Mangum 1 August 1901, probably in Atascosa Co., Texas. She was born 6 February 1876 in Poteet, Atascosa Co., Texas, and died in Phoenix about 1959.

4. SARAH A.[5] WRIGHT, b. September 1859 in
Georgia.
5. FREDRICK[5] WRIGHT, b. about 1863 in Georgia.

ii. MARTHA[4] WRIGHT, b. 1830, Putnam Co., Ga.

iii. REBECCA[4] WRIGHT, b. 1832 Putnam Co., Ga.; m. JAMES A.
ROGERS about 1849 Putnam Co., Ga.; b. 1826 Georgia.

Rebecca Wright was identified as a daughter of
Richard Wright by John E. Ellis in his letter. James A.
and Rebecca Rogers are living in Putnam Co., Ga., in
1850 with daughter, Georgia, b. Sept. 1850.[33]

The letter states that he had two daughters: Georgia
and Jimmie and that they both married a Bellflower. M.
J. Bellflower married E. G. Rogers 24 December 1870
Terrell Co., Ga. M. J. Bellflower married Mary J.
Rogers 15 January 1882 in Terrell Co., Ga.

M. J. Bellflower is widowed, stating he got married
in 1870, and living with his sister in Cowarts, Houston
Co., Alabama, in 1910.[34] He was also a widower when
listed in the 1900 census for Newton, Dale Co., Ala.[35]
Mary J. Belflower, b. 2 December 1851, d. 1 October
1894, is buried in Bethel Baptist Church Cemetery,
Newton, Alabama.[36] She was listed as the wife of
Milton J. Belflower.

Milton J. Belflower is buried in New River
Cemetery, Tift Co., Ga. He was born 26 March 1848
and died 16 July 1930.[37]

Children of REBECCA WRIGHT and JAMES A. ROGERS are:

1. ELIZABETH GEORGIA[5] ROGERS, b. September 1850
Putnam Co., Ga.; d. about 1880 Terrell Co., Ga.;
m. MILTON J. BELFLOWER 24 December 1870
Terrell Co., Ga., son of ELIJAH BELFLOWER and
SUSAN MORRIS;[38] b. 26 March 1848 Randolph
Co., Ga.; d. 16 July 1930 Tift Co., Ga.

---

[33] 1850 Census Putnam Co., Ga., District 70, p. 296B, #332/332.

[34] 1910 Census Cowarts, Houston Co., Ala., ED 145, p. 6B.

[35] 1900 Census, Newton, Dale Co., Ala., ED 61, p. 9B.

[36] Located at http://www.findagrave.com, #68587409. Accessed 21 March 2013.

[37] Located at http://www.findagrave.com, #54819720.

[38] Additional information on the Belflower family obtained from Batdorf, Forrest.
Batdorf. 5 September 2005. Located at http://wc.rootsweb.ancestry.com, (db. fbatdorf.).

Children of GEORIGA ROGERS and MILTON BELFLOWER:

> a. ELLA F. BELFLOWER, b. 1872 Putnam Co., Ga.
>
> b. JODIE BELFLOWER, b. 1874 Putnam Co., Ga.
>
> c. MARY J. BELFLOWER, b. 1878 Putnam Co., Ga.

2. MARY JIMMIE[5] ROGERS, b. 2 December 1851 Putnam Co., Ga.; d. 1 October 1894 Newton, Dale Co., Ala.; m. MILTON J. BELFLOWER 15 January 1882 Terrell Co., Ga.. son of ELIJAH BELFLOWER and SUSAN MORRIS; b. 26 March 1848 Randolph Co., Ga.; d. 16 July 1930 Tift Co., Ga.

Child of JIMMIE ROGERS and MILTON BELFLOWER:

> a. G. EVELYN BELFLOWER, b. 1884 Ga.; d. 25 April 1952 Tift Co., Ga.; m. HENRY EARL BELFLOWER 1 November 1903 Newton, Dale Co., Ala.

iv. ELIZABETH[4] WRIGHT, b. 25 December 1835 Putnam Co., Ga.; d. 2 January 1884 Liberty Co., Florida; m. CHARLES B. EDWARDS 12 November 1854 Decatur Co., Ga.;[39] b. 1831 Florida.

Although recorded in the marriage transcript as Charles D., he is almost certainly Charles B. Edwards. In 1850 Charles B. Edwards is a 19 year old overseer in the household of Mary Rogers in Gadsden Co., Florida.[40] I have not found them in the 1860 or 1870 Census. In 1880 Charles B. Edwards and wife Elizabeth E. Edwards, born about 1835 in Georgia, are living in Bristol, Liberty Co., Florida.[41] He is listed as a miller, with both parents born in North Carolina. Both of her parents are reported to have been born in South

---

[39] Decatur Co., Ga., Marriage Book A:233. Located online at http://usgwarchives.org/ga/decatur/vitals/marriage/marbrwz.txt. Accessed 26 December 2012.

[40] 1850 Census Gadsden Co., Fla., Dist. 7, p. 201A, #338. He said he was born in Florida.

[41] 1880 Census Liberty Co., Fla., Bristol, ED 95, p. 467D, #33.

Carolina. While this does not agree with the data developed here, I have not been able to identify another Elizabeth Wright in Decatur County at the appropriate time to be the woman in Liberty County, Florida in 1880. Furthermore, Charles B. Edwards was recorded in the 1885 Census for Liberty County as age 54 and born in Florida, widowed, father born in South Carolina and mother born in Georgia.[42]

Elizabeth E. Wright is buried in Bristol Cemetery, Bristol, Liberty Co., Florida.[43]

Children of ELIZABETH WRIGHT and CHARLES EDWARDS are:

1. ADOLPHUS[5] EDWARDS, b. 12 September 1862 Gadsden Co., Florida; d. 13 May 1934[44] Gadsden Co., Fla.; m. BELL CHESTER,

2. FRANK[5] EDWARDS, b. 25 August 1864 Gadsden Co., Fla.; d. 23 April 1931 Gadsden Co., Fla.[45]

3. FANNIE[5] EDWARDS, b. 1867 Florida

4. RALPH[5] EDWARDS, b. 1873 Florida

5. CLIFTON CLAUD[5] EDWARDS, b. 14 November 1878 Gadsden Co., Fla.; d. 10 February 1944 Gadsden Co., Fla.[46]

---

[42] 1885 Florida State Census, Liberty Co., p. 10, #86. All of the children are there.

[43] http://www.findagrave.com, memorial #95783852.

[44] http://www.findagrave.com, memorial #97217413. Helen Strickland, who posted this also posted his obituary from the Gadsden County Times, 17 May 1934. Funeral services for Adolphus Edwards, 71, who died Sunday, were held from the Methodist church at Old Mount Pleasant at 10 a. m. Tuesday, the Rev. J. E. Skipper, pastor of the Greensboro Methodist church, officiating. Burial was made in the church cemetery nearby. Mr. Edwards was born at Old Mount Pleasant in this county on September 12, 1862. During the major part of his business career he engaged in the turpentine business in Georgia and in the southern part of Florida. After retiring from this vocation, he engaged in farming in this county. Surviving relatives are two sons, A. M. Edwards, St. Petersburg, and Chester Edwards, Apalachicola; four daughters, Mrs. T. E. Whittle, Greensboro; Mrs. H. W. Bishop, Bishopville; Mrs. W. C. Prince, Greenville; Mrs. R. E. Smith, DeLand. One brother, Ralph Edwards, of Blountstown, also survives. The late Frank Edwards, formerly proprietor of the Quincy Hotel, was a brother. Mr. Edwards was united in marriage with Miss Bell Chester, of Wetumpka, who died April 15, 1924. The deceased was a member of the Methodist church and throughout his life was a man of fine Christian character. He was affiliated with the order of the Knights of Pythias."

[45] Buried Eastern Cemetery, Quincy, Gadsden Co., Fla. Located 26 December 2012 at http://findagrave.com., memorial #66645937.

[46] Buried McAlpin Cemetery, Gadsden Co., Florida. Located 26 December 2012 at http://findagrave.com, memorial #27570830.

6. CHARLES B.[5] EDWARDS, b. 14 April 1881 Liberty Co., Fla.; d. 13 December 1889 Liberty Co., Fla.[47]

v. VIRGINIA A.[4] WRIGHT, b. 17 March 1839 Putnam Co., Ga.; d. September 1864 in Texas; m. (1) WILLIAM T. EDWARDS 23 December 1853 Decatur Co., Ga.[48]; d. before December 1855 Decatur Co., Ga.; m. (2) WILLIAM RANDOLPH JETER 16 January 1859 Decatur Co., Ga.,[49] son of WILLIAM MADISON JETER and ELIZA W. BATTLE; b. 1836 Georgia.[50]

Richard W. Wright applied to be appointed administrator of the estate of William T. Edwards on 3 December 1855, which confirms that the Virginia Wright listed in the marriage book is his daughter.[51] He filed the return on Edwards' estate 6 July 1860.[52]

Virginia H. Jeter, 22, born Georgia, and W. R. Jeter, 24, born in Georgia, have W. T. Edwards, 5, GA, and R. M. Jeter, 5/12, Texas, are living in Newton County, Texas, next door to W. M. Jeter and E. W. Jeter, 56 and 49 respectively, who are probably his parents.[53] I have not been able to find her in the 1870 or 1880 census.

An online file reports that William Randolph Jeter was born 21 November 1835 in Meriwether Co., Georgia, and died 11 August 1864.[54] The same source was used for Virginia's date of birth and the data on Richard Jeter.

Child of VIRGINIA WRIGHT and WILLIAM T. EDWARDS is:

1. WILLIAM T.[5] EDWARDS, b. 1855 Decatur Co., Ga.

---

[47] http://www.findagrave.com, memorial #95783837.

[48] Decatur Co., Ga., Marriage Book A:221. Accessed 26 December 2012 at http://usgwarchives.org/ga/decatur/vitals/marriage/marbrwz.txt.

[49] Jeter, Richard. 9 Apr 1999. http://boards.ancestry.com/mbexec? htx=message&r=an&p=localities.northam.usa.states.georgia.counties.decatur&m=16, confirmed in Georgia Marriages 1851-1900. Online database at Ancestry.com.

[50] William Jeter and Eliza, along with their children are living in 1850 in Gadsden Co., Fla., District 7, p. 183A, #78. Marriage records show that William Jeter married Eliza W. Battle 15 April 1830 in Upson Co., Ga.

[51] Decatur Co., Ga., Court of Ordinary Minutes, Book B:125

[52] Decatur Co., Ga., Court of Ordinary Minutes, Book B:319

[53] 1860 Census Newton Co., Texas, p. 264, #245. Parents are #246.

[54] http://trees.ancestry.com/tree/28713057/person/12084494093.

Children of VIRGINIA WRIGHT and WILLIAM R. JETER are:

2. RICHARD RANDOLPH[5] JETER, b. 11 December 1860 Burke, Newton Co., Texas; d. 8 November 1940 Dade City, Pasco Co., Fla.; m. LUELLA ROBERTSON 1 July 1891 Natchitoches Parish, La., dau.of JOHN H. ROBERTSON and JULIE ANN COOPER; b. 10 December 1863 Newbern, Dyer Co., Tenn.[55]

3. NATHANIEL[5] JETER, b. 1862 Newton Co., Texas; d. 1864 Newton Co., Texas.

vi. JOHN N.[5] WRIGHT, b. 1841, Putnam Co., Ga.; d. December 24, 1861, Albany, Dougherty Co., Ga.; m. ELIZA E. FREEMAN, March 5, 1861, Decatur Co., Ga.

John N. Wright enlisted in the Decatur Guards, subsequently known as Co. D, 17th Regt., Georgia Volunteer Infantry on 13 August 1861, and he died on active duty at Albany, Ga., on 24 December 1861. [56] Richard W. Wright applied to be the guardian of Eliza E. Wright on May 4, 1863. [57] In the application it was noted that she was the daughter of Eliza Freeman. Eliza E. Freeman was the daughter of James Voland Freeman and Hannah Freeman.[58] She subsequently married Henry W. Lester on 23 November 1865 shortly after the death of R. W. Wright.[59] Henry W. Lester and Eliza (Wright) Freeman are living in Gadsden Co., Fla., in 1870.[60] She had no living children from her marriage to John N. Wright.

---

[55] Jeter, Richard R., III. http://www.rootsweb.ancestry.com/~latangip/queries98.htm.

[56] Jones, Frank S. History of Decatur County, Georgia. (1971, n. p. d.), p. 369.

[57] Decatur Co., Ga., Court of Ordinary Minutes, Book B:612.

[58] Her will was written 29 September 1856 and specifically names her daughter Eliza. Olivent, Chad. Will of Hanna Freeman. 31 Jan 1999. (Decatur Co., Ga., Message No. 469, located on http://boards.ancestry.com.) cf. also message 25.117

[59] Decatur Co., Ga., Marriage Book A, #491

[60] 1870 Census Gadsden Co., Fla., Quincy, p. 828A, #98. Henry W. Lester was born in Massachusetts about 1844. She was born about 1845 in Georgia.

3. PURITHA[3] WRIGHT was born 1802 in Virginia, and died about 1855 in Putnam Co., Ga. She married BOYKIN BASS, son of JACOB BASS and ANN _____ 27 September 1822 in Franklin Co., N. C. He was born about 1800 in Franklin Co., N. C., and died before December 1827 in Franklin Co., N. C.

The kinship of Puritha Bass to John Wright is established by her correspondence reproduced under his entry. Her marriage bond to Boykin Bass is of record in Franklin County, with Jacob Bass serving as his son's bondsman.

Boykin Bass died in Franklin Co., N. C., between 31 May 1827, when his will was dated, and December 1827 when it was probated. In his will, he names his heirs as his wife Puritha and his son and daughter, John and "Francis."[61]

She is listed as the head of household in the 1830 Census for Franklin County, with one boy and one girl under ten, herself, and one other female over 45.

Puritha moved to Putnam Co., Georgia about 1836, as she applied for guardianship of her minor son, John Bass, 22 December 1836 in Putnam Co., Ga.[62] Since no record of Frances was found, she is presumed to have died between 1830 and 1836. I do not think this is the Frances referred to by Puritha in her letter to Lucy Andrew Wright, as she reportedly died about 1844 in Harris County, Ga. I think she was probably named after her aunt.

Puritha Bass was also listed as the head of household in Putnam Co., Ga., in 1840 and 1850.[63] From these censuses she was born in 1802 in Virginia, and from her correspondence with Lucy Andrew Wright, we know she was living in Putnam Co., Ga., in 1855, but in poor health, and that her married name was Bass. She is not in the 1860 Census for Putnam Co., and her son was living with his uncle, Isham Wright. She is presumed to have died in Putnam County between those two dates, and perhaps near the date of the later letter.

Jacob Bass appears in the Halifax District of Franklin Co., N. C. in the 1790 census in a household containing three males

---

[61] Franklin Co., N. C., Will Books H, I, J, 1824-1834, p. 37.

[62] Data from Lea L. Dowd via e-mail 30 Sep 2000.

[63] 1850 Census Putnam Co., Ga., Dist. 70, p. 306, #485. Interestingly, #481 is James W. Wright 74 NC, Frances Wright 54 F VA, John Wright, 32 GA, dentist, and Ann E. Wright 25 GA. Also living in the household are Rebecca Hall 14 GA, Mary Hall 8 GA, and Sarah Person 12 GA.

over 16, three females over 16, and one female under 16, and ten slaves. Jacob Bass, Jr., is also listed in that census having one male over 16, one female under 16, four females over 16, and four slaves.

Numerous land transactions involving Jacob Bass are recorded and by 1797 he appears to have acquired around 1,000 acres along the south bank of Sandy Creek. He sold 200 acres to his son Jacob Bass, Jr., in 1791. [64]

Jacob Bass, Jr., died in 1812 and was survived by his widow and at least three children: Boyakin, Sally, and Cynthia. Court records show that he had eight children, and that his widow, Ann, died before 1827. [65]

Boykin Bass sold his interest in his mother's dower land to David Sills, who had earlier served as guardian to his younger brother, Wyatt.[66] His brother Jacob had sold his land to David Sills on 27 November 1825 and his brothers Wyatt and Guilford sold to David Sills on 26 May 1826.[67] David Sills is also shown as having bought land "drawn by Mrs. Jacob Gupton in the division of the lands of Jacob Bass, deceased, in 1813 and was since sold as the property of her husband, 15 March 1826." [68] Jacob Bass, brother of Boykin. had moved to Warren Co., N. C., while Wyatt and Guilford Bass had moved to Tennessee.

Children of PURITHA WRIGHT and BOYKIN BASS are:

i. JOHN[4] BASS, b. 2 July 1823 Franklin Co., N. C., d. 4 January 1894 Johnson Co., Ga.; m. FRANCES BATCHELOR, 1 January 1861 Putnam Co., Ga., daughter of BLAKEY BATCHELOR and SARAH REYNOLDS. [69] She was b. 12 November 1842 Putnam Co., Georgia; d. 15 August 1931 Johnson Co., Ga.[70]

---

[64] Watson, Joseph W. Kinfolks of Franklin Co., N. C., 1793-1844. (Rocky Mount, N. C., 1985) Deed Book 7:103, 13 Aug 1791, 200 acres.; Deed Book 21:56.

[65] Franklin Co., Court, December session, 1812; petition for inheritance of land along Sandy Creek.

[66] Watson; Deed Book 16:68.

[67] Watson; Deed Book 16:164.

[68] Watson; Deed Book 16:169.

[69] Frances Batchelor was the fifth child of Blakey B. Batchelor, b. 1804 Franklin Co., N. C., d. 19 May 1879 Putnam Co., Ga.; m. Sarah Reynolds 19 December 1830 Putnam Co., Ga. [Williams, Lyle K. The Batchelor Family. (Fort Worth, 1991), p. 82-83.]

[70] Allen, James W. Williams Cemetery, Rehoboth. Located online at

John Bass, 28, is a tailor, living with his mother in the 1850 Census.[71] He is living with his uncle, Isham B. Wright in the 1860 Census, age 32.[72] He and Frances and their children are present in Putnam Co., Ga., in 1870[73] and 1880.[74] His neighbors include his wife's Batchelor family. He is not in the 1900 Census. Mary Elizabeth, 14, and Susan Bass, 10, are still at home. Sarah Bass is not.

The Muster Roll for Co. F, 66th Regt. Ga. Volunteer Infantry, Army of Tennessee, CSA, shows that John Bass enlisted as a private 2 Aug 1863, that he was hospitalized in Macon, Ga., with intermittent fever 29 Nov 1863, and pension records show he "served until surrender," and died 4 April 1896.[75] Also shown on the muster roll are Owen Jefferson Batchelor and Joseph Batchelor. There is a tombstone, though, for John Bass in Williams Cemetery, Johnson Co., Ga., that lists his date of birth as 2 July 1823 and his date of death as 4 January 1894. I have chosen to use the tombstone dates.

Children of JOHN BASS and FRANCES BATCHELOR are:

1. SARAH[5] BASS, b. about 1863 Putnam Co., Ga.
2. ELIZABETH[5] BASS, b. about 1866 Putnam Co., Ga.
3. SUSAN[5] BASS, b. b. 19 November 1869 Putnam Co., Ga.; d. 20 January 1912 Johnson Co., Ga.; m. JOHN R. STEPHENS 1890 in Georgia; b. November 1864 in Georgia.

    The 1900 Census for Pullen, Johnson Co., Georgia, shows Frances Bass, b. November 1839 in Georgia, both parents born in Georgia living

---

http://files.usgwarchives.net/ga/johnson/cemeteries/williams390cm.txt. Accessed 24 December 2012.

[71] 1850 Census Putnam Co., Ga., 70th Dist., p. 306, #485.

[72] 1860 Census Putnam Co., Ga., p. 424, #430/430.

[73] 1870 Census Putnam Co., Ga., Popcastle, p. 24, #624 (age 47), Frances, age 28.

[74] 1880 Census Putnam Co., Ga., Rockville, p. 489, #79/82, age 56, NC, NC, VA, Frances, age 37 (p. 490) GA/NC/SC.
[75]

http://ftp.rootsweb.com/pub/usgenweb/ga/putnam/military/civilwar/rosters/cof66reg.txt.

with John Stephens and Susie Stephens.[76] She is buried in Williams cemetery, but he does not have a marker in that cemetery. There is also an online Bible outlining the children of Isham Stephens that shows a John Daniel Stephens, b. 10 June 1872, but this is probably a different man.[77]

The obituary of Sara Frances Tyson of Johnson County, Ga., states she was the daughter of Johnny Stephens and Mrs. Susan Bass Stephens.[78] She was reportedly born 12 September 1890 according to her death certificate. The obituary lists surviving family members.

ii. FRANCES[4] BASS, b. about 1826, Franklin Co., N. C.; d. about 1835, Franklin Co., N. C.

4. ISHAM BROOKS[3] WRIGHT was born 1809 in Virginia, and died 19 February 1890 Putnam Co., Ga. He married EMILY BARKSDALE 17 January 1831 Putnam Co., Ga. She was born in Virginia, and died 8 May 1897 Putnam Co., Ga.

Isham Wright was born in Virginia, but his calculated birth year varied from 1803 to 1809. The most common seems to

---

[76] 1900 Census Johnson Co., Ga., Pullen, ED 52, p. 15B, #275. She identified herself as the mother of one child, with one still living. I interpret this to mean that Sarah and Mary Elizabeth were dead.

[77] http://files.usgwarchives.net/ga/johnson/bibles/davisbible.txt. Accessed 24 Dec 2012.

[78] Wrightsville (GA) *Headlight*, 18 May 1967. Accessed online 24 December 2012 at http://files.usgwarchives.net/ga/johnson/obits/t/tisontys13115ob.txt. Mrs. Sara Frances Tyson, 76, of Meeks, died in a Swainsboro hospital Sunday night. Mrs. Tyson was a lifetime resident of Johnson County, a daughter of the late Johnny Stephens and Mrs. Susan Bass Stephens. She was a member of Rehobeth Baptist Church and was married to the late Henry Green Tyson. Surviving are one son, M. C. Tyson, Meeks; two sisters, Mrs. Lillian Odom, Wrightsville and Mrs. Iris Lord, Toombsboro' one brother, Artis Stephens, Milledgeville; two grandchildren and one great-grandchild. Funeral services were conducted at four o'clock Tuesday from Rehobeth Baptist Church with the Rev. A. W. Franklin and the Rev. H. A. Hiers officiating. Burial was in the church cemetery with Sammons Funeral Home in charge. Pallbearers were C. M. Norris Jr., R. T. Brantley, Robert Webb, Palmer McGee, M. T. Riner Jr., and W. E. Jackson (Sara was born 12 Sep 1890. Georgia death certificate #014681. Her husband, Henry Green Tison/Tyson is also buried at Rehobeth Baptist Church Cemetery.)

be 1809, which is what I have shown. Isham Wright died on 18 February 1890, and was buried on 22 February 1890 at Crooked Creek Primitive Baptist Church, Eatonton, Ga. This is still an active church, and he was associated with the church as a deacon. His obituary was published in the Eatonton *Messenger* issue of Saturday, 22 February 1890:

> It is with great regret we announce the death of another one of the old citizens of Putnam. Mr. Isham B. Wright died at his home last Wednesday afternoon at 2 o'clock. Sitting in his chair in his usual health, death came suddenly and the good man's spirit was transpered [sic] from its earthly tabernacle to a mansion in a better world. He was about 87 years of age, a member of the Primitive Baptist church and was true to his faith. He was an honest and upright citizen and his walk in the religious life was such that no one doubts his preparation for the change. His remains were buried in the cemetery near Crooked creek church.

He is recorded in Putnam Co., Ga., in Censuses from 1830 through 1860, is in Hancock Co., in 1870, and in Putnam Co., in 1880. His farm is apparently located near the Hancock Co. line, as there is no suggestion that he moved. Marriage records for Putnam County show his marriage to Emily Barksdale 27 January 1831. The names of his children were listed in the 1850 census.

He was a "fortunate drawer" in the 1832 Cherokee Land Lottery as an "orphan of John Wright," and is described in Puritha Wright Bass' letters as "living ten miles from Eatonton."

Isham Wright served as a militia private in Capt. James A. Meriwether's Company in the Indian Wars of 1836.[79] Emily

---

[79] Ayres, Linda. She posted a copy of an article from the *Federal Union*, Milledgeville, Ga., 29 January 1836, which reported an order requiring a draft of 110 men from the first brigade, and 230 men of the second brigade, 3rd Division, Ga. Militia. The men were part of a general draft ordered by the Governor of Georgia for 3,500 men to be mobilized to march to the defense of Florida. Meriwether's company, known as the State Fencibles, was ordered to assemble and march forthwith. Accessed 16 January 2013 at http://files.usgwarchives.net/ga/military/indian/meriwether.txt.

Wright, widow of Isham Wright, filed for a pension benefit based on this service in 1892.[80]

On 4 February 1845 Isham B. Wright bought 210 acres of land, "plus the acres of the widow's land" from the estate of Ransom Ballard adjacent to Ross, Lancaster and Roughton for $399. [81] Isham Wright was a beneficiary of the will of Jesse Batchelor, probated in Putnam County, Ga., in July 1856. [82] And on 5 November 1861 Isham B. Wright sold land in his capacity as administrator for the estate of Francis Ross of Hancock County.[83]

His will was written 3 May 1879, Putnam Co., Ga., and probated there in 1890.[84]

State of Georgia
Putnam County
Last Will of Isham B. Wright
In the name of God Amen. Isham B. Wright of said state and county—being of advanced age but being of sound and disposing mind and memory deem it both right and proper as respects myself and family that I should make a disposition of the property with which a kind providence has blessed me. I do therefore make my last will and testament hereby revoking and annulling all others by me heretofore make.
Item 1st I desire and direct that all of my just debts be paid without delay by my executor hereafter named and appointed.
Item 2nd I give bequeath and devise to my beloved wife Emily all that tract of parcel of land in Putnam County and state aforesaid in which I am now living known as the Bryant place containing one hundred and thirty five acres more or less with all the rights members and appurtenances to said lot of land in anywise belonging free from all charges and limitations whatever to her own

[80] "United States, Index to Indian Wars Pension Files, 1892-1926," index and images, FamilySearch (https://familysearch.org/pal:/MM9.1.1/KDR1-D6T: accessed 17 Jan 2013), Isham B Wright, 1892.
[81] Putnam Co., Ga., Deed Book Q:322.
[82] Putnam Co., Ga., Will Book B:284-285.
[83] Putnam Co., Ga., Deed Book S:283.
[84] Putnam Co., Ga., Unbound papers., Ga. Department of Archives and History. Transcribed by Kathryn Wright Myers, October 2001.

proper use benefit and behoof forever with the full power to dispose of the same by will or otherwise as she may deem proper. I also give and bequeath to my beloved wife in the same unreserved right all the stock of every kind farming utensils household and kitchen furniture provisions carriages together with everything else in or connected in any way with the said farm described above.
Item 3rd I hereby constitute and appoint my wife Emily Wright Executrix of this my last will and testament.
May 3rd 1879   Isham B. Wright
Signed sealed delivered and published by Isham B. Wright as his last will and testament in the presence of us the undersigned who subscribed our names hereto in the presence of the Testator at his special instance and request and in the presence of each other.
May 3rd 1879 Joe Ashfield, W.C.Branan, Thomas Branan
Test by James W. Hargrove, J.P.

Emily Barksdale was born in Virginia, and was illiterate based upon information recorded in the census and the fact that she signed her will with a mark. [85]

Will of Emily Wright, wife of Isham Brooks Wright, 8th June 1893
Georgia, Putnam County)
In the name of God Amen. I Emily Wright of the County of Putnam and State of Georgia being of sound and disposing mind and memory and being desirous to settle my worldly affairs while I have strength so to do, do make and publish this my last will and testament hereby revoking all wills by me heretofore made.
And first I commit my soul to the God who gave it, and my body I desire to be buried in the family plot at Crooked Creek Church in the county of Putnam in the state of Georgia, and my worldly estate I dispose of as follows.

---

[85] Putnam Co., Ga., Unbound papers., Ga. Department of Archives and History. Transcribed by Kathryn Wright Myers, October 2001.

Item 1st I give to my daughter Puritha Emma Marchman all of the property by me held during her natural life and at her death to be legally divided between my other children share and share alike.

In witness whereof I the said Emily Wright have to this will consisting of one page of foolscap paper set my hand and seal this the 8th day of June 1893.

her
Emily x Wright
Mark

Signed sealed and published and declared by the above named Emily Wright as her last will and testament in presence of me who at her request in presence of each other have subscribed our names as witnesses hereto.

A.J. Rasser

T.J. Branon

James W. Hargrove

PS} I hereby appoint my daughter Puritha Emma Marchman executrix of this my last will and testament. This was written before being signed.

Puritha Emma Marchman probated this will and stated that Emily (Barksdale) Wright had died on 8 May 1897. However, Puritha Marchman apparently died in 1905, as William H. Wright, the youngest son, petitioned to be made a substitute administrator on 6 December 1905. He stated that Emily Wright died 15 April 1897.

Puritha Emma (Wright) Marchman's name is further evidence of connection between Puritha (Wright) Bass and Isham Wright as established by her letters cited earlier.

John Ellis' letter to L. S. Wheeler in 1932, cited above, states the Isham B. Wright had a Sarah Fox Wright who married a Bomgartel. The name seems to come up as Baumgardner most of the time. I have not located a marriage record for this couple, nor have I found evidence for Sarah associated with Isham Wright. He lists daughters Mary Wheeler, Elizabeth Ross, and sons William, John, James, and Joseph. The census data show all of these except

John,[86] and also show Puritha Emma, Rebecca and Martha J., who are not on Mr. Ellis' list.

Children of ISHAM WRIGHT and EMILY BARKSDALE are:[87]

    i. MARY[4] FRANCES WRIGHT, b. 1833 Putnam Co., Ga.; d. 1898 Hancock Co., Ga.; m. ELIJAH WHEELER 28 December 1854 Putnam Co., Ga.;[88] b. 13 June 1832 Granville Co., N. C.; d. 17 January 1903 Hancock Co., Ga.;[89] m. (2) PURITHA EMMA (WRIGHT) MARCHMAN 2 July 1899 Hancock Co., Ga.

    E. Wheeler, 38, is listed as an overseer in the 1860 Census of Hancock Co., Ga., along with his wife, two daughters and a son.[90]

    He enlisted as a private in Co. I, 49th Regt., Ga. Volunteer Infantry, 14 May 1862. He was wounded at Cold Harbor, Va., 27 June 1862. He was appointed 4th Corporal in January 1863, and 4th Sergeant in March of that year. He was wounded in the left leg and placed on disability leave at the Wilderness, Va., 6 May 1864. He evidently recovered quickly, as he was appointed 2nd Sergeant in June 1864. He was wounded yet again at Petersburg, Va., in February 1865, and was disabled when the surrender occurred.[91]

---

[86] There are no men named John Wright listed in either 1850 or 1860 who could be this man. The closest is John Wright, b. 1838, living with John Braddy and P. Braddy in Hancock Co., Ga., [p.254, #303/334]. However, in the 1850 Census John Brady,50, Apenita Brady 50, have Ann A. Wright 14, John Wright 12, and Apenita Wright 10, living together in Greene Co., Ga., (Dist. 140, p. 101A, #437.) Apenita Brady was likely Mrs. Wright, and married Mr. Brady sometime in the 1840's. No marriage record found for John Brady, though.

[87] 1850 Census Putnam Co., Ga., p. 299, #387/387. "Isham B. Right." B. H. Batchelor is on the same page at #383/383.

[88] Information courtesy of John Wheeler, lineal descendant of Elijah Wheeler. He stated that Elijah Wheeler was from Granville Co., N. C., and moved to Putnam Co., Ga., in 1853. (17 April 2012.)

[89] His date of birth was listed in the record of his Civil War service; date of death was in the pension application of Emma (Wright) (Marchman) Wheeler, who applied for his pension after his death, (John Wheeler.) John says he was born in Granville Co., N. C., where he appears in the 1850 Census. In the Census records in Georgia, he says he was born in Georgia in all entries until 1880 and 1900 where he says he was born in North Carolina as were his parents.

[90] 1860 Census Hancock Co., Ga., p. 242, #204/223. They are all listed by first initial.

[91] Johnson, Carolyn. Muster Roll of Company I, 49th Regiment, Georgia Volunteer Infantry, Army of Northern Virginia, CSA: Hancock County, Georgia, Pierce Guards. Accessed 18 April 2012 at

In 1870, Elijah Wheeler and his wife "M. F." are living in Sparta, Militia Districts 101 and 102, along with Emma, 14, Paul E., 12, Ella, 11, SF, 9, JE, 5, and JA, 2.[92]

In 1880, the children are all named, although there are a couple that may have died young when comparison is made to the 1870 list.

Children of MARY FRANCES WRIGHT and ELIJAH WHEELER:

1. MARY EMMA[5] WHEELER, b. 1856 Hancock Co., Ga.
2. PAUL EZEKIEL[5] WHEELER, b. 1858 Hancock Co., Ga.; d. 1938 Hancock Co., Ga.; m. SARAH ADELA MCNATT.
3. ELLA[5] WHEELER, b. 1859 Hancock Co., Ga.
4. LUCY F.[5] WHEELER, b. 1861 Hancock Co., Ga.
5. J. ELIJAH[5] WHEELER, b. 1864 Hancock Co., Ga.
6. JULIA[5] WHEELER, b. 1866 Hancock Co., Ga.
7. ISHAM[5] WHEELER, b. 1875 Hancock Co., Ga.

ii. JOSEPH[4] WRIGHT, b. 1838, Putnam Co., Ga.

Joseph Wright, 22, is living with his parents in 1860.[93] He would have been about 23 when enlistments started for Confederate service in the spring of 1861, so I have looked for evidence of his service. Although Joseph Wright is a common name, Civil War units were usually recruited from single counties. An online source identified that Co. G, 12th Regt., Co. F., 44th Regt., and Co. F., 66th Regiment of Georgia Volunteer Infantry were recruited in Putnam County.[94] I have found no one who could be this Joseph Wright in those three companies. I also considered that he might have served from Hancock County, since his father's farm was close to the county line. The same source identified Co. E,

---

http://files.usgwarchives.net/ga/hancock/military/civilwar/rosters/coi49reg.txt

[92] 1870 Census Hancock Co., Ga., Militia District 101 & 102, p. 395B, #443/451. He is now listed as a farmer and is living in the middle of a large number of black families, so is likely living on the land for which he was an overseer before the Civil War.

[93] 1860 Census Putnam Co., Ga., Dist. 308, p. 424, #430/430.

[94] http://freepages.military.rootsweb.ancestry.com/~pudig/GAInfantry.htm. Accessed 16 January 2013.

and Co., K, 15th Regt., Co. D and Co. I, 58th Regiment, Georgia Volunteer Infantry as being recruited from Hancock County.[95]

The muster rolls show J. B. Wright originally enlisted in Co. F, 12th Regt., Ga., Infantry 11 June 1861 and was appointed musician. He was discharged because of disability 16 June 1861, but re-enlisted as a private in Co. K, 15th Regt. 24 February 1862 and was paroled at Appomattox C. H., 9 April 1865.[96]

The muster roll for the 15th Regiment shows J. B. Wright, private in Co. K, and Joseph Wright, private, then Sergeant, Co. E, and Joseph Wright, private in Co. K.[97] In the 1860 Joseph Wright, 13, was living in a household headed by Jas. D. Lester, 69, and Rebecca Lester, 38, with S. S. Wright, 36, and a number of other persons, none of whom were named Wright.[98] At least one of the men named Joseph Wright is probably the man born about 1840 living with George Wright and wife Mary in Hancock County in 1860.[99] The other may be Joseph Wright, son of Isham. One Joseph Wright enlisted in Co. E, 15th Infantry Regt., on 15 July 1861, and was mustered out 9 May 1864.[100]

The 1870 Census showed Joseph Wright, 28 and born in Georgia, with wife Sarah and children Mary, 9, Ida, 5, William H., 4, and Harriet J., 2, living in Heard Co., Ga.[101] Joseph Wright married Sarah Hubbard 10

---

[95] The same source confirms Elijah Wheeler in Co. I, 49th Regiment, Ga. Volunteer Infantry, suggesting not everyone enlisted in his home county. There was no one who could be Joseph Wright in this regiment.

[96] http://www.researchonline.net/gacw/rosters/15thcomk.htm. Accessed 16 January 2013.

[97] http://www.rootsweb.ancestry.com/~gatroup2/15thregimentinfantry4.htm. Accessed 16 January 2013.

[98] 1860 Census Dooly Co., Ga., p. 537. I found one online source that identifies him as Joseph Steele Wright, b. 13 January 1847, son of William Henry Thomas Wright and his wife, Sarah S. Bass. [http://trees.ancestry.com/tree/20746901/person/1022196323.] He is probably the Joseph "L." Wright who married Isabelle J. Speer 5 December 1867 Monroe Co., Ga., and who was living at 78 Fraser St., Atlanta, Ga., in the 1903 City Directory. (all located on Ancestry.com). Joseph 23, Isabel, 22, Henry, 1, and Sarah S. Turner, 46, are living together in Macon, Bibb Co., Ga., in 1870, p. 861A.

[99] 1860 Census Hancock Co., Ga., p. 280, #571.

[100] "U. S. Civil War Soldier Records & Profiles." Database locate on Ancestry.com, accessed 16 January 2013.

[101] 1870 Census Heard Co., Ga., Dist. 761, p. 343A.

October 1861 in Fayette Co., Ga. Joseph Wright, 60, was still living in Heard Co., Ga., in 1900, and said both of his parents were born in Georgia.[102]

I have not located anyone in the 1880 Census who fits the demographic of this Joseph Wright. I also have not located an obituary or a tombstone for him as of this time.

iii. MARTHA J.[4] WRIGHT, b. 1839, Putnam Co., Ga.

Martha J. Wright is not living with her parents in 1860 and presumably married during the prior decade.

iv. ELIZABETH[4] WRIGHT, b. April 1841, Putnam Co., Ga.; d. 11 August 1923 Hardwick, Baldwin Co., Ga.; m. JAMES A. ROSS 24 March 1858 Putnam Co., Ga. He was b. 1818 Hancock Co., Ga., d. before 1900 Hancock Co., Ga.[103]

James Ross, 35, Elizabeth 20, and M. E. are living in Mayfield, Hancock Co., Ga., in 1860. On 12 May 1863 the newspaper reported the death of Martha Emma Ross, age 2 years, 10 months, and 4 days on the 4th of May at the home of IB Wright.[104]

The 1870 Census for Hancock Co., Ga., shows James Ross and Elizabeth living next door to William H. Wright and Isham B. Wright.[105] They have James 8, Joseph 5, Mary E. 4, and Susan B. 1 living with them. Joseph Ross, 16, is living with his grandfather, Isham B. Wright in the 1880 census.[106]

In 1880 James A. Ross, 62, is living with "Lizzie" 38.[107] Susan Ross has evidently died in the interim, as she is not listed.

The 1910 Census shows Elizabeth Ross living in Baldwin Co., Ga., in the household of her son-in-law

---

[102] 1900 Census Heard Co., Ga., Texas, ED 73, p. 7B, #143. He is also in the 1880 Census in Dist. 761, ED 65, p. 76D, #152. He did have a son, William H., b. 1866. His grave is registered and records a death date of 29 August 1919, [http://findagrave.com, memorial #11519A.]

[103] Jane Sims. Personal communication 6 November 2005.

[104] Ibid.

[105] 1870 Census Hancock Co., Ga., Dist. 102, p. 404, #1087/1095. Isham B. Wright, Emily and Sarah are at #1085/1093 and William H. Wright and Catherine are at #1086/1094.

[106] 1880 Census Putnam Co., Ga., Papcastle Dist., p. 47B. He is specifically identified as a grandson. He was born in Georgia as were both of his parents.

[107] 1880 Census Hancock Co., Ga., Dist. 103.

Simeon H. Renfroe, and her daughter, Willie P. Ross.[108] Also living in the house is Joseph W. Ross, 44, a brother-in-law who is not married. She says that she had 11 children, and seven survived. Thus, there are two more children, whose names cannot be determined from the census or the obituary, who must have died young.

The 1920 Census shows Elizabeth Ross now living with her son, James D. Ross, and his wife Julia B. Ross, again with unmarried son Joseph W. Ross.[109]

The obituary of Elizabeth (Wright) Ross was published in August 1923.

"Mrs. Elizabeth Ross died at the home of her son, Mr. J. D. Ross in Hardwick Monday morning, August 11, at three o'clock.

Mrs. Ross had been in declining health for the past several months on account of old age, having lived far beyond her three score years, and she peacefully and quietly passed away.

The funeral services were held at the residence Tuesday morning, Rev. Will Green, of Jones County, officiating, and her remains were buried in the cemetery in this city.

Mrs. Ross, before her marriage was Miss Elizabeth Wright, daughter of Mr. And Mrs. I. B. Wright of Putnam County, and was eighty-two years of age last April. In early womanhood she married Mr. James A. Ross, who preceded her to the grave. Her home was in Hancock County until fifteen or sixteen years ago, when she came to Baldwin County to live with her children.

Mrs. Ross was a member of the Primitive Baptist Church, and was faithful to the teachings and lessons of her faith. She was a woman of a kind and sympathetic nature, possessing those traits of character which made her a kind and devoted wife and mother, friend and neighbor. She has gone to her reward leaving a heritage of a well-spent life to her children and grandchildren.

---

[108] 1910 Census Baldwin Co., Ga., Salem, Dist. 2, (Militia Dist. 115).
[109] 1920 Census Baldwin Co., Ga., Midway, Dist. 8.

She is survived by three sons, Messers. J. D. Ross, J. W. Ross, and George Ross; three daughters, Mrs. O. D. Herringdine, Mrs. W. B. Renfroe, (and Mrs. S. H. Renfroe.)"

Children of ELIZABETH WRIGHT and JAMES M. ROSS are:

1. MARTHA EMMA[5] ROSS, b. 1 July 1859 Hancock Co., Ga.; d. 4 May 1863 Putnam Co., Ga.
2. JAMES[5] D. ROSS, b. about 1862 Hancock Co., Ga.; m. JULIA B. _____.
3. JOSEPH[5] W. ROSS, b. about 1865 Hancock Co., Ga.
4. MARY ELIZABETH[5] ROSS, b. about 1866 Hancock Co., Ga., d. after 1910 and before 1923.[110]
5. SUSAN R.[5] ROSS, b. about 1869 Hancock Co., Ga.; d. before 1880 Hancock Co., Ga.
6. WILLIE[5] P. ROSS, b. 1871 Hancock Co., Ga.; m. SIMEON H. RENFROE.
7. GEORGE[5] ROSS, b. 1873 Hancock Co., Ga.
8. AUGUSTA[5] ROSS, b. 1876 Hancock Co., Ga.; m. O. D. HERRINGDINE.
9. LUELLA[5] ROSS, b. 1877 Hancock Co., Ga.; m. W. B. RENFROE.

v. REBECCA[4] WRIGHT, b. 1843, Putnam Co., Ga.

Rebecca Wright, 13, is living with her parents in 1860, but not in 1870, and so presumably married during that decade.

vi. WILLIAM H.[4] WRIGHT, b. September 1846 Putnam Co., Ga.; d. after 1905; m. CATHERINE _____, about 1870 Hancock Co., Ga. She was b. Jan. 1848 in Ga.

In 1870 Wm. H. Wright is living between his father, I. B. Wright and his brother-in-law James Ross in Hancock Co., Ga.[111] He is 23 and his wife Catherine is 24, born in Georgia. No children are listed, so I assume they married about 1870 in either Putnam or Hancock Co., Ga.

---

[110] This calculation is based on Elizabeth Ross' statement in 1910 that she had seven surviving children. There are two early deaths that can be accounted for from the census: Martha Emma and Susan. The names of the other two children, who died young, are not known to me or to Jane Sims.

[111] 1870 Census Hancock Co., Ga., Dist. 102, p. 404, #1086/1094.

W. H. Wright was living in Jones Co., Ga., in 1905 when he became substitute administrator for his sister, Emma Marchman. With this clue, I am confident that he is listed in Jones Co., Ga., in both 1880[112] and 1900.[113] However, I have not been able to find him with certainty afterward.[114]

Given the lack of an 1890 Census, it seems likely that there are children born in the interval between Gordon and Lawson Wright.[115]

Children of WILLIAM H. WRIGHT and CATHERINE are:

1. WILLIAM[5] WRIGHT, b. about 1871 in Georgia
2. JAMES HARRIS[5] WRIGHT, b. 4 September 1875 Jones Co., Ga.; d. 4 July 1950 Jones Co., Ga.; m. LOIS M. SMITH about 1895 Jones Co., Ga.; b. 7 July 1873; d. 23 Jan 1941.

   James H. Wright is living in Davidson, Jones Co., Ga., in 1910. I have not been able to identify him for certain after this.[116] The names of the last three daughters are my attempt to translate the script, and are quite likely wrong. The dates of birth and death, as well as Lois Wright's maiden name are from their tombstones.[117]

Children of JAMES H. WRIGHT and LOIS SMITH are:

---

[112] 1880 Census Jones Co., Ga., Dist. 304, p. 67, #636/636. The month of birth is from this census.

[113] 1900 Census Jones Co., Ga., Davidson, Enumeration Dist. 63, p. 12 B, #212/214.

[114] There is a William H. Wright, b. about 1844 in Georgia present in the 1920 Census for Wheeler, Jefferson Co., Fla., Enumeration Dist. 76, p. 1B, family 16, living with his wife, whose name appears to be Mastria J., but could possibly be Martha J. She is 74 and b. Fla. This William Wright say his father was b. NC, mother was b. Georgia. I have no information that allows me to say with certainty this is, or is not the same W. H. Wright.

[115] Thomas G. Wright and his wife Leola, both 32, b. GA, with parents born in Ga., along with daughters Catherine 2, and Luvenia, 5/12 are listed in the 4th Ward Macon, Bibb Co., Ga., in 1910, p. 235A, Enumeration District 42, p. 12A, #258/317. Also listed was Lawrence L. Wright, 23, and wife Lillie, also 23, along with son Worth, 9/12 in Enumeration District 12, p. 41B, line 19. Since this is near Lawson L. Wright, it is possible that the information about him is incorrect.

[116] 1910 Census Jones Co., Ga., Davidson, p. 310A, Enumeration Dist. 87, part 1, line 1, family #27.

[117] The names were originally from the census. Data amplified by readings from their tombstones in Bradley Baptist Church Cemetery, Bradley, Ga. Cited in Colvin, Earl and Colvin, Beth. Fields of Stone: Cemeteries of Jones County, Georgia. (2004), p. 53, person #177. Cited hereafter as Colvin.

a. JAMES EVERETTE[6] WRIGHT,., b. 31 December 1895 Jones Co., Ga.; d. 29 August 1969 Jones Co., Ga.; m. ALMA GILES; b. 14 June 1902; d. 19 Feb 1989 Jones Co., Ga.[118]

b. HELEN H.[6] WRIGHT, b. about 1898 Jones Co., Ga.

c. EMORY N.[6] WRIGHT, b. about 1901 Jones Co., Ga.

d. PRIAM E.[6] WRIGHT, (f), b. about 1907 Jones Co., Ga.

e. ELVIN M.[6] WRIGHT, (f), b. about 1907 Jones Co., Ga.

f. RICHARD H.[6] WRIGHT, b. about 1907 Jones Co., Ga.

g. ALICE P.[6] WRIGHT, b. September 1909 Jones Co., Ga.

3. GORDON[6] WRIGHT, b. about 1877 in Georgia

4. LAWSON L.[6] WRIGHT, b. March 1887 in Jones Co., Ga.

Lawson L. Wright is living in the 4th Ward, Macon, Bibb Co., Ga. in the 1910 Census, living in the house of James Daniels.[119]

vii. JAMES A. R.[4] WRIGHT, b. March 1850 Putnam Co., Ga.

James Wright, 10, is living with his parents in 1860. He has not been located with certainty in the 1870 Census.[120]

vii. PURITHA EMMA[4] WRIGHT, b. 1852 Putnam Co., Ga.; d. 1905, Putnam Co., Ga.; m. (1) WALTER B. MARCHMAN about 1870 Putnam Co., Ga., son of STEPHEN MARCHMAN and ELIZABETH _____. He was b. about 1847 Putnam Co., Ga., d. before 1880 Putnam Co., Ga.; m. (2) ELIJAH WHEELER 2 July 1899 Hancock Co., Ga.

---

[118] Bradley Baptist Church Cemetery, Bradley, Ga. Colvin, p. 53, person #175.

[119] 1910 Census Bibb Co., Ga., 4th Ward, Macon, Enumeration Dist. 12, p. 50B, line 29.

[120] The only possible identified so far is James Wright, 20, in Marshall Co., Ala., p. 160, #292. His wife Evalina is 22, and he has two sons, John Alfred, 1, and William H., 4/12. Evalina and both sons were born in Alabama. I am not confident this is the correct person, and a search using the Ancestry.com search engine has not identified any certain candidates.

Puritha E. Marchman, 18,is living with her husband, Walter B. Marchman, 23, as part of the household of his father Stephen Marchman and "Lizzie."[121] Also living in the household are his sister, Amanda J., 34, and brother Francis E., 20.

Emma Marchman is living in the household of her father, Isham B. Wright in 1880.[122] She is listed as the wife of Elijah Wheeler, b. June 1832 in the 1900 Census.[123]

4. FRANCES[3] WRIGHT, died about 1842 Muscogee Co., Ga. She married WILLIAM BARKSDALE 19 August 1830 in Putnam Co., Ga., son of NATHAN BARKSDALE and ANGELINE HILL.[124] He was born 1807 Hancock Co., Ga. and died after 1880, probably in Chambers Co., Alabama.

The marriage records of Putnam County list the marriage of Frances Wright to William "Bagsdell"[125] on 19 August 1830.[126] Puritha Bass said that Frances had died in

---

[121] 1870 Census Putnam Co., Ga., Rockville Dist., p. 109, #891, with his parents as family #890.

[122] 1880 Census Putnam Co., Ga., Papcastle Dist., p. 47B, #139/141.

[123] 1900 Census Hancock Co., Ga., Militia District 101, ED 11, p. 7A, #114/121. This appears to be the same location he lived at with her sister, Mary Frances from 1854 onward. This marriage appears to have been a way to provide for her, as her husband died young without any property and no children, and she lived with her father and mother until their deaths, at which point her sister had died, so she married Elijah Wheeler presumably to obtain access to his pension. John Wheeler has documents from the pension file showing that her nephews and nieces were happy with the arrangement.

[124] Hubert, Sarah Donelson. Genealogy of Part of the Barksdale Family of America. (Atlanta: Franklin Printing & Publishing, 1895,) p. 10. Copy located online 20 March 2013 https://dcms.lds.org/view/action/ieViewer.do?dps_pid=IE92258&dps_dvs=1363791891173 ~445&dps_pid=IE92258&change_lng=en. Nathan Barksdale, son of Joseph Barksdale, married, moved to Putnam county, Georgia. Issue, two sons—Judge and Nathan. Judge died unmarried. Nathan married Angeline Hill. Issue ten children. Mrs. Emma Wright of Eatonton, is a daughter of his. Some of his family are living in Barnesville, Pike county, Georgia.

[125] According to John Ellis' letter, Frances Wright married William Barksdale.

[126] Putnam Co., Ga., Marriage Records. Viewed online at both Ancestry.com and Familysearch.org. Both are compiled record sites. The original microfilm would have to be examined to see if Barksdale is a better reading of the manuscript, but it is phonetically probable.

Forsyth about 10 years ago, meaning about 1844.[127] It is unclear, but I assume she meant the town of Forsyth, which is in Monroe County. There are no persons named Barksdale in the county in either 1840 or 1850.

Search of the 1840 Census suggested the most likely candidate was William Barksdale of Muscogee Co., Ga.[128] He was 30-40, with a wife of similar age, and had two boys under five, three 5-10, and one girl under 5. This would give them six children in 10 years. While not biologically impossible, it is implausible.

The 1850 Census shows William Barksdale in Muscogee Co., Ga., as a 41 year old male, born in Hancock Co., Georgia.[129] He is living in the household of James and Jane T. Jones along with William Barksdale, 13, born in Putnam Co., Georgia. There are no other persons named Barksdale living in Muscogee Co., Ga. This matches reasonably well with the information at hand, except with the information in the 1840 Census.

There are still three boys who should have been 15-20 unaccounted for. There are no Barksdale children living with Richard, Puritha, or Isham Wright in Putnam County. He may have sent other children to his sisters and brothers, but they would be difficult to identify in the census.

I have not found William Barksdale in the 1860 Census, but he is in Muscogee Co., Ga., in 1870, where he was working as a farm hand and living in what appears to have been a boarding house. He is in Chambers Co., Ala., again working as a farm hand at age 75, and living with a servant.

Children of FRANCES WRIGHT and WILLIAM BARKSDALE are:

   i. WILLIAM[4] BARKSDALE, b. 1837 Putnam Co., Ga.

  ii. LAVINIA[4] BARKSDALE, b. 1839 Putnam or Muscogee Co., Ga.

 iii. FRANKLIN[4] BARKSDALE, b. 1842 Muscogee Co., Ga.

---

[127] Certainly the appearance of two children named Barksdale, 11 and 8, in the household of Mary Gossett, her sister, support the statements in the letters.

[128] 1840 Census Muscogee Co., Ga., Militia District 772, p. 223B, #677.

[129] 1850 Census Muscogee Co., Ga., District 8, p. 413A, #48

5. MARY[3] WRIGHT was born about 1803 in Mecklenburg Co., Va., and died after 1870 in Fort Bend Co., Texas. She married JOHN GOSWICK (GOSSETT) 15 December 1827 in Franklin Co., North Carolina. He was born about 1809 in Franklin Co., N. C., and died after 1860 in Fort Bend Co., Texas.

The marriage of Mary Wright to John Goswick is of record.[130] John Gossett was living with his wife and two sons in Putnam County, Ga., in 1840.[131] John Gossett was taxed on 400 acres of land in Putnam Co., Ga., in 1852, but was listed in Jones Co., Ga., in 1850.[132]

John "Gassett" and wife Mary are living in the household of Thomas DeWalt in Fort Bend Co., Texas, in 1860,[133] while son Samuel, 30, is an overseer a few doors away.[134] Samuel has a wife, "L. H." and "Linton" 7/12, both born in Georgia.

In 1870, "L. H." is probably Lora H. Hartney, 32, born in Georgia, who is married to George D. Hartney, 50, merchant from Canada, along with Mary Gossit, 8, Samuel Gossit, 5, and Emmer Gossit, 2, all born in Texas, and Mary Gossit, 60, born in Virginia. Samuel Gossett died about 1868, and his widow re-married and moved in with her three children and her mother-in-law.[135]

Children of MARY WRIGHT and JOHN GOSSETT are:

  i. JOHN[4] GOSSETT, b. about 1828 Franklin Co., N. C.; d. after 1850.

  ii. SAMUEL[4] GOSSETT, b. about 1830 Franklin Co., N. C.; d. about 1868 Fort Bend Co., Texas; m. LORA H. _____

---

[130] Kennemore, Henry H., Kennemore, Keuttah Goswick. Goswick Genealogies. http://freepages.genealogy.rootsweb.ancestry.com/~keuttah/censusfindings.htm#top. Accessed 19 March 2013. "In my many years of research on the surname of Goswick, I have found that many of the Goswick descendants are "Gossett" today. There are several Gossett of today that prove they descend from the Goswick's of North Carolina. For reasons that I do not know, Joseph Goswick of Franklin Co. N.C. is found as: Goswick and Gossett in many records, and it is from his lineage that we find many of the Gossett descendants."

[131] 1840 Census Putnam Co., Ga., Militia District 310, p. 195. [011001-000001]. He is on the same page as Meredith Kendrick and Lewis Wright. (see #3 above.)

[132] He was 44, born in N. C., wife Mary was 47, born in Virginia, and sons John 23, a teacher, and Samuel, 21, were born in North Carolina. Also in the household were Lavinia Barksdale, 11, and Franklin, 8, both born in Georgia. These latter two are orphans of her sister, Frances.

[133] 1860 Census Fort Bend Co., Texas, p. 370, #232/212.

[134] 1860 Census Fort Bend Co., Texas, p. 370, #227/207.

[135] I have not found these people in 1880.

about 1858 in Georgia; b. about 1838 Ga.; m. (2) GEORGE D. HARTNEY about 1869 Fort Bend Co., Texas.

Children of SAMUEL GOSSETT and LORA H. are:

1. LINTON[5] GOSSETT, b. December 1859 Georgia; d. young.
2. MARY[5] GOSSETT, b. 1862 Fort Bend Co., Texas.
3. SAMUEL[5] GOSSETT, b. 1865 Fort Bend Co., Texas.
4. EMMER[5] GOSSETT, b. 1868 Fort Bend Co., Texas.

Chapter 8: John Andrew Wright

John Andrew Wright was born 9 October 1831[1] in Clarke Co., Georgia. His father, John Wright, married Lucy Garland Andrew on 10 May 1830.[2] John Wright died, testate, in Clarke Co., Ga., after 9 July 1832 and before 22 October 1832.[3] Lucy Garland Andrew was the fourth of twelve children born to the Rev. John Andrew and his wife, Mary Overton Cosby.[4]

John A. Wright's father died before he was a year old, and his mother probably lived in the household of her brother, James O. Andrew, who was elected a bishop of the Methodist Episcopal Church at the General Conference of 1832, and moved to Oxford, Georgia, to take his seat. Lucy Wright married there, as his second wife, William Roe Henry 28 November 1843. Mr. Henry was an attorney and judge who moved to Campbell Co., Ga., by 1857.[5]

John A. Wright clearly spent time in the Henry household, as the second of twelve letters he wrote between 1853 and 1858[6] was addressed to William R. Henry, Jr.[7] In the 1850 Census, he was listed as a farmer, and living in the household of his uncle, Hardy Harbert Andrew.[8] He started studying for the law sometime before 10 July 1853, when he wrote a letter addressed to "Judge Henry and Lady."

---

[1] The dates of birth and death were recorded by his son. They were probably living in Farmington in the household headed by James O. Andrew.

[2] Clarke Co., Ga., Marriage Book B:155.

[3] Clarke Co., Ga., Will Book B:111.

[4] Revolutionary Soldiers and Their Descendants. Georgia Pioneers. 13-14:99,1976-77.

[5] Campbell Co., Ga., Deed Book F:267, [26 Jan 1857.] Transcribed by Beth Collins. Located at http://files.usgwarchives.org/ga/campbell/deeds/dd180.henry.txt. Accessed 8 May 2008. They are in the 1860 Campbell Co., Ga., p. 235, #378/362.

[6] Lucius Horace Featherston Papers, (Collection 504, Series 3, Box 10). Manuscript, Archive, and Rare Book Collection, Emory University, Atlanta, Georgia. There are a total of 12 letters written by John A. Wright in this file, plus two written by Puritha Bass to Lucy (Wright) Roe, which document the adult children of John Wright.

[7] William was two years older than John A. Wright, judging by the 1850 Census data. There is a letter in the same series, folder one, that was written to Kathleen F. Wright from an elderly resident of Macon, Ga., who knew the Roe household, and he confirmed that John A. Wright was raised along with the Henry children. She had written inquiring about any knowledge he had about her first husband, John Wright, but he had none.

[8] Hardy H. Andrew, (17 March 1811-30 May 1854), was apparently a teacher and also an ordained elder in the Methodist church. [Holcomb, Brent H. Marriage & Death Notices from the Southern Christian Advocate, Vol. 1, (1837-1860.) (Easley, SC: Southern Historical Press, 1979,) p. 344, citing the edition of 30 June 1854.]

I will have from 20 to 25 school avg and I have in hopes I will please the people. So far I am doing very well and very well pleased. I have a good boarding house at Mr. White's & feel perfectly at home there among such friends and relations. I have practiced the *Discussion* at New Hope and to address them on Saturday week.

The letter goes on to discuss the weather and the prospects for the crops before closing. He wrote "Bill" Henry a longer letter dated 14 July 1853 from Palmetto, (Campbell Co.,) Georgia. In addition to offering the use of his spare clothing, as noted before, he goes on to report:

But let the clothing be as plenty as they will I should like to have some of your cigars. 500 I understand you've got. Schools might go to Texas if I was just then to smoke a few—never would take up another school as long as I live if I could get cigars enough to smoke. I have got fourteen and Monday morning will have 19 sure. I would have had them all this week, but I have been sick. I have had the Diarrhea a week and am now well except I am too feeble to go about. I tell you Bill if I had just been at home while I was at my worst schools might have gone to Guinea. But my Spirits have returned again and by Saturday morning I shall be entirely well I think. I am to go up to Uncle Davenport's Sunday to meeting. I made a speech up there last Saturday night on this Liquor question. I had to take the anti side. I heard next morning that a man was present said that Mr. Wright gave his views 100 percent better than he could have done it himself, so [ ] Good Saturday evening week I will make an attempt to advise the Division up there any way to rub the green off. I intend to embrace every opportunity of speaking whether I say much or little very good idea I think. But I have quit chewing tobacco or using it in any way. And have found you a wife in Campbell. Her father owns a plantation on the Chatahooochee has 2 or 3 children and a quantity of Negroes about 40 I think little & big come out here to the Campbell camp meeting & you shall have an interview with her. Her name is Harrallson.

John A. Wright makes no mention of any romantic interests of his own, but on 29 September 1854 he married Sarah J. Camp in Campbell County.[9] He was about to celebrate his 23rd birthday, and she was 19. That same year, he announced the opening of his law practice at "Campbellton, Georgia, (now part of Atlanta) and "Blue Ridge and portions of the Flint circuit."[10] In this notice he gives as references Rev. James O. Andrew, Oxford, Georgia; Messrs. Harper & Lamar, Covington, Georgia; Hon. C. D. Pace, Covington, Georgia; Dr. William Brown, Savannah, Georgia; and Gen. A. Austell, Campbellton, Georgia. He was also socially active, being a member of the Grand Lodge of Georgia #76, which was headed by Benjamin Camp.[11]

The next surviving letter was addressed to Lucy Henry and dated Campbellton, [Ga.] 11 December 1854.

Dear Ma

Nothing interesting to write you. Will not be surprised at a short letter. We got home safely Friday night after supper, eat and went to a show where they had a bear that could tell the time by a watch, could tell the value of a piece of money, could play cards, that knew the multiplication tables by heart and was equally good in Division, Subtraction, and addition. So we [ ] for singing and [ ] came off with a half Dollar less in my pocket. We are well—all send their love. Write soon, give my love to all.

Your son,
John A. Wright

---

[9] There are two women named Sarah Camp in the 1850 Census, Campbell Co., Ga. She is probably the girl shown on p. 447, #616, where she was listed as 15. She was the daughter of Langley Billups Camp and Christian McClure. Mr. Camp died in 1848 Campbell Co., Ga. [Blackman, Elaine. Camp Descendants. 23 June 2008. Located at http://wc.rootsweb.ancestry.com, (db camp_descendants).]

[10] Card in my possession.

[11] Grand Lodge of Georgia 1854, Campbellton Lodge No. 76. Located at http://files.usgwarchives.net/ga/campbell/history/76camp.txt. Accessed 23 October 2008. There is a letter from 1866 written by Thyrza Frances (Fleming) Wright to the lodge, inquiring about his membership, and apparently from the context of his reply, asking if there was any support for her a widow with an orphaned son. The letter confirmed that he had joined the Lodge that year, but there was no evidence of any further activity.

Tragedy struck, as he wrote in a letter to his mother dated 10 January 1855.[12]

Dear Ma,

It pains me to write yet it is my duty. Sallie was taken sick last Saturday and died Monday at two o'clock. Nothing in life ever affected me so. Years only will remove it. No man ever had a better. I feel so unpleasant that you must not expect anything farther. Give my love to all.

Your affectionate son,
John A. Wright

He then wrote a hasty note to his mother dated Palmetto, [Ga.] 27 March 1855, which contains an ominous remark.

I am doing well here, better than I ever did before in my life. I am making money. I think I know I am safe if nothing happens. A gang moving here tried to injure me of these. I ask nothing.

He does not specify exactly what he was doing that caused the "gang moving here" to try and injure him. One piece of legal business that did occupy him was to represent the estate of his uncle, H. H. Andrew.

Upon the application of John A. Wright for Letters of Administration on the estate of Harvey H. Anderson, late of Newton County, deceased, it appearing to the Court that due and legal notice of said application has been published in the Southern Recorder and no objections being filed, it is therefore ordered by the Court that he be hereby appointed Administrator of the estate of said Harvey H. Anderson, late of said County, deceased, and

---

[12] 10 January 1855 was a Wednesday, so Sarah Camp died 8 January 1855. In March 1855, he applied for and received letters of administration on her estate. [Campbell Co., Ga., Ordinary Court Minutes A:512. "It appearing to the court that John A. Wright has made application for letters of administration on the estate of his wife Sarah J. Wright, dec'd, and it further appearing that no objections have been place in office it is therefore ordered that letters of administration be issued accordingly he having given bond and security in term of law."]

290

that Letters of Administration issue upon his giving bond and security in the sum of $8,000 provided the said John A. Wright shall and does comply with the above ordered and renders bon of $8,000 with sufficient security by the Oct. term of said Court.[13]

In the April 1855 term of the Ordinary Court of Campbell County, Georgia, John A. Wright applied for Temporary Letters of Administration on the estates of James M. Knox, George W. Knox, and Augustus P. Knox, which was granted, with an appearance scheduled for the August session. In August, "It being _____ to appear to the Court that the Health of John A. Wright would not permit his appearance at this term of Court. It is therefore ordered that application for...[letters of administration]...be continued to September term 1855."[14] In September 1855, John A. Wright was granted letters of administration, and in November 1855 he was given leave to sell the personal property of James M. Knox and Augustus P. Knox. In December 1855, Samuel Knox, 14, selected John A. Wright as his guardian.

John A. Wright wrote his mother a letter dated 26 August 1855, outlining that his law practice was going well, although indicating he had been ill, as reported in the court minutes.

Dear Ma,
Since I wrote you my last I have been at Court. It was a very bad time for me to be out yet I done very well. I got sixty five Dollars in fees at court on two cases—one a Divorce case the other a True bill for selling Liquor to Slaves. Uncle [ ] says in three months I will be crowded with business. I do not expect to make but little more by my practice than my expenses this year. But next year I think I shall bring it *up* if all things should work well. Shall have in my hands, the first of next year over Ten thousand Dollars.

---

[13] Newton Co., Ga., Ordinary Court Minutes (1852-1857):87, [8 Aug 1854]. Cited in Bruno, John I. *Newton County, Georgia, Minutes of the Inferior Court for Ordinary Purposes 1852-1857.* (Mansfield, GA: Wolfe Publ., 1999,) pp. 68-69. I have not consulted the original, but this is certainly H. H. Andrew.
[14] Campbell Co., Ga. Ordinary Court Minute Book A:524.

If you will write me I will come to Newton at Camp meeting if you will let me know the time. I fell tolerable well. I think I shall go to Uncle Davenport's this evening after it gets cool. I will start out there. I shall stay about two weeks with you.

Let me know at once when Camp meeting *convenes*. Cousin Sarah Davenport will come with me. I am feeble yet & not as prudent as I should be yet I have fattened a little. Give my love to all and [ ].

Your unworthy son,
John A. Wright

John A. Wright probably felt his prospects were good, as on 7 February 1856 he married Thyrza Frances Fleming of Coweta County, daughter of John Fleming and Frances Bailey. He was 24 and she was 26. No information as to how or when they met has survived. Unfortunately, his business affairs began to unravel almost immediately after his marriage. In February 1856 term of court: [15]

The petition of A. H. Cochran showeth that your petitioner is security for John A. Wright in his administration bond as administrator of the estates of James M. Knox, George W. Knox, and Augustus P. Knox, deceased. That your petitioner conceives himself in danger of suffering from his said securityship of as aforesaid in this: to wit, because said John A. Wright is mismanaging the effects of said estates of said deceased. Therefore your petitioner prays that such order may be made in the premises as will relieve your petitioner and save him from injury and as in duty pound your petitioner ever pray be this February 4th, 1856.

A. H. Cochran

The court, presided over by Mr. R. C. Beavers, ordered John A. Wright to appear in the March term and show cause why Mr. Cochran should not be released from his securityship and John Wright made security or relieved of his right of administration.

---

[15] Campbell Co., Ga. Ordinary Court Minute Book A:544.

It appearing to the Court that citation was granted at the February term of this court 1856 on the petition of A.H. Cockran setting forth that he was security on those bonds given by John A. Wright as administrator on the several estates or James M. Nox [sic], George W. Nox, and Augustus P. Nox all three late of said county deceased. That said John A. Wright was mismanaging said three estates administrator and said citation having been served on said John A. Wright to come forward and show cause why said A.H. Cockran should not be released as security and said three bonds at this term of the Court to give other good security as administrator on said estates. The said John A. Wright having failed to appear and show cause why said A.H. Cockran should not be released on said three bonds as his security. It is therefore ordered by the Court that said [Cockran] be released from his securityship on said bonds and from all liability on said Bonds from this date & he is hereby released and exonorated from al liability on said three bonds.[16]

Granted: March 4th, 1856   R.C. Beavers

On March 13, 1856, Letters of Administration for John A. Wright on the Knox estates was revoked.[17] It seems likely this was the business that John A. Wright had thought would bring him $10,000. His reputation collapsed, and his former in-laws sued to have him relived as administrator of his first wife's estate the next month. Things went rapidly from bad to worse, and he fled. The next surviving letter was written from Memphis, dated 15 July 1856.

Darling,
My love I am 450 miles from you. May heaven help you sweet one. You know that when that little self of

---

[16] Campbell Co., Ga. Ordinary Court Minute Book A:548.

[17] In May 1856, Samuel Knox, presumably now 16, was granted Letters of Administration on the three Knox estates, and in January 1857, Samuel Knox was granted leave to sell the property of James M. Knox. In February 1857, Samuel Knox was ordered to appear on petition of his securities and accused of mismanagement. He failed to appear at the March 1857 term of court, and was replaced as administrator by DeBerry Watts, one of the sureties.

yours all my affections are centered That I love you better than all the world. Do you love me the same way. I know I have acted wrong in many instances that you will forgive it all would all want you darling and still love one unworthy of you. Do you ever think of me. Do you ever think of him who although now [ ] trouble is yet determined to size, Besides my own love. I have gained the good will of Lewis ___ a member of the Governor's Cabinet of Texas he offers to lend me his assistance. I am going with him to Texas. I expect to leave here to day for Texas. I have to write to you a [ ] day or two. If I could just have a letter from you and know that you still thought of me and prayed for me I would have an easy heart. My prospects one tonight love

Good bye sweet darling Oh that I could see you.

Your lasting and affectionate husband
John A. Wright

This proposed trip to Texas apparently did not take place, as the next letter was addressed from Monticello, [Drew Co.], Arkansas, and dated 22 August 1856. This letter comes as close to outlining what caused his flight from Georgia as any that he wrote.

You know that I am away from Palmetto. You know that I have bitter enemies there. You know too that it is natural for almost every man to tell things that he cannot establish when he know the subject of his hate is away and cannot confront him and answer the charges. You know that such men live in Palmetto and you know as well as I do that they will tell anything on me that will injure me. You spoke of a debt in Campbellton of $400. I never owed such a debt. You spoke of borrowed money to Viney and I never borrowed any from him. I told you when I left that I had made a sham trade with him and that he was accountable to me for a portion of it after he sold them. I say so yet, but I told you to say nothing of it, but you see you have done it. You ought never to have mentioned the fact of his knowing anything about my leaving. It might turn things to [ ]. I have no fears of anyone following me.

He would never follow another. Still it might damage my plans were it known. I made an arrangement with Vineyard[18] to sell all the things under them fi fa[19] and send them to me. I was to write to him at Gainesville, which I did the day I wrote you after I got here...

I don't drink a drop now and have not since I left you. What I told you about it before I left was true. But you seem to do as you have always done—believe everybody else and get it down that everything I say is a lie. Now I am not hurt Love.You know I am not [ ]. My darling to defend myself and if they could in any way estrange me and cause you to quit me they would ask nothing more. You will see if you live long enough that most of these large tales will dwindle into nothing after awhile, but don't believe me wait and see for yourself. Believe everything you hear and put it down I am a professed liar and not to be believed about anything I say to you [ ] not think my darling would have done me so just believe every prejudicial report about me. You must suspect that there are two sides to every question and although one way be dark yet it is often be improved and made bright by explanation. It might be so in my case. Now let me suggest an [ ]. Do you determine that you will believe nothing you hear about me till you see me and tell you how it is, just do that. If you believe everything you hear you will never come to me   You believe me not other people or else if I am just a liar that you can't believe me, believe nobody. Don't let people be telling you about me.

---

[18] The 1850 Census for Campbell Co., Ga., p. 416A, family 185, lists James U. Vinyard, 24, school teacher born in Georgia, living with his mother, Margaret D., 48, and siblings, Toliver, 19, William F., 16, John M., 14, and Martha E. 12. A search of world connect showed a file identifying him as James Hayes Vineyard, who died 12 February 1875 in Chattanooga, Tenn, son of Samuel L. Vineyard and Margaret D. Haynie. Samuel L. Vineyard was born 13 May 1800 in Elbert Co., Ga., and died 16 October 1844 in Campbell Co., Ga. He married Margaret 9 January 1823. [Poore, Jackie. Poore Family. 5 April 2008. Located at http://wc.rootsweb.ancestry.com, (db. 7angels.).] Another source says he was born 2 January 1828 in Madison Co., Ga., and died 9 October 1903 in Fayette Co., Ga. This source gives the same parents and wife. [Kerr, William. Compton's Place of Georgia Connections. 25 May 2008. Located at http://wc.rootsweb.ancestry.com, (db. gilead07.)

[19] Fieri fascias, literally "that you cause to be made." In law a writ of execution after legal action for debt or damages, which addresses the sheriff and orders him to make good the amount owed out of the goods of the person against whom the judgment was obtained.

Whenever they [ ] it tell them to close at once. Allow no one to tell you tales about me. If you love me you will not. Do you think people could run to me with reports about you. You think now that if some man were to write to me that you had since I left been too intimate with another man that I would believe it. Never. But yet knowing as you do that I am not present to meet these charges, you still allow them to come to your ear and believe some and take the rest for granted. And here you go you set it down among them all that I am a liar scoundrel gambler and every thing else.

A month later things had apparently stabilized somewhat, for he was able to write that he wanted her to come to Arkansas and be with him.[20]

I received yours of the 6th inst. today. You recollect I told you to listen to nothing you heard of me but wait until I had a chance to vindicate myself, wait untill you see me then I will answer these questions. But you are my wife and I think as good and true a one as a man ever had and as fine. I love you too as well as you can ask and better than you can know or conceive. I love you because I conceive you worthy [of] any man's love. And believe me it would be the happiest moment of my life would I now hold you to my bosom and have you with me. But you know my situation. I have no money, only as I make it and if you have not enough to bring you here you will have to wait till I make it. With me is your proper place....

But I am to settle here. I am now clerking. You ask me about the country. I like it—land is cheap and will bring from 1500 to 2000 pounds seed cotton to the acre & can be bought from 25 cts to $2.50 per acre. I don't know whether Parks[21] would like it or not he might and I think would, but tell him not to come to this western country till

[20] Letter dated Monticello, Ark., Sept. 24th, 1856.

[21] Joshua Parks Fleming, her brother, born 20 January 1814 in Abbeville Dist., S. C., died 15 December 1892 Newnan, Coweta Co., Ga.; m. Martha Maxey 6 July 1837 in Newnan. She died 4 October 1852 in Coweta Co., Ga. They had six children, but there is no evidence he ever left Coweta County.

he has first looked for himself. I think it the best country I ever saw...Talk about me giving up and you giving me advice when at the same time you are giving way to the worst feelings in the world. Come you must cheer up and if people talk about you let them do it. You have the consciousness to know it is false. I will never believe it though an angel from the throne of God were to tell me. Then what do you care you are mine. I am yours, though I confess a poor piece of property. Yet I am all yours every bit and feel proud that I have the good luck to belong to such a woman. Then what need you care, you are not wanting to remain in Georgia, etc. Say, I will live a long time yet and I have no idea you will be a widow, at least in many a long day, nor do I expect to be a widower. I believe we will yet be happy and that numbers of little Wrights will yet come into the world to honor and bless us. That is my greatest desire. I want a little girl just like you. Then come to me and be with me and we will be happy together and love each other. All I ask is for you to love me. You are my wife. You so must not be giving up to unpleasant feelings and allowing fearful forebodings to change your mind and perplex you.

Thyrza Fleming Wright did come to Monticello and was living there with him when he wrote her sister Melissa Fleming Mc Lin and her husband, James, on 11 July 1857.

Your letter reached us a few days ago. We were glad to hear from you and to know that you were well. Nothing gives me more heartfelt happiness from loves & the dear ones it holds. I feel more keenly my situation when I reflect that I am banished forever from my native State. My pride and my feelings would not let me go back were I worth thousands. I don't know what will become of us. God knows. And I think I can see where in his providence has aided me even since I saw you. I felt until lately as if I could not approach my maker with any assurances that he would hear me after my great wrongs. I have reached that point that I long ago should have reached. I believe there is no solid happiness for me or piece of mind apart from a strict observance of my duties. I can see now where if I had have hung to my religious views __ to now I could have been in very different circumstances. Now about my business. I am doing very well—the man I am with likes me and I find myself daily cultivating strict business habits. I don't think there will be any doubt of my getting business next year.

Thyrza next. She is the same as ever, sets in my lap every time she gets the chance. Says she loves me more than ever. I sometimes pretend as if I thought she didn't., but I have every reason to believe that my wife is as true to me as ever woman was true. She has only one fault in my eyes. She has a little temper, and when that's aroused she blows alarmingly for awhile and then cools off, generally says after a storm that she was hurt, not mad, but you know more about her than I could tell you. I love my wife & her little tempers I sometimes think is good for her. We get along smooth I stay in my room when not at business & we always find enough to keep us alive in this backwoods country we have all kinds of people here. But Thyrza will write some. Old Cowart turned out just as ~~and better than~~ I expected. My love to you all. Kiss your baby for me.

Yours ever
John A. Wright

The letter confirms that his earlier attendance at religious meetings had been mostly opportunities to develop his reputation for public speaking, as well as indicating that he had grown up. He was then 25. Although he does not say so in his letter, Thyrza Wright was pregnant, and delivered a son they named Henry Summerfield Wright on 18 September 1857, shortly before John A. Wright's 26th birthday. This letter, and the additional one on the same page addressed to her husband, suggest that John thought things were settling down, but that it would take many years to accumulate the money necessary to clear his debts in Georgia.

Unfortunately, he was not to have that time. On 23 July 1858 he wrote Melissa Mc Lin again. This letter has suffered physical damage, so parts of the paper are lost (indicated by brackets). However, the meaning is still clear.

298

Yours of the 11th reached us today. We were glad to hear from you to know that you yet live though your bodily sufferings are great. Yet we believe that you have faith in God and he will uphold you. You advise me to return to Georgia and see you all [...]eld I have half or one fourth of the money [...]ay my debts then I would entertain [...] proposition. But as it is I could [...] could raise no more than one fourth of the [...] if that ___ and it would be an injustice [...] my family to leave them and take what [...] I can raise to pay debts and deprive [...] of the means of support. Then should [...] my creditors would be certain [...]mprison me and having acted as I have [...] man would have any mercy for me [...] sympathy. Then I could not get business [...] my case would be worse than ever. [...] here I have some credit and I believe that I can in a year or two pay a part of these things. Well you say if I die if I do then like others I must die nobly. I have consumption no doubt. That is a fact that would not admit of controversy nor do I think I will live long. Every day carries me nearer death. Already he whispers in my ear—Prepare to they god. I have thrown myself upon god's mercy. I have not asked him to lengthen out the thread of my misspent life. No. But I have asked him to keep my wife and my little one and to pardon my manifold sins. An then to do as it pleases him. I make no requisitions of him. No, I am willing to do just his way not mine. I have no demands at God's hands now—he owes me nothing was I live a thousand years and spend it all in his service I could not repay the simple debt I owe for being suffered to live this long and had time and warning to repent. Well as to my health I look upon that as just Judgement of an ___ for having sinned with all the lights I had [...] before me. I would like to live to a ripe [...] age. But I have no right to ask it. I don't even petition God to restore my he[...] I don't deserve it. I don't think that I [...] ever regain my health here under an[...] circumstances. I want in a few wee[...] to go to Hot Springs and spend a few days [...] That may help me a while yet I feel disease working on my hourly and I [...] convinced that I am as doomed man. I [...] even a doubt but that I have Consumption. Yet I may live a year or two. But I will die. And I will exert all my powers to live right and do god's will just in his way. Was my health good I feel that god would call me to do his work in the great vineyard of Souls. But I am too near gone I health. I once felt that I was called to preach and had I have done God's will then my acct would not have been as bitter as it is now. I had tasted of the world's flattery and my aspirations were worldly. My aspirations were to Law. I wanted to mix in the heat of Debate. To call for the applause of listening Senate and hand enraptured millions on my Tongue. But now I find myself further back than I started. I can't look back over my life and point to one good deed. And under these circumstances I can't ask my Maker to give me health if he will but admit me to his ___ as one of the meanest of his worshippers then I have all [...]sts. I would like to leave my wife {...}competency and to pay my debts. But [...] do nothing. I can only say God's will [...]one. Enclosed you will find a letter [...]a. May God bless her and pardon [...]way I have treated her. Please send [...] her.

Yours Truly
John A. Wright

My dearest Mother,

I know that I have mistreated you. But I ask your forgiveness. I write you to tell you that my health is not good. The physicians tell me that I have Consumption. I feel it daily and hourly gnawing at my vitals. I am a doomed man. My days are numbered and the grim messenger is whispering in my ear/ prepare to meet they God. I have known myself at god's feet and claimed his mercy, not in my way but his. I don't even ask him to restore my health. I feel that it is but the Judgment of a justly engaged haven on one who has sinned with all the lights before him. I would like to pay my debts and leave my wife a *comfaltenoy* and was I to live I would do it. God bless her a finer a nobler a truer woman never breathed and was I to live I could never repay her for half she has done. I have a bright eyed boy. His name is Henry

Sommerfield. I would have named him John Sommerfield as you asked me, but I didn't want him to have any part of my name. I have worked hard and have been economical but it is no use. My intentions in leaving Georgia was not to avoid paying my debts. I knew that I would be finished and I wanted no man to suffer on my account. And could I be healthy in a year or two pay them off. I had to quit clerking on account of my health—had I been well I could have demanded any wages in reason. I had to fall back on the law and have up to this time made a support. I have kept out of debt here. As I said at first my health is gone. I will soon die and I don't even want my relations to know where I am buried. I do not want any aid. I will make a support as long as I live and when I am dead let them forget me. Don't even shed a tear over me when I am dead. God will pardon me and take me to his rest and thought. I will die with a thousand regrets. Yet it is just and I can't grumble. I am only thankful that he has had mercy on me and spared me to this hour. I never expect to see you again. But recollect that I am an altered man. I live in a beautiful place and if I had health I could do well. I feel it my duty to write to you. I feel as if a load had passed off. I never could muster the courage to do it before. Forgive me. I wish you could see my boy. I love him better than I do my own life. But as to my health I may live a year or two. But no longer.

John A. Wright

John A. Wright died in Monticello, Drew County, Arkansas, 16 January 1859. His widow and son returned to Georgia, and probably stayed with her sister, Melissa Mc Lin in Atlanta, as it was her portrait that had the place of honor in Henry S. Wright's home.[22] Thyrza Wright lived with her various relatives for the rest of her life, dying in Troup Co., Georgia, on 12 September 1907. Her obituary was published in *The Atlanta Constitution* 14 September 1907.

---

[22] They were certainly in Atlanta in 1864, as there were oft told tales of the family's adventures during the battle for Atlanta.

West Point, Ga., September 13th. Mrs. Thursa Wright died at the home of her nephew, Dr. J. L. Askew, last night, aged 78 years. She is survived by one son, Dr. H. S. Wright of Atlanta. The body was interred in Pinewood Cemetery this afternoon, Rev. A. R. Bond officiating.[23]

Genealogical Summary

1. JOHN ANDREW[3] WRIGHT, b. 9 October 1831 Clarke Co., Ga.; d. 16 January 1859 Monticello, Drew Co., Ark.; m. (1) SARAH J. CAMP 29 September 1854 Campbell Co., Ga., daughter of LANGLEY BILLUPS CAMP and CHRISTIAN MCCLURE; b. 1835 Campbell Co., Ga.; d. 8 January 1855 Campbell Co., Ga.; m. (2) THYRZA FRANCES FLEMING 7 February 1856 Campbell Co., Ga., daughter of JOHN FLEMING and FRANCES BAILEY; b. 28 November 1829 Abbeville Dist., South Carolina; d. 12 September 1907 Troup Co., Ga.

Child of JOHN A. WRIGHT and THYRZA FRANCES FLEMING is:

i. HENRY SUMMERFIELD[4] WRIGHT, b. 18 September 1857 Monticello, Drew Co., Ark.; d. 9 April 1911 Atlanta, Fulton Co., Ga.; m. MARY EMMA FEATHERSTON, dau. of LUCIUS HORACE FEATHERSTON and MARIA ANN TOMPKINS; b. 10 February 1856 Franklin, Heard Co., Ga.; d. 25 February 1945 Atlanta, Fulton Co., Ga.

[23] Brantley-Wilson, Judy K. Cited at http://www.findagrave.com, memorial #30422793. Accessed 22 December 2011.

Chapter 9: Descendants of Henry Summerfield Wright

Henry S. Wright was born in Monticello, Arkansas, but moved to Georgia with his mother following the death of his father in January 1859. He and his mother probably moved in with her sister and brother-in-law, Melissa Isabel Fleming and J. G. McLin. The McLins resided at the corner of Cain and Ivy Streets in Atlanta from 1862 until their deaths. Henry spent all of his youth with them and Melissa's portrait had a place of honor in the living room of his family's home at 1335 W. Peachtree Street for many years. In the 1880 Census, "S. Henry Wright," is a boarder in Palmetto, Campbell Co., Ga., occupation pharmacist.[1] Head of the household was S. William Zellers, a 49 year old druggist born in Va., along with his wife, Margaret Zellers, 40, born in Ga., and their son, A. William Zellers, 30, a physician. L. Thomas Camp, a boarder, was living in the household as well.[2] James G. McLin was living in Atlanta, and listed his occupation as "Sheriff of the Georgia Supreme Court."[3]

According to his daughter Kathleen, Henry and Thyrza were in Atlanta during the battle in 1864. As the cannon balls started coming closer, they decided to relocate to the basement of the "doctor's house, which was across the lot from them." Just as they got into the middle of the field, a cannon ball exploded, knocking both of them down and covering them with dirt. Henry related sitting up and frantically brushing the dirt off of his mother's face. They left Atlanta, reputedly on the cowcatcher of the last train to leave Atlanta, and went to a hospital encampment near Augusta. There Thyrza attended the sick and then became ill herself. Henry reported sneaking into the tent where she was being kept by lifting the flap of the tent wall and sliding under her bed.

---

[1] 1880 Census, Campbell Co., Ga., p. 592, line 6, dwelling 382, family 387.

[2] Benjamin Camp was father of Margaret Zellers based upon his will, written 27 May 1880 and proved 1 December 1884.[2] Benjamin Camp was a first cousin to Wesley Camp, father of Sarah Camp, and first wife of Henry S. Wright's father, John A. Wright. [Nelson, James B. Nelson Cousins, Descendants of James F. Nelson. 23 Feb 2006. Located at http://worldconnect.rootsweb.com, (db. jbnel3957). They shared as a grandfather, Benjamin Camp, b. 1757 King & Queen Co., Va., d. 1832 Walton Co., Ga.; m. Elizabeth Dykes.]

[3] 1880 Census, Fulton Co., Ga., p. 527, family 439. He is listed as 63, and his wife, Melissa was 56.

A number of letters from Thyrza to Henry are extant. Most exhort him to avoid alcohol without ever quite saying that his father was an alcoholic. They also advise him to secure a trade as quickly as possible. She was apparently moving around and living off of the charity of her family, with Henry being virtually adopted by the McLins.

By 1884 "Dr. H. S. Wright opened a new drug store on the southwest corner of the square" in Newnan, Georgia.[4] In 1885 he was listed as third lieutenant of the Newnan Guards.[5] He married Mary Emma Featherston in Newnan 28 November 1882. Her father was a prominent retired local judge. Kathleen recalled visiting her grandfather's mansion as a child, and even today there is a subdivision in Newnan known as Featherston Heights. She particularly recalled one visit where she and "Brother" were playing in the hay in the barn, when he became stuck. Unfortunately he attracted the attention of a goat, who proceeded to butt him on his posterior while he was stuck. She recalled thinking it was terribly funny, but conceded that Brother had likely not found it so.

Henry apparently was not satisfied being a pharmacist, and enrolled in the Atlanta Medical College.[6] His diploma listed his graduation as 1892. He opened his practice in Atlanta following graduation, and lived on Juniper Street.

As a new physician in Atlanta, Henry Wright applied for the position of physician to the 6th Ward.[7] The position carried an annual stipend of $800, but required the physician to attend the police station house as well as provide medical and surgical care to any persons in the ward not able to afford a physician. The position was evidently desirable, as 14 physicians applied. Although Henry S. Wright was named first in the list of applicants, he was apparently not selected.

I found one more mention of his name in connection to his medical practice. On 22 July 1902, one C. L. Edwards knocked a loaded pistol off of his bureau top and the weapon discharged,

---

[4] Jones, Mary G. and Reynolds, L. Coweta County Chronicles for One Hundred Years. Stein Printing Co., Atlanta, Ga., 1928, p. 258.

[5] Jones, p. 267.

[6] This institution subsequently became the basis for the Emory University School of Medicine following the appearance of the Flexner report in 1909.

[7] *The Atlanta Constitution*, 10 March 1896, p. 3. Located online at Ancestry.com.

shooting him in the abdomen. Dr. Wright was one of three doctors summoned to attend the man, but it appears that he died.[8]

Dr. and Mrs. Wright desired to be part of Atlanta society, as they and their children started appearing regularly in the social pages of Atlanta newspapers. In 1897 Henry S. Wright had returned from a trip to New York and Baltimore.[9] The next year a photo of their youngest child, Marie Louise Wright, sitting in a cart that was part of a parade for Confederate Veterans in Newnan appeared.[10] Mary F. Wright did her part, too, being a member of the Ladies Auxiliary to the YMCA,[11] and recording visits from her family.[12]

Although his family appeared in the society notices of both *The Atlanta Constitution* and *The Atlanta Georgian and News* during the early 1900's, Henry S. Wright did not appear in the newspaper until an article reported his impending death.[13]

Dr. Henry S. Wright Very Ill At Hospital
Well-Known Physician Has Suffered Relapse From Apoplectic Stroke

Dr. Henry S. Wright, one of the leading physicians of Atlanta, who has been seriously ill at Wesley Memorial hospital for two months, suffering from a stroke of apoplexy, underwent a relapse Saturday, and his condition is regarded as serious.

Dr. Wright is a native of Arkansas, having been born in Monticello, Ark. But when a small boy, his family moved to Georgia, and he was forced to undergo the privations all true southerners suffered during the reconstruction period. In spite of these handicaps, Dr. Wright secured an education, and graduated from the Atlanta College of Physicians and Surgeons.

---

[8] The Atlanta Constitution, 23 July 1902, p. 7. Located online at Ancestry.com.

[9] *The Atlanta Constitution*, 30 May 1897, p. 7. Located online at Ancestry.com.

[10] *The Atlanta Constitution*, 8 October 1899, p. 31. Located online at Ancestry.com.

[11] *The Atlanta Constitution*, 14 May 1902, p. 5. Located online at Ancestry.com.

[12] *The Atlanta Constitution*, 14 August 1904, p. 30. "Mr. and Mrs. J. E. Featherstone, of Newnan, on their way home from St. Louis, are the guests of Dr. and Mrs. Henry S. Wright on Juniper street." There were several similar instances. Located online at Ancestry.com.

[13] *The Atlanta Constitution*, 30 March 1911, p. 10. Located online at Ancestry.com. Essentially the same item appeared in *The Atlanta Georgian and News*, 30 March 1911, p. 2. Located online at http://atlnewspapers.galileo.usg.edu/atlnewspapers/.

For twenty years he has been practicing his profession in this city, and is well known throughout the state.

Dr. Henry Wright Claimed by Death
Prominent Physician Succumbs to Attack of Apoplexy[14]

Dr. Henry S. Wright, one of the most prominent physicians of Atlanta, died at a private sanitarium last night at 6:30 o'clock. He was stricken with apoplexy on the last of January, and, after appearing to recover suffered a relapse two weeks ago which proved fatal.

Dr. Wright was a leading and well-beloved member of his profession and was also a prominent Mason. He was born in Monticello, Arkansas, fifty three years ago. While he was but a small boy his parents moved to Georgia, and he was brought up in the country.

After receiving an academic education he came to Atlanta and matriculated at the Atlanta College of Physicians and Surgeons. He graduated four years later and since that time has been among the leading practitioners of the city.

Surviving Dr. Wright are his wife Mrs. Mary F. Wright, two daughters, Misses Kathleen and Marie Louise Wright, and a son, Dr. Lucius Wright, a rising young doctor.

The funeral will be held Tuesday morning at 10:30 o'clock at the First Methodist Church. The interment will be at West View.

An invitation to the funeral issued by the family was printed the next day, and the formal announcement of the funeral was published on the 12th. After his death, the family appeared in the social pages briefly in 1912, and then disappeared. Presumably, with his death, they no longer had the money to afford the price of being "society."

Genealogical Summary

1. HENRY SUMMERFIELD[4] WRIGHT was born 18 September 1857 Monticello, Drew Co., Arkansas, and died 9 April 1911 in

---

[14] *The Atlanta Constitution*, 10 April 1911, p. 10. Located online at Ancestry.com.

Atlanta, Fulton Co., Georgia. He married MARY EMMA FEATHERSTON, daughter of LUCIUS HORACE FEATHERSTON and MARIA ANN TOMPKINS, 28 November 1882 Newnan, Coweta Co., Ga. She was born 10 February 1856 Franklin, Heard Co., Ga., and died 25 February 1945 in Atlanta, Fulton Co., Ga.

Children of HENRY WRIGHT and MARY FEATHERSTON are:

2.   i. KATHLEEN FEATHERSTONE[5] WRIGHT, b. 10 November 1883 Newnan, Coweta Co., Ga.; d. 30 June 1970 Atlanta, Fulton Co., Ga.

3.   ii. LUCIUS FEATHERSTONE[5] WRIGHT, b. 9 November 1885 Newnan, Coweta Co., Ga.; d. 3 November 1956 Atlanta, Fulton Co., Ga.; m. KATHRYN PEARL DENNY, 3 February 1920 Denver, Denver Co., Colo., daughter of BARTON STONE DENNY and MARY ELIZABETH MASSIE. She was b. 26 July 1896, Hampton, Iowa; d. 10 July 1943, Alexandria, Rapides Par., La.

4. iii. MARIE[5] WRIGHT, b. 14 May 1889 Newnan, Coweta Co., Ga.; d. before 1955 Mercer Co., New Jersey; m. (1) CLIFTON COX CALLOWAY about 1912 Atlanta, Fulton Co., Ga., son of WILLIAM R. CALLOWAY and MARY E. _____; b. 20 June 1886 Meigs, Thomas Co., Ga.; d. A.; m. (2) RAYMOND HALE CURLIS, son of GEORGE H. CURLIS and SARAH FRANCES MOORE; b. 12 October 1894, Hope, Mercer Co., N. J.; d. 29 January 1972, Titusville, Mercer Co., N. J.; he m. (2) ANNA ELIZABETH FOOTE 12 April 1955 Newtown, Bucks Co., Pa., daughter of JAMES LOTT FOOTE and ELIZABETH IDA FITZPATRICK; b. 1 August 1903 Fallsington, Bucks Co., Pa.; d. 7 November 1993 Fallsington, Bucks Co., Pa.

2.   KATHLEEN FEATHERSTONE[5] WRIGHT was born 10 November 1883 in Newnan, Coweta Co., Georgia. She died 30 June 1970 in Atlanta, Fulton Co., Georgia.

Although "Aunie" never married and had children, much of the story of the family would have been lost without her efforts. She was unusually well educated for a woman of her times. She appeared as an honorable mention on the 5th grade honor roll for her school in 1895.[15] She made the honor roll the next year.[16] She attended high school at Lucy Cobb Institute[17] in Athens, Georgia, and graduated in 1902.[18]

She received her BA from Hollins College in Virginia,[19] and a master of science degree from Emory in biology. Her mother had a reception for her in 1905,[20] but she appears only a few times in the social pages, usually in conjunction with visits from family or other family celebrations, and, as noted, these were drastically curtailed following the death of her father in 1911.

She taught art in the Atlanta public schools for many years,[21] and was also actively associated with the High Museum of

---

[15] *The Atlanta Constitution*, 9 June 1895, p. 6. Copy located online at Ancestry.com. She was at the Calhoun Street School and had a GPA of 96.7.

[16] *The Atlanta Constitution*, 1 March 1896, p. 7. Copy located online at Ancestry.com. She was at Fair Street School and had a GPA of 96.4.

[17] The Lucy Cobb Institute, a secondary school for young women in Athens, was founded in 1859 by Thomas R.R. Cobb, a prominent lawyer and proslavery writer. Between 1880 and 1928 Cobb's niece Mildred Lewis Rutherford, a Lucy Cobb graduate, taught at the school. She served as principal for twenty-two of those years...Her national reputation as a historian of the Civil War (1861-65) and the Old South brought the school widespread recognition and respect...Most Lucy Cobb students came from wealthy and well-established families...Under the leadership of Rutherford and her sister Mary Ann Lipscomb, the curriculum became even more rigorous. Students, or "Lucies," in the collegiate track studied sciences (including chemistry and physics), higher mathematics (algebra, geometry, trigonometry), logic, rhetoric, languages, history, and literature. After 1918, once the University of Georgia (UGA) began accepting women students, graduates of Lucy Cobb's collegiate program could enroll. Indeed, the school aimed its curriculum to prepare graduates to attend the university. In her extensive 1916 report on women's education in the South, Elizabeth Avery Colton of the Southern Association of College Women listed Lucy Cobb as one of the very best schools for young women in Georgia. Along with academics, Rutherford and other faculty members emphasized the importance of a modest appearance and proper manners and etiquette. Students were prohibited from venturing beyond the school's front yard un-chaperoned, entertaining male visitors, attending parties in town, dancing, and wearing makeup or short skirts. The combination of academic rigor with education in gentility, their teachers believed, prepared students for both private and public life." Located online 28 December 2012 at http://www.georgiaencyclopedia.org/nge/Article.jsp?id=h-2624.

[18] *The Atlanta Constitution*, 21 December 1901, p. 12. Copy located online at Ancestry.com. "Miss Kathleen Wright has returned from Lucy Cobb to spend the Christmas Holidays."

[19] *The Atlanta Constitution*, 12 April 1903, p. 33. Copy located online at Ancestry.com. "Miss Kathleen Wright is making an excellent record at Hollins, Va., where she was elected president of the literary society of the school, an honor bestowed only on honor students. She was one of a party spending the Easter holidays in Washington city."

[20] *The Atlanta Constitution*, 25 Nov 1905, p. 5. Copy located online at Ancestry.com. "Mrs. Henry S. Wright has issued invitations for a reception Wednesday afternoon, November 29th, from 5 to 7 o'clock in compliment to her daughter, Miss Kathleen Wright and Miss Marguerite Hemphill."

[21] In 1923 she was listed as a 6th grade teacher at Fernwalt Street Elementary School in an article listing all of the teaching and administrative appointments by the Board of

308

Art in Atlanta through the late 1950's. I think she retired after the Paris plane crash in 1962 that killed so many of the citizens associated with that institution.

After her father's death in 1911, she and her mother moved to the residence at 1335 W. Peachtree Street. Her brother retired from the U. S. Army in 1945 and moved into the home with her until his death in 1956. The house remains a central memory of both her nephew and great-nephew.

Aunie died of colon cancer on 30 June 1970. Although she had no children, she was the keeper of the family lore, and it is due to her that we have any information at all about John Andrew Wright or John Wright. Even though she told many stories, and had made some efforts at genealogical research, she had had no success in finding out more about John Wright. Although she had the letters of John Andrew Wright in her possession, she never indicated that she knew anything about the scandal that had caused her grandfather to move so abruptly to Arkansas. If she knew, she would not have said, since she did not really want to know anything bad about the ancestors. However, she did not destroy the letters, which clearly show that John Andrew Wright had left town under dubious circumstances and with a clouded reputation. As noted in the discussion of her sister, Marie, she also did what she could to provide parental guidance to her nephew, Wright Callaway.

3. LUCIUS FEATHERSTONE[5] WRIGHT, SR., was born 9 November 1885 Newnan, Coweta Co., Ga., and died 3 November 1956 Atlanta, Fulton Co., Ga. He married KATHRYN PEARL DENNY 3 February 1920 Denver, Denver Co., Colorado, daughter of BARTON STONE DENNY and MARY ELIZABETH MASSIE. She was born 26 July 1896 Hampton, Iowa, and died 20 July 1943 Alexandria, Rapides Parish, Louisiana.

Lucius F. Wright was listed as a graduate of Boys High School in Atlanta in 1904.[22] Like his sisters, he also appeared in

---

Education for the upcoming year. *The Atlanta Constitution*, 9 June 1923, p. 3. Copy located online at Ancestry.com.

[22] *The Atlanta Constitution*, Friday 3 June 1904, p. 7. Graduation was stated to have occurred the night before. Copy located online at Ancestry.com.

the society columns from time to time. In 1907 the following article appeared.[23]

To Baseball Teams

The buffet supper which Miss Marie Wright and Mr. Lucius Wright will give Friday evening in honor of the Tech and Georgia baseball teams will be a delightful event. The decorations will include cut flowers and the college colors.

Assisting in the entertainment of the guests will be Miss Kathleen Wright, Miss Harriet Calhoun and her guest, Miss Phinlay of Athens; Misses Clifford West, Aurelia Speer, Mabel Swift, Lucille Kiser, Messers. Milton Dargan, Edward Brown, Harrison and Saunders Jones, Inman Gray, Ralph Ragan, Stewart Witham.

He appeared sporadically in the society pages until 1911, usually in association with a dinner for a friend who was getting married. A good example was published 26 October 1911.[24]

Dr. Calhoun Mc Dougall will be host to a stag supper in honor of Dr. Francis Jones, whose marriage to Miss Lucille Jeter takes place soon, on Monday evening at nine o'clock at the University Club, his guests to include Dr. Jones, Dr. E. M. Sanderson of Jacksonville, Fla., Judge W. H. Baker of Jacksonville, Mr. Angus Baker of Jacksonville, Mr. Robert H. Jones, Mr. Robert H. Jones, Jr., Dr. Hugh M. Lokey, Dr. G. F. Spearman, Dr. Lucius Wright, Mr. James Jones, and Mr. Robert Mc Dougall.

Lucius F. Wright, Sr., graduated from Emory University and received his M. D. from the Atlanta Medical College in 1911. He did post-graduate studies at Grady Hospital in Atlanta.

---

[23] *Atlanta Georgian and News*, 17 May 1907, p. 8. Copy located online at http://atlnewspapers.galileo.usg.edu/atlnewspapers/. When I mentioned this to the family in December 2012, they were totally surprised, since this sort of thing seemed out of character for the people we had known after they had reached their "mature" years. The same paper also included announcement of a garden party for the graduating seniors of Washington Seminary being hosted by Marie Wright. (see under her entry.)

[24] Atlanta Georgian and News, 26 October 1911, p. 10. Copy located online at http://atlnewspapers.galileo.usg.edu/atlnewspapers/.

Growing up, my father heard a story from his aunt, Kathleen F. Wright, that Dr. Wright had received a "rising vote of thanks" from the Georgia Legislature for his action in entering an isolation ward during an epidemic.The availability of The Atlanta Constitution archives online allowed me to find a more complete description of that experience.[25]

Undaunted By Dread Disease, "Fighting Four" Labors To Stamp Out Meningitis
By Britt Craig

Much of the success attained by Atlanta's first contagious hospital is due to a quartet of young internes and trained nurses who volunteered to submit to isolation in the meningitis clinic at Grady and to remain on duty there either until the plague had been driven from the city, or they themselves had succumbed to its ravages.

Within less than a month the contagious clinic will be closed. Meningitis is almost extinct. The influx of patients stopped a week or more ago. Authorities now have to content only with the sufferers who already have been installed in the hospital, of whom there are only seventeen.

A great victory has been won over a situation which a month ago, threatened to burden Atlanta with an epidemic. City officials are elated over the triumph.

On one page of the account which will go down in history will be the statistics of the amazing number of cases discovered in the city. The installation of a contagious hospital will be chronicled for the first time in Atlanta's career.

And, if the whole story is to be told, the drama of the four internes and nurses will occupy pages as conspicuous as the proud statistics. The history of the dangers and hardships they underwent will be a more noble record than the cold spiritless facts and figures which tell only that meningitis was driven from the city, and leave the reader to his or hew own conception of the particular processes by which it was driven out.

---

[25] *The Atlanta Constitution*, Sunday, 4 May 1913, p. 37. Copy located online at Ancestry.com.

How meningitis was defeated is a story of heroism of the two young internes and their two co-workers, the trained nurses. It is the story of submittance to quarantine in a pest house in the face of peril inconceivable—the story of denial and hardship—and a story that brinked on martyrdom.

Liable to Contagion

It is a popular impression that physicians and nurses are equipped with means of preventing the contraction of contagious diseases with which they come in contact. That belief is a fallacy, pure and simple, and probably originated in the same way as did the superstition of the mistake of walking under a ladder.

Meningitis is no respecter of persons or professions. The human system is the same with the two internes and their assistants, the trained nurses, as it is with blacksmiths or gardeners. The disease would have gripped either of them as quickly and as fatally as it had gripped any of the patients under their care.

To a normal person, confinement in a contagious ward would seem like abiding in the anteroom to the graveyard. Some men might put their heads in the lion's mouth, but those same men would not go into the ward.

Yet the contagious clinic holds no fears for Miss Annie Butler, Mrs. Mamie Ashford, Dr. L. L. Blair, or Dr. Lucius Wright, the guardians of the meningitis ward at Grady. While his call for volunteers for service in the new ward was being disdained by some thirty or more nurses and physicians, Dr. W. B. Summerall, superintendent of Grady, found this quartet eager and ready for the perilous duty.

For the last month, they have been quarantined to the service. The prospects are that they will remain for a month to come. The success with which they have met is causing medical experts throughout the south to marvel. Although death has been braved by them every hour spent in the death-laden atmosphere of the clinic, none have yet contracted the malady.

And, as optimistic as on the day they entered, the "Fighting Four" still expect to emerge alive and unscathed.

Miss Butler is a pretty girl of 22, with a wealth of auburn hair, a perpetual smile and a buoyant spirit, quite unlike the spirit of the martyr she would be. Mrs. Ashford is a middle-aged woman, industrious and enthusiastic, with twenty years of medical experience.

Dr. Blair and Dr. Wright are both from the Grady staff of internes. They have been attached to the hospital for several years, having entered the service upon leaving college. Both are single. Married men hardly would venture so close to verge of martyrdom unless premiums were fully paid on heavy life insurance.

Interviewed by Phone

Members of the "Fighting Four" were interviewed yesterday by telephone, of course. Even a reporter isn't going to invade a contagious hospital.

It is unethical for physicians and nurses to talk for publication on subjects pertaining to their duties or profession. Gently, they informed the reporter of this fact. A story of their heroism wouldn't pass muster without at least a few words from the courageous four, though, therefore the reported insisted.

"Aren't you afraid you'll catch the disease and die?" he asked.

"Certainly not," retorted one of the "Fighting Four." "If we were, we wouldn't be here. This is no place for nerves or fright."

"Apparently not. Do you like it?"

"We do," they chorused.

"Would you do it again?"

"We would: every day of the week and Sundays, too."

"When do you expect to get out?"

"We're not worrying about that. Our interest is only in the sufferers of whom we're taking care."

The interview was brief. The reporter pleaded, by the treatment of cerebrospinal meningitis requires constant attention, infinite care and caution and systematic methods. The task is a 24-hour one, and a single careless nap at the switch may cost a life.

Day and Night Merge

Dr. Blair and Miss Butler are in charge of the hospital during the day, and Dr. Wright and Mrs. Ashford at night. Night and day, though, are only too often merged into one long, fatiguing watch of incessant labor. A flickering life to be snatched from the portal of eternity must be attended to upon the instant, whether at midnight or noon.

And the combined efforts of the entire "Fighting Four" are required in the snatching. Energy and alertness play roles as important as the knowledge of medical science and the deft touch of the surgeon's finger. To be perpetually on the job is a prime qualification for service in the treatment of contagious disease. It is one of the many secrets of the "Fighting Four's" success.

What time they are not ministering to their afflicted charges, Miss Butler, Mrs. Ashford, Dr. Blair, and Dr. Wright are employing this formula to prevent becoming victims of the plague:

Eight percent cleanliness.

Two percent caution.

Two percent sterilization, and

Eighty eight percent trust in Providence.

Fate is impartial to the courageous. It is the timid and fearful who walk out of the way to avoid the slightest of dangers, finally to be killed by a banana peel. Webster gives a number of definitions to the word bravery, chief of which is:

"Ready to meet or incur danger without flight, or flinching; encountering peril or enduring pain without surrendering to one's fears or weakness." It applies aptly to Grady's "Fighting Four."

No Coward Could Last

A person who is brave as bravery is defined by Webster generally dies a natural death and dies it at a venerable age. A coward wouldn't last in contagious quarantine. The odds are he would die before they got him thoroughly sterilized.

If soldiers of those particular periods had been of the cast of Grady's "Fighting Four," the chances are that Napoleon never would have lost his Waterloo, or Lee his Appomattox.

Their salaries are not above the average. In fact, they are underpaid considering the hardships they undergo, and the dangers they incur. It isn't a matter of pay, though, as they themselves admit. It's the success they achieve and the lives they save.

In all, thirty-eight patients suffering from meningitis have been admitted to the contagion hospital. Ten were whites. The only fatalities among these were three, who died within thirty hours after they had reached the clinic. The disease had reached a stage from which there is no recovery before their cases had been discovered. Two of the whites have been cured and released. Five, all of whom are convalescent, remain. Twenty-eight Negro patients have been given treatment. Four were cured. Seven died, each succumbing within thirty hours after admittance. The entire number had suffered for four weeks before being removed to the hospital. Of the seventeen patients in all, seven are recovering, while the probabilities of future deaths are few.

The expense of maintaining the contagious clinic for two months will reach $2,500. Equipment is the biggest item. The cost of serum is next. The salaries paid the corps of internes and nurses is smallest.

The clinic will be abolished upon extermination of the present epidemic. Meningitis is a seasonal malady and mercifully, of but short duration. The building will be torn down to make way for a new structure. No plans have been made to fight contagion next season. Future operations depend entirely upon the existence of a probable epidemic. If the plague is not as great in 1914 as it was this year, it is doubtful if a clinic will be installed.

But, in case a similar situation arises, hospital authorities have been assured beforehand that the "Fighting Four" will be subject to call and ready for volunteer duty.

After internship he entered private practice with his office at 803 Peachtree St. He was appointed as an assistant inspector of health by the Atlanta Board of Education in 1915 and charged with the assisting in school physicals, which at that time were an important tool in controlling infectious diseases.[26] He was listed as a new member of the Chamber of Commerce on 1 January 1916.[27]

He was commissioned as a First Lieutenant in the Medical Section Officers Reserve Corps, Army of the United States, on 30 June 1917[28] and served for the duration of the War. At the end of the war, he decided he preferred practice in the military and applied for a commission in the Regular Army Medical Corps. He was one of six physicians who passed a competitive examination involving patients with tuberculosis and was assigned to Fitzsimons General Hospital, which was the Army's principal tuberculosis hospital. There he met Kathryn Pearl Denny. Her father was suspicious of this Army doctor and arranged for him to be investigated by private detectives. Apparently he passed that inspection, too, as they were married at First Methodist Church in Denver on 3 February 1920.

Following the birth of his sons, he was ordered to duty in the Philippine Islands. Dad has some memories of the voyage and there are photos of them during the long sea voyage in the family photo albums. The overseas tour was scheduled to last three years, but Kathryn almost died as a result of severe asthma, and Dr. Wright received permission to return to the United States with her. He took her to her sister, Bertha Mae "Auntie Bae" Coffman, in Spokane, Wash. While awaiting transportation back to the Philippine Islands, he worked at Fort George Wright in Spokane. He was required to make up the time missed before being allowed to return to the U. S. where he was assigned to duty at Douglas, Arizona. He subsequently served as a battalion surgeon at Fort Williams in Portland, Maine, then went overseas again on assignment at Tripler General Hospital, Honolulu, Hawaii, and then returned to Fitzsimons.

---

[26] *The Atlanta Constitution*, 8 August 1915, p. 1. Copy located online at Ancestry.com.

[27] *The Atlanta Constitution*, 12 January 1916, p. 9 Copy located online at Ancestry.com.

[28] His commission is in my possession.

With the onset of World War II, he was assigned as hospital commander at Camp Claiborne, La., near Alexandria. A clipping from page 2 of the *Alexandria (La.) Town Talk* of 20 February 1945 headlined "Claiborne Hospital Treats 96,000 men in 4 Years" reported:

Completion of four years of service during which time more than 96,000 men have been treated for wounds and injuries, will be observed February 20, when the Camp Claiborne Station Hospital begins the fifth year of operations.

At 1:15 PM February 20, 1941, the first patient was admitted to the hospital, thus launching a medical program dedicated to task of providing adequate medical care to the soldiers encamped here. At the time of the admission of the first soldier, about 80 buildings, including warehouses, were in the process of construction over the 240 acre plot. Since that date, over the four year period, buildings have covered the original plot and overflowed onto additional ground.

Many times the 96,000 soldier-patients have been examined and treated in the out-patient department since the time of formal opening, when the hospital was little more than an architect's drawing. Only 90 patients have died from injury or disease during the entire life of the hospital.

"We do not boast of phenomenal achievements," Col. Lucius F. Wright, commanding officer of the Station Hospital said. "We do have the pleasure of knowing that members of the staff and the personnel of the enlisted detachment have done an excellent job caring for the health and welfare of the soldiers stationed here."

The hospital has served as a clinic for various phases of the army's medical program as well as a medical center for members of the armed forces. Five days after Pearl Harbor, members of the Board for the Investigation of and Control of Influenza and Epidemiological Diseases under the direction of the Surgeon General of the Army, met here with local medical officers.

Results of the investigation were published in War Medicine March, 1943, after the project was completed the year before.

During the past year the hospital has organized and put into practice a reconditioning program. The program consists of educational features, physical training adapted to the condition of each patient, occupational training, and education pictures. Instructors assigned to carry out this program are graduates of the Educational and Physical Reconditioning course of the School for Personnel Services in Lexington, Va.

Cantonment type, the hospital is one of the most modernly equipped units of its kind operated by the army. Almost every conceivable instrument and piece of equipment known to science may be found in surgery, laboratories and wards. The staff is manned by skilled medical and dental officers, and trained enlisted assistants, a few of whom have been with the hospital since it was opened for patients four years ago this week.

Following the war, he retired from active duty and moved back to the family home in Atlanta, where he lived with his sister, Kathleen F. Wright, until his death from a myocardial infarction in 1956.

Kathryn Pearl Denny was born in Hampton, Iowa, to Barton Stone Denny and Mary E. Massie. B. S. Denny was superintendent of the Christian (Disciples) Church in Iowa. In an application for appointment as a reconstruction aide (occupational therapist) on 20 March 1919, she listed her education as grammar school in Des Moines, high school in Spokane, Washington, and three years' study of liberal arts at the University of Spokane where she majored in Geology and Chemistry. She studied art and design at the Cumming Art School in Des Moines, had one year's experience supervising drawing in the Columbus and Hawthorne Schools of Cicero, Illinois, and completed a two year Normal, Graphic, Manual and Industrial Art Course offered by the Chicago Academy of Fine Arts.

She apparently decided to get married without discussing the matter with her parents. A letter from her father to Dr. Wright dated 5 February 1920 makes it clear that he was notified of the

318

marriage by telegram. In a later letter to her, dated 14 May 1920, he writes that he was disappointed not to perform the marriage ceremony himself, but that he was pleased that she had not married someone named Lloyd, whom the superintendent had not thought likely to be much of a success. In his letter to Dr. Wright he describes the Denny family as "good pioneer stock," and apparently was reassured that this applied to the Wright family as well.

Kathryn Pearl Wright suffered from asthma all of her adult life and died 10 July 1943 in Alexandria, La from heart failure caused by repeated injections of epinephrine (Adrenaline®), then the only available drug for treatment of asthma.

In 2000, their son, Lucius F. Wright, Jr., recalled stories he had heard about his parents while he was growing up. "Dad didn't talk much about himself to us. Aunie told us about Dad and another young Doctor going into quarantine during an epidemic of spinal meningitis. I learned this because I was looking through a bunch of old pictures. She said they were given a "Rising Vote of Thanks" by the Georgia Legislature."

"Dad used to tell about Mom hurting her foot somehow. He took her out to Fitzsimons Hospital (in Denver) for an X-ray.The technician reached up to adjust something and grabbed a hot wire. Dad was busy shutting off the power and attending to the corpsman. When he looked up, he couldn't find Mom. He finally located her about a half block away and had to help her back to get the X-ray."

"Dad hated to drive a car. It's probably a good thing because he was absent-minded. Mom told of driving into the Ford garage in Denver for maintenance on their first car, a Model T Ford. Fortunately the place had two doors, because Dad couldn't remember how to stop the car until they had done a couple of laps. Mom said she should have been in fear of her life but, being a preacher's kid, she had never before heard language like Dad was using and was doubled up with laughter. It might help to explain that the Model T could be braked to a stop but it could also be stopped by pressing a reverse pedal."

Dad used to tell other stories about his father's driving skills. Once, when turning right onto West Peachtree Street from Lombardy Way, he had the passenger's side fenders and running

319

board taken off by someone who passed him on the right as he was pulling into traffic. He also recalled that once, when his mother had been hospitalized with pneumonia, his father was so upset he drove all the way home on the wrong side of the road. Fortunately, on post there was no traffic and the speed limit was only 15 MPH. When Dad was 15, Dr. Wright was given 30 days' leave, so his mother took him to the examiner's station and lied about his age, so he could replace his father behind the wheel.

Children of LUCIUS F. WRIGHT, SR., and KATHRYN PEARL DENNY are:

5. i. LUCIUS FEATHERSTONE[6] WRIGHT, JR, b. 20 November 1921 Denver, Denver Co., Colo.; m. MARY MINA WHITENER 27 January 1947 Alexandria, Rapides Par., La.; dau. of GEORGE ALVIN WHITENER and AUGUSTA AMIS; b. 8 September 1925 Meridian, Lauderdale Co., Miss.

6. ii. RALPH DENNY[6] WRIGHT, b.10 February 1923 Denver, Denver Co., Colo.; d. 6 March 2006 Mobile, Mobile Co., Ala.; m. ANNE GRIFFIN 10 March 1945 New Orleans, La.; b. 9 August 1925 Montgomery, Ala.

4. MARIE LOUISE[5] WRIGHT was born 14 May 1889 in Newnan, Coweta Co., Georgia, and died before 1955 in Mercer Co., New Jersey. She married (1) CLIFTON COX CALLOWAY 1911 in Atlanta, Fulton Co., Ga., son of WILLIAM R. CALLOWAY and MARY E. _____. He was born about 1887 in Georgia, and died after 1940. She married (2) RAYMOND HALE CURLIS about 1920 in Chester, Delaware Co., Pennsylvania, son of GEORGE H. CURLIS and SARAH FRANCES MOORE. He was born 12 October 1894 in Hope, Mercer Co., New Jersey, and died 29 January 1972 in Titusville, Mercer Co., New Jersey. He married (2) ANNA ELIZABETH FOOTE 12 April 1955 Newtown, Bucks Co., Pa., daughter of JAMES LOTT FOOTE and ELIZABETH IDA FITZPATRICK. She was born 1 August 1903 in Fallsington, Bucks Co., Pa., and died 7 November 1993 Fallsington, Bucks Co., Pa.

Marie Louise Wright was known to her siblings as "Babe" or "Teedee," although I never heard where the nickname came from. My grandfather disapproved of her decision-making in regards to her marriage and forbade speaking of her, and I did not know about her at all until the early 1960's, although my father and uncle knew a little about her. I did have conversations with both of her children, but do not remember that they provided any information about her. Aunie told me that when news of her death reached them in Atlanta, she saw him become tearful, an experience that was very unusual for him, and he decided to go out to Westview and visit the graves of their parents.

Marie Louise Wright was photographed riding a cart pulled by two ponies at the time of a parade for Confederate veterans in 1899.[29] In May 1907, she was a junior at Washington Seminary[30], and hosted a party for the graduating seniors.[31] Another typical entry was recorded 11 July 1908.[32]

Miss Wright's Lawn Party For Miss Elizabeth Smith
A pretty party of Tuesday evening will be the one Miss Marie Wright will give at her home on Juniper St. in

---

[29] *The Atlanta Constitution*, 8 October 1899, p. 31. Photo of two girls in a cart drawn by two ponies and each pony being ridden by a boy. Caption reads: "This little cart, decorated in blue hydrangeas, was greatly admired during the floral parade given by the ladies of Newnan in honor of the Confederate Veterans in July. Marie Louise Wright, the little daughter of Dr. and Mrs. Henry S. Wright, of this city, and little Marian Ellen Dibble, of Newnan, with Masters Stacy Capers and Evans Brown as honorary escorts."

[30] "Washington Seminary...was established in the parlor of General W. S. Walker's home in 1878 by Anita and Lola Washington, the two great nieces of George Washington.The original school was called The Misses Washington School for Girls, even though that first group of eight pupils included boys as well as girls. In 1882 the school's name was changed to Washington Seminary. There were several different owners after Miss Anita passed away and Miss Lola retired; and in 1904, Llewellyn Scott and his sister Emma inherited the school. In 1913 they purchased the spacious Clifford Anderson Home on Peachtree Street. Llewellyn Scott with the help of his sister directed the school with great success for the next 25 years."
http://www.westminster.net/academics/libraries/archives/collections/washington-seminary/index.aspx. Accessed 27 December 2012.

[31] *Atlanta Georgian and News*, 17 May 1907, p. 8. Located online at http://atlnewspapers.galileo.usg.edu/newspapers/. "The junior class of Washington Seminary gave a lawn party Friday afternoon at the home of Miss Marie Wright on Juniper Street, in honor of the senior class. Miss Wright and Miss Caro Stearns, president of the junior class, received the guests wearing dainty toilets of white mull, trimmed with embroideries and lace. Miss Clifford West, treasurer and secretary of the class, and Miss Helen Thorn, vice-president, served punch. Miss West wore a frock of pink silk and Miss Thorn was gowned in pale blue. The guests were entertained at a guessing contest, the prizes being a gold hat pin and a book. During the afternoon dainty refreshments were served."

[32] *The Atlanta Georgian and News*, 11 July 1908, p. 6. Located online at http://atlnewspapers.galileo.usg.edu/newspapers/.

complement to Miss Elizabeth Smith, of Goldsboro, N. C., who is now the guest of Miss Martha Francis and will go on Tuesday to be with Miss Marjorie Brown.

The party will be on the lawn, which will be brilliantly lighted with Japanese lanterns.

Miss Wright will be charmingly gowned in rose pink silk mull elaborately finished with round thread lace.

Invited to meet with the guest of honor are Miss Passie Mae Ottley, Miss Marjorie Brown, Miss Lucy Stockard, Miss Mary Traylor, Miss Clifford West, Miss Martha Francis, Miss Mildred Fort, Mr. Frank Sims, Mr. Ralph Ragan, Mr. Joe Blount, Mr. Stewart Witham, Mr. Fred Crandell, Mr. Calhoun Mc Dougall, Mr. Lucius Wright, and Mr. Charles LeCraw.

After completion of high school at Washington Seminary, Marie attended Cox College[33], although I do not know if she graduated.[34] She appeared in the funeral announcement for her father in 1911. Significantly, I find no announcements in the social pages for her marriage to Clifton Callaway, no parties, and no receptions. In 1912 the following notice appeared.[35]

Mr. and Mrs. Clifton Callaway announce the birth of a son, Wright Summerfield Callaway, Monday, April 29th, at the home of Dr. L. F. Wright, 803 West Peachtree. Mrs. Callaway was formerly Miss Marie Wright.

The combination of no parties and the convoluted life of Wright Callaway suggest to me that this was a forced marriage due to Marie becoming pregnant. While the family might have

[33] "Cox College was a private women's college located in College Park, Georgia that operated from 1842 to 1934. Cox College was originally called LaGrange Female Seminary in 1842 when it opened in LaGrange, Georgia. It changed names several times: to LaGrange Collegiate Seminary for Young Ladies in 1850, Southern and Western Female College in 1852, Southern Female College in 1854; and finally to Cox College by the 1890s. Part of the school moved to East Point, Georgia in the 1890s, however the main institution moved to Manchester, Georgia in 1895, which renamed itself College Park in 1896. By 1913 it was sometimes referred to as Cox College and Conservatory. It closed several times, including ten years between 1923-1933. It reopened one more time in 1933, but closed for a final time in 1934, leaving the city of College Park without a college."

[34] *The Atlanta Constitution*, 3 January 1909, p. 38. Copy located at Ancestry.com.

[35] *The Atlanta Constitution*, 30 April 1912, p. 8. Copy located at Ancestry.com.

been able to overcome this,[36] she then left her husband and left her son in the care of her mother and sister as documented in census data and by family report. This action appears to be the reason Lucius F. Wright, Sr., refused to discuss her during the rest of his lifetime.

Marie appears in the family home in the 1900 Census, with her birth recorded as May 1889.[37] The date I have was recorded by Aunie, and I have accepted it as correct as it lines up with the documented timing of her graduation from high school. Marie is at home, unmarried, in 1910. Clifton C. Calloway, 22, a commercial traveler, is living in the home of his parents, William R., and Mary E. Calloway.[38] The elder Calloway was a life insurance agent. The address was not far from the 800 block of Peachtree Street where Dr. Wright was living and where he had his practice.

In 1920 Marie Calloway was living as a boarder in Chester, Delaware Co., Pennsylvania, and worked as a finisher in a silk mill.[39] She said she was 30 years old, born in Georgia, with both parents born in Georgia, and said she was married.

I have encountered some difficulty in being sure where Clifton Calloway was after 1910. The one entry that seems most likely is in the 1940 Census, where C. C. Calloway, 53, born in Georgia, is listed at 1428 Peachtree Street, Apartment 502, with his wife, Frances P. Calloway, also 53, born in Alabama. He was listed as a superintendent of operations for Gulf Oil Corporation, and had completed high school.[40]

There are two entries for Clifton C. Calloway in the 1930 Census. One was living in Frostproof, Polk Co., Florida, with a 30 year old wife, Nellie, a 14 year old son, Aurel L., 14, a daughter Lera N., 5, and another son, Allen H., 2 11/12.[41] He is described as being 44, a sawyer, born in Georgia, with both parents born in Georgia. The eldest child, who would have been born about 1916, was also born in Georgia, although Nellie was born in Alabama.

---

[36] *The Atlanta Constitution*, 24 November 1912, p. 18. "Mr. and Mrs. W. S. Featherston gave a beautiful reception Friday at their home on Boulevard to celebrate their silver wedding anniversary....punch was served by Miss Kathleen Wright, Mrs. Clifton Callaway..." This was the last entry I found for her in *The Atlanta Constitution* archives.

[37] 1900 Census Fulton Co., Ga., Atlanta, Ward 6, ED 79, p. 14A.

[38] 1910 Census Fulton Co., Ga., Atlanta, Ward 4, ED 74, p. 1B, family #20.

[39] 1920 Census Delaware Co., Pa., Chester Ward 11, ED 149, p. 35B, #784.

[40] 1940 Census Fulton Co., Ga., Atlanta, ED 160-198, p. 5A, #118.

[41] 1930 Census Polk Co., Fla., Frostproof, District 38, p. 13A/B, family 303.

However, there is a second entry for Clifton C. Callaway, age 44, born in Georgia. This one was a patient at the U. S. Veterans Hospital in Rapides Parish, Louisiana.[42] He was described as married at age 34, or in other words, about 1920, and a veteran of the World War. These certainly could be the same man, but I cannot be sure. Certainly, the timing was about right, given the remarriage of Marie Wright Calloway to Raymond Curlis about 1920.

I have not found Clifton Calloway in the 1920 Census. Clifton C. Callaway registered for the draft on 5 June 1917, was described as single and born 19 October 1886 in Meigs, Thomas Co., Ga.[43] While this fits with the man at the VA Hospital in Alexandria, La., in 1930, it is not clear this is the man living in Atlanta in 1940.

The Social Security Death Index does have an entry for Clifton Callaway, confirmed by Florida records as Clifton C. Callaway, born 20 June 1886, who died in September 1972 in Orlando, Orange Co., Florida.[44] Taken as a whole, the evidence is most easily interpreted as one man, born in 1886 in Thomas Co., Ga., who moved extensively, took a variety of jobs, and was involved in at least three marriages. I suspect the patient at the VA and the man in Florida are indeed the same man; he was double-counted because of the "usual residence" instructions given for completing the form.

In 1930 Marie Curlis was living in Chester, Delaware Co., Pa., with her husband, Raymond and daughter, Frances, 5, at 1103 Clover Lane. She said she was 35, had been married 10 years, and was working as a finisher at a silk mill. I have not found her in the 1940 Census, although in 1942, when he registered for the draft, Raymond H. Curlis listed her as his wife, and reported that they

---

[42] 1930 Census Rapides Par., La., Police Jury Ward 10, ED 47, p. 4A.

[43] Ancestry.com. *U.S., World War I Draft Registration Cards, 1917-1918* [database on-line]. Provo, UT, USA: Ancestry.com Operations Inc, 2005. Original data: United States, Selective Service System. *World War I Selective Service System Draft Registration Cards, 1917-1918*. Washington, D.C.: National Archives and Records Administration. M1509, 4,582 rolls. Imaged from Family History Library microfilm. There is also a Clifton Carter Callaway, b. 22 September 1872, living in Montgomery, Alabama, working as a machinist on the L&N Railroad, married to Edna. It seems unlikely this man is being confused with Clifton Cox Callaway.

[44] Ancestry.com. *Florida Death Index, 1877-1998*.

lived at Skillman Village, Somerset Co., N. J.[45] Investigation shows this was the State Home for Epileptic Children[46], and was surveyed separately as part of Montgomery Twp. I reviewed the individual listings for the staff at the hospital and they are not listed. On the other hand, Frances Curlis, 16, born in Pennsylvania, was a lodger attending school in Ewing, Mercer Co., New Jersey.[47] She was recorded as having completed the 7th grade, which implies she was then in the 8th grade. She had apparently fallen at least one year behind, suggesting moves and dislocation associated with the Depression. I have not been able to determine if the family where she was staying were kin to Raymond Curlis, although it seems likely.

Raymond Curlis was born 12 October 1894 in Hope, Mercer Co., N. J., son of George H. Curlis, then 27, and Sarah F. (Frances) Moore, then 21.[48] He married Anna Elizabeth Foote 12 April 1955 in Newton, Pa.[49] Her obituary was published 8 November 1993.[50]

---

[45] Ancestry.com. WWII Draft Registration Cards, 1942. Data also available from FamilySearch.org.

[46] See en.wikipedia.org/wiki/Skillman,_New_Jersey. Accessed 21 December 2012.

[47] 1940 Census Mercer Co., N. J., Ewing, ED 11-5, p. 9A.

[48] "New Jersey Births and Christenings, 1660-1931."

[49] Thompson, Vickie B. The Ancestors of Verna Fowler Beckstead. 8 March 2012. Located at http://www.rootsweb.ancestry.com, (db. vernabeckstead.) Newtown (PA) Enterprise, 14 April 1955. Cited by Thompson Cited hereafter as Thompson. "In a nuptial mass ceremony performed Tuesday morning at 9:30 o'clock in St. Andrew's R. C. Church, Newtown, Miss Anna Elizabeth Foote of 304 E. Washington Avenue, Newtown, daughter of the late Mr. and Mrs. James L. Foote, became the bride of Raymond H. Curlis of Trenton, New Jersey, son of the late George Curlis. The Rev. Daniel J. Daly officiated. Miss Judith Chustion of Trenton, New Jersey sang "Ave Maria", "Mother At Thy Feet Is Kneeling", "O Sacred Heart", "O Love Divine", "O Lord I Am Not Worthy" and "Panis Angelicus" accompanied at the organ by Mrs. Alois Metzel of George School. For her wedding the bride chose an afternoon dress of pink peau-de-soie with matching hat and pink accessories. She carried a white prayer book and a white orchid. Mrs. John O'Hara of White Haven served as her sister's only attendant in a navy ensemble and matching accessories. She carried a nose-gay of assorted pink flowers. John O'Hara, brother-in-law of the bride, was the best man. Following the ceremony, a wedding breakfast was held at the Temperance House. Upon their return from a trip to New York City, the couple will reside at the home of the new bride until their newly built home in Titusville, New Jersey is completed. Mrs. Curlis is a faculty member at the Fisk School, Ewing Township, New Jersey. Her husband is associated with the State Department of New Jersey."

[50] Falsington (PA) Courier 8 November 1993. Cited by Thompson. "CURLIS - Anna (Foote) died on November 7, 1993 at St. Mary's Hospital. Born in Fallsington. Survived by 2 nephews, Thomas J. Foote, MD of Newtown and Dr. William Andrew Foote of Hamilton Square, New Jersey and 4 nieces, Helen Foote of Jenkintown, Pennsylvania., Mrs. Patricia Anderson of Maine, Mrs. Alice Yoder of Trenton and Mrs. Ellen Scott of Manahawkin, N.J. Mass of Christian Burial 10 a.m. at St. George's Church, Titusville, N.J. on

Child of MARIE LOUISE WRIGHT and CLIFTON COX CALLAWAY is:

i. HENRY (ANTHONY) WRIGHT[6] CALLAWAY, b., 29 April 1912 Atlanta, Fulton Co., Ga.; d. 9 April 1976. Atlanta, Fulton Co., Ga.; m. MATTIE _____; d. Atlanta, Fulton Co., Ga.

Wright, as he was known in the family, was living with his grandmother, Mary Emma Featherston, and his aunt, Kathleen F. Wright, in 1920. He was described as being 6 and 8/12 years old, and since the census was done on 6 January, this implies he was born in May 1913.[51] Since his birth announcement clearly shows he was born 29 April 1912, this seems to me to be an attempt to cover his "premature" birth.

His name was mangled as Callaway H. Wright, 17, grandson of Mary F. Wright, and "son" of Kathleen F. Wright in the 1930 Census completed 9 May 1930.[52] He is probably the Henry W. Callaway, 28 year old WM, born in Georgia, who had completed his second year of college, but who was an inmate at the Maryland State Penal Farm on 1 April 1940.[53] Interestingly, he is also listed, at age 27, as inmate #43281 at the Maryland House of Correction & Hospital in Anne Arundel County in the census taken 8 May 1940.[54]

I was told by Aunie that his first name was Anthony, and as Anthony W. Callaway, he appears in the SSDI with a birth date as 29 April 1912 and a death date of April 1976 in Atlanta, Ga. The 29 April is likely correct, but he was born in 1913 according to the information recorded by his grandmother in the 1920 census, which was most likely correct. Ancestry.com has a listing of online Georgia death certificates, which

Wednesday. Calling hours 9-10 at the church. Arrangements by Blackwell Memorial Home, Pennington, N.J."

[51] 1920 Census Fulton Co., Ga., Atlanta, Ward 8, ED 126, p. 6A

[52] 1930 Census Fulton Co., Ga., Atlanta, ED 111, p. 6A, 1335 West Peachtree Street.

[53] 1940 Census Washington Co., Maryland, ED 22-55, p. 61A. When I asked Dad in 2012 if he knew about it, he said Wright was often in trouble with the law, so it was certainly possible, but he did not know for sure. It would certainly explain his lack of draft registration in 1942.

[54] 1940 Census Anne Arundel Co., Maryland, ED 2-21, p. 16B, #77.

shows that he died 9 April 1976 in Atlanta, Fulton Co., Ga. I have not examined the original death certificate.[55] From the Social Security Number it was identified as having been issued prior to 1951 in Maryland, which certainly fits the previous information. I presume he changed his first name sometime between his release from prison and his acquisition of a social security number.

I met Wright on two occasions, once in 1966 when I visited with Aunie after doing a visit for prospective students at Emory University. At that time he was living in a house downtown. I found out later that Aunie had been providing the housing. When her brother died, her nephews had placed his estate into a conservator account to be used for her support. Denny Wright, in particular, was incensed that she had diverted some of the money to support Wright Callaway. Interestingly, this property is listed online. The address was 325 Newington Court, and is just north of the intersection of I-20 and the I-75/85 corridor. The property was acquired by Mobility Financial Cendant Corp., from Anthony W. Callaway and Patricia Callaway on 8 January 2002. It had apparently been leased to a Alpesh Patel prior to that, and it was sold to him on 8 January 2002 for $384,900![56] The area now appears to be inhabited by people of apparent Vietnamese extraction judging by the names on the deeds.

The second time I met him was when Aunie was in the hospital shortly before her death. She knew she was dying, and gave me a ring she had inherited from her father to keep as a memento. Wright and Mattie came by to visit while Dad, Uncle Denny, and I were all there. With the benefit of hindsight, it is clear that Wright was an alcoholic, and if he was an ex-convict, he probably found it difficult to obtain meaningful employment. Presently, I do not know if alcohol was at the root of the incarceration, but it seems likely, since

[55] Death certificate #011069. Located on Ancestry.com, 23 December 2012.
[56] www.city-data.com/fulton-county/N/Newington-Court-1.html. Accessed 23 December 2012.

the Penal Farm was commonly used for non-violent offenses.[57]

Child of MARIE WRIGHT and RAYMOND CURLIS is:

ii. FRANCES MARIE[6] CURLIS, b. 25 April 1924 Chester, Delaware Co., Pa.; d. 9 November 2007 Lawrenceville, Mercer Co., New Jersey; m. WILLIAM ANDREW STAM 23 June 1948 Mercer Co., N.J., son of WILLIAM STAM and OLIVE E. STAM[58]; b. 11 October 1922 Mercer Co., N. J.; d. 17 July 2005 Mercer Co., New Jersey.[59]

I never met Frances, but Dad did remember meeting Ray and Marie at some point about the time he was at West Point and that he thought they lived in Trenton, which they certainly did in 1935 according to Frances' census entry in 1940. I talked to Frances on the telephone perhaps twice about 1965 when she called us after we had returned from Germany. She gave me the information about the dates of birth for her children and herself. Unfortunately, I neglected to ask for the date of death for her mother.

Frances Curlis, age 5, was living with her parents at 1130 Clover Lane in Chester, Delaware Co., Pennsylvania, in 1930.[60] In 1940, she was living as a boarder in the house of Paul and Jeannette Haney. She is reported as being in school, and having completed the 7th grade. This suggests she was a couple of years behind the usual time frame, suggesting some dislocations, perhaps associated with the Depression. At the time of her father's draft registration in 1942, her parents were living at Skillman Village, Montgomery Twp., Somerset Co., N. J., but I have not located them there, or anywhere else, in 1940.

---

[57] Julius, E. and Hanna, K. From Penal Farm to Prison Complex. Hagerstown (MD) Herald-Mail 29 July 2007. Located online at http://articles.herald-mail.com/2007-07-29/news/25089191_1_mci-h-third-prison-fellow-prisoners. Accessed 21 December 2012.

[58] 1940 Census Mercer Co., N. J., Trenton, Trenton City, ED 27-119, p. 1A, #6. It shows an older brother, Albert E, and wife Viola, as well as younger brothers Elmer H., and Albert E., and sister Verna M.

[59] SSDI.

[60] 1930 Census Chester, Delaware Co., Pa., ED 38, p. 8B, #156.

Her obituary was located online.[61] It does not mention William Stam, and I assume this reflects a divorce.

"Bordentown, NJ resident Frances M. Stam, age 83, passed away Friday, November 9th, 2007 in Lawrenceville, NJ. Born in Chester, PA, she has retired in the Bordentown area since 1970. She retired as a principal clerk from the New Jersey Motor Vehicle Commission in Trenton, NJ after seventeen years of service. Daughter of the late Raymond and Marie Wright Curlis. She is survived by her son, William C. Stam and his wife Kimberly of Burlington Township; daughter, Susan Kraus and her husband Donald of Connecticut; two grandchildren, Laura Lynch and Alexander Stam and a great-grandson, Ian Lynch.

Funeral services will be conducted Monday, November 12th, 2007 at 11 AM from the Huber-Moore Funeral Home, 517 Farnsworth Avenue, Bordentown, NJ, with Rev. Julie Jensen of the First Presbyterian Church of Bordentown officiating. Burial will follow in Ewing Presbyterian Church Cemetery, Scotch Road, Ewing, NJ. Calling hours will be Sunday, November 11th, 2007 from 7 to 9 PM and Monday from 10 AM until the time of service at the funeral home."

Children of FRANCES CURLIS and WILLIAM STAM are:

1. SUSAN[7] STAM, b. 27 November 1950 Mercer Co., N. J.; m. DONALD KRAUS.
2. WILLIAM CURLIS[7] STAM, b. 17 September 1959 Mercer Co., N. J.; m. (1) MICHELE ANNETTE ARCHER 21 August 1982; m. (2) KIMERLEY DELORES BENSON 20 May 1995.

Child of WILLIAM STAM and MICHELLE ARCHER is:

a. LAURA MICHELE[8] STAM, b. 6 May 1984; m. _____ LYNCH; child: IAN, b. before 9 November 2007.

---

[61] Burlington County (NJ) Times, 10 November 2007. Posted online by Bohony, Jo, at http://www.findagrave.com, memorial # 22801129. The cemetery was also known as Ewing Presbyterian Church cemetery.

Child of WILLIAM STAM and KIMBERLEY BENSON is:

> b.   ALEXANDER WILLIAM[8] STAM, b. 24 July 1996.

5. LUCIUS FEATHERSTONE[6] WRIGHT, JR., was born 20 November 1921 in Denver, Denver Co., Colorado. He married MARY MINA WHITENER 27 January 1947 in Alexandria, Rapides Parish, Louisiana, daughter of GEORGE ALVIN WHITENER and AUGUSTA AMIS. She was born 8 September 1925 in Meridian, Lauderdale Co., Mississippi.

      Lucius F. Wright, Jr., was born at Fitzsimons General Hospital in Denver, Colorado, where his father was a staff physician treating patients with tuberculosis. Shortly after the birth of his brother there in 1923, his father was reassigned to the Philippine Islands, then a territory of the United States. Dad remembered snatches of the trip on the *S. S. Thomas* from San Francisco to Manila, which took a couple of weeks. He also remembered being told that his mother had a steamer trunk full of old sheets that were cut up to serve as diapers, and they exhausted their supply of fresh linens before they had even gotten out of San Francisco Bay. There is a picture of him taken in Manila showing him looking at the camera while the amah carries his brother, Denny, on her back. The expression on his face is one that was seen often throughout his life.
      Pearl Wright's asthma got dramatically worse in the tropical air, to the point where Dr. Wright requested a temporary reassignment to take her home. He was sent to Fort George Wright in Spokane, near where her sister, known to Dad as "Aunie Bae" was living, and where Pearl had gone before for her health. Dad and the family stayed there while Dr. Wright returned, alone, to the Philippines to complete his tour of duty.
      Upon his return Dr. Wright was then assigned to Camp Douglas, Arizona. In those days the Army had segregated units, and typically they assigned white officers with Southern backgrounds to the "colored" units. Such was the case with Dr. Wright. Dad often commented that he was practically grown before he realized that enlisted men "came in white, too." Dad recalled going to school on the school "bus," which was a wagon

drawn by mules, and driven by an enlisted man. This was the place where he and his brother started a range fire while playing with matches. (See under Denny Wright's entry for details.)

When Dad was in the second grade, his father was reassigned to Portland, Maine, as support for a coast artillery unit. They are listed there in the 1930 Census. Dad recalled that the trip took quite a long time, and that they spent long enough in Atlanta *en route* that he went to three different schools that year, and always seemed to be reading "The Little Red Hen."

Dr. Wright was reassigned to Fitzsimons General Hospital in the mid 1930's, and his son graduated from East High School in Denver, Colo., in 1939. He went to Bean's Preparatory Academy in Washington, D. C., to study for the entrance exam. He received a Congressional appointment to the United States Military Academy from Colorado in 1940 and graduated in the class of June 1943. He was commissioned as a 2nd Lieutenant of field artillery. He did his officer basic training at Camp Chaffee, Arkansas, and was then sent to England, where he was assigned to a replacement depot. On D+11, (June 17, 1944) he was assigned as a forward observer with the 2nd Armored Division. At the end of the war, he was the only regular Army first lieutenant in his battalion, so was promoted to Captain and given command of a battery.

While home on leave in the winter of 1945 he attended a party hosted by Mrs. George Powell in Alexandria, Louisiana, where he met Mary Mina Whitener. He returned to Europe for occupation duty and married her upon his return. He was then stationed at Fort Sill, Okla., where he taught gunnery, served as a battery commander, and also as an aide-de-camp for Major General Cecil Andrus. He was at Fort Sill at the time of the 1950 Census.

In 1951 he was sent to Fort Bliss, Tex., where he was involved in developing methods for integrating missiles into traditional artillery roles. This was a time when the traditional division of field artillery and coast artillery was abolished and air-defense artillery was being developed. Dad always maintained his identity as a field artilleryman, though. He was promoted to major about the time of assignment to Fort Bliss.

He was sent to attend the Command and General Staff College at Fort Leavenworth, Kansas, from 1954 to 1955.

Following graduation, he was sent to Korea, where he worked in the G-3 (Air) section of 8th Army HQ, and then as a battalion commander. The family stayed in Meridian, Mississippi, while he was overseas.

Upon his return, he was assigned as a professor of military science at Xavier University in Cincinnati, Ohio, where he was promoted to lieutenant colonel. He served there from 1957 to 1961. The family was in the suburb of Reading, Ohio, at the time of the 1960 census.

In the summer of 1961, he was assigned as battalion commander for the 5th Missile Battalion, 42nd Artillery, and went to Fort Sill for specialized training in the workings of the La Crosse missile, the weapon being served by this battalion. While there, the Berlin wall was erected, so rather than going as a family, he went ahead to take command of the battalion, located in Aschaffenburg-am-Main, West Germany. He then sent for us, and we went overseas in November 1961. In 1963, he was reassigned to the G-4 section (logistics) of 7th Army HQ at Patch Barracks, Vaihingen, near Stuttgart, West Germany.

In 1964, he was reassigned to the Deputy Chief of Staff, Logistics, at the Pentagon. The family came home on the *U. S. S. Patch*, landed at the Brooklyn Navy Yard, and established in rental housing in McLean, Virginia. He was promoted to Colonel in 1966, and retired from the Army in 1968.

Upon retirement, he moved to Memphis, Tenn., initially working for Wurzburg Brothers before becoming an agent for General Business Services. During his years in Memphis, he was active in the United Methodist Church, the West Tennessee Historical Society, and the Tennessee Genealogical Society. They lived at 6330 Coteswood Road in Memphis from the time the house was built in 1969 until the fall of 2009, when they moved to Lutheran Village, also in Memphis.

Mary Mina Whitener was born in Meridian, Miss. Her father George Alvin Whitener, worked from the Swift Meat Packing Company. The company moved the family from Meridian to Alexandria, La., where she graduated from Bolton High School in 1943. She attended Sophie Newcomb College for three years, from 1943-1946. In 1946 she served as the society editor for the Alexandria *Daily Town Talk*. She was on the tennis team in high school and remains an active tennis player until age 80, when she had a heart attack and needed bypass surgery. She has also been active in the DAR at the local and state level, and has represented the state at the national level.

My sister recalled: "Living in Meridian was interesting. Daddy left to go to Korea and we stayed in a brown house on 34th street. I remember the day Daddy left to go overseas. I had no clue why everyone was so upset that day. Daddy kept hugging everybody and even Mama was crying a little. Then, after we had taken a bunch of pictures, we all got in the car and went to the airport. My first understanding of the occasion was when I stood behind a high fence and watched Daddy walk across the pavement to the airplane. He kept turning around to wave and I finally understood that he was leaving for a long time. I did not understand, however, that he was coming back. I had nightmares for years after that about not being able to find my real parents. Mama and I didn't always get along then and I really missed my Daddy. When he did come home, Luke walked around for days telling me "The Whip" was coming home. I was so terrified, I didn't speak to Daddy for quite a while.

When I was ten years old, we went to live in Aschaffenburg, Germany. I had never flown before and was very apprehensive about my first flight. Daddy met us at the Frankfurt airport. We rode a really strange bus to the American side and then drove to A'burg. He took us to the Officer's Club for lunch and we were waited on by "Little Margaret." It seemed that she had adopted him while he was waiting for us because she treated him like family. It was my first introduction to a German person.

I was exhausted from the trip and totally out of my comfort zone. The first night, we went to bed and slept on top of and under feather beds. I think I was given a tranquilizer to calm me down so I could sleep. The second night, I woke up and had to go to the bathroom. Daddy had already warned me that I was not to come to their room for that and should go to the room marked OO down the hall. I braved it down a cold hallway in the semi-darkness. I met a man coming the other way who was wearing a nightshirt and had a hat on. He started speaking German to me and gesturing to me to go in the bathroom. I am sure today that he was only being kind and allowing a child to go first, but at the time, I was sure he was going to kill me. I bolted the door, went to the bathroom and then raced back to bed and cried myself back to sleep.

Random memories of Germany: Readiness tests—especially the one where Daddy thought I was in the bathroom and yelled "Judy, get the hell out of there!" I knew the "balloon" had gone up and I would be dead by morning. Control cards designed to make it possible to trace how far I got in case we had to be evacuated. Sharing a passport with Mama. Not having confidence in Mama's ability to follow her NEO route. (She kept telling me she would just follow the crowd to the airport.) She never ran the route the same way twice. I just knew we would be lost and at the mercy of the Germans.

Kennedy was assassinated during the evening—I heard it on the radio while I was baby sitting for the Gersitz girls) in Germany, so that I will forever be out of sync with Americans who remember it happened in the morning. The Cuban Missile crisis. Seeing JFK at Hanau and Mama telling everybody in front of us that if she had to sit down, so did they. (She could embarrass a couple of kids fairly easily) Mama falling down the stairs and around the corner and halfway down the next flight of stairs and clearing out the fourth floor library. She got mad at us for laughing at her, but I had never seen anyone fall around a corner before!

My brother recalled: "One summer, I believe it was 1986, Dad was mowing the front lawn with the tractor when he stopped moving forward but the engine was still running. While pushing the mower back to the carport, we noticed that the right side rear wheel and axle were coming out of the transmission. The repair folks wanted more money than Dad thought reasonable so he decided we should try to fix it ourselves. I suspect that, if nothing else, he just wanted to see how it worked.

We took the tractor up under the oak tree, used a rope to jack up the back end and set to work removing the transmission. The bolts holding the transmission to the chassis had frozen and no amount of WD-40 would break them free. Dad showed me how to drill out the bolts to free up the transmission. After taking the transmission off of the chassis, we placed it on the workmate under the same tree. We removed the bolts holding the upper section from the lower section and carefully lifted the cover off of the transmission. Before we could get a good look at the orientation, the lower section fell off the workmate and greasy gears rolled everywhere through the dirt. After the usual expletives, we picked up the pieces and set to work on the screen porch cleaning off the grease using gasoline. Unfortunately, the grease got out of control and we coated the screen porch floor with it. I spent the better part of two days reassembling five forward speeds and one reverse. The problem that originated this ordeal was a simple 35 cent retaining clip. In the end, the tractor was repaired, I learned about shade tree mechanics, Dad paid me for the repair, and Mom made me paint the porch floor the same color as the carport floor."

Children of LUCIUS WRIGHT and MARY MINA WHITENER are:

i. LUCIUS FEATHERSTONE[7] WRIGHT, III, b. 10 April 1948 Fort Sill, Comanche Co., Okla.; m. CYNTHIA MANN 23 June 1973 Memphis, Shelby Co., Tenn., dau. of ORIAN CLARKE MANN and LOTTIE RUTH SMITH; b. 5 May 1950 Memphis, Shelby Co., Tenn.

Children of LUCIUS WRIGHT and CYNTHIA MANN are:

1. KATHRYN[8] WRIGHT, b. 11 November 1975 Denver, Denver Co., Colo.; m. WILLIAM WEBB MYERS 19 August 2000 Jackson, Madison Co., Tenn.; b. 30 September 1975 San Antonio, Bexar Co., Texas; children: Mary Olive, b. 30 September 2004 Atlanta, Fulton Co., Ga.; Charles Allen, b. 11 March 2007 San Antonio, Bexar Co., Texas.

2. DAVID CLARKE[8] WRIGHT, b. 20 September 1977 Fort Sam Houston, Bexar Co., Texas; m. VICKIE IRENE ELLIS 27 December 2010 Jackson, Madison Co., Tenn.; b. 10 October 1960 Atlanta, Fulton Co., Ga.

3. FRANCES[8] WRIGHT, b. 2 June 1980 Fort Sam Houston, Bexar Co., Texas; m. DUNCAN KIRK BRELAND 11 October 2008 Jackson, Madison Co., Tenn.; b. 8 July 1980 Flowood, Rankin Co., Miss.; children: Eli Augustus, b. 31 July 2011 Memphis, Shelby Co., Tenn.; David Lawrence, b. 20 January 2013 Memphis, Shelby Co., Tenn.

4. MARIAN[8] WRIGHT, b. 8 August 1983 Fort Sam Houston, Bexar Co., Texas.

ii. JUDITH[7] WRIGHT, b. 17 December 1950 Fort Sill, Comanche Co., Okla.; m. WALTER EDWIN PIERCE 14 August 1976 Memphis, Shelby Co., Tenn.; b. 24 December 1948 Montgomery, Alabama.

Children of JUDITH WRIGHT and WALTER PIERCE are:

1. MELISSA LEIGH[8] PIERCE, b. 15 August 1979 Little Rock, Pulaski Co., Arkansas; m. EMMETT JOSEPH WEBB 14 February 2004 Hoover, Jefferson Co., Alabama; b. 19 October 1977 Winchester, Frederick Co., Virginia; children: Caroline Leigh, b. 11 October 2008 Williamson Co., Tenn.; Ella Marie, b. 31 October 2009 Williamson Co., Tenn.; Emmett Joseph, Jr., b. 4 June 2013 Williamson Co., Tenn.

2. MICHAEL EDWIN[8] PIERCE, b. 19 September 1983 Homewood, Jefferson Co., Ala.; m. BELEE JONES 25 May 2012 Montgomery, Montgomery Co., Alabama.

iii. GEORGE DENNY[7] WRIGHT, b. 26 November 1966 Washington, D. C.; m. SUSAN DAWN MILLER 3 June 1989 Memphis, Shelby Co., Tenn.; b. 18 January 1967 Memphis, Shelby Co., Tenn.

Children of DENNY WRIGHT and SUSAN MILLER are:

1. REBECCA SUZANNE[8] WRIGHT, b. 14 August 1997 Baton Rouge, La.

2. AMY ELIZABETH[8] WRIGHT, b. 28 March 2000 Baton Rouge, La.

3. STEPHEN DANIEL[8] WRIGHT, b. 10 June 2003 Baton Rouge, La.

6. RALPH DENNY[6] WRIGHT was born 10 February 1923 in Denver, Denver Co., Colorado, and died 6 March 2006 in Mobile, Mobile Co., Alabama. He married ANNE GRIFFIN 10 March 1945 in Montgomery, Montgomery Co., Alabama. She was born 9 August 1925 in Montgomery, Montgomery Co., Alabama.

In 2003, Denny Wright recalled that when his father died, he had reviewed the "201 File," which was the Army's term for a soldier's personal record of official actions. He noted the file mostly contained rebukes for the behaviors of his two sons. Some of the episodes that he recalled, not in chronological order, included a time in Hawaii where he made a pea-shooter out of a papaya branch, which was naturally hollow, and using the berries as ammunition, shot at the adults attending a party next door. He remembered that one of the berries hit a man in the glasses and ran red, looking like he had drawn blood. He did not recall his punishment for that adventure.

He also recalled that he and his brother had found a box of kitchen matches while they were at Camp Douglas, Arizona, and took to playing with them and succeeded in lighting a tumbleweed. As it rolled, it started a range fire, which required the soldiers to be mustered to put it out. After that one of the sergeants took to asking them if they had started any fires, warning them that if he caught them doing it, he would "cut their ears off and pin them to his pet alligator."

He remembered several episodes from their time at Fort Williams, (Portland), Maine. He recalled that they had lit candles in the basement of their quarters to smoke their initials into the floorboards overhead. He also recalled that there was an old Civil War cannon located near the Colonel's quarters at Fort Williams, which they loved to play on. Once, his brother jumped on the cannon's trail while Denny was sitting on the cannon, causing the cannon and caisson to move, nearly hitting Denny.

He also recalled a time when he and his brother took two boxes of Xylitone tablets, a cathartic used for preparation for gastrointestinal radiographs, and "shared" them with their unsuspecting schoolmates. He had bet everyone in the class they could not "hold it" for 10 minutes after taking the pills. He did not lose the bet. The event was traced back to him, since his brother had given his box to him.

He commented that "Dad" typically administered punishment with his Sam Browne belt, which was a standard part of an officer's uniform in those days. On at least one occasion, when they knew they were going to do something to merit that punishment, they took the precaution of hiding all of the belts first.

He also recalled that when he and Ann visited the family in Atlanta, they were put in the twin beds in the front room. They would pull the beds together, but the next morning Aunie would have them pulled apart and back in their usual place. They finally used belts to lash the two beds together, and that put a stop to it.

Dr. Wright's obituary was published in the *Mobile (Alabama) Register* on 8 March 2006.

Dr. Ralph Denny Wright, a longtime Mobile internist and a former assistant professor with the University of South Alabama College of Medicine, died Monday at an area hospital. He was 83.

A native of Denver, Wright came to Mobile in 1955 and maintained a private practice and partnership in internal medicine for nearly 50 years in Mobile.

His daughter, Katherine "KD" Wright Inge of Mobile, remembered him as a man with an incredible sense of humor.

"Medicine and his family were truly his passions," she said.

She said her father had been in poor health lately.

He attended the University of Colorado in Boulder and graduated from the University of Alabama in Tuscaloosa and later received his medical degree from the Tulane University School of Medicine.

Wright, who interned at the City Hospital in Mobile, was an officer in the U.S. Army, serving as a medical resident at Brooke Army Hospital in San Antonio and later at Walter Reed Hospital in Washington, D.C. In 1952, he became chief of medicine at 20th Station Hospital in Bad Kreuznach, Germany.

Wright had served as president of the Medical Society of Mobile County; president of the medical staff of the Mobile General Hospital and Suburban Hospitals, Mobile Infirmary and Providence Hospital; consultant at the Foley and Thomas Hospitals; and medical director of Degussa Corp. He had also been chairman of the department of medicine at Spring Hill Memorial Hospital.

Survivors include his wife of 61 years, Anne Griffin Wright of Mobile; and four daughters, Inge and Elisabeth

Wright Gilmer, both of Mobile, Anne Wright Greaves of Birmingham and Margaret Wright Beasley Martin of Nashville, Tenn.; his brother, Col. Lucius Featherstone Wright, Jr. of Memphis, Tenn.; 10 grandchildren; and three great-grandsons.

A memorial service will be at noon Thursday at St. Paul's Episcopal Church, with a visitation in the church's parish hall from 10:30 a.m. until the noon memorial service. Pine Crest Funeral Home on Dauphin Island Parkway handled arrangements.

Memorials may be made to the Dr. Ralph Denny Wright Scholarship Fund at the University of South Alabama College of Medicine, Attn: GinnyTurner, 307 University Blvd., HSB 2150, Mobile, AL 36688.

Children of DENNY WRIGHT and ANNE GRIFFIN are:

i. KATHERINE DENNY[7] WRIGHT, b. 24 February 1947 Mobile, Mobile Co., Ala.; m. DAVID UNGER INGE 4 August 1970 Mobile, Mobile Co., Ala.; b. 28 March 1947 Mobile, Mobile Co., Alabama.

Children of KATHRYN WRIGHT and DAVID INGE are:

1. KATHERINE BURGETT[8] INGE; b. 15 December 1972 Birmingham, Jefferson Co., Ala.; m. WILLIAM ALEXANDER HINSON 3 January 2004 Mobile, Mobile Co., Alabama; child: William A. Hinson, III.

2. RICHARD DENNY[8] INGE; b. 15 August 1975 San Antonio, Bexar Co., Texas; m. ELIZABETH ANN WATSON 3 February 2001; child: Coleman Watson Inge, b. 2 August 2002.

3. DAVID GORDON[8] INGE; b. 4 November 1979 Colorado Springs, Colo.;

ii. ANNE TENNENT[7] WRIGHT, b. 17 October 1950 San Antonio, Bexar Co., Texas; m. MAC BELL GREAVES 22 December 1972 Mobile, Mobile Co., Ala.; b. 28 November 1949

Children of ANNE WRIGHT and MAC GREAVES are:

1. MAC BELL[8] GREAVES, JR., b. 29 July 1978.

2. ANNE CATHERINE[8] GREAVES, b. 24 February 1981.

iii. MARGARET[7] WRIGHT, b. 17 August 1956 Mobile, Mobile Co., Ala.; m. CYRUS GARNETT BEASLEY 12 July 1980 Mobile, Mobile Co., Ala.; b. 24 August 1950; d. 29 March 2001; m. (2) PHILLIP M. MARTIN 31 January 2004 Birmingham, Jefferson Co., Ala.; b. 28 April 1954.

Children of MARGARET WRIGHT and CYRUS BEASLEY are:

1. CYRUS GARNETT[8] BEASLEY, JR., b. 8 November 1984; m. MELANIE KAYE ALVAREZ 23 June 2007; child: CATHERINE GRIFFIN BEASLEY, b. 13 August 2012 Hong Kong, China.
2. MARGARET MCKENZIE[7] BEASLEY, b. 16 March 1988; m. ALLEN LEE BEFORT 10 September 2011.

iv. ELIZABETH[7] WRIGHT, b. 8 February 1962 Mobile, Mobile Co., Ala.; m. WALTER THOMPSON GILMER, JR., 6 December 1986 Mobile, Mobile Co., Ala.; b. 8 February 1962.

Children of ELIZABETH WRIGHT and WALTER GILMER are:

1. JOHN MARSHALL[8] GILMER, b. 19 May 1990 Mobile, Mobile Co., Ala.
2. WILLIAM LEE[8] GILMER, b. 19 May 1990 Mobile, Mobile Co., Ala.
3. WALTER THOMPSON[8] GILMER, III, b. 4 January 1995 Mobile, Mobile Co., Ala.

Appendix A: Brunswick Co., Virginia, Tax Lists 1782-1814

1782 A, p. 9[1]   Wright, John   1-1-4-0[2] 0/13/0

               Wright, William Stanhope   1-0-3-0 0/10/9

1783 A, p. 13   Estate of Robert Wright, deceased: 5-10-2-35 5/12/9

        David, George, Dina, Milley, Phebey

        Jacob, Lucy, Nancy, Peter, Silvey

               Reuben Wright: 3-6-2-17   3/8/3

        Jack, Sarah, Amey, Meck, Phill

1783 B, p. 11   John Wright: Taylor, Charlotte, Milley 3-2-2-8 1/16/0

1783 C, none

1783 D, p. 9   George Wright   1-1-2-6 0/15/6

1783 E, none

1783 F, p. 8   James Wright   1-1-2-7 0/15/9

1784 A, p. 8

        Reuben Wright   10-4-0-4-17

        John Wright, John Wright < 21   1-2-1-1-8

        Mary Wright   5-4-0-3-11

1784 B, none

1784 C, none

1784 D, p. 35   George Wright   1-1-0-2-12

1784 E, none

1785 A, p. 14 John Wright, John Wright <21; Glasgow 3-2-1-2-4

        p. 15   Reuben Wright; Jack, Sall, Aggy, _____,

        Mike, Phill, Roling   8-3-0-4-17

        James Wright, Labon Wright, David Wright 3-3-2-3-2

        Mary Wright; Milley, Terry, Amy, Geo.   4-2-0-1-12

1785 4th District p. 28   George Wright   1-1-0-3-4

               Sarah Wright, widow son (?)   0-1-1-0-5

1786 A p. 31   Mary Wright; George, Miley, Suzy, Peter

       Silvey, Amey   6-2-0-1-10

               Reuben Wright; Jack, Sall, _____, Aggy,

       Mike, Phill, _____, Silvia   9-3-0-4-18

               John Wright (Taylor), John Wright;

       Chance   2-3-1-1-6

1786 4th District (Meherrin Parish)

        p. 48   George Wright   1-1-0-2-0-0

               Sarah Wright   0-1-1-0-3-0

        p. 61   James Wright   1-1-0-1-8-0

               John Wright   1-1-0-1-0-0

---

[1] Remainder illegible due to faded ink.

[2] 1=number of taxables; 2=number of tithables; 3=whites < 21; 4=horses; 5=cattle

1787 A	p. 26	Jno. Wright/Jno. Wright	1-0-0-1-5
		Reuben Wright/Reuben Wright	0-2-6-5-7
		Mary Wright/	0-2-4-1-11
		William Wright/William Wright	0-0-0-1-0
		Elizabeth Wright	0-1-0-0-0
1787 B	p. 15	James Wright/James Wright	3-0-0-3-6
		Thomas Washington/Thos. Washington	
		/John Wright	0-10-11-5-23
		James Wright/David Wright	0-1-1-2-8
1788 A	p. 30	John Wright/John Wright	1-0-0-2
		Reuben Wright/Reuben Wright	2-2-2-5
		Mary Wright/	0-2-1-1
	p. 31	William Wright/William Wright	0-0-0-1
1788 B	p. 19	George Wright	1-0-0-1
	p. 20	Thomas Washington	1-8-1-5
	p. 21	James Wright	4-0-0-3
		James Wright	1-0-0-2
	p. 22	John Wright	1-0-0-1
	p. 23	Sarah Wright	2-0-0-1
1789 A	p. 31	Reuben Wright	3-4-0-4
	p. 32	John Wright (Tailor)	2-0-0-3
		Mary Wright	1-2-2-1
1789 B	p. 59	James Wright	3-0-0-3
		George Wright	1-0-0-3
	p. 60	Sarah Wright	2-0-0-1
	p. 61	James Wright	1-0-0-2
	p. 42	John Wright	1-0-0-0
1790 A	p. 31	Reuben Wright	3-4-0-4
		Robert Wright	1-0-0-1
		John Wright (tailor)	2-0-0-3
	p. 32	Mary Wright	1-3-1-1
		John Wright	1-0-0-1
1790 B	p. 24[3]	John Wright	1-0-0-0
1791 A	p. 28	George Wright	1-1-0-1
		Samuel Wright	1-0-0-1
	p. 29	Nancy Wright	1-0-0-2
		John Wright	1-0-0-1
		James Wright	2-0-0-3
	p. 32	Sarah Wright	0-3-1-1
1791 B	p. 65	Reuben Wright	3-4-0-4
	p. 66	Robert Wright	0-3-1-1
		Mary Wright	0-3-1-1

[3] Several pages after this badly faded.

1792 A	p. 24	John Wright	1-0-0-0
		George Wright	1-0-0-0
	p. 25	James Wright	2-1-0-3
	p. 26	George Wright	1-1-1-1
		Samuel Wright	1-0-0-1
	p. 27	Laban Wright	1-0-0-1
		John Wright	1-0-0-2
		Nancy Wright	0-0-0-4
		Jarrott Wright	1-0-0-1
	p. 28	Sarah Wright	1-0-0-2
1792 B	p. 64	Reuben Wright	2-4-0-5
		Robert Wright	1-0-0-1
		John Wright	1-0-0-2
		Mary Wright	0-1-1-1
1793 A	p. 29	James Wright	2-0-0-2
		Sarah Wright	1-0-0-2
		Jarrott Wright	1-0-0-2
		Labon Wright	1-0-0-2
		Nancy Wright	0-0-0-5
		John Wright, Junr.	1-0-0-0
	p. 31	George Wright	1-7-0-6
		Samuel Wright	1-0-0-1
	p. 32	John Wright, Senr.	1-0-0-0
1793 B	p. 65	Reuben Wright	2-4-2-4
		Mary Wright	0-3-0-1
	p. 66	Robert Wright	1-0-0-1
1794 A	p. 26	Nancy Wright	1-0-0-4
		John Wright, Junr.	1-0-0-1
		Laborn Wright	1-0-0-2
		Jarrott Wright	1-0-0-2
	p. 28	Samuel Wright	1-0-0-1
		Dilley Wright	1-0-0-1
		John Wright, Senr.	1-0-0-0
		James Wright	2-0-0-2
	p. 29	Lewis Wright	1-0-0-1
1794 B	p. 57	Reuben Wright	1-4-1-5
		Mary Wright	0-2-0-1
1795 A	p. 43	Reuben Wright	1-4-1-4
1795 B	p. 25	Samuel Wright	1-0-1-1
	p. 26	Nancy Wright	1-0-0-4
		John Wright, Junr.	1-0-0-2
		Laban Wright	1-0-0-1
		John Wright, Senr.	1-0-0-0
		James Wright	2-0-0-3

		Jarratt Wright	1-0-0-0	
1796 A		none[4]		
1796 B	p. 27	James Wright	1-0-0-2	
		Jarrett Wright	1-0-0-1	
		George Wright	1-2-0-3	
		Samuel Wright	1-0-0-1	
	p. 28	Nancy Wright	1-0-0-3	
		John Wright, Junr.	1-0-1-2	
		John Wright, Senr.	1-0-0-1	
1797 B	p. 26	George Wright	1-2-1-2	
		John Wright	1-0-0-2	
		Nancy Wright	1-0-0-3	
	p. 27	John Wright, Senr.	1-0-0-1	
		James Wright	1-1-0-2	
		William Wright	1-0-0-1	
		Samuel Wright	1-0-0-1	
1798 B	p. 24	George Wright	1-2-0-2	0.00
		Samuel Wright	1-0-0-1	0.09
		Nancy Wright	1-0-0-4	0.36
		John Wright	1-0-1-1	0.44
	p. 25	James Wright	1-1-0-2	0.53
		William Wright	1-0-0-1	0.09
		John Wright, Senr.	1-0-0-1	0.35
1799 B	p. 24	George Wright	2-1-0-2	
		Samuel Wright	1-2-0-1	
		Nancy Wright	1-0-1-1	
		John Wright	1-0-1-1	
	p. 25	John Wright, Senr.	1-0-0-0	
1800 B	p. 24	George Wright	2-1-0-2	
		Samuel Wright	1-2-0-1	
		Nancy Wright	0-0-0-3	
		John Wright	1-0-1-1	
	p. 25	John Wright, Senr.	1-0-0-0	
1801 B	p. 21	George Wright	2-1-0-2	
		Samuel Wright	1-1-0-1	
		Nancy Wright	1-0-0-1	
		John Wright	1-0-0-2	
		John Wright, Sr.	1-0-0-0	
	p. 22	Reuben Wright	1-0-0-1	
1802 B	p. 23	Samuel Wright	1-2-0-1	
		Nancy Wright	1-0-0-1	

---

[4] There are no Wrights in the upper district until 1805 when Sterling Wright makes his first appearance here. For convenience, I will list all book B only.)

		John Wright	1-1-0-1
	p. 24	John Wright, Senr.	1-0-0-0
		Reuben Wright	1-0-0-1
1803 B	p. 22	George Wright	2-1-0-2
		Samuel Wright	1-1-0-1
		Nancy Wright	1-0-0-2
		John Wright	1-0-0-1
		Reuben Wright	0-0-0-2
	p. 23	John Wright, Senr.	1-0-0-0
		Reuben Wright	1-0-0-1
1804 B	p. 20	George Wright	2-1-0-2
		Samuel Wright	1-1-1-1
		John Wright	1-0-0-0
	p. 21	Nancy Wright	1-0-0-1
		John Wright, Sr.	1-0-0-0
1805 A	p. 34	Sterling Wright	1-0-0-1
1805 B	p. 22[5]	Nancy Wright	1-0-0-2
		John Wright, Senr.	1-0-0-0
1806 A	p. 34	Sterling Wright	1-0-0-1
1806 B	p. 19	George Wright	2-1-0-3
		Samuel Wright	1-2-0-1
		John Wright, Jr.	1-0-0-2
		Nancy Wright	1-0-0-1
		John Wright	1-0-0-0
	p. 21	Josias Wright	1-0-0-1
1807 A		no Wrights	
1807 B	p. 19	George Wright	2-1-0-2
		Willey Wright	1-0-0-1
		Samuel Wright	1-1-0-1
		John Wright	1-0-0-0
	p. 21	Josias Wright	1-0-0-1
1808		No taxes collected	
1809 A		No Wrights	
1809 B	p. 20	George Wright	2-0-0-3
		Willie Wright	1-0-0-1
		John Wright	1-0-0-0
	p. 21	Josias Wright	1-0-0-1
	p. 22	Merritt Wright	1-0-0-1
		Samuel Wright	1-1-0-1
1810 A		No Wrights	
1810 B	p. 20	George Wright	2-1-0-2
		Willie Wright	1-0-0-1

---

[5] A number of entries were quite faded and could not be read.

	p. 22	Josiah Wright	1-0-0-1
	p. 23	Merritt Wright	1-0-0-1
		Samuel Wright	1-2-0-1
1811 A		No Wrights	
1811 B	p. 14	George Wright	2-1-0-3
		Wesley Wright	1-0-0-1
	p. 15	Samuel Wright	1-1-0-1
	p. 16	Josiah Wright	1-0-0-0
1812 A	p. 37	Sterling Wright	1-0-0-0
1812 B	p. 17	George Wright	2-0-1-4
1813 A	p. 38	Robert Wright	1-0-0-0
		Sterling Wright	1-0-1-1
1813 B	p. 14	Wesley Wright	1-0-0-1
		George Wright	3-0-1-3
1814 A	p. 33	Sterling Wright	1-0-1-1
1814 B	p. 14	Wesley Wright	1-0-0-1
		George Wright	1-0-0-2

Appendix B: Lunenburg Co., Virginia, Tax Lists 1782-1812

1782[6]	p. 21	Joseph Wright
	p. 22	Thomas Wright, Parsons Wright
		James Wright
		John Wright
1783	p. 25	John Wright
		Joseph Wright
		James Wright
		Parsons Wright
		Thomas Wright, Thomas Wright, jr., J. Wright
1784	p. 27	James Wright/Labon Wright/David Wright
		Joseph Wright
		Parsons Wright
	p. 28	John Wright
1785	p. 34	Joseph Wright
		John Wright
	p. 35	Parsons Wright
		Thomas Wright
1786	p. 38	Parsons Wright
		Joseph Wright
		Thomas Wright, David Wright
1787	p. 26	John Wright (separated from the others by
many names)		
	p. 27	James Wright
		Joseph Wright
		Thomas Wright
		James Wright
		John Wright
		Parsons Wright
1788	p. 27	Parsons Wright
		Joseph Wright
		John Wright
1789	p. 26	Thomas Wright
		John Wright
		David Wright
	p. 27	Parsons Wright
1790	p. 26	Joseph Wright
	p. 27	Thomas Wright
		David Wright

---

[6] All men named Wright were listed in the lower district. Sometimes the lower district appears first on the microfilm reel, but I have ignored that.

1791	p. 29	Joseph Wright	
	p. 31	Parsons Wright	
		John Wright	
		Thomas Wright	
		David Wright	
1792	p. 24	Parsons Wright[7]	
	p. 25	John Wright	
		Charles Wright	
		Thomas Wright	
		Joseph Wright	
1793	p.25	Parsons Wright	
	p. 26	Joseph Wright	
		John Wright	
		Charles Wright	
		Thomas Wright	
1794	p. 27	Parsons Wright	
		Thomas Wright	
	p. 28	Joseph Wright	
1795	p. 28	Joseph Wright	
		Parsons Wright	
		Thomas Wright	
1796	p. 31	Joseph Wright	
		Thomas Wright	
	p. 31	Parsons Wright	
1797	p. 33	Parsons Wright	
	p. 34	Thomas Wright	
		Joseph Wright	
1798	p. 35	Joseph Wright	
		Parsons Wright	
		Thomas Wright	
1799	p. 35	Parsons Wright	
		Joseph Wright	
		Thomas Wright	(2 white tithes)
1800	p. 34	Joseph Wright	1-1
		Parsons Wright	1-0
		Thomas Wright	2-1
1801	p. 39	Joseph Wright	1-1
		Parsons Wright	1-0
		Thomas Wright	2-1
1802	p. 40	Thomas Wright	2-0
		Parsons Wright	2-0
		Joseph Wright	1-1

---

[7] (Shadrack Whitt is the only intervening name)

1803	p. 32	Parsons Wright	1-0
		John Wright	1-0
		Thomas Wright	3-0
	p. 33	Joseph Wright	1-1
1804	p. 36	Thomas Wright, estate	(done 10 April 1804)
		Parsons Wright	1-0
		Joseph Wright	1-1
1805	p. 37	Thomas Wright, est.	1-0
	p. 39	Joseph Wright	1-1
		David Wright	1-1
		Parsons Wright	1-0
1806	p. 29	David Wright	1-1
		Parsons Wright	1-0
		Thomas Wright, est.	0-0
		Joseph Wright	1-1
		John Wright	1-0
1807	p. 37	Joseph Wright	
		Robert Wright	
		David Wright	
		Hannah Wright	
		John Wright	
		Parsons Wright	
1808		No tax	
1809	p. 19	Wright, Robert	1-0-0-1
		Wright, David	1-1-0-2
		Wright, Joseph	1-1-0-2
		Wright, Parsons	2-1-1-2
		Wright, John	1-0-0-1
1810	p. 17	Wright, Robert	1-0-0-2
		Wright, David	1-1-0-1
		Wright, Joseph	1-1-0-2
		Wright, John	1-0-0-0
	p. 18	Wright, Parsons	1-2-0-2
1811	p. 17	Wright, Parsons	1-2-0-2
		Wright, John	1-0-0-0
1812		No Wrights in the Tax Rolls	

1782	p. 16[8]	Wright, Bolling	1-0-0-1
		Wright, Lucy	0-0-9-1
1783	p. 26	Wright Lucy, Bolling Wright	1-0-0-6-1
1784	p. 17	Wright, Augustine (+10 Negroes)	1-3-7-27-3
		Wright, Lucy	0-0-0-5-1
		Wright, Bolling	1-0-0-0-0
		Wright, Laban	1-2-0-15-3
1785	p. 9	Wright, Laban (Caesar & Hannah)	1-1-1-9-3
		Wright, Austin (Jacob, Katie, Jim, Beck, Jacob	
		Phillis, Milley, ____, Edy, ____, Fanny	
	p. 36	Wright, James	1-0-0-0-1
1786	p. 37	Wright, Laban (Caesar & Lidia)	1-1-1-18-3
		Wright, Austin	1-4-9-29-3
	p. 38	Wright, Bolling	1-0-0-5-2
		Wright, Sterling	1-0-0-0-0
1787	p. 38	Wright, Laban	
		(Caesar, Jimmy, Elijah, Jinny)	1-0-2-2-9-10
		Wright, Claiborne	0-1-0-0-0-0
	p. 39	Wright, James, Lucy	1-0-1-0-2-5
		Wright, Laban, jr.	1-0-0-0-1
	p. 40	Wright, Augustine	1-0-4-8-3-27
1788 A	p. 37	Wright, Job	1-0-0-0
1788 B	p. 29	Wright, James	1-0-0-2
	p. 31	Wright, Augustine	1-5-1-3
		Wright, Sterling	1-0-0-0
	p. 32	Wright, Laban, jr.	1-0-0-1
1789 A	p. 38	Wright, John (himself exempt)	0-0-0-2
	p. 39	Wright, Job	1-0-0-0
1789 B	p. 48	Wright, Augustine	1-6-1-3
	p. 49	Wright, James	1-0-0-1
1790 A	p. 38	Wright, John (exempt)	0-0-0-2
	p. 39	Wright, Job	1-0-0-0
1790 B	p. 47	Wright, Augustine	1-6-1-5
	p. 50	Wright, James	1-0-1-2
1791 A	p. 44	Wright, Job	1-0-0-0
		Wright, John	1-0-0-1
1791 B	p. 14	Wright, Augustine	2-6-1-7
		Wright, James	1-0-0-1
		Wright, Claiborne	1-0-0-1

---

[8] Some damaged pages that may be relevant.

1792 A	p. 29	Wright, Augustine, Wright, John	2-6-1-6
	p. 30	Wright, James	1-0-0-1
		Wright, William	1-0-0-0
		Wright, Laban	1-0-0-1
		Wright, Anderson	1-0-0-0
	p. 31	Wright, Claiborne	1-0-0-1
1792 B	p. 33	Wright, Job	1-0-0-0
1793 A	p. 33	Wright, Job	1-0-0-1
1793 B	p. 35	Wright, James (Molley)	1-1-0-2
		Wright, Augustine, Wright, John	2-7-1-5
		Wright, Claiborne	1-0-0-0
1794 A	p. 28	Wright, William	1-0-0-0
	p. 29	Wright, Austin	1-6-1-5
		Wright, Anderson	1-1-0-1
		Wright, Claiborne	1-0-0-1
1794 B	p. 30	Wright, Job	1-0-0-0
1795 A	p. 62	Wright, Job, Thos. _____	2-0-0-0
1795 B	p. 35	Wright, Claiborne	1-0-0-1
		Wright, James	1-0-0-3
	p. 36	Wright, Anderson	1-0-0-1
		Wright, Augustine	1-7-2-5
1796 A	p. 31	Wright, Claiborne	1-0-0-1
		Wright, Anderson (Nealon)	1-0-1-1
	p. 32	Wright, Robert (Milly, Mike)	1-2-0-1
		Wright, Reuben	
		(Jack, P----, Sall, Isaac, Lucy)	1-5-0-8
		Wright, Austin	1-7-2-4
1796 B	p. 26	Wright, Job	1-0-0-1
1797 A	p. 36	Wright, Job	1-0-0-1
1797 B	p. 38	Wright, Robert (Mike, Milley)	1-2-0-1
	p. 39	Wright, John	1-0-0-1
		Whitlow, James; Francis Whitlow	
	p. 40	Wright, Anderson	1-0-0-0
	p. 41	Wright, Claiborne	1-1-0-1
		Wright, James	1-0-0-2
		Wright, Augustine	1-7-2-1
		Wright, Reuben (Jack, etc.)	1-5-1-2
1798 A	p. 49	Wright, John (Chancey)	1-1-0-0
		Wright, David List Judy	1-1-0-2
		Wright, Reuben, List son Thomas, Jack,	
		Phill, Sall, Lucy, _____	2-3-0-4
		Wright, William List	1-0-0-1
		Wright, Austin, son John, Jacob,	
		Jacob, Jim, etc	2-7-1-3

		Wright, John, son of Reuben	1-0-0-1	
		Wright, Robert List (Mike, Milley)	1-2-0-2	
	p. 50	Wright, Claiborne List	1-0-0-1	
1798 B	p. 35	Wright, Job	1-0-0-1	
1799 A	p. 33	Wright, Job	1-0-0-1	
1799 B	p. 64	Wright, John (Georgia)	1-0-0-1	
		Wright, Robert	1-3-0-2	
	p. 65	Wright, Austin	1-7-4-3	
	p. 66	Wright, Reuben	1-5-0-4	
	p. 67	Wright, Claiborne	1-0-1-0	
		Wright, John (Fanny 12)	1-0-1-0	
	p. 68	Wright, John	1-0-0-1	
		Wright, Thomas	1-0-0-1	
1800 A	p. 24	Wright, John	1-0-0-1	
		Wright, John (Fox) (Eady H.)	1-1-0-0	
		Wright, James	1-0-0-2	
		Wright, William	1-0-0-0	
	p. 25	Wright, Austin	1-7-3-4	
	p. 26	Wright, Thomas	1-0-0-0	
		Wright, Claiborne[9]	1-0-0-1	
1801 A	p. 34	Wright, Job	1-0-0-1	
1801 B	p. 40	Wright, Reuben, son Thomas	1-5-0-4	
	p. 41	Wright, James	1-0-0-2	
	p. 42	Wright, John (Fox)	1-1-0-1	
		Wright, John	1-1-0-1	
		Wright, Claiborne	1-0-0-1	
1802 A	p. 34	Wright, Job	1-0-0-1	
1802 B	p. 39	Wright, James	1-1-0-3	
		Wright, Reuben, sons Thomas & Joshua		3-5-1-4
		Wright, David	1-1-0-1	
		Wright, John (Fox)	1-1-0-1	
	p. 40	Wright, John (son of Austin)	1-3-0-1	
		Wright, Austin	1-9-1-4	
		Wright, William	1-0-0-0	
		Wright, Robert	1-2-0-1	
	p. 41	Wright, John	?-0-0-0	
1803 A	p. 46	Wright, Robert	1-2-0-1	
		Wright, Austin, son Austin	2-9-2-5	
		Wright, John (Fox)	1-1-0-2	
	p. 47	Wright, Reuben	1-5-1-4	
	p. 48	Wright, James	1-1-0-3	
		Wright, Joshua	1-0-0-0	

---

[9] Plus ordinary license.

		Wright, John (son of Reuben)	1-1-0-1
		Wright, John (son of Austin)	1-1-2-2
		Wright, David	1-1-0-1
1803 B	p. 35	Wright, Job	1-0-0-1
1804 A	p. 37	Wright, Job	1-0-0-1
1804 B	p. 49	Wright, David	1-1-0-1
		Wright, John (Fox)	1-1-0-2
	p. 50	Wright, Austin, son Austin	2-9-2-6
		Wright, Lewis	1-0-0-0
		Wright, James	1-0-0-3
		Wright, Robert	1-2-0-2
	p. 52	Wright, Reuben	1-5-1-4
		Wright, William	1-0-0-1
		Wright, John, (son of Austin)	1-2-0-1
1805 A	p. 52	Wright, Reuben	1-6-1-2
		Wright, John (Fox)	1-1-0-2
		Wright, William	1-2-0-5
	p. 53	Wright, James	1-0-0-3
		Wright, John (son of Reuben)	1-0-0-1
		Wright, Austin, son Austin	2-8-1-5
	p. 54	Wright, John (son of Austin)	1-1-1-2
		Wright, Robert	1-1-0-2
1806 B	p. 45	Wright, John (son of Reuben)	1-0-0-1
		Wright, Austin, Jr.	2-7-7-4
	p. 46	Wright, Reuben	1-5-1-4
		Wright, James	1-0-0-2
		Wright, John (Fox)	1-0-0-2
		Wright, Thomas	1-0-0-0
	p. 47	Wright, Lewis	1-0-0-0
1807 B	p. 39	Wright, Austin	1-0-0-0
	p. 40	Wright, John (Fox)	1-3-1-3
		Wright, Thomas	1-0-0-0
		Wright, Reuben	1-4-1-5
		Wright, Joshua	1-1-0-2
	p. 43	Wright, Austin, Jr.	1-6-2-4
1808		no tax collected	
1809 B	p. 45	Wright, John	1-1-2-1
	p. 46	Wright, Reuben	2-4-0-4
		Wright, Thomas	1-0-0-0
		Wright, Austin	1-7-1-5
		Wright, John Fox	1-0-0-1
		Wright, Austin, Jr.	1-0-0-0
		Wright, Joshua	1-0-0-1
		Wright, Lewis	1-0-0-0

1811 B	p. 33	Wright, Francis	1-0-0-0
		Wright, John (son of Reuben)	1-1-1-2
	p. 35	Wright, John	1-0-0-2
		Wright, Reuben, jr.	1-0-0-0
	p. 36	Wright, Thomas	1-0-0-0
		Wright, Reuben	1-4-0-4
		Wright, Joshua	1-0-0-2
		Wright, Austin, jr.	1-0-0-1
1812 B	p. 50	Wright, John	1-2-0-3
	p. 52	Wright, Robert	1-1-1-2
	p. 54	Wright, Joshua	1-0-0-1
	p. 55	Wright, Austin, Sr.	1-7-2-5
		Wright, Austin, Jr.	1-3-0-1
		Wright, Thomas	1-0-0-0
		Wright, Reuben, Jr.	1-0-0-1
		Wright, Reuben, Sr.	1-4-1-4
1813 B	p. 49	Wright, John	1-2-0-0
		Wright, James	1-0-0-0
	p. 55	Wright, Robert	1-0-0-0
		Wright, Reuben, Sr.	2-4-1-4
		Wright, Austin, jr.	1-3-0-0
		Wright, Robert, Jr.(?)	1-1-2-0
		Wright, Joshua	1-0-0-0
1814 B	p. 31	Wright, Reuben, Sr.	1-4-2-5
	p. 32	Wright, Reuben, Jr.	1-0-0-3
		Wright, Austin, Sr.	2-9-1-6
		Wright, Joshua	1-0-1-1
		Wright, Benjamin	1-0-0-1
		Wright, Robert	1-2-1-3
		Wright, Austin, jr.	1-3-1-2

Holmes, Samuel, 8. 250
Holmes, Samuel Jr., 131, 220
Holmes, William, 220
Hopkins, Arthur, 198
Hopkins, John, 42, 61
Hopkins, Samuel, Jr., 42, 52, 219
Horton, Winnifred, 183
Howell, John, 119
Howell, Tabitha, 172
Hubbard, Bartlett, 66
Hubbard, John, 251
Hubbard, Sarah, 277
Hubbard, Thomas, 192
Huddleston, Robert, 51
Hudgins, Aaron, 93
Hudson, William, 124
Hughes, Ashford, 198
Hughes, Robert, 195, 196
Huling, Edmund, 118
Hulm, Ann, 140, 141
Hulm, Elizabeth, 140
Hulm, Hamblen, 141
Hulm, Henry, 145
Hulm, John, 140. 141
Hulm, John W., 145
Hulm, Robert, 141
Hulm, Thomas, 141
Hundley, John A., 138
Hundley, Nancy A., 138
Hundley, William A., 138
Hundley, William H., 134, 136
Hunt, John, 213
Hunt, Patience A., 213
Hurt, Henry, 259
Hutt, Daniel, 124

-I-

Inge, David, 339
Inge, David G., 339
Inge, Katherine B., 339
Inge, Richard D., 339
Ingles, Nathaniel, 217
Ingram, Bartholomew, 35
Ingram, John, 19
Inscoe, William, 249
Irby, Charles, 108
Irby, William, 110
Ivey, Henry, 71

-J-

Jackson, Jordan, 183

Jackson, Mark, 99, 240, 249
Jackson Mark L., 248
Jackson, Martha A., 184
Jackson, Susan, 183
James, Cary, 95
James, John A., 94
James, William, 93, 94
James, William Jr., 95
Jannua, William, 188
Jarrett, Ada, 118, 150
Jarrett, Nancy, 177, 186
Jarrett, Peter, 169
Jarrett, Thomas, 102, 113, 116,
    119, 146, 150, 156, 169, 173,
    176
Jarrett, Thomas Jr., 117, 157
Jarrett, William B., 169
Jefferson, Field, 114
Jeffries, Mary, 213
Jeffries, Osborne, 72
Jenkins, Philemon, 139
Jeter, Lucille, 310
Jeter, Nathaniel, 266
Jeter, Richard R., 266
Jeter, William M., 265
Jeter, William R., 265
Johnson, Isaac, 119
Johnson, James, 142, 148, 152
Johnson, Robert R., 133
Johnson, William M., 38
Johnston, Bushrod, 259, 260
Johnston, Mary, 85
Jones, Belee, 336
Jones, Edward, 232
Jones, Elizabeth, 74
Jones, Francis, 310
Jones, Goodrich, 219
Jones, Harrison, 310
Jones, James, 233, 310
Jones, Jesse, 178
Jones, John, 44
Jones, Nancy, 168
Jones, Obedience, 233
Jones, Peter, 124
Jones, Rebecca, 208
Jones, Robert, 232
Jones, Robert H., 132, 310
Jones, Robert H., Jr., 310
Jones, Sarah, 232

Mims, David A., 198
Mims, John, 198
Mims, Robert, 197, 200
Mims, William, 76
Mize, Anderson, 4
Mize, Elizabeth, 115
Mize, Hannah, 21, 148
Mize, James, 4, 92, 112-116, 146,
    148, 156, 157, 176
Mize, James Jr., 112, 115
Mize, Jeremiah, 112-116, 156
Mize, John, 118, 150, 157, 162,
    177, 241
Mize, Lavender, 241
Mize, Mary, 148
Mize, Rhoda, 150
Mize, Sarah, 148, 157
Mize, Shepherd, 148, 150
Mize, Stephen, 112, 115, 149, 175
Mize, Susan M., 4
Mize, William, 112, 115, 146
Mizell, Owen K., 130
Mizell, Perry S., 130
Mobley, David C., 123
Mobley, Jemima, 123
Monk, John 23
Monk, Silas, 238
Montgomery, Martha, 21, 236-238
Mooney, Bryant, 97
Moore, Hartwell, 182
Moore, Joel, 118, 151
Moore, John, 92, 93
Moore, Mary, 98
Moore, Rebecca, 127
Moore, Sarah F., 320
Moore, William, 188
Moore, Wilson, 182
Morgan, Benjamin, 106, 245, 248
Morgan, Betsy, 103, 245
Morgan, Edith, 103, 245, 249
Morgan, Edward, 232
Morgan, Elizabeth, 245, 246
Morgan, Frederick, 246
Morgan, John, 245
Morgan, Mary, 248
Morgan, Mary A., 243, 245
Morgan, Nancy, 103, 245
Morgan, Philip, 102, 104, 245, 246

Morgan, Reuben, 103, 104, 106,
    243, 245-247, 249
Morgan, Reuben W., 104
Morgan, Sally, 245
Morgan, Sterling, 246, 248
Morgan, Susan, 103
Morris, Catherine, 183
Morris, John, 188
Morris, Mary, 251
Morris, Susan, 262, 263
Morrison, George, 129
Moss, David, 51, 113, 114, 116,
    156
Moss, David J., Sr., 44
Moss, Nathaniel, 246
Moss, Ray, 51
Motheral, Margaret, 143
Motheral, Samuel, 143
Motheral, Sarah, 143, 144
Mott, Richard S., 130
Mullins, John, 198, 200
Murphy, Drury, 243
Murphy, John, 259
Murphy, William, 243
Myers, Charles A., 335
Myers, Mary O., 335
Myers, William W., 335
Myrick, Charles, 139
Myrick, Jesse, 140
Myrick, Lafayette B., 140
Myrick, Owen, 185
            -N-
Nance, Aggie, 210
Nance, Frederick, 210
Nance, Isham, 240, 241, 244, 249
Nance, Mary, 229
Nance, Nancy S., 83
Nance, Thomas, 244
Nanney, Benjamin, 106
Nanney, Hughberry, 128, 252
Nanney, Patsy, 128
Nanney, William, 106, 248
Nash, Thomas, 108
Neal, Brooks, 209
Neal, John, 240, 243
Neal, Richard, 209
Neal, Robert, 143
Newman, Daniel, 51
Newman, George, 134

Ragland, Richard, 12
Ragsdale, John, 117
Ramsey, Richard, 18, 47
Rainey, Allen, 229
Rainey, Betsey, 250
Rainey, Buckner, 240, 244, 247-
    249
Rainey, Christian, 108
Rainey, Christiana, 252
Rainey, Dicey, 247
Rainey, Drucilla, 250
Rainey, Edith, 246
Rainey, Francis, 239-242
Rainey, Frederick, 240, 243-247
Rainey, James, 220, 221
Rainey, James F., 242-243
Rainey, John, 244
Rainey, Lucretia, 247
Rainey, Mary (Morgan), 103
Rainey, Mary (Davis), 21, 220-223
Rainey, Reuben M., 244
Rainey, Sarah, 247
Rainey, Smith, 244, 245
Rainey, William, 108, 243, 250-
    252
Rainey, Williamson, 240, 244, 246,
    248, 249-250
Randle, Apphia, 98
Randle, Edmund, 96
Randle, James, 96, 184
Randle, John, 89, 97
Randle, Josias, 96, 97, 98
Randle, Matilda, 98
Randle, Polly, 97
Randle, Richard, 96, 97
Randle, Susanna, 97
Randle, Thomas, 97
Randolph, Joseph, 163
Rankin, William, 195
Rasser, A. J., 274
Read, Stephen P., 65
Reddick, Peter, 129
Redding, Ezekiel, 56
Reed, Alexander, 195
Reed, Anne, 195
Reed, Clement, 108, 118, 151
Reese, Daniel, 73
Renfroe, Simeon, 280
Renfroe, W. H., 280

Reynolds, Sarah, 268
Rhodes, Randolph, 18, 47
Richardson, John C., 70
Richardson, Rosa, 30
Rideout, Elijah, 9, 52, 225
Riggan, Daniel, 137
Roach, Alexander, 145
Roach, Emily, 142
Roach, Finis, 145
Roach, Frank, 97
Roach, James G., 145
Roach, John A., 145
Roach, Samuel, 145
Roach, Thomas, 145
Roach, William, 145
Roberson, Israel, 234, 235
Roberson, Susannah, 234, 235
Roberts, Eugene S., 28
Roberts, Grant, 28, 29
Roberts, James, 109
Roberts, John, 106
Roberts, Joseph, 179
Roberts, Sally, 108, 252
Roberts, Thomas, 102, 106, 244
Roberts, Thomas S., 29
Roberts, William, 252
Robinson, John, 97
Rodwell, Elizabeth, 136, 139
Roffe, Lewis, 124
Rogers, Elizabeth A., 262
Rogers, George, 250
Rogers, James A., 262
Rogers, Mary J., 262
Rose, Thomas, 119
Ross, Augusta, 280
Ross, George, 280
Ross, James A., 278
Ross, James D., 280
Ross, Joseph W., 280
Ross, Luella, 280
Ross, Martha E., 280
Ross, Mary E., 280
Ross, Susan R., 280
Ross, Willie E., 280
Ross, Martha E., 280
Ross, Francis, 272
Rosser, John K., 205
Rottenbury, Ann, 250
Rottenbury, Elizabeth A., 239, 241

367

Made in the USA
Charleston, SC
15 April 2014